# Incorporate in Nevada from Any State

# Incorporate in Nevada from Any State

## Second Edition

Mark Warda
Attorney at Law

SPHINX® PUBLISHING
AN IMPRINT OF SOURCEBOOKS, INC.®
NAPERVILLE, ILLINOIS
www.SphinxLegal.com

Second Edition: 2008

Published by: **Sphinx® Publishing, An Imprint of Sourcebooks, Inc.®**

<u>Naperville Office</u>
P.O. Box 4410
Naperville, Illinois 60567-4410
630-961-3900
Fax: 630-961-2168
www.sourcebooks.com
www.SphinxLegal.com

This publication is designed to provide accurate and authoritative information in regard to the subject matter covered. It is sold with the understanding that the publisher is not engaged in rendering legal, accounting, or other professional service. If legal advice or other expert assistance is required, the services of a competent professional person should be sought.

*From a Declaration of Principles Jointly Adopted by a Committee of the American Bar Association and a Committee of Publishers and Associations*

**This product is not a substitute for legal advice.**

*Disclaimer required by Texas statutes.*

Library of Congress Cataloging-in-Publication Data

Warda, Mark.
 Incorporate in Nevada from any state / by Mark Warda. -- 2nd ed.
   p. cm.
 Includes index.
  ISBN 978-1-57248-662-1 (pbk. : alk. paper)  1.  Incorporation--Nevada--Popular works.  2. Incorporation--Nevada--Forms.  I. Title.
 KFN813.5.W37 2008
 346.793'06622--dc22
                            2008015096

Printed and bound in the United States of America.
SB 10  9  8  7  6  5  4  3  2  1

# Contents

# Using Self-Help Law Books

Before using a self-help law book, you should realize the advantages and disadvantages of doing your own legal work and understand the challenges and diligence that this requires.

**The Growing Trend**

Rest assured that you will not be the first or only person handling your own legal matter. For example, in some states, more than 75% of divorces and other cases have at least one party representing him- or herself. Because of the high cost of legal services, this is a major trend and many courts are struggling to make it easier for people to represent themselves. However, some courts are not happy with people who do not use attorneys and refuse to help them in any way. For some, the attitude is, "Go to the law library and figure it out for yourself."

We write and publish self-help law books to give people an alternative to the often complicated and confusing legal books found in most law libraries. We have made the explanations of the law as simple and easy to understand as possible. Of course, unlike an attorney advising an individual client, we cannot cover every conceivable possibility.

**Cost/Value Analysis**

Whenever you shop for a product or service, you are faced with various levels of quality and price. In deciding what product or service to buy, you make a cost/value analysis on the basis of your willingness to pay and the quality you desire.

When buying a car, you decide whether your top priority is transportation, comfort, status, or sex appeal. Accordingly, you decide among such choices as a Neon, Lincoln, Rolls Royce, or Porsche. Before making a decision, you usually weigh the merits of each option against the cost.

When you get a headache, you can take a pain reliever or visit a medical specialist for a neurological examination. Given this choice, most people, of course, take a pain reliever since it costs only pennies, whereas a medical examination costs hundreds of dollars and takes a lot of time. This is usually a logical choice because it is rare to need anything more than a pain reliever for a headache. But in some cases, a headache may indicate a brain tumor and failing to see a specialist right away can result in complications. Should everyone with a headache go to a specialist? Of course not, but people treating their own illnesses must realize that they are betting on the basis of their cost/value analysis of the situation. They are taking the most logical option.

The same cost/value analysis must be made when deciding to do one's own legal work. Many legal situations are very straightforward, requiring a simple form and no complicated analysis. Anyone with a little intelligence and a book of instructions can handle the matter without outside help.

But there is always the chance that complications are involved that only an attorney would notice. To simplify the law into a book like this, several legal cases often must be condensed into a single sentence or paragraph. Otherwise, the book would be several hundred pages long and too complicated for most people. However, this simplification necessarily leaves out many details and nuances that would apply to special or unusual situations. Also, there are many ways to interpret most legal questions. Your case may come before a judge who disagrees with the analysis of our authors.

Therefore, in deciding to use a self-help law book and to do your own legal work, you must realize that you are making a cost/value analysis. You have decided that the money you will save in doing it yourself outweighs the chance that your case will not turn out to your satisfaction. Most people handling their own simple legal matters never have a problem, but occasionally people find that it ended up costing them more to have an attorney straighten out the situation than it would have if they had hired an attorney in the beginning.

Keep this in mind if you decide to handle your own case, and be sure to consult an attorney if you feel you might need further guidance.

**Local Rules**    The next thing to remember is that a book that covers the law for the entire nation, or even for an entire state, cannot possibly include every procedural difference of every county court. Whenever possible, we provide the exact form needed; however, in some areas, each county, or even each judge, may require unique forms and procedures. In our state books, our forms usually cover the majority of counties in the state, or provide examples of the type of form that will be required. In our national books, our forms are sometimes even more general in nature but are designed to give a good idea of the type of form that will be needed in most locations. Nonetheless, keep in mind that your state, county, or judge may have a requirement, or use a form, that is not included in this book.

You should not necessarily expect to be able to get all the information and resources you need solely from within the pages of this book. This book will serve as your guide, giving you specific information whenever possible and helping you find out what else you will need to know. This is just like if you decided to build your own backyard deck. You might purchase a book on how to build decks. However, such a book would not include the building codes and permit requirements of every city, town, county, and township in the nation; nor would it include the lumber, nails, saws, hammers, and other materials and tools you would need to actually build the deck. You would use the book as your guide, and then do some work and research involving such matters as whether you need a permit of some kind, what type and grade of wood is available in your area, whether to use hand tools or power tools, and how to use those tools.

Before using the forms in a book like this, you should check with your court clerk to see if there are any local rules of which you should be aware, or local forms you will need to use. Often, such forms will require the same information as the forms in the book but are merely laid out differently, use slightly different language, or use different color paper so the clerks can easily find them. They will sometimes require additional information.

**Changes in the Law**

Besides being subject to local rules and practices, the law is subject to change at any time. The courts and the legislatures of all fifty states are constantly revising the laws. It is possible that while you are reading this book, some aspect of the law is being changed.

In most cases, the change will be of minimal significance. A form will be redesigned, additional information will be required, or a waiting period will be extended. As a result, you might need to revise a form, file an extra form, or wait out a longer time period; these types of changes will not usually affect the outcome of your case. On the other hand, sometimes a major part of the law is changed, the entire law in a particular area is rewritten, or a case that was the basis of a central legal point is overruled. In such instances, your entire ability to pursue your case may be impaired.

Again, you should weigh the value of your case against the cost of an attorney and make a decision as to what you believe is in your best interest.

# Introduction

While most states are finding new ways to tax and keep records on their citizens, one state stands out for supporting low taxes and citizen privacy—Nevada.

Always a little freer than most states with legalized gambling, prostitution, and easy divorces, Nevada has now decided to be at the forefront of low taxation and privacy. In recent years, Nevada has liberalized its corporation laws and decided to offer itself as a haven for those seeking to avoid the high taxes of most states.

Thousands of businesses around the country decide to incorporate or form a limited liability company (LLC) in Nevada every year. This has spawned a growth industry of registered agent companies that help Nevada maintain its low tax status.

Anyone who is thinking of forming a corporation or LLC should consider the benefits of Nevada and weigh them against the small costs involved.

The main reason people incorporate or form an LLC is to avoid personal liability. While sole proprietors and partners have all their personal assets at risk, corporate shareholders and LLC members risk only what they paid for their stock and membership interests. With so many people ready to sue for any reason or for no reason at all, the corporation and LLC are two of the few inexpensive protections left.

Creating a simple corporation or LLC is very easy, and it is the purpose of this book to explain, in simple language, how you can do it yourself. A *simple corporation* or *LLC* as used in this book is one in which there are five or fewer participants and all of them are active in the business. If you plan to sell interests to someone who is not active in the business or plan to have many more participants, you should seek the advice of an attorney. However, some guidance is provided throughout this book as to what some of the concerns will be in these circumstances.

If your situation is in any way complicated or involves factors not mentioned in this book, you should seek the advice of an attorney practicing business law. The cost of a short consultation can be a lot cheaper than the consequences of violating the law.

If you plan to sell shares to outside investors, you should consult with a lawyer who specializes in securities laws. Selling a few thousand shares to friends and neighbors may sound like an easy way to raise capital for your business, but it is not! Since the stock market crash of 1929, there have been federal laws regulating the sale of securities. There are harsh criminal penalties for violators and the laws do not have many loopholes. The basic rules are explained in Chapter 7.

This book also explains the basics of corporate taxation, but you should discuss your own particular situation with your accountant before deciding what system to use for your business. He or she can also set you up with an efficient system of bookkeeping that can save both time and money.

Good luck with your new business!

# Should You Incorporate in Nevada?

## chapter 1

Before you take the big step of organizing a Nevada corporation or limited liability company (LLC), you should understand the advantages and disadvantages of corporations and LLCs in comparison to the advantages and disadvantages of incorporating in the state of Nevada. For simplicity, when we say *incorporate* in this book, we will be referring to forming either a corporation or an LLC.

## ADVANTAGES OF CORPORATIONS AND LLCS

For nearly any type of business, the corporation or LLC is preferred over the sole proprietorship or partnership. Except for the smallest home-based business, it is foolish to operate without the protections these entities offer. This section will review the advantages of using a corporation or LLC as your business entity.

**Limited Liability**
The main reason for forming a *corporation* or *limited liability company (LLC)* is to limit the liability of the owners. In a *sole proprietorship* or *partnership*, the owners are personally liable for the debts and liabilities of the business, and creditors can often go after their assets to collect business debts. If a corporation or LLC is formed and operated properly, the owners can be protected from all such liability.

## Example:

If several people are in a partnership and one of them makes many large extravagant purchases in the name of the partnership, the other partners can be held liable for the full amount of all those purchases. The creditors can take the bank accounts, cars, real estate, and other property of any partner to pay the debts of the partnership. If only one partner has money, he or she may have to pay all the debts accumulated by all the other partners. When doing business in the corporate form, the corporation may go bankrupt and the shareholders may lose their initial investments, but the creditors cannot touch the personal assets of the owners.

## Example:

If a person runs a taxi business and one of the drivers causes a terrible accident, the owner of the taxi company can be held liable for the full amount of the damages. If the taxi driver was on drugs and killed several people and the damages amount to millions of dollars more than the insurance coverage, the owner may lose everything he or she owns. With a corporation, only the corporation would be liable. The owner could not be touched, even if there was not enough money or insurance to cover the damages.

One real-life example of this was a business owner who owned hundreds of taxis. He put one or two taxis into each of hundreds of different corporations that he owned. Each corporation only had minimum insurance coverage, and when one taxi was involved in an accident, the owner only lost the assets of that corporation.

**NOTE:** *The corporation will not protect an owner from the consequences of his or her own act or from the debt if a corporate officer or shareholder does something negligent him- or herself, signs a debt personally, or guarantees a corporate debt. Also, if a corporation does not follow the proper corporate formalities, it may be ignored by a court and the owners or officers may be held personally liable. The formalities include having separate bank accounts, holding meetings, and keeping minutes. When a* *court ignores a corporate structure and holds the owners or officers liable, it is called* piercing the corporate veil.

**Continuous Existence**

A corporation or LLC may have a perpetual existence. When a sole proprietor or partner dies, the assets of his or her business may go to his or her heirs, but the business does not exist any longer. If the surviving spouse or other heirs of a business owner want to continue the business in their own names, they will be considered a new business even if they are using the assets of the old business. With a partnership, the death of one partner could cause a dissolution of the business.

---

### Example:

If a person dies owning a sole proprietorship, his or her spouse may want to continue the business. That person may inherit all the assets but will have to start a new business. This means getting new licenses and tax numbers, registering the name, and establishing credit from scratch. With a corporation or LLC, the business could continue with all the same licenses, bank accounts, etc.

---

### Example:

If one partner dies and no prior agreements allow for the continuation of the business, the partnership may be forced to close. The heirs of the deceased partner may be able to force the sale of their share of the assets of the partnership, even if the surviving partner needs them to continue the business. If he or she does not have the money to buy out the heirs, the business may have to be dissolved. With a corporation or properly drawn LLC agreement, the surviving member could be allowed to buy out the interest of the deceased one.

---

**Ease of Transferability**

A corporation and all its assets and accounts may be transferred by the simple assignment of a *stock certificate*. An LLC may be transferred with an assignment of a *membership interest*. With a sole proprietorship, each of the individual assets must be transferred, and the accounts, licenses, and permits must be individually transferred.

### Example:

If a sole proprietorship is sold, the new owner will have to get a new occupational license, set up his or her own bank account, and apply for a new taxpayer identification number. The title to any vehicles and real estate will have to be put in his or her name and all open accounts will have to be changed to his or her name. He or she will probably have to submit new credit applications. With a corporation, all of these items remain in the same corporate name. As the new shareholder, he or she would elect him- or herself director, and as director, he or she would elect him- or herself president, treasurer, and any other offices he or she wanted to hold.

**NOTE:** *In some cases, the new owners will have to submit personal applications for such things as credit lines or liquor licenses.*

**Transfer of Ownership**

By distributing stock or different types of membership interests, the owner of a corporation or LLC can share the profits of a business without giving up control. This is done by keeping a majority of ownership or by issuing different classes of ownership—some with and some without voting rights.

### Example:

If a person wants to give his or her children some of the profits of his or her business, he or she can give them stock and pay dividends to them without giving them any control over the management. This would not be practical with a partnership or sole proprietorship.

**Ease of Raising Capital**

A corporation or LLC may raise capital by selling stock or membership interests. A corporation or LLC does not pay taxes on money it raises by the sale of stock or membership interests.

### Example:

If a company wants to expand, the owners can sell off 10%, 50%, or 90% of the stock and still remain in control of the business. The people putting up the money may be more willing to invest if they know they will have a piece of the action than if they were making a loan with a limited return. They may not want to become partners in a partnership.

---

**NOTE:** *There are strict rules about the sale of stock, with criminal penalties and triple damages for violators. See Chapter 7.*

**Separate Record Keeping**
A corporation or LLC has all its own bank accounts and records. A sole proprietor may have trouble differentiating which of his or her expenses were for business and which were for personal items.

**Tax Advantages**
There are some tax advantages that are available only to corporations or LLCs, such as:

- ✪ medical insurance for your family may be fully deductible;

- ✪ a tax deferred trust can be set up for a retirement plan; and,

- ✪ losses are fully deductible for a corporation, but an individual must prove there was a profit motive before deducting losses.

**Ease of Estate Planning**
With a corporation or LLC, shares of a company can be distributed more easily than with a partnership or sole proprietorship. Different heirs can be given different percentages, and control can be limited to those who are most capable. This is called *estate planning*.

**Prestige**
The name of a corporation or LLC sounds more prestigious than the name of a sole proprietor to some people. John Smith d/b/a Acme Builders sounds like one lone person. Acme Builders, Incorporated, or Acme Builders, LLC, sounds like it might be a large operation.

**Separate Credit Rating**
A corporation or LLC has its own credit rating, which can be better or worse than the owner's credit rating. A corporation or LLC can go bankrupt while the owner's credit remains unaffected, or an owner's credit may be bad but the corporation may maintain a good rating.

## DIFFERENCES BETWEEN CORPORATIONS AND LLCS

The limited liability company is the newest form of business entity, and some have suggested that every business should adopt the form today. However, a closer look at the entities will show that they may offer advantages for some businesses, but for others, the corporate form may be better.

**Advantages of
Corporations**

The main advantages that a corporation has over an LLC are as
follows.

*History.* The corporation has a long history and many thousands of
court cases have decided the rights and obligations of the participants.
Since the LLC was only invented just over a decade ago, there have
been few court cases to spell out its rights. Thus a large business, especially one that plans to go public, might prefer the certainty of a
corporation.

*Taxes.* The main advantage of certain corporations—namely S corporations—over an LLC is that profits taken out other than salary are
not subject to Social Security and Medicare taxes, whereas all profits
of an LLC are subject to these taxes. However, LLCs are able to opt to
be taxed as corporations and then opt to be treated as S corporations.

There would not be much difference for a large business where the
owners take out salaries of $68,400 or more plus profits. But for a
smaller business where an owner would take out, say, $30,000 salary
and $20,000 profit, the extra taxes would be over $3,000.

*Reorganizations.* An S corporation is allowed—under Internal
Revenue Code (I.R.C.), Section (Sec.) 368—to have a tax-free *merger*
(joining with another company to form one company) or *asset divesti-
ture* (selling off a major portion of its assets) under certain
circumstances, but an LLC is not. However, an LLC may switch to a
corporate structure prior to reorganization to use these benefits.

**Advantages
of LLCs**

The main advantages that an LLC has over a corporation are as
follows.

*Asset protection.* In some states, the interest a member owns in an
LLC can be protected from the member's creditors. While corporate
stock can be seized and sold by a creditor, in some states an interest
in an LLC is only subject to a creditor's *charging order.* This means
that the creditor only gets what the other members of the LLC decide
to give him or her. He or she cannot sell the interest because the
interest is not *assignable.* The creditor cannot vote in place of the
former member and cannot require the LLC to be dissolved.

*Formality.* It is presumed by most legal experts that an LLC requires
less formality than a corporation. While improper procedures in a
corporation may allow a creditor to *pierce the corporate veil* and hold
shareholders liable, the LLC is clearly meant to be a safe harbor to
protect business owners from liability.

*Taxes.* An LLC can make special allocations of profits and losses among members (as long as the tests of Federal Treasury Regulation, Section 1.704(b) are satisfied), whereas an S corporation cannot. An S corporation must have one class of ownership in which profits and losses are allocated according to the percentage of ownership.

In an LLC, money borrowed by the company can increase the tax basis of the owners (and lower the taxes), whereas in an S corporation, it cannot.

Contributing property to set up an LLC is not taxable even for minority interest owners; however, contributing property to set up a corporation is only tax-free for the contributors who have control of the business, and not for minority interest owners. (I.R.C., Sec. 351.)

An S corporation may lose its favorable tax status for five years if an interest is acquired by a foreign person, another corporation, or a certain kind of trust, and it may not have more than seventy-five shareholders. An LLC has no such limitations.

When an LLC buys out a member, it may increase its basis in a portion of the receivables and tangible assets, but an S corporation may not. (This makes the taxable profit lower when they are sold.) When a third party buys the interest of a member, the LLC may make an election to increase its basis in assets. (I.R.C., Sec. 754.) An S corporation cannot.

Upon death of an owner, the person inheriting an S corporation interest may need to pay taxes on more income than a person inheriting a similar LLC. (I.R.C., Sec. 691.)

*Newness.* Another advantage may be psychological. The LLC is a new entity, and in the twenty-first century it may look more up-to-date to be an LLC than an ordinary corporation.

## ADVANTAGES OF NEVADA

**Views of Secretary of State**

The state of Nevada and many promoters have lists of the advantages of Nevada corporations over those in other states. However, not all of these work for everyone.

The Nevada secretary of state lists the following as advantages.

*No corporate income tax.* Most states impose a corporate income tax, although many exempt S corporations. If you need a C corporation or live in a state that does not exempt S corporations, then a Nevada corporation can offer substantial tax savings.

One method for saving taxes is to form two corporations, one in Nevada and one in your home state. Your local corporation engages in business and is subject to state taxes, but has no assets and makes no profit. Any assets can be leased from the Nevada corporation or can be subject to a lien by the Nevada corporation. Any income of the local corporation would be paid to you as salary or to the Nevada corporation as lease payments, purchases of supplies, etc. See the next chapter for more information on this.

*No taxes on corporate shares.* Many states tax corporate shares either initially (on issuance) or annually. If you are in one of these states, Nevada can save you money.

*No franchise tax.* This is an annual tax that some states assess on the privilege of having a corporation. (California charges a minimum of $800 a year, which increases to thousands of dollars for larger businesses.)

*No personal income tax.* Since most states impose a personal income tax, forming a Nevada corporation would not exempt you from your home state's tax on your personal income. However, you may be able to leave profits in your Nevada corporation and avoid paying your state income tax on them.

*Nominal annual fees.* Nevada's $85 per year fee is lower than most states, but there are a few states that have lower annual fees.

*Nevada corporations may purchase, hold, sell, and transfer shares of its own stock.* Some states may not allow this, but most do.

*Nevada corporations may issue stock for capital, services, personal property, and real estate, including leases and options.* The directors may determine the value of any of these transactions, and their decision is final. Some states may not allow this.

*No franchise tax on income.* Some states may have such a tax.

*No inheritance or gift taxes.* Many states have such taxes. However, if you are a resident of a state that does, it may still apply to you even if your corporation is based in Nevada.

*No unitary tax.* Some states may have such a tax.

***No estate tax.*** Many states have such taxes. However, if you are a resident of a state that does, it may still apply to you even if your corporation is based in Nevada.

***Competitive sales and property tax rates.*** Many states have higher taxes.

***Minimal employer payroll tax—0.7% of gross wages with deductions for employer-paid health insurance.*** Many states have such taxes. However, if your business is located in another state, then this does not apply.

***Nevada's business court.*** Developed on the Delaware model, Nevada's business court minimizes the time, cost, and risks of commercial litigation through early, comprehensive case management, active judicial participation in settlements, priority for hearing settings to avoid business disruption, and predictability of legal decisions in commercial matters. This would be advantageous if you expected to be involved in litigation in Nevada.

The secretary of state used to list "No IRS reporting," meaning they did not share information with the IRS, but this advantage has been deleted. It is unclear if they started to share such information or if they no longer want to advertise it as a benefit.

**Views of Promoters**

Some other promoters of Nevada corporations have suggested that the following are also benefits of the Nevada corporation.

***Nominee officers.*** All states require companies to list some officers, members, or directors, which are public records, usually searchable on the state website. Nevada allows companies to list *nominees*—that is, people you hire to be listed so employees' real names are not in the public record. Nominee officers, members, or directors can be hired at the same companies that serve as your Nevada registered agent. In some states you can achieve the same result by listing a trust as an officer or manager.

***Bearer stock.*** The advantage of *bearer stock* is that if you do not possess it, you do not own it; therefore, if you are put under oath and asked if you own any stock, you may be able to answer no if you gave the certificate to someone else. However, a smart lawyer will ask you to name any stocks you have owned in the recent past. Failure to disclose this information under oath would be perjury. Also, Nevada law requires that a corporation keep a list of its shareholders, either at its Nevada registered office or at a location that is listed at the Nevada registered office. Thus, a corporation that does not require shareholders to disclose their ownership would be in technical violation of Nevada law.

*No interim filings.* Some states require that the current directors or officers be kept on record with the state. Nevada only requires that such information be filed once a year. The theory is that you can hire someone to be a director and officer for the one day the filing is made, then fire him or her and elect yourself for the next 364 days until the next filing is due, and never have yourself on record.

> *Warning:* While tactics such as this are legal under the technical reading of the statutes, you should keep in mind that courts have wide leeway in redressing wrongs. If someone uses technically legal tactics to defraud people, a court can still hold him or her liable. Sometimes these things can be fit into criminal statutes such as *conspiracy* or *scheme to defraud*. And there are legal principles that are not always in the statutes that allow courts to reach what they feel is a just result, even when someone followed all the technical rules.

*Piercing the corporate veil.* When a court ignores a corporate structure and holds an owner personally liable for corporate debt, this is called *piercing the corporate veil*. In Nevada, this is more difficult to do than in most states because the law requires a *sham to perpetrate fraud* in addition to the mere undercapitalization required in other states.

## DISADVANTAGES OF NEVADA

For most people, the advantages of a Nevada corporation outweigh the disadvantages, but for people in states with no income tax and minimum corporate requirements, they may not. The following are the disadvantages of incorporating your business in Nevada, rather than in your home state.

**Nevada Registered Office and Agent**

First, as a Nevada corporation, you will need to have a *registered office* and *registered agent* in the state of Nevada. If you incorporate in your own state, you can usually use your own business office as the registered office and you or one of your employees could be the registered agent.

However, the fee to hire a Nevada registered office and registered agent is around $100 a year, so this should not be a burden except for the smallest enterprise. A list of corporate agents is included in Appendix C.

**Home State Registration**

Second, as a Nevada corporation, you may need to register as a *foreign corporation* in the state in which you are actually doing business. However, this is usually a simple procedure of filing a form and paying a fee each year. In some states this is a small fee, but in others it is considerable. A list of state offices with which you must register is included in Appendix B.

One exception is if the corporation is not actually doing business anywhere. If it merely owns real estate or passive investments, it may not have to register. Some people form a Nevada corporation to own their assets and then form a second corporation to engage in business in another state. The Nevada corporation loans money or assets to the local corporation and sometimes sells goods or services to it. The local corporation never has any net worth or makes a profit and is therefore judgment-proof and tax-free. Meanwhile, the Nevada corporation is not subject to income tax if it is far away and not involved in any risky activities.

**Lawsuits**

A third disadvantage is that as a Nevada corporation, you can be sued in Nevada. If you are doing business with anyone in or near Nevada, it would be easier for them to sue you and harder for you to defend yourself far away from where you reside.

## chapter 2

# Tax Considerations

## CORPORATION TAX ISSUES

A corporation has a choice of how it wants to be taxed. It can make the election at the beginning of its existence or at the beginning of a new tax year. The choices are as follows.

**S Corporation**

Formerly called a *Subchapter S corporation*, an *S corporation* pays no income tax and may only be used for businesses with a limited number of shareholders. All the income or losses of the corporation for the year are passed through to the shareholders who report them on their individual returns. The corporation files an *information return* at the end of each year, listing all its income, expenses, depreciation, etc., and sends each shareholder a notice of his or her share as determined by percentage of stock ownership.

***Advantages.*** Using this method avoids double taxation and allows the pass-through of losses and depreciation. The business is treated like a partnership. Since many businesses have tax losses during the first years due to start-up costs, it can be advantageous to elect S status in the beginning and switch over to C corporation status in later years. Once a corporation terminates its S status, there is a five-year waiting period before it can switch back.

***Disadvantages.*** If stockholders are in high tax brackets, their share of the profits will be taxed at those rates. Shareholders who do not *materially participate* in the business cannot deduct losses. (This means they cannot be mere investors; they have to be actual participants in the operations of the business.) Some fringe benefits, such as health and life insurance, may not be tax deductible in an S corporation, whereas they would be in a C corporation or LLC.

***Requirements.*** To qualify for S corporation status, the corporation must:

- ✪ have no more than seventy-five shareholders, none of whom are nonresident aliens or corporations, all of whom consent to the election (shares owned by a husband and wife jointly are considered owned by one shareholder);

- ✪ have only one class of stock;

- ✪ not be a member of an *affiliated group* of companies;

- ✪ generate at least 20% of its income in this country and have no more than 20% of its income from *passive sources* (interest, rents, dividends, royalties, securities transactions); and,

- ✪ file **Election by a Small Business Corporation (IRS form 2553)** before the end of the fifteenth day of the third month of the tax year for which it is to be effective and have it approved by the IRS. This form and instructions are in Appendix D. (see form 16, p.251.)

***Multiple Corporations.*** The Internal Revenue Service (IRS) has approved the use of two or more S corporations in partnership to increase the number of allowable investors in a venture. It may also be possible for an S corporation to form a partnership with a C corporation.

**C Corporation**

A *C corporation* pays taxes on its net earnings at corporate tax rates. Salaries of officers, directors, and employees are deducted from income so they are not taxed to the corporation, but money paid out in dividends is taxed twice. It is taxed at the corporation's rate as part of its profit, and then the stockholders must include the amounts they receive as dividends in their income.

***Advantages.*** If taxpayers are in a higher tax bracket than the corporation and the money will be left in the company for expansion, taxes are saved. Fringe benefits such as health, accident, and life insurance are deductible expenses.

*Disadvantages.* Double taxation of dividends by the federal government is the biggest problem with a C corporation. But this tax does not apply to money taken out as salaries, and many small business owners take all profits out as salaries to avoid double taxation. But there are rules requiring that salaries be reasonable, and if a stockholder's salary is deemed to be too high in relation to his or her job, the salary may be considered dividends and subject to double taxation.

*Requirements.* There are no requirements to incorporating. All corporations are C corporations unless they specifically elect to become S corporations.

## LLC TAX ISSUES

When LLCs were first started, they had to follow strict rules in order to qualify for advantageous tax treatment. Single business owners could not qualify for pass-through taxation because it was not considered logical to treat a single person as a partnership.

Now, you merely obtain **ENTITY CLASSIFICATION ELECTION (IRS FORM 8832)** and check the box indicating whether you wish to be taxed like a corporation or to pass the income through to the owners and have them declare it on their personal returns. **IRS FORM 8832** and instructions are included in this book in Appendix D. (see form 33, p.299.)

Since one of the reasons LLCs were developed was to allow businesses to enjoy partnership taxation with corporate protections from liability, not many LLCs will select to be taxed as corporations. However, an LLC opting to be taxed as a corporation can also opt to be taxed as an S corporation, so there should be no tax reason to choose a corporation rather than an LLC structure.

## DUAL CORPORATION TAX ISSUES

As mentioned in the previous chapter, an advantage of the Nevada corporation is that Nevada has no corporate or personal income taxes. One way to take advantage of this if you are doing business in a state that does have a corporate income tax is to form two corporations—one in Nevada and one in your state. Have the Nevada corporation make the profits and the local corporation break even.

For example, suppose you were a painting contractor who owned a building and equipment. You could incorporate in your home state as a painting contractor but put the building and equipment into a Nevada corporation. The Nevada corporation would then lease these to the local corporation. After paying the workers, buying supplies, paying your salary, and making lease payments to the Nevada corporation, your local company could break even with no taxable profit. The profit would all be in the Nevada corporation, which does not pay taxes in your state.

From a federal tax standpoint, there would seldom be an issue because taxes would have to be paid on the profits of any corporation, whether or not it was a Nevada corporation.

There would be a couple of issues from a state tax standpoint. One is whether the Nevada corporation was doing business in your state. It might not even need to register as doing business in your state if the acts of the Nevada corporation are passive enough. For example, if it just loaned money to your corporation, it would not have to register (especially if you happened to go to Las Vegas to sign the papers). In most states, merely owning rental real estate does not require a corporation to register.

A second issue would be whether your state has any catch-all tax laws that would prevent this kind of setup. If you are going to start two corporations for this purpose, you should meet with a local tax specialist to be sure that it is done correctly under your state requirements.

## SALES AND USE TAX ISSUES

**In-State**    In most states, you will need to collect a *sales and use tax* on each sale if your business will be providing goods or services to the public. Most states exempt various items such as food, medicines, and certain types of services. You should contact the state department of revenue in each state in which you do business to register as a collector of the tax and obtain the rules and regulations. Your business is liable for the tax even if you do not collect it, and must remit the taxes even if the state does not send you the forms on time. If your registration materials do not arrive in time for your first filing, you may be able to get temporary forms from your local tax office to avoid a penalty for late filing.

**Out-of-State**    In 1992, the United States Supreme Court safeguarded the rights of small businesses by ruling that state tax authorities cannot force them to collect sales taxes on interstate mail orders (*Quill Corporation v. North Dakota*). This means, for example, that a business in Iowa that sells something by mail to someone in New York does not have to figure out New York tax laws, collect New York taxes, and send them to New York tax authorities. If this case had ruled the other way, every small business would have to keep track of taxes in all fifty states (and many cities), many of which require annual fees and a bond. This would have put all but the biggest companies out of business.

Unfortunately, the court left open the possibility that Congress could allow interstate taxation of mail-order sales. Several bills that would do so have since been introduced.

At present, companies are only required to collect sales taxes for states in which they do business. Exactly what business is enough to trigger taxation is a legal question and some states try to define it as broadly as possible.

If you have an office in a state, clearly you are doing business there, and any goods shipped to consumers in the state are subject to sales taxes. If you have a full-time employee working in the state most of the year, many states will consider you to be doing business there. In some states, attending a two-day trade show is enough business to trigger taxation for the entire year for every order shipped to the state. One loophole that often works is to be represented at shows by persons who are not your employees.

Because the laws are different in each state, you will have to do some research on a state-by-state basis to find out how much business you can do in a state without being subject to its taxation. You can request a state's rules from its department of revenue, but keep in mind that what a department of revenue wants the law to be is not always what the courts will rule that it is.

## BUSINESS TAX ISSUES

Being subject to a state's income or other business taxes is even worse than being subject to its sales taxes. For example, California charges every company doing business in the state a minimum $800 a year fee and charges income tax on a portion of the company's worldwide income. Doing a small amount of business in the state is clearly not worth getting mired in California taxation.

Some trade shows have been moved from California for this reason, and this has resulted in a review of the tax policies and some *safe-harbor guidelines* to advise companies on what they can do without becoming subject to taxation. Write to the department of revenue of any state with which you have business contacts to see what might trigger your taxation.

## INTERNET TAX ISSUES

In 1998, Congress passed a moratorium on taxation of the Internet, which was extended through 2007. Perhaps the Internet can be used as an *enterprise zone* to encourage business growth. Keep an eye out for any news stories on proposals to tax the Internet.

However, while there is no current *Internet tax*, sometimes you will have to pay sales tax for items you buy on the Internet. While a lot of online retailers avoid having to charge sales tax, if a company has an actual physical presence in the same state where an Internet sale is made, then the company does have to collect sales tax on the sale and send it to the IRS.

## CANADIAN TAX ISSUES

The Canadian government expects American companies, which sell goods by mail order to Canadians, to collect taxes for them and file returns with Revenue Canada, its tax department.

Those that receive an occasional unsolicited order are not expected to register, and Canadian customers who order things from the United States pay the tax plus a $5 fee upon receipt of the goods. But companies that solicit Canadian orders are expected to be registered if their worldwide income is $30,000 or more per year. In some cases, a company may be required to post a bond and to pay for the cost of Canadian auditors to visit its premises and audit its books! For these reasons, you may notice that some companies decline to accept orders from Canada.

# EMPLOYER IDENTIFICATION NUMBER

It is important to know about identification for tax purposes. Prior to opening a bank account, the corporation must obtain an *employer identification number* (EIN), sometimes called a *taxpayer identification number*. This would be the corporate equivalent of a Social Security number. This is done by filing the **APPLICATION FOR EMPLOYER IDENTIFICATION NUMBER (IRS FORM SS-4)**. (see form 3, p.217.) This usually takes two or three weeks, so it should be filed early.

You can get an EIN more quickly by faxing the form in, and you can get one immediately by applying online. The online form is much longer than the SS-4, but it can be completed quickly. It can be found at: **https://sa2.www4.irs.gov/modiein/individual/index.jsp.**

You can apply online during the following hours:

Monday–Friday, 6:00 a.m.–12:30 a.m., EST
Saturday, 6:00 a.m.–9:00 p.m., EST
Sunday, 7:00 p.m.–12:00 a.m., EST

If you are forming a single-member limited liability company that will be owned by one member and will have employees within the next twelve months, then you must have two EINs. One EIN is assigned to the individual owner (as a sole proprietor) and the other is assigned to the LLC. If you do not already have an EIN as a sole proprietor, you cannot use the online EIN application to apply for the LLC EIN. You should call the IRS Business and Specialty Tax Line at 800-829-4933 between 7:00 a.m. and 10:00 p.m. local time in order to be assigned the two EINs.

When you apply for this number, you will probably be put on the mailing list for other corporate tax forms. If you do not receive these, you should call your local IRS office and request the forms for new businesses. These include: *Circular E* explaining the taxes due, the W-4 forms for each employee, the *tax deposit coupons*, and the *Form 941* quarterly return for withholding.

# Business Name

## chapter 3

The very first thing to do before starting a new business is to choose a great name and thoroughly check it out to be sure that no one else already has legal rights to it.

## CHOOSING YOUR BUSINESS NAME

While the quality of your goods or services will improve the value of your name, having a great name can give the initial image of your company the boost it needs for people to give it a try. Consider if you were looking for a flight to Paris and the two airlines you had to choose from were Air International and Barney's Airline and Baitshop. Or if you needed a repair made to your office computer and the two computer repair shops you had to choose between were called Heather's Techsters on Wheels and Micro Systems Services.

These are exaggerations of course, but you get the idea that when all you have to go on is a name, one that sounds more knowledgeable or established will probably attract more business.

Some people have started a business as a lark, used a silly name, and watched it grow so big that the name became embarrassing. You may think that if you are lucky enough to have your business explode, you will not mind changing the name. Perhaps a silly name can be used to challenge fate. You can just hope to get so big that the name has to be changed.

But changing a business name is more complicated than you think. After years of establishing a name and reputation, changing it can be costly, in time and expense and in lost business.

**Guidelines**    In choosing a name, you should use the following guidelines.

*Use the right suffix.* Nevada law requires that certain words or suffixes be a part of the name of a company. In Chapter 4 is a list of those required for a corporation and in Chapter 5 is a list of those required for an LLC.

*Do not use forbidden words.* Certain words are not allowed to be used as part of a company name without approval or special licensing. (See later chapters for more details.)

*Do not be too similar.* While there might seem to be some advantage to having your name sound like a more successful competitor, it may be more trouble than it is worth. If a court finds a name to be confusingly similar, it can order the second user to stop using the name and to pay damages to the company that had the name first. The legal costs of fighting a large corporation with deep pockets can bankrupt a small business.

For example, Toys "R" Us® sues any company that it finds using "R Us" in its name (Insurance R Us, Flowers R Us). While the company's claim was not strong—because legally, using the same name in another field of commerce was not an infringement of a trademark—it won because little companies could not afford to spend tens of thousands of dollars fighting in court. Now, however, the law protects famous trademarks from anyone using similar names.

On the other side, if you are looking for some free publicity for your fledgling business, you are sure to get written up in the local papers if an international corporation complains of your innocent use of a similar name.

*Be sure it is not confusing.* Many words, especially in the English language, are spelled differently from how they sound. Be sure that the name you choose is easy for people to spell and to look up in the phone book, on the Internet, or elsewhere.

**Software**    There is computer software available that is supposed to be helpful in the process of choosing a name. While it is costly for a one-time use, it may be worthwhile if you plan to name several products, or you may be able to find someone who will let you use it once for a fee.

**Consultants**
There are consultants who offer their services in choosing an ideal name; however, for a new business, the fee is usually too high. A business magazine once ran a story about a major corporation that paid a consultant $50,000 to come up with a name for a new breakfast cereal. The magazine also polled its own staff for suggestions based on the criteria given to the consultant and its staff produced the same name.

## SEARCHING THE NAME

Once you have chosen the perfect name, you need to be sure that no one else has established legal rights to it. Many businesses have been forced to stop using their name after spending thousands of dollars promoting it.

Legal rights can be established by registering a name as a trademark or by merely using the name. Consequently, you cannot be sure that no one has rights to a name just by checking registered names. You need to check to see if anyone is using the name who has not registered it yet.

The following are places you should check.

**Division of Corporations**
You should first check with the *Nevada Division of Corporations* to see if there is another corporation with the same name. It publicizes a nine-hundred number you can use to reserve up to three names for thirty days for $10 (900-420-8042). You can also go online to the secretary of state's website and do a search at **https://esos.state. nv.us/sosservices/AnonymousAccess/CorpSearch/CorpSearch. aspx**.

**Trademarks**
Next, you should check the *United States Patent and Trademark Office* (USPTO) to see if anyone has registered your name as a trademark. There are several ways you can do this.

***Online search.*** The records of the trademark office were put online in 1999. You can now search every registered and pending trademark at the following site:

> http://tess2.uspto.gov/bin/gate.exe?f=tess&state=esu7al.1.1

If you do not have access to the Internet at your home or office, you may be able to access it on a computer at a public library. If you are not familiar with how to get online, you may be able to have someone at the library perform the search either for a small fee or for free.

*Federal depository libraries.* You can also search trademarks at the numerous federal depository libraries around the country. These are usually connected with universities. Either your local public library or university library can tell you where the nearest federal depository library is located.

*Search firms.* If you would rather have someone else do the search, you can hire a professional search firm. In addition to a trademark search, a professional search firm can check other records around the country and give you a more accurate answer as to whether the name is being used anywhere. The cost can range from about $100 to over $500 depending on how thorough the search is and who is doing it. The following are a couple firms that do searches. You can call them for a quote.

**Government Liaison Services, Inc.**
200 North Glebe Road, Suite 321
P. O. Box 10648
Arlington, VA 22203
800-642-6564
www.trademarkinfo.com

**Thomson CompuMark**
500 Victory Road
North Quincy, MA 02171
800-692-8833
www.compumark.thomson.com

**Telephone Listings**

Since some businesses neglect to properly register their names (yet still may have superior rights to it), you should also check phone books and business directories. Some libraries have phone books from around the country as well as directories of trade names, but using the Internet is much easier.

If you have a computer with Internet access, you can search every Yellow Pages listing for free. Just search for "yellow pages" with any Web search engine (e.g., Google, Dogpile, Yahoo). You can select a state, enter your business name, and it will tell you if any other companies are listed with that name. One site that allows you to search all states at once is:

http://yellowpages.superpages.com

If you do not have access to a computer, you may be able to use one at your public library or have the search done at your library for free or for a small fee.

## REGISTERING YOUR NAME

Once you have chosen the right name for your new company, you should register your company before someone else registers one with the same name.

**Division of Corporations**

By forming your corporation with the state of Nevada, you have insured that no other person can register a company with the same name. However, this does not stop someone from registering the name with another state or getting a trademark for it.

**Federal Trademark**

A federal *trademark* gives the owner the right to use the name anywhere in the United States and to stop most others from using it.

---

### Example:

Suppose you want to start a motel chain and find that no one has registered the name Rip Van Winkle Inns as a trademark. You checked the Internet, business directories, and Yellow Pages listings, and no one is using it. Once you register a federal trademark, you can stop anyone else from using the name except those who have previously used it. Suppose a small motel in Arizona has used the name, but it did not show up in your search. Because the motel used the name first, it has legal rights to it in its area. You have rights everywhere else. You cannot use the name in its immediate area in competition with it, but it cannot expand outside its area now that you own the name.

---

Before attempting to register the name, you should know that the following rules apply to federal trademarks.

- ✪ You cannot register just the name of a business. You must first use it on goods or services that are sold to the public.

- ✪ A *trademark* is a name, symbol, or other device used to identify goods. A *service mark* is a name, symbol, or other device used to identify services.

✪ You cannot be fully registered until you actually use the mark. You can file an application indicating your intent to use a mark, but you must actually use it before registration is accomplished.

✪ In order to qualify for federal registration, you must use your mark in *commerce*, which means between states or with a foreign country. The use must be bona fide, meaning you cannot just mail a copy to a relative or friend.

✪ You can register your trademark with each state. If you plan to get a federal trademark immediately this is not necessary, but if you plan to limit your business to one state or do not plan to expand out of state for a number of years, state registration is faster and cheaper than federal registration.

✪ Trademarks are registered according to classes of goods. If you plan to use your mark on such different products as tires, lubricants, and window glass, you will need to register and pay a filing fee for each class. (Fees are $325 if filed online or $375 if filed by mail.)

**Fictitious Names**

Registering a federal trademark is beyond the scope of this book, but you can get more information from the following USPTO website:

www.uspto.gov

Sometimes it seems like every good name is taken. Nonetheless, a name can sometimes be used if it is modified slightly or used for a different type of goods.

---

**Example:**

If you want to use the name Flowers by Freida in San Francisco and there is already a Flowers by Freida, Inc., in Los Angeles, you might incorporate under the name Freida Jones, Inc., and then register the corporation as doing business under the fictitious name Flowers by Freida. Unless Flowers by Freida, Inc., has registered a trademark for the name either in California or nationally, you will probably be able to use the name.

---

**Subclasses**    **NOTE:** *You should realize that you might run into complications later, especially if you decide to expand into other areas of the state. One protection available would be to register the name as a trademark. This would give you exclusive use of the name anywhere that someone else was not already using it.*

If someone else is already using a trademark you want to use and in the same class in which you plan to use it, it is possible to register the mark if your goods are different enough.

---

### Example:

If you wanted to use the word *bud* (as in buddy) on an electronic game for boys, but someone else had registered *bud* (picturing a rosebud) as the name of a doll, you might be able to register in the same category (games and playthings) since the products are different and are aimed at different audiences. However, being so close is inviting trouble, and if you were in the same category as Bud, as in Budweiser®, you probably would not be allowed to use it.

---

# Corporate Paperwork

## chapter 4

This chapter explains the specific paperwork you must file to form a corporation. If you are forming an LLC, you should skip this chapter and go on to Chapter 5. After completing the paperwork in this chapter, you should continue to Chapter 6 for the rest of the start-up procedures.

As this book goes to press, the Nevada Secretary of State will not yet accept the online filing of the required paperwork, but it says to check back and it will eventually accept it.

## ARTICLES OF INCORPORATION

The act that legally creates the corporation is the filing of the **ARTICLES OF INCORPORATION** with the Nevada Secretary of State. Some corporations have long, elaborate articles that spell out numerous powers and functions, but most of this is unnecessary. The powers of corporations are spelled out in Nevada law and do not have to be repeated. (Nevada Revised Statutes (Nev. Rev. Stat.), Section (Sec.) 78.060.) The main reason to keep the **ARTICLES OF INCORPORATION** short is to avoid having to amend them later. Putting all but the basics in the bylaws of the corporation makes altering the corporate structure much easier. The **ARTICLES OF INCORPORATION** included in this book are as simple as possible for this reason. (see form 13, p.237.)

Nevada law requires that only seven things be included in the **ARTICLES OF INCORPORATION**. These items are as follows:

1. the name of the corporation;

2. the name and street address of the resident agent;

3. the number of shares authorized;

4. whether the people on the governing board are called directors or trustees, and the names and addresses of the first board;

5. the purpose of the corporation;

6. the names and addresses of incorporators (may be post office box); and,

7. acceptance by resident agent.

**Rules**   Some of the rules you must follow when preparing the articles are as follows.

*Name of the corporation.* If the name of the corporation looks like the name of a person, it must include one of the following words, abbreviations, or other words that identify the business as not being a natural person.

| | |
|---|---|
| Company | Co. |
| Corporation | Corp. |
| Incorporated | Inc. |
| Limited | Ltd. |

While it is not required by the statutes, it is wise for all corporations to use one of these words or abbreviations. If a corporation does not, someone may successfully argue in court that he or she did not know he or she was dealing with a corporation and that the owners should be held personally liable.

One cannot use the words *bank* or *trust* or other words indicating that the company is a financial institution without approval of the commissioner of financial institutions. (Nev. Rev. Stat., Sec. 78.045.) The company must get the approval of the commissioner of insurance if the name of the company or anything else in the articles indicates that the company will be in the insurance business. Except for publicly traded companies, i.e., companies that are not in the professional engineering businesses, no business may use words such as *engineer* or *engineering* unless the principals of the company are certified to be licensed or exempt from licensing by the state board of professional engineers.

***Name and address of the resident agent.*** The name and street address in the state of Nevada of the resident agent must be provided. If the mailing address is different than the street address, this must be provided as well. If you will not be using your own office in Nevada, you will need to make arrangements with a resident agent in the state. Some of those that provide this service are listed in Appendix C of this book. The resident agent must either sign the articles accepting the position or sign a separate paper stating that he or she accepts.

***The classes of stock.*** If more than one class is authorized, the classes, the series, and the number of shares of each class or series must be included unless the articles give the directors the power to set classes, series, and numbers of shares under Nevada law. (Nev. Rev. Stat., Secs. 78.195 and 78.196.)

***Whether there are directors or trustees.*** A Nevada corporation may call its controlling board members either trustees or directors. The members of the first board must be listed with their addresses, which can be their home, their business, or a post office box. They must all be at least 18 years of age. If you wish to have provisions for changing the number of directors, as provided in Nevada Revised Statutes, Section 78.115, they should be included here.

***Purpose.*** This is optional. Usually the best answer is: "Any and all lawful business."

***The name and address of the incorporator(s).*** The address can be a home, business, or post office box. The incorporator is usually one of the parties starting the business, but it may be any person, even if that person has no future interest in the corporation. For people who need to be incorporated quickly, there are companies in Nevada that can, on a moment's notice, have someone sign and run over to the Division of Corporations to file a certificate of incorporation. It is later assigned to the real parties in interest. Each incorporator must sign and the signature(s) must be notarized.

**Forms**     The secretary of state provides a form for the **ARTICLES OF INCORPORATION**, which is included in Appendix D. (see form 13, p.237.) It is not required that you use this form. You can type the document on blank paper.

**Fees**　According to the schedule provided below, the filing fee is at least $75.

**Stock with no par value**
$1 per share

**Stock with par value**

| | |
|---|---|
| Capital $75,000 or less | $75.00 |
| Capital $75,001 to $200,000 | $175.00 |
| Capital $200,001 to $500,000 | $275.00 |
| Capital $500,001 to $1,000,000 | $375.00 |

**Over $1,000,000**

| | |
|---|---|
| First $1,000,000 | $375.00 |
| Each additional $500,000 (or fraction thereof) | $275.00 |
| Maximum fee | $35,000.00 |

You must also include $10 plus a photocopy of the articles for each certified copy you need. You will need at least one copy because one certified copy must be kept with the registered agent in Nevada.

The return time for the articles is usually a week or so. If there is a need to have them back quickly, you may request expedited filing for an additional $50 fee. A complete fee schedule is included in Appendix A.

**Filing**　Your articles can be filed with the secretary of state of Nevada by fax, mail, courier, or over the counter. To pay by credit card, use the **CREDIT CARD CHECKLIST** form in Appendix D. (see form 1, p.213.) The fax number is 775-684-5724. The address is:

> New Filings Division
> 101 N. Carson Street #3
> Carson City, NV 89701

**Expedited Service**　The secretary of state offers four levels of expedited service—twenty-four hours for $75, four hours for $125, two hours for $500, and one hour for $1,000. More details are included in Appendix A.

**Initial List**　After your articles have been filed, you must file an *Initial List of Officers, Directors, and Resident Agent* by the end of the month following filing. You can file online at **www.sos.state.nv.us /business/forms**. There is an additional $125 filing fee for this.

## BYLAWS AND MINUTES

Every corporation must have bylaws and must maintain a set of minutes of its meetings. The bylaws must be adopted at the first meeting, and the first minutes of the corporation will be of the organizational meeting.

The bylaws are the rules for the organization and operation of the corporation. Two sets of **Bylaws** are included with this book. One is for simple corporations (see form 14, p.239), and one is for professional associations. (see form 15, p.245.) In order to complete form 14:

- ✪ fill in the name of the corporation at the top;

- ✪ write the city of the main office of the corporation in the first paragraph;

- ✪ in the "Shareholders" section, write the proposed date of the annual meeting (this can be varied each year as needed);

- ✪ in "Article III," write in the number of directors to be on the board;

- ✪ in "Article VI, Section 1," fill in the number of appropriate months for annual reporting; and,

- ✪ finally, write the date this form is signed at the end of the document.

To complete form 15:

- ✪ fill in the name of the corporation at the top;

- ✪ in "Article I," write the city of the main office of the corporation;

- ✪ at "Article II," write what professional field the corporation will act in (i.e., engineering, construction, etc.);

- ✪ in "Article III, Section 2," write the proposed date of the annual meeting;

- ✪ in "Article IV, Section 2," write in the number of directors to be on the board;

- ✪ in "Article VIII, Section 1," write in the number of shares the corporation can issue, along with value per share; and,

- ✪ finally, write the date this form is signed at the end of the document.

Nevada law allows corporate officers to execute incorporation papers without a meeting, but it is better to have a formal meeting to prove to possible future creditors that you conducted the corporation in a formal manner.

## SHAREHOLDER AGREEMENT

Whenever there are two or more shareholders in a corporation, they should consider drawing up a *shareholder agreement*. This document spells out what is to happen in the event of a disagreement between them. For example, the minority shareholders in small corporations have a risk of being locked into a long-term enterprise with little or no possibility of withdrawing their capital. A shareholder agreement is a fairly complicated document, and you should consider having it drawn up by an attorney. This may be costly, but the expense should be weighed against the cost of going to court should the parties separate. A less expensive alternative is to sit down and decide what will happen in the event of a shareholder's death, divorce, retirement, or decision to sell. Write that up, and have everyone sign it. Some of the things that may be addressed in such an agreement are as follows:

- veto by minority shareholder;

- greater than majority voting requirement;

- cumulative voting;

- deadlocks;

- arbitration;

- dissolution;

- compulsory buyout;

- preemptive rights;

- restrictions on transfers of shares; and,

- refusal of a party to participate.

## IRS FORM 2553

If your corporation is to be taxed as an S corporation, you must file **ELECTION BY A SMALL BUSINESS CORPORATION (IRS FORM 2553)** with the IRS within seventy-five days of incorporation. (see form 16, p.251.) As a practical matter, you should sign and file this at your incorporation meeting because otherwise you may forget. To make the S corporation status official, you should also fill out a **RESOLUTION (ADOPTING S CORPORATION STATUS)** electing to be taxed as an S corporation and keep it in your minute book. (see form 20, p.267.)

## CORPORATE SUPPLIES

A corporation needs to keep a permanent record of its legal affairs, including:

- ✪ the original charter;

- ✪ minutes of all meetings;

- ✪ records of the stock issued, transferred, and canceled;

- ✪ fictitious names registered; and,

- ✪ any other legal matters.

The records are usually kept in a ring binder. Any ring binder will do, but it is possible to purchase a specially prepared *corporate kit* that has the name of the corporation printed on it and usually contains forms such as minutes, stock certificates, etc. Most of these items are included with this book, so purchasing such a kit is unnecessary unless you want to have something different, such as specially printed stock certificates.

Some sources for corporate kits are:

**Corpkit Legal Supplies**
888-888-9120
info@corpkit.com
www.corpkit.com

**Blumberg Excelsior**
800-529-6278
weborders@blumb.com
www.blumberg.com

**Corpex**
800-221-8181
corpex@markscorpex.com
www.markscorpex.com

One thing that is not included with this book is a *corporate seal*, which must be specially made for each corporation. Most corporations use a metal seal like a notary's seal to emboss the paper. These can be ordered from many office supply companies. In recent years, many companies have been using rubber stamps for corporate seals. These are cheaper, lighter, and easier to read. Rubber stamp seals can also be ordered from office supply stores, printers, and specialized rubber stamp companies. Your seal may be round or rectangular. The corporate seal should contain:

- the full, exact name of the corporation;

- the word "Seal"; and,

- the year of incorporation.

Corporations are no longer required to issue stock certificates to represent shares of ownership. However, as a practical matter, it is a good idea to do so. This shows some formality and gives each person tangible evidence of ownership. If you do issue shares, the face of each certificate must show:

- the corporate name;

- that the corporation was organized under Nevada law;

- the name of the shareholder(s);

- the number, class, and series of the stock; and,

- the signature of one or more officers designated by the bylaws or the board of directors.

If there are two or more classes or series of stock, the front or back of the certificate must disclose that upon request and without charge. The corporation will provide to the shareholder the preferences, limitations, and relative rights of each class or series; the preferences of any preferred stock; and, the board of directors' authority to determine rights for any subsequent classes or series. If there are any restrictions, they must be stated on the certificate, or a statement must be included that they are available without charge.

The stock certificates can be fancy, such as with engraved eagles, or they can be typed or handwritten. Sample **STOCK CERTIFICATES** are included in Appendix D. (see form 22, p.271.) For *professional associations*, the following statement should be typed on the certificate: "The transfer of the shares represented by this certificate is restricted by the bylaws of the corporation."

**NOTE:** *Do not forget to make copies if you intend to use the stock certificates in this book so that you do not run out.*

# LLC Paperwork

## chapter 5

This chapter explains the specific paperwork you must file to form a limited liability company. If you are forming a corporation, you should ignore this chapter, use the instructions in Chapter 4, and then go on to Chapter 6.

As this book goes to press, the Nevada Secretary of State's office will not yet accept online filings, but it says to check back and it will eventually be set up to accept them.

## ARTICLES OF ORGANIZATION

The act that creates a limited liability company is the filing of articles of organization with the secretary of state in Carson City. Some LLCs have long, elaborate articles that spell out numerous powers and functions. Most of this is unnecessary. The powers of LLCs are spelled out in Nevada law and do not have to be repeated. (Nev. Rev. Stat., Sec. 86.281.) The main reason to keep the articles of organization short is to avoid having to amend them later. Putting all but the basics in an operating agreement makes altering the structure much easier. The **LIMITED-LIABILITY COMPANY ARTICLES OF ORGANIZATION** included in this book are as simple as possible for this reason. (see form 32, p.297.) Instructions accompany the form.

**Rules**     Nevada law requires that only the name, registered address, resident agent, and management be listed in the articles of organization. The following are the specific rules.

***Name of the limited liability company.*** The company must include one of the following designations or abbreviations as part of the name:

| | | |
|---|---|---|
| Limited Liability Company | L.L.C. | LLC |
| Limited Company | LC | |
| Limited | Ltd. | |

The word *Company* can be abbreviated *Co.*

***Name and address of the registered agent.*** The name and street address in the state of Nevada of the resident agent must be provided. If the mailing address is different from the street address, this must be provided as well. If you will not be using your own office in Nevada, you will need to make arrangements with a resident agent in the state. (Some of those that provide this service are listed in Appendix C.) The resident agent must either sign the articles accepting the position or sign a separate paper stating that he or she accepts.

***The name and address of the organizer(s).*** The address given for the organizer can be from a home, business, or post office box. The organizer is usually one of the parties starting the business, but it may be any person, even if that person has no future interest in the company. For people who need to form their business quickly, there are companies in Nevada that can, on a moment's notice, have someone sign the LIMITED-LIABILITY COMPANY ARTICLES OF ORGANIZATION and run over to the Division of Corporations to file it. Each organizer must sign and the signature(s) must be notarized.

***Management.*** The articles must specify whether the company is to be managed by the members or separate managers.

**Form**   The secretary of state provides a form for the LIMITED-LIABILITY COMPANY ARTICLES OF ORGANIZATION, which is included in Appendix D. (see form 32, p.297.) It is not required that you use this form. You can type the document on blank paper.

**Filing**   The filing fee is $75. A file-stamped copy of the articles will be returned to you at no additional charge. To receive a certified copy, you must enclose an additional $30 per certification.

Your articles can be filed with the Nevada secretary of state by fax, mail, courier, or over the counter. To pay by credit card, use the CREDIT

**Card Checklist** in Appendix D. (see form 1, p.213.) The fax number is 775-684-5724. The address is:

> New Filings Division
> 101 N. Carson Street #3
> Carson City, NV 89701

**Expedited Service**

The secretary of state offers four levels of expedited service—twenty-four hours for $75, four hours for $125, two hours for $500, and one hour for $1,000. More details are included in Appendix A.

**Initial List**

After your articles have been filed, you must file an *Initial List of Managing Members and Resident Agent* by the end of the month following filing. You can file online at **www.sos.state.nv.us/business/forms**. There is an additional $125 filing fee for this.

## OPERATING AGREEMENT

As mentioned in the previous chapter, an LLC must decide if it will be managed by all the members or a limited number of managers. If it is to be run by managers, there may be one or more and they may or may not be members.

In either case, it is important to have a written agreement spelling out the rights and duties of the members and managers, if any. This is also a good document in which to include other rules governing the LLC. Even if an LLC has only one member, a membership agreement should be signed to formalize the LLC and make it clear that the member is not personally liable for the debts of the business.

The law of LLCs is very new, and since corporations that do not follow procedures can be *pierced* (and their shareholders held liable), it is possible that a court may try the same on an LLC. Therefore, following the old formula is the safest. Of course, if you set up procedures and do not follow them, this could backfire, and a court could use that as a reason to impose liability.

**Membership Operating Agreement**

In Appendix D there is a generic **Limited Liability Company Member-Managed Operating Agreement**. (see form 34, p.305.) Use this form if your LLC will either have just one member or if it will have two or more members and be managed by all the members.

This form has basic terms that can be useful to most businesses. If all the terms apply to your business, you should execute a copy and keep it with your company records.

If there are other terms you would like to include in your agreement, you can add them in paragraph 21 or you can draw up an addendum to the membership agreement.

**Management Agreement**

In Appendix D there is a generic LIMITED LIABILITY COMPANY MANAGEMENT AGREEMENT. (see form 35, p.307.) Use this form if your LLC will have two or more members and be managed by a limited number of members, or if it will be managed by someone who is not a member.

This form has basic terms that can be useful to most businesses. If all the terms apply to your business, you should execute a copy and keep it with your company records.

If there are other terms you would like to include in your agreement, you can add them in paragraph 21 or you can draw up an addendum to the management agreement.

Both operating agreements use SCHEDULE A TO LIMITED LIABILITY COMPANY OPERATING OR MANAGEMENT AGREEMENT to include the specific information for your company. (see form 36, p.309.)

**Certificate of Authority**

When people do business with an LLC, they occasionally ask for some proof that the person they are dealing with has authority to sign things in the name of the LLC. For this purpose you can use a CERTIFICATE OF AUTHORITY, which is included in Appendix D. (see form 39, p.315.)

# IRS FORM 8832

The ENTITY CLASSIFICATION ELECTION (IRS FORM 8832) is used by the IRS to allow LLCs to chose their tax status. (see form 33, p.299.) It is basically a choice between partnership taxation and corporate taxation. For a single-member LLC, it is a choice between sole proprietorship taxation and corporate taxation.

The difference between the two is that a sole proprietorship or partnership is not taxed at all, but a corporation is treated like a separate taxpayer. A sole proprietorship or partnership just reports its income and expenses and the proprietor or partners report the net profit or loss on their personal tax return. A corporation files a tax return and pays tax on any profits. If it distributes any of the profits to the members, those profits are taxed again. Therefore, in most cases, it is better not to choose corporate taxation.

One way around the double taxation is paying all the profits to the members as salary; this makes them deductible and the corporation has no profit on which to pay tax. The problem arises when the company makes more money than would be reasonable to pay as salaries. The IRS can then impose extra corporate taxation on the excess amounts.

If you are unsure how you wish to be taxed, you should consult a book on the taxation of businesses or check with a tax professional. Once you decide, you should file the **ENTITY CLASSIFICATION ELECTION (IRS FORM 8832)**. This form must be filed within seventy-five days of starting your LLC. (see form 33, p.299.) Instructions accompany the form in Appendix D.

# Start-Up Procedures

## chapter 6

This chapter contains the steps to start your Nevada business after you have prepared either the corporate forms in Chapter 4 or the limited liability company forms in Chapter 5.

## NEVADA BUSINESS LICENSE

Nevada does have one tax that does not fit into its usual free-wheeling scheme—the quarterly state business tax of $25 per employee. Fortunately for Nevada corporations and LLCs that do not do business in Nevada, the fee only has to be paid once.

Once you have formed your Nevada corporation or LLC, you should use the **NEVADA BUSINESS REGISTRATION** to register for a license. (see form 7, p.225.) Instructions accompany the form. Check with the Nevada Secretary of State to see if your business requires the **SUPPLEMENTAL INFORMATION** form as well. (see form 8, p.227.)

## REGISTERING WITH YOUR HOME STATE

Once you have formed your Nevada corporation or LLC, you must register it as a foreign corporation in the state in which you will have your main office (and any other states in which you will be doing business). This usually requires filling out a simple form and paying the filing fee. You must contact your state corporation division (usually the secretary of state) to obtain this form. The addresses of these offices for all fifty states are included in Appendix B of this book.

For some states, you can download the forms from the Internet. Others will send them to you if you call, and a few require you to send a letter. You should send for this material right away, because some states take weeks to send it. You can use a form like the one in Appendix D entitled **REQUEST FOR CORPORATE FORMS**. (see form 2, p.215.)

Check to see exactly what your state requires for registration—it might be a certified copy of your corporate or LLC documents, or a certificate of status—and be sure to get the right form from Nevada. Once your company has been successfully registered in your state, you will be able to legally do business.

## ORGANIZATIONAL MEETING

The real birth of the business takes place at the organizational meeting of the corporation or LLC. This is when the payment is made for the stock or membership interests, and the officers and directors or members are named.

As discussed earlier, an LLC has much less formality than a corporation. However, the more formally an LLC conducts itself, the less likely it is that the members will have to face questions of liability. So it is best to use formal procedures for the LLC whenever it is not too inconvenient.

Usually minutes, tax forms, and other forms are prepared before the organizational meeting and used as a script for the meeting. They should be signed at the end of the meeting.

**Agenda for a Corporation**   The following is the usual agenda for a corporation:

1. signing the **WAIVER OF NOTICE OF THE ORGANIZATIONAL MEETING** (form 17, p.259);

2. noting persons present in the **MINUTES OF THE ORGANIZATIONAL MEETING** (form 18, p.261);

3. presentation and acceptance of a copy of the articles of incorporation;

4. election of directors;

5. adoption of **BYLAWS** (form 14, p.239, or form 15, p.245);

6.  election of officers;

7.  presentation and acceptance of corporate seal;

8.  presentation and acceptance of **STOCK CERTIFICATES** (form 22, p.271);

9.  designation of bank with a **BANKING RESOLUTION** (form 4, p.219);

10. acceptance of **OFFER TO PURCHASE STOCK** (form 19, p.265); (use **BILL OF SALE** (form 6, p.223) if property is traded for stock);

11. **RESOLUTION TO REIMBURSE EXPENSES** (form 5, p.221);

12. adoption of special resolutions such as S corporation status; and,

13. adjournment.

At the end of the meeting, the stock certificates are usually issued, but in some cases, such as when a prospective shareholder does not yet have money to pay for them, they are issued when payment is complete.

To issue the stock, the certificates at the end of this book should be completed as follows.

- ✪ Add the name of the corporation in the gray box.

- ✪ Make sure a statement that the corporation is organized under the laws of Nevada is beneath the name.

- ✪ Insert the name of the shareholder, the number of shares the certificate represents, and the type of stock issued in the first paragraph.

- ✪ Number the certificate in the top left box. (Each certificate should be numbered in order to keep track of them.)

- ✪ Write the number of shares the certificate represents in the top right box.

- ✪ Sign and date at the bottom. (These certificates should be signed by officers designated in the bylaws.)

- ✪ Make a record of the stock issuance on the **STOCK LEDGER** (see form 21, p.269.)

**Agenda for An LLC**

The following is the usual agenda for an LLC:

1. note persons present in minutes;

2. presentation and acceptance of a copy of the articles of organization;

3. presentation and acceptance of LIMITED LIABILITY COMPANY MEMBER-MANAGED OPERATING AGREEMENT (form 34, p.305) or LIMITED LIABILITY COMPANY MANAGEMENT AGREEMENT (form 35, p.307), plus SCHEDULE A TO LIMITED LIABILITY COMPANY OPERATING OR MANAGEMENT AGREEMENT (form 36, p.309);

4. presentation and acceptance of ENTITY CLASSIFICATION ELECTION (IRS FORM 8832) (form 33, p.299);

5. designation of bank with a BANKING RESOLUTION (form 4, p.219);

6. RESOLUTION TO REIMBURSE EXPENSES (form 5, p.221); and,

7. adjournment.

## RECORDS BOOK

After the organizational meeting, you should set up your *company records book*, sometimes called the *minute book*. As noted earlier, this can be a simple ring binder.

**Corporation**

The minute book for a corporation usually contains the following:

1. a title page ("Company Records of _____");

2. a table of contents;

3. the letter from the Nevada Secretary of State acknowledging receipt and filing of the articles of incorporation;

4. a copy of the articles of incorporation;

5. the letter from the local secretary of state acknowledging registration as a foreign company doing business in the state;

6. a copy of the document filed with the local state to register as a foreign corporation able to transact business in the state;

7. a copy of any fictitious name registration;

8. a copy of any trademark registration;

9. a **WAIVER OF NOTICE OF THE ORGANIZATIONAL MEETING** (form 17, p.259);

10. **MINUTES OF THE ORGANIZATIONAL MEETING** (form 18, p. 261);

11. **BYLAWS** (form 14, p.239, or form 15, p.245);

12. **SAMPLE STOCK CERTIFICATES** (form 22, p.271);

13. **OFFER TO PURCHASE STOCK** (form 19, p.265);

14. tax forms

&#9673; **APPLICATION FOR EMPLOYER IDENTIFICATION NUMBER (IRS FORM SS-4)** (form 3, p.217);

&#9673; **ELECTION BY A SMALL BUSINESS CORPORATION (IRS FORM 2553)** (form 16, p. 251); and,

**LLC**    15. a **STOCK LEDGER** (form 21, p.269).

The minute book for an LLC usually contains the following:

1. a title page ("Company Records of _____");

2. a table of contents;

3. the letter from the Nevada Secretary of State acknowledging receipt and filing of the certificate of formation;

4. a copy of the certificate of formation;

5. the letter from the local secretary of state acknowledging registration as a foreign company doing business in the state;

6. a copy of the document filed with the local state to register as a foreign LLC able to transact business;

7. a copy of any fictitious name registration;

8. a copy of any trademark registration;

9. a copy of the operating agreement;

10. tax forms

&#9673; **EMPLOYER IDENTIFICATION NUMBER (IRS FORM SS-4)** (form 3, p. 217);

✪ **ENTITY CLASSIFICATION ELECTION (IRS FORM 8832)** (form 33, p.299); and,

11. a list of member names and addresses.

## BANK ACCOUNTS

A corporation must have a bank account. Checks payable to a corporation cannot be cashed—they must be deposited into an account.

Unfortunately, many banks charge high rates to corporations for the right to put their money in the bank. You can tell how much extra a corporation is being charged when you compare a corporate account to a personal account with similar activity.

Usually, there is a complicated scheme of fees, with charges for each transaction. Many banks today may even charge companies for the right to make a deposit. (Twenty-five cents for the deposit plus ten cents for each check that is deposited. Deposit thirty checks and this will cost you $3.25.) Often the customer is granted an interest credit on the balance in the account, but it is usually small and if the credit is larger than the charges, you lose the excess.

Fortunately, some banks have set up reasonable fees for small corporations, such as charging no fees if a certain balance is maintained. Because the fees can easily amount to hundreds of dollars a year, it pays to shop around. Even if the bank is relatively far from the business, using bank-by-mail can make the distance meaningless. But do not be surprised if a bank with low fees raises them. Companies have been known to change banks multiple times in one year as banks raise fees or are bought out by a bank with higher fees.

One trick to finding an affordable bank is to open a checking account and a money market account. (Money market accounts pay higher interest and do not charge for making deposits. You can only write three checks a month, but you can usually make unlimited withdrawals.) Make all your deposits into the money market account and just pay bills out the regular checking account, transferring funds as needed.

Another way to save money in bank charges is to order checks from a private source rather than through the bank. These are usually much cheaper than those the bank offers because the bank makes a profit on the check printing. If the bank officer says it cannot be done when you are opening the account, just wait until your first batch of checks runs out and switch over without telling the bank. The bank probably will not even notice, as long as you get the checks printed correctly. While most business checks are large (and expensive), there is no reason you cannot use small personal-size checks for your business. They are easier to carry around and work just as well unless you want to impress people with the size of your check.

All you should need to open a corporate bank account is a copy of your articles of incorporation and your federal tax identification number. Some banks, however, want more, and they sometimes do not even know what it is they want.

---

### Example:

After opening numerous corporate accounts with only the two items previously listed, the author once encountered a bank employee who wanted "something certified so we know who your officers are. Your attorney will know what to draw up." I explained that I was my own attorney and was the president, secretary, and treasurer of the corporation, and I would write out and sign and seal whatever the bank wanted. No, it had to be a nice certificate signed by the secretary of the corporation and sealed. So, I typed out a statement in legalese, put a gold foil seal on it, and the bank opened the account.

---

If you have trouble opening the account, you can use the **BANKING RESOLUTION** included with this book, or you can make up a similar form. (see form 4, p.219.)

## LOCAL LICENSES

In some states, counties and municipalities are authorized to levy a license tax on the privilege of doing business. Before opening your business, you should obtain a county occupational license, and if you will be working within a city, you should obtain a city occupational license. Businesses that perform work in several cities, such as builders, must obtain a license from each city in which they work. This does not have to be done until you actually begin a job in a particular city.

**Home Businesses**

County occupational licenses can usually be obtained from the tax collector in the county courthouse. City licenses are usually available at city hall. Be sure to find out if *zoning* allows your type of business before buying or leasing property, because the licensing department will check the zoning before issuing your license.

Problems occasionally arise when persons attempt to start a business in their home. Small new businesses cannot afford to pay rent for commercial space, and cities often try to forbid businesses in residential areas. Getting a county occupational license often gives notice to the city that a business is being conducted in a residential area.

Some people avoid the problem by starting their business without occupational licenses, figuring that the penalties are nowhere near the cost of office space. Others get the county license and ignore the city rules. If a person has commercial trucks and equipment parked on his or her property, there will probably be complaints by neighbors and the city will most likely take legal action. But if a person's business consists merely of making phone calls out of the home and keeping supplies inside the house, the problem may never arise.

If the problem does surface regarding a home business that does not disturb the neighbors, a good argument can be made that the zoning law that prohibits the business is unconstitutional. When zoning laws were first instituted, they were not meant to stop people from doing things in a residence that had historically been part of the life in a residence. Consider a painter. Should a zoning law prohibit a person from sitting in his or her home and painting pictures? Is there a difference if he or she sells them for a living? Can the government force him or her to rent commercial space?

Similar arguments can be made for many home-based businesses. But court battles with a city are expensive and probably not worth the effort for a small business. The best course of action is to keep a low profile. Using a post office box is sometimes helpful in diverting attention away from the residence. However, the secretary of state and the occupational license administrator will want a physical street address. There should be no problem using a residential address and explaining to the city that it is merely the corporate address and that no business is conducted on the premises.

# Capital Structure and Selling Stock

## chapter 7

## CAPITAL STRUCTURE

There is no hard and fast rule as to how much capital you should put into a new corporation or LLC. The more you put in as capital, the more you have at risk in the business, so you would want to put in as little as possible. But if you put in too little, a court might someday say you were undercapitalized and find you personally liable for company debts, just as it could for a corporation. Also, there could be tax problems with not counting enough of your contributions as capital or for contributing appreciated property. These matters should be discussed with a tax specialist.

If you are starting a small business that does not need a lot of expensive equipment, a few thousand dollars would be a safe amount with which to start. If you do need to buy expensive equipment, and the company can borrow the money from a third party to cover it, you would probably be safe as well. But if you need to purchase expensive equipment and personally loan the money to the company rather than contribute it as capital, you should weigh the risks of a lawsuit and consider consulting an attorney or accountant who specializes in business start-ups.

One thing to keep in mind is that if you do not put in the amount of capital you state in your initial agreement and are later sued or file bankruptcy, you may be required to come up with any unpaid amount.

For a corporation, the purchaser should submit an **OFFER TO PURCHASE STOCK** before any stock is issued. (see form 19, p.265.) The offer states that it is made "pursuant to Sec. 1244 I.R.C." The advantage of this section is that in the event the business fails or the value of the stock drops, the shareholder can write off up to $50,000 ($100,000 for married couples) as ordinary income, rather than as a long-term capital loss, which would be limited to $3,000 a year.

Some thought should be given to the way in which the ownership of the stock or membership interests will be held. Stock owned in one person's name alone is subject to probate upon death. Making two persons *joint owners* of the stock (joint tenants with full rights of survivorship) would avoid probate upon the death of one of them. However, taking a joint owner's name off in the event of a disagreement (such as divorce) could be troublesome. Where a couple jointly operates a business, joint ownership would be best. But where one person is the sole party involved in the business, the desire to avoid probate should be weighed against the risk of losing half the business in a divorce.

Another way to avoid probate is to put ownership of the stock in a living trust. You are allowed to list your securities as *pay on death* or *transfer on death* in about half the states. This avoids probate as well. (For living trusts or information on pay on death registration, you should consult an attorney or a book on estate planning.)

## CLASSES OF INTERESTS

When different shareholders or members have different types of interests in the business, it is possible to issue different classes of stock or levels of membership. For example, stock can be issued as *common* or *preferred* and as *voting* or *nonvoting* (except that S corporations can have only one class of stock). Membership interests in an LLC may have different types of memberships to suit the needs of the participants.

**Classes of Stock**

The following are some classes of stock that can be used.

- ✪ *Common stock* is the basic stock issued to owners of a corporation.

- ✪ *Preferred stock* can be used to give some shareholders special rights, such as first claim to the profits or to the assets of the corporation upon dissolution.

**Example:**

If you have an investor in your corporation who will be paid a guaranteed rate of return before other shareholders get any profits, you might issue him or her preferred stock and the other owners common stock.

✪  *Voting* and *nonvoting stock* can be issued when some shareholders will have control of the corporation and others will not.

**Example:**

The owner of a business might want to give $10,000 worth of stock to each of his or her children each year to avoid estate taxes at death, but he or she might not want the children to have a vote in the affairs of the corporation. To do so, he or she can create both voting and nonvoting stock and give the children the nonvoting stock.

The creation of different classes of stock has various legal and tax consequences. You should not use anything other than common stock until you have consulted with an accountant or attorney who can make sure your plan will work best.

## PAYMENT FOR INTERESTS

Stock or membership interests may be paid for with money, property, services, or a promissory note. The important thing to remember is that if a person fails to make the specified payment or takes return of the payment, he or she may be liable to the company or its creditors for the full amount that should have been paid. To make this less likely, the board of directors or managers should pass a resolution stating that they have determined that the property is being accepted at its fair market value in the exchange.

**LLCs**    The following are some other things for an LLC to consider.

✪  If a member trades services for an interest in the capital of the company, he or she must pay income tax on the value of interest at the time the services are exchanged for the interest. (If the interest is only a share of future profits, the tax does not have to be paid until the profits are received.)

✪ When appreciated property is traded to an LLC in exchange for a membership interest, the tax basis of the property carries over to the membership interest. Taxes on the appreciation are paid when the member sells his or her LLC interest.

✪ If the LLC sells the property, it may have to pay a tax on the amount received over the contributor's basis.

**Corporations**    The most important thing to know for a corporation is that the Internal Revenue Code allows the tax-free exchange of property for stock if the persons receiving the stock for the property or for cash end up owning at least 80% of the voting and other stock in the corporation. If more than 20% of the stock is issued in exchange for services instead of property and cash, the transfers of property will be taxable and treated as a sale for cash. (I.R.C., Sec. 351.)

Also, if the stock has par value and the payment is in cash, the payment should not be less than par value but may be more. (*Par value* is the assigned amount the share is worth when it is first issued.)

Tax rules are complicated and ever-changing. You should consult with a tax expert or a tax guide if you will be doing creative financing.

## SECURITIES LAWS

The issuance of securities is subject to both federal and state securities laws. A *security* is equity interest in a company and debt (i.e., notes, bonds). The laws covering securities are so broad that any instrument that represents an investment in an enterprise, such as where the investor is relying on the efforts of others for profit, is considered a security. Even a promissory note has been held to be a security. Once an investment is determined to involve a security, strict rules apply. If the rules are not followed, there can be criminal penalties. Civil damages can also be awarded to purchasers.

The rules are designed to protect people who put up money as an investment in a business. In the stock market crash of 1929, many people lost their life savings in swindles. The government wants to be sure that this does not happen again. Unfortunately, the laws can also make it difficult for many honest businesses to raise capital.

The goal of the laws covering sales of securities is for investors to be given full disclosure of the risks involved in an investment. To accomplish this goal, the law usually requires that the securities must either be registered with the federal *Securities and Exchange Commission* (SEC) or a similar state regulatory body, and that lengthy disclosure statements be compiled and distributed.

The law is complicated and strict compliance is required. The penalties are so harsh that most lawyers will not handle securities matters. You most likely would not be able to get through the registration process on your own. But, like your decision to form your business without a lawyer, you may wish to consider some alternatives when attempting to raise capital without a lawyer.

- ✪ Borrow the money as a personal loan from friends or relatives. The disadvantage is that you will have to pay them back personally if the business fails. However, you may have to do that anyway if they are close relatives or if you do not follow the securities laws.

- ✪ Tailor your stock issuance to fall within the exemptions in the securities laws. There are some exemptions in the securities laws for small businesses that may apply to your transaction. (The antifraud provisions always apply, even if the transaction is exempt from registration.) Some exemptions are explained in the next section, but you should make at least one appointment with a securities lawyer to be sure you have covered everything and that there have not been any changes in the law. You can often pay for an hour or so of a securities lawyer's time for $200 and just ask questions about your plans. He or she can tell you what not to do and what your options are. You can then make an informed decision.

## FEDERAL EXEMPTIONS FROM SECURITIES LAWS

In most situations where one person, a husband and wife, or a few partners run a business and all parties are active in the enterprise, securities laws do not apply to their issuance of stock to themselves. As a practical matter, if your father or aunt wants to put up some money for some stock in your business, you might not get into trouble. They probably will not seek triple damages and criminal penalties if your business fails.

However, you may wish to obtain money from additional investors to enable your business to grow. This can be done in many circumstances as long as you follow the rules carefully. In some cases, you do not have to file anything with the SEC, but in others, you must file a notice.

**Federal Private Placement Exemption**

If you sell interests in your business to a small group of people without any advertising, you can fall into the private offering exemption if all the following are true:

- all persons to whom offers are made are financially astute, are participants in the business, or have a substantial net worth;

- no advertising or general solicitation is used to promote the stock;

- the offer is made to a limited number of persons;

- the shares are purchased for investment and not for immediate resale;

- the persons to whom the stock is offered are given all relevant information (including financial information) regarding the issuance and the corporation. (Again, there are numerous court cases explaining each aspect of these rules, including such questions as what is a *financially astute person*); and,

- a filing claiming the exemption is made upon the United States Securities and Exchange Commission.

**Federal Intrastate Offering Exemption**

If you only offer your securities to residents of one state, you may be exempt from federal securities laws. This is because federal laws usually only apply to interstate commerce. Intrastate offerings are covered by SEC Rule 147. If it is followed carefully, your sale will be exempt from federal registration.

**Federal Small Offerings Exemptions**

The SEC has liberalized the rules in recent years in order to make it easier for business to grow. Under Regulation D, adopted by the SEC, there are three types of exemptions under SEC Rules 504, 505, and 506.

The offering of securities of up to $1,000,000 in a twelve-month period can be exempt. (SEC Rule 504). Offers can be made to any number of persons, no specific information must be provided, and investors do not have to be sophisticated.

An offering of up to $5,000,000 can be made in a twelve-month period. (SEC Rule 505.) However, no public advertising may be used and only thirty-five nonaccredited investors may purchase stock. Any number of accredited investors may purchase stock. (*Accredited investors* are sophisticated individuals with high net worths or high incomes, sophisticated individuals with large trusts or investment companies, or persons involved in the business.)

SEC Rule 506 has no limit on the amount of money that may be raised, but, like SEC Rule 505, it does not allow advertising, and it limits the amount of nonaccredited investors to thirty-five.

## STATE SECURITIES LAWS

One reason there are exemptions from federal securities laws is that there are so many state laws covering securities that additional registration is not needed. Every state has securities laws, which are called *blue sky laws*. If you wish to offer your stock in all fifty states, you must be registered in all fifty states unless you can fit into one of the exemptions. However, exemptions are very limited.

**Typical State Law Private Placement Exemption**

The most common one is the *private placement exemption*. This can apply if all the following are true:

- ✪ there are thirty-five or fewer purchasers of shares;

- ✪ no commissions are paid to anyone to promote the stock;

- ✪ no advertising or general solicitation is used to promote the stock;

- ✪ all material information (including financial information) regarding the stock issuance and the company is given to or accessible to all shareholders; and,

- ✪ a three-day right of rescission is given.

These rules may sound simple on the surface, but there are many more rules, regulations, and court cases explaining each one in more detail.  For example, what does "thirty-five persons" mean? Sounds simple, but it can mean more than literally thirty-five people. Spouses, persons whose net worths exceeds a million dollars, and founders of the company may not be counted in some circumstances.

As you can see, the exemption does not give you much latitude in raising money. Therefore, if you wish to raise money from a wider group of people, you will have to register. You should contact the securities commission of your state to find out more about your state's requirements. The contact information for your state's securities commission can be found in the following pages.

Another good source of information for the securities laws of all fifty states is the *Blue Sky Reporter*, a multivolume loose leaf service that summarizes the securities laws of the states. A copy should be available in most law libraries.

## INTERNET STOCK SALES

With the advent of the Internet, promoters of business interests have a new way of reaching large numbers of people, most of whom are financially able to afford investments in securities. However, all securities laws apply to the Internet, and they are being enforced. Recently, state attorneys general have issued *cease and desist orders* to promoters not registered in their states in order to get them to stop business there.

Under current law, you must be registered in a state in order to sell stock to its residents. If you are not registered in a state, you must turn down any residents from that state who want to buy your stock.

You may wonder how the famous Spring Street Brewing Company raised $1.6 million for its Wit Beer on the Internet. The main reason it was successful was because its president is a securities lawyer and could prepare his own prospectus to file with the SEC and the states. That would have cost anyone else about $100,000. Also, most of its stock sales were inspired by newspaper and magazine articles about the company and not from the Internet.

Some Internet sites that may be helpful in raising capital are:

**Angel Capital Electronic Network (SBA)**
www.sba.gov

**NVST**
www.nvst.com

# STATE SECURITIES REGISTRATION OFFICES

The following are the addresses of the offices that can provide information on securities registration requirements for each state.

**Alabama Securities Commission**
770 Washington Avenue, Suite 570
Montgomery, AL 36130
Phone: 800-222-1253
Fax: 334-242-0240
www.asc.state.al.us

**Alaska Division of Banking and Securities**
150 3rd Street, Suite 217
Juneau, AK 99801
Phone: 888-925-2521
Fax: 907-465-2549
www.dced.state.ak.us/bsc/bsc.htm

**Arizona Corporation Commission**
Securities Division
1300 West Washington Street, 3rd Floor
Phoenix, AZ 85007
Phone: 866-837-4399
Fax: 602-594-7470
www.azcc.gov/divisions/securities

**Arkansas Securities Department**
Heritage West Building
201 East Markham, Suite 300
Little Rock, AR 72201
Phone: 800-981-4429
Fax: 501-324-9268
www.securities.arkansas.gov

**California Department of Corporations**
320 West 4th Street, Suite 750
Los Angeles, CA 90013
Phone: 866-275-2677
Fax: 213-576-7188
www.corp.ca.gov

**Colorado Division of Securities**
1560 Broadway, Suite 900
Denver, CO 80202
Phone: 303-894-2320
Fax: 303-861-2126
www.dora.state.co.us/securities

**Connecticut Department of Banking**
260 Constitution Plaza
Hartford, CT 06103
Phone: 800-831-7225
Fax: 860-240-8178
www.state.ct.us/dob

**Delaware Department of Justice**
Division of Securities
820 North French Street, 5th Floor
Wilmington, DE 19801
Phone: 302-577-8424
Fax: 302-577-6987
www.state.de.us/securities

**District of Columbia**
Department of Insurance, Securities, and Banking
801 1st Street, NE, Suite 701
Washington, DC 20002
Phone: 202-727-8000
Fax: 202-535-1196
http://disb.dc.gov

**Florida Office of Financial Regulation**
200 East Gaines Street
Tallahassee, FL 32399
Phone: 800-848-3792
www.flofr.com/licensing

**Georgia Division of Securities and Business Regulation**
2 MLK Jr. Drive, SE
West Tower, Suite 802
Atlanta, GA 30334
Phone: 404-656-3920
Fax: 404-657-8410
http://sos.georgia.gov

**Hawaii Business Registration Division**
King Kalakaua Building
335 Merchant Street, Room 201
Honolulu, HI 96813
Phone: 808-586-2744
Fax: 808-586-2733
http://hawaii.gov/dcca/areas/breg

**Idaho Securities Bureau**
800 Park Boulevard, Suite 200
Boise, ID 83712
Phone: 208-332-8000
Fax: 208-332-8099
http://finance.idaho.gov/SecuritiesBureau.aspx

**Illinois Secretary of State**
Securities Department
300 West Jefferson Street, Suite 300A
Springfield, IL 62702
Phone: 800-628-7937
Fax: 217-782-8876
www.cyberdriveillinois.com/departments/
securities/home.html

**Indiana Securities Division**
Office of the Secretary of State
302 West Washington, Room E-111
Indianapolis, IN 46204
Phone: 800-223-8791
Fax: 317-233-3675
www.in.gov/sos/securities/invadval/html

**Iowa Securities Bureau**
Enforcement Section
330 Maple Street
Des Moines, IA 50319
Phone: 515-281-4441
Fax: 515-291-3059
www.iid.state.ia.us/ia_securities_bureau/index.asp

**Kansas Securities Commissioner**
618 South Kansas Avenue
Topeka, KS 66603
Phone: 800-232-9580
Fax: 785-296-6872
www.securities.state.ks.us

**Kentucky Department of Financial Institutions**
1025 Capitol Center Drive, Suite 200
Frankfort, KY 40601
Phone: 502-573-3390
Fax: 502-573-0086
www.kfi.ky.gov

**Louisiana Office of Financial Institutions**
Securities Division
8660 United Plaza Boulevard, 2nd Floor
Baton Rouge, LA 70809
Phone: 225-925-4660
Fax: 225-925-4548
www.ofi.state.la.us

**Maine Office of Securities**
121 State House Station
Augusta, ME 04333
Phone: 877-624-8551
Fax: 207-624-8590
http://maine.gov/pfr/securities/index.shtml

**Maryland Office of the Attorney General**
Securities Division
200 Saint Paul Place
Baltimore, MD 21202
Phone: 888-743-0023
Fax: 410-576-6532
www.oag.state.md.us/Securities/index.htm

**Massachusetts Securities Division**
One Ashburton Place, 17th Floor
Boston, MA 02108
Phone: 800-269-5428
Fax: 617-248-0177
www.sec.state.ma.us/sct/sctidx.htm

**Michigan Office of Financial and Insurance Services**
Division of Securities
611 West Ottawa Street
Lansing, MI 48933
Phone: 877-999-6442
Fax: 517-335-4978
www.michigan.gov/cis/0,1607,7-154-10555---00.html

**Minnesota Department of Commerce**
Securities Division
85 7th Place East, Suite 500
St. Paul, MN 55101
Phone: 651-296-4973
Fax: 651-296-4328
www.state.mn.us

**Mississippi Secretary of State's Office**
Securities Division
700 North Street
Jackson, MS 39202
Phone: 800-804-6364
Fax: 601-359-2663
www.sos.state.ms.us/regenf/securities/securities.asp

**Missouri Office of the Secretary of State**
Securities Division
600 West Main Street
Jefferson City, MO 65101
Phone: 800-721-7996
Fax: 573-526-3124
www.sos.mo.gov/securities

**Montana State Auditor's Office**
Securities Department
840 Helena Avenue
Helena, MT 59601
Phone: 800-332-6148
Fax: 406-444-3497
http://sao.mt.gov/securities/secintro.asp

**Nebraska Department of Banking & Finance**
Bureau of Securities
1230 "O" Street, Suite 400
Lincoln, NE 68508
Phone: 402-471-3445
www.ndbf.org

**Nevada Secretary of State**
Securities Division
555 East Washington Avenue, Suite 5200
Las Vegas, NV 89101
Phone: 702-486-2440
Fax: 702-486-2452
http://sos.state.nv.us/securities/general/info.asp

**New Hampshire Bureau of Securities Regulation**
Department of State
107 North Main Street #204
Concord, NH 03301
Phone: 603-271-1463
Fax: 603-271-7933
www.sos.nh.gov/securities

**New Jersey Division of Consumer Affairs**
Bureau of Securities
153 Halsey Street, 6th Floor
Newark, NJ 07102
Phone: 866-446-8378
Fax: 973-504-3601
www.state.nj.us/lps/ca/bos/index.html

**New Mexico Regulation and Licensing Department**
Securities Division
2550 Cerrillos Road
Santa Fe, NM 87505
Phone: 800-704-5533
Fax: 505-984-0617
www.rld.state.nm.us/securities/index.html

**New York State Attorney General's Office**
Bureau of Investor Protection and Securities
120 Broadway
New York, NY 10271
Phone: 212-416-8000
Fax: 212-416-8816
www.oag.state.ny.us/investors/investors.html

**North Carolina Securities Division**
2 South Salisbury Street
Raleigh, NC 27601
Phone: 800-688-4507
Fax: 919-821-0818
www.secretary.state.nc.us/sec

**North Dakota Securities Department**
State Capitol, 5th Floor
600 East Boulevard Avenue
Bismarck, ND 58505
Phone: 800-297-5124
Fax: 701-328-2946
www.ndsecurities.com/department-info/default.asp

**Ohio Department of Commerce**
Division of Securities
77 South High Street, 22nd Floor
Columbus, OH 43215
Phone: 614-644-7381
Fax: 614-466-3316
www.com.ohio.gov/secu

**Oklahoma Securities Commission**
Department of Securities
First National Center
120 North Robinson, Suite 860
Oklahoma City, OK 73102
Phone: 405-280-7700
Fax: 405-280-7742
www.securities.ok.gov

**Oregon Division of Finance and Corporation Securities**
350 Winter Street, NE, Suite 410
Salem, OR 97301
Phone: 503-378-4140
Fax: 503-947-7862
www.dfcs.oregon.gov

**Pennsylvania Securities Commission**
Eastgate Office Building, 2nd Floor
1010 North Seventh Street
Harrisburg, PA 17102
Phone: 800-600-0007
Fax: 717-783-5122
www.psc.state.pa.us

**Puerto Rico Securities Division**
Office of the Commissioner of Financial
Institutions
Edif. Centro Europa—Suite 600
1492 Ave. Ponce de León
San Juan, PR 00907
Phone: 787-723-3131
Fax: 787-723-4042
www.cif.gov.pr/index_eng.html

**Rhode Island Department of Business Regulation**
Securities Regulation Division
233 Richmond Street
Providence, RI 02903
Phone: 401-222-3048
Fax: 401-222-5629
www.dbr.ri.gov

**South Carolina Attorney General's Office**
Securities Division
P.O. Box 11549
Columbia, SC 29211
Phone: 803-734-9916
Fax: 803-734-0032
www.scattorneygeneral.com//securities/
index.html

**South Dakota Division of Securities**
445 East Capitol Avenue
Pierre, SD 57501
Phone: 605-773-4823
Fax: 605-773-5953
www.state.sd.us/drr2/reg/securities

**Tennessee Department of Commerce and Insurance**
Securities Division
Davy Crockett Tower
500 James Robertson Parkway
Nashville, TN 37243
Phone: 615-741-2241
www.state.tn.us/commerce/securities

**Texas State Securities Board**
208 East 10th Street, 5th Floor
Austin, TX 78701
Phone: 512-305-8300
Fax: 512-305-8310
www.ssb.state.tx.us

**Utah Division of Securities**
160 East 300 South, 2nd Floor
Salt Lake City, UT 84111
Phone: 800-721-7233
Fax: 801-530-6980
www.securities.utah.gov

**Vermont Department of Banking, Insurance, Securities, and Health Care Administration**
Securities Division
89 Main Street
Montpelier, VT 05620
Phone: 802-828-3420
Fax: 802-828-2896
www.bishca.state.vt.us/SecuritiesDiv/
securindex.htm

**Virginia Division of Securities and Retail Franchising**
1300 East Main Street, Ninth Floor
Richmond, VA 23218
Phone: 800-552-7945
Fax: 804-371-9911
www.scc.virginia.gov/division/srf/webpages/homepage.htm

**Washington Department of Financial Institutions**
Securities Division
P.O. Box 9033
Olympia, WA 98507
Phone: 877-746-4334
Fax: 360-902-0524
www.dfi.wa.gov/sd

**West Virginia Securities Commission**
State Capitol Building 1, Room W100
Charleston, WV 25305
Phone: 888-368-9507
Fax: 304-558-4211
www.wvsao.gov/securities/securities.asp

**Wisconsin Department of Financial Institutions**
Division of Securities
P.O. Box 1768
Madison, WI 53701
Phone: 608-266-1064
Fax: 608-264-7979
www.wdfi.org

**Wyoming Securities Division**
The Capitol Building
200 West 24th Street
Cheyenne, WY 82002
Phone: 307-777-7370
Fax: 307-777-5339
http://soswy.state.wy.us/securiti/securiti.htm

# Running a Corporation or an LLC

## chapter 8

## DAY-TO-DAY ACTIVITIES

There are not many differences between running a corporation, LLC, or any other type of business. The most important point to remember is to keep the company affairs separate from your personal affairs. Do not make frequent loans to yourself from company funds, and do not commingle funds.

Another important point to remember is to always refer to the corporation as a corporation or to the limited liability company as an LLC. Always use the designation *Inc.*, *Corp.*, or *LLC* on everything. Always sign company documents with your title. If you do not, you may lose your protection from liability. There have been many cases where a person forgot to put the word "president" after his or her name and was held personally liable for a corporate debt.

## RECORDS

**Corporations**    A Nevada corporation is required to keep the following records at its registered office in Nevada:

- ✪ a copy of its **ARTICLES OF INCORPORATION** (form 13, p.237) and any amendments certified by the secretary of state;

- ✪ a copy of its **BYLAWS** (form 14, p.239, or form 15, p.245) and any amendments certified by an officer of the corporation; and,

○ a STOCK LEDGER (form 21, p.269) or duplicate stock ledger listing the names of stockholders in alphabetical order, the number of shares they own, and, if known, their residences. (However, the corporation can keep this item at another location and just include the name and address of the custodian in Nevada instead.)

*Form of records.* The minutes may be in writing or in "another form capable of being converted into written form within a reasonable time." This means that the minutes can be kept on a computer or possibly on a videotape. However, it is always best to keep at least one hard copy. Accidents can easily erase magnetic media. (Nev. Rev. Stat., Sec. 78.105 (2).)

*Examination of records.* Any shareholder of the corporation who has been a shareholder for at least six months or who has written authorization from 5% of the stockholders has the right to examine and copy the corporation's books and records after giving written notice of at least five days. (Nev. Rev. Stat., Sec. 78.105 (3).)

The shareholder may have his or her attorney or agent examine the records, but the attorney or agent must have a written power of attorney.

**LLCs**    An LLC may provide in its operating agreement that it does not need to keep any records in the state of Nevada. (Nev. Rev. Stat., Sec. 86.241.) If it does not so provide, the company must keep the following at an office within the state:

○ a current alphabetical list of all members and managers;

○ a copy of the articles of organization and any amendments, along with any powers of attorney that apply to them; and,

○ copies of any effective operating agreements.

## MEETINGS

**Corporations**    The corporation must hold an *annual meeting* of the directors and shareholders. These meetings may be formal or informal, and need not be held in Nevada. The bylaws should specify when and where meetings will be held.

A sole shareholder and director can hold an annual meeting in his or her mind without reciting all the verbiage or taking a formal vote. But the important thing is that the meetings are held and that minutes are kept. Regular minutes and meetings are evidence that the corporation is legitimate if the issue ever comes up in court. Various minute forms for the annual meetings are included with this book. (form 25, p.283, and form 27, p.287.) You can use them as master copies to photocopy each year. Unless you actually change officers or directors, or need to take some other corporate action, all that needs to be changed on the form is the date.

Under most bylaws, a corporation must either give notice in advance of each meeting or the attendees must waive the right to receive notice. Waiver of notice forms are included in this book in Appendix D for this purpose. A waiver should be signed by all attendees whenever a meeting is held, unless formal notice was sent in advance as provided in the bylaws.

When important decisions must be made by the board of shareholders between the annual meetings, the corporation can hold *special meetings*. Minutes should be taken then, too, on the form **MINUTES OF SPECIAL MEETING OF SHAREHOLDERS**. (see form 31, p.295.)

Nevada Revised Statutes explain the rules for whether there is a *quorum*, or when action can be taken without a meeting, and how to hold meetings over the telephone. (Nev. Rev. Stat., Secs. 78.315 and 78.320.)

Under Nevada procedures, action may be taken by the directors without a formal meeting. (Nev. Rev. Stat., Sec. 78.325.) However, it is best for a small corporation to use formal meetings in case someone later tries to pierce the corporate veil.

**LLCs**     There is no requirement for regular meetings of the members of a limited liability company. But once again, since the law is not settled in this area, the more formality you use, the greater protection you have against potential liability.

Holding a meeting when major decisions are being made is a good idea. If you are a one-member company, you can hold the meeting in your head. Just remember to fill out a **MINUTES OF A MEETING OF MEMBERS** form for the company records. (see form 38, p.313.)

## COMMITTEES

Both corporations and LLCs have the power to appoint committees to carry out their business functions.

**Corporations**
The committees for a corporation may be authorized by a resolution of the board of directors or by the bylaws. The committees may have the power to act for the board of directors. The committee must have a name as stated in the bylaws or a resolution and must have at least one director as a member. (Nev. Rev. Stat., Sec. 78.125.)

**LLCs**
There are no specific requirements for LLCs. Under the general power to "exercise all powers necessary or convenient to effect any of the purposes for which the company is organized," it could legally form a committee. (Nev. Rev. Stat., Sec. 86.281(11.) However, the committee would not have the power to manage the business or to do such things as incur debt or acquire real estate, unless such power was assigned in the articles of organization. (Nev. Rev. Stat., Secs. 86.291, 86.301, and 86.311.)

## DISTRIBUTIONS

A corporation or LLC is usually free to make any distributions of money or property to its shareholders or members. The exception is where the distribution would make the company *insolvent*, meaning unable to pay its debts.

For the specific rules regarding distributions that may make the company insolvent, see Nevada Revised Statutes Section 78.288 for corporations, and Sections 86.341 and 86.343 for limited liability companies.

## ANNUAL LISTS

Each year, every corporation and LLC registered in Nevada must file an *annual list* of its officers and directors or managers, managing members, and resident agent.

**Corporations**
A corporation files a (profit) **ANNUAL LIST OF OFFICERS, DIRECTORS, AND RESIDENT AGENT** (form 23, p.279), which must include a president, secretary, treasurer (or equivalents), and all directors.

The filing fee is a minimum of $125 based on the value of the current total of the authorized stock as follows:

| | |
|---|---|
| $75,000 or less | $125.00 |
| Over $75,000, but not over $200,000 | $175.00 |
| Over $200,000, but not over $500,000 | $275.00 |
| Over $500,000, but not over $1,000,000 | $375.00 |

**Over $1,000,000**

| | |
|---|---|
| For the first $1,000,000 | $375.00 |
| For each additional $500,000 (or fraction thereof) | $275.00 |
| Maximum fee | $11,100.00 |

If an Annual List is filed late, there is a late fee of $75.

**LLCs**    A limited liability company files an **ANNUAL LIST OF MANAGERS OR MANAGING MEMBERS AND RESIDENT AGENT** (form 37, p.311), which must include at least one manager or managing member. The filing fee is $125, and there is a late fee of $75.

## EMPLOYMENT REQUIREMENTS

If you will be paying wages to anyone, even just yourself, you will need to comply with all the *employer reporting and withholding laws* of both your state and the federal government. Explaining every requirement is beyond the scope of this book, but the following is a summary of most of the requirements.

**Summary**    *New hire reporting.* To improve the enforcement of child support payments, all employers must report the hiring of each new employee to an agency in the state in which the employee is working.

*Employment eligibility.* To combat the hiring of illegal immigrants, employers must complete the Department of Justice I-9 form for each employee.

*Federal tax withholding.* Social Security and income taxes must be withheld from employees' wages and deposited to an authorized bank quarterly, monthly, or more often, depending on the amount. The initial step is to obtain a form W-4 from each employee upon hiring. (This same form can also be used to fulfill the previously discussed new hire reporting law.)

***State withholding.*** In states that have income taxes, there is usually a withholding and reporting requirement similar to the federal one.

***Local withholding.*** In cities that have income taxes, there is usually a withholding and reporting requirement similar to the federal one.

***Unemployment compensation.*** There are taxes on employee wages—which employers must pay—that must be paid to the state and federal governments regularly. Employers are also required to send reports quarterly and annually.

***Workers' compensation.*** Depending on the number of employees and type of work, the state may require that workers' compensation insurance be obtained by the employer.

## CORPORATIONS

**Correction of
Instruments**

Whenever an instrument that has been filed with the Nevada secretary of state is found to be inaccurate, defective, or erroneously executed, attested, sealed, verified, or acknowledged, it may be corrected by filing a *certificate of correction* with the secretary of state that includes:

- ✪ the name of the corporation;

- ✪ a description of the document to be corrected, including the filing date;

- ✪ a description of the incorrect statement or defective execution;

- ✪ a correction of the incorrect statement or defective execution; and,

- ✪ the signature of an officer of the corporation.

**Articles of
Incorporation**

The articles of incorporation may be amended for any reason as long as the provisions are all lawful under Nevada Revised Statutes Sections 78.035 and 78.037. (Nev. Rev. Stat., Sec. 78.385.) The statute specifically allows changes:

- ✪ to modify the name of the corporation;

- ✪ to add or subtract corporate powers or purposes;

- ✪ to substitute powers or purposes;

- ✪ to increase, decrease, or reclassify stock; and,

- ✪ to alter the par value, number, or other rights of its stock.

***Before stock is issued.*** The articles of incorporation may be amended before stock is issued by filing with the secretary of state a certificate of amendment signed by at least two-thirds of the incorporators. (Nev. Rev. Stat., Sec. 78.380.) The certificate must state:

- ✪ the corporation's name;

- ✪ that the signers comprise two-thirds of the incorporators;

- ✪ the date the original articles were filed; and,

- ✪ that no stock has been issued.

***After stock is issued.*** After stock has been issued, the corporation must adhere to the following procedures to amend the articles.

- ✪ The board of directors must pass a resolution setting forth the proposed amendment and stating that it is advisable to adopt. It must then call a meeting of stockholders and give notice to each stockholder entitled to vote.

- ✪ If the amendment passes at the stockholders' meeting, the president or vice president and the secretary or assistant secretary must execute a certificate stating the vote by which the amendment passed and either the amendment or the amended articles, and it must be signed by the president or vice president and notarized. (Nev. Rev. Stat., Sec. 78.390.)

***Restated articles.*** After the articles have been amended, the corporation may prepare *Restated Articles of Incorporation* to consolidate all the changes into one document. These can be filed with the secretary of state, accompanied by either a resolution or a form provided by the secretary of state. (Nev. Rev. Stat., Sec. 78.403.) The restated articles can include new changes to the articles, but if they do, they must comply with the rules for amending the articles.

**Bylaws**     Nevada has few requirements regarding bylaws of the corporation. The board of directors may make (and presumably amend) bylaws for the corporation, subject to any bylaws made by the stockholders. (Nev. Rev. Stat., Sec. 78.120.)

**Registered Agent or Registered Office**

To change the resident agent or registered office, a corporation must file a certificate with the secretary of state signed by an officer, stating:

- ✪ the name of the corporation;

- ✪ that the change is authorized by Nevada Revised Statutes Section 78.110 and is effective upon filing;

- ✪ the street address of the present registered office;

- ✪ the address of the new registered office, if the address is changing;

- ✪ the name of the present resident agent;

- ✪ the name of the new resident agent, if the agent is changing; and,

- ✪ an acceptance by the new resident agent, if the agent is changing.

If the resident agent changes his or her name or address, he or she must follow the Nevada procedures. (Nev. Rev. Stat., Sec. 78.095.)

If a resident agent resigns and appoints a successor, he or she must also follow the Nevada procedures. (Nev. Rev. Stat., Sec. 78.097.)

## LLCS

**Articles of Organization**

The LIMITED-LIABILITY COMPANY ARTICLES OF ORGANIZATION (form 32, p.297) may be amended either by all the members or as otherwise provided by the articles or any operating agreement in effect.

The amendment must be filed with the Nevada secretary of state and in the form of a certificate that includes:

- ✪ the name of the company;

- ✪ the date of the filing of the original articles;

- ✪ the amendment to the articles; and,

- ✪ the signature and acknowledgment by a member or, if manager-managed, by a manager.

**Registered Agent or Registered Office**

***Restated articles.*** After the articles have been amended, the company may prepare *Restated Articles of Organization* to consolidate all the changes into one document.

To change the resident agent or registered office, an LLC must file a certificate with the secretary of state signed by an officer, stating:

- ✪ the name of the company;

- ✪ that the change is authorized by Nevada Revised Statutes Section 86.235 and is effective upon filing;

- ✪ the street address of the present registered office;

- ✪ the address of the new registered office, if the address is changing;

- ✪ the name of the present resident agent;

- ✪ the name of the new resident agent, if the agent is changing; and,

- ✪ an acceptance by the new resident agent, if the agent is changing.

If the resident agent changes address, he or she must follow the Nevada procedures. (Nev. Rev. Stat., Sec. 86.231 (2.).)

If a resident agent resigns and appoints a successor, he or she must also follow the Nevada procedures. (Nev. Rev. Stat., Sec. 86.251.)

**Operating Agreement**

The operating agreement of a limited liability company may be amended only by unanimous consent of the members at the time of the amendment. (Nev. Rev. Stat., Sec. 86.286.)

# Glossary

## A

**annual report.** A document filed by a corporation or limited liability company each year that usually lists the officers, directors, and resident agent.

**articles of incorporation.** The document that demonstrates the organization of a corporation. Called *certificate of incorporation* in some states.

**articles of organization.** The document that demonstrates the organization of a limited liability company.

## B

**blue sky laws.** Laws governing the sales of securities.

**bylaws.** Rules governing the conduct of a corporation's affairs.

## C

**C corporation.** A corporation that pays taxes on its profits.

**common stock.** The basic ownership shares of a corporation.

**contract.** An agreement between two or more parties.

**corporation.** An organization recognized as a person in the law that is set up to conduct a business owned by shareholders and run by officers and directors.

# D

**distributions.** Money paid out to owners of a corporation or limited liability company.

**domain name.** The address of a website.

# E

**employee.** A person who works for another under that person's control and direction.

**employer identification number (EIN).** A number issued by the Internal Revenue Service to identify taxpayers who do not have Social Security numbers.

**estate planning.** Preparing such documents as a will, trust, and other arrangements to control the passing of one's property at death.

**exemption.** The ability to sell certain limited types of securities without full compliance with securities registration laws.

# F

**fictitious name.** A name used by a business that is not its personal or legal name.

# G

**general partnership.** A business that is owned by two or more persons.

# I

**intangible property.** Personal property that does not have a physical presence, such as the ownership interest in a corporation.

**intellectual property.** Legal rights to the products of the mind, such as writings, musical compositions, formulas, and designs.

# L

**liability.** The legal responsibility to pay for an injury.

**limited liability company.** An entity recognized as a legal person that is set up to conduct a business owned and run by members.

**limited liability partnership.** An entity recognized as a legal person that is set up to conduct a business owned and run by professionals, such as attorneys or doctors.

**limited partnership.** A business that is owned by two or more persons of which one or more is liable for the debts of the business and one or more has no liability for the debts.

# M

**management agreement.** A contract controlling the operation of a limited liability company in which the company is run by its managers.

**membership agreement.** A contract controlling the operation of a limited liability company in which the company is run by members.

**minutes.** Records of the proceedings of corporate meetings.

# N

**nonprofit corporation.** An entity recognized as a legal person that is set up to run an operation in which none of the profits are distributed to controlling members.

# O

**occupational license.** A government-issued permit to transact business.

**operating agreement.** A contract among members of a limited liability company spelling out how the company is to be run.

**option.** The right to buy stock at a future date, usually at a predetermined price.

**organizational meeting.** The meeting of the founders of a corporation or limited liability company in which the company is structured and made ready to begin business.

# P

**partnership.** A business formed by two or more persons.

**par value.** A value given to newly issued stock that used to have legal significance, but now usually does not relate to anything except, in some states, taxation.

**personal property.** Any type of property other than land and the structures attached to it.

**piercing the corporate veil.** When a court ignores the structure of a corporation and holds its owners responsible for its debts or liabilities.

**professional association.** An entity recognized as a legal person that is set up to conduct a business of professionals, such as attorneys or doctors.

**promoters.** Persons who start a business venture and usually offer interests for sale to investors.

**proprietorship.** A business that is owned by one person.

# R

**resident agent.** The person authorized to accept legal papers for a corporation or limited liability company.

**resident alien.** A person who is not a citizen of the country but who may legally reside and work there.

# S

**S corporation.** A corporation in which the profits are taxed to the shareholders.

**securities.** Interests in a business such as stocks or bonds.

**shareholder agreement.** A contract among the owners of a corporation that spells out their rights.

**shares.** Units of stock in a corporation.

**stock.** Ownership interests in a corporation.

# T

**tangible property.** Physical personal property such as desks and tables.

**trademark.** A name or symbol used to identify the source of goods or services.

**transferability.** The ability to sell shares of stock in a corporation.

# U

**usury.** Charging an interest rate higher than that allowed by law.

# W

**withholding.** Money taken out of an employee's salary and remitted to the government.

# Z

**zoning.** A governmental regulation controlling the use of a piece of real property.

# Selected Nevada Statutes and Fee Schedules

Included in this appendix are the Nevada corporation statutes that will be most useful in organizing your corporation or limited liability company.

Sections from the following statutes are included in this appendix:

The next few pages contain an outline of all corporation and LLC statutes. Those in italics are not included but may be found at your library, law library, or on the Internet at:

http://sos.state.nv.us/business/comm_rec/statutes.asp

## CHAPTER 78 PRIVATE CORPORATIONS

### General Provisions

### Formation

### Powers

### Registered Office and Resident Agent

### Directors and Officers

## Meetings, Elections, Voting and Notice

## Acquisition of Controlling Interest

## Amendment and Restatement of Articles of Incorporation

## Combinations with Interested Stockholders

## Sale of Assets; Dissolution and Winding Up

## Insolvency; Receivers and Trustees

NRS 78.710 Distribution of money to creditors and stockholders.

NRS 78.715 Acts of majority of receivers effectual; removal and vacancies.

NRS 78.720 Employees' liens for wages when corporation insolvent.

## Reincorporation; Renewal and Revival of Charters

NRS 78.725 Domestic corporations in existence on April 1, 1925, may reincorporate under this chapter.

NRS 78.730 Renewal or revival: Procedure; fee; certificate as evidence. [Effective through June 30, 2008.]

NRS 78.730 Renewal or revival: Procedure; fee; certificate as evidence. [Effective July 1, 2008.]

NRS 78.740 Renewal or revival: Status of corporation.

## Suits Against Corporations, Directors, Officers, Employees, Agents and Stockholders

NRS 78.745 Action against stockholder for unpaid subscriptions; limitation of action.

NRS 78.746 Action against stockholder by judgment creditor; limitations.

NRS 78.747 Liability of stockholder, director or officer for debt or liability of corporation.

NRS 78.750 Service of process on corporations. [Effective through June 30, 2008.]

NRS 78.750 Service of process on corporations. [Effective July 1, 2008.]

NRS 78.7502 Discretionary and mandatory indemnification of officers, directors, employees and agents: General provisions.

NRS 78.751 Authorization required for discretionary indemnification; advancement of expenses; limitation on indemnification and advancement of expenses.

NRS 78.752 Insurance and other financial arrangements against liability of directors, officers, employees and agents.

## Secretary of State: Duties and Fees

NRS 78.755 Duties: Collection of fees; employment of new technology to aid in performance.

NRS 78.760 Filing fees: Articles of incorporation.

NRS 78.765 Filing fees: Certificate changing number of authorized shares; certificate of amendment to articles; certificate of correction; certificate of designation; certificate of termination; certificate of withdrawal.

NRS 78.767 Filing fees: Certificates of restated articles of incorporation.

NRS 78.780 Filing fee: Certificate of dissolution.

NRS 78.785 Miscellaneous fees. [Effective through June 30, 2008.]

NRS 78.785 Miscellaneous fees. [Effective July 1, 2008.]

## Miscellaneous Provisions

NRS 78.795 Registration of natural person or corporation willing to serve as resident agent for corporation, limited-liability company or limited partnership. [Effective through June 30, 2008.]

NRS 78.795 Registration of natural person or corporation willing to serve as registered agent for corporation, limited-liability company or limited partnership. [Effective July 1, 2008.]

\* \* \*

## General Provisions

### NRS 78.010 Definitions; construction. [Effective through June 30, 2008.]

1. As used in this chapter:

(a) "Approval" and "vote" as describing action by the directors or stockholders mean the vote of directors in person or by written consent or of stockholders in person, by proxy or by written consent.

(b) "Articles," "articles of incorporation" and "certificate of incorporation" are synonymous terms and, unless the context otherwise requires, include all certificates filed pursuant to NRS 78.030, 78.180, 78.185, 78.1955, 78.209, 78.380, 78.385, 78.390, 78.725 and 78.730 and any articles of merger, conversion, exchange or domestication filed pursuant to NRS 92A.200 to 92A.240, inclusive, or 92A.270. Unless the context otherwise requires, these terms include restated articles and certificates of incorporation.

(c) "Directors" and "trustees" are synonymous terms.

(d) "Receiver" includes receivers and trustees appointed by a court as provided in this chapter or in chapter 32 of NRS.

(e) "Record" means information that is inscribed on a tangible medium or that is stored in an electronic or other medium and is retrievable in perceivable form.

(f) "Registered office" means the office maintained at the street address of the resident agent.

(g) "Resident agent" means the agent appointed by the corporation upon whom process or a notice or demand authorized by law to be served upon the corporation may be served.

(h) "Sign" means to affix a signature to a record.

(i) "Signature" means a name, word, symbol or mark executed or otherwise adopted, or a record encrypted or similarly processed in whole or in part, by a person with the present intent to identify himself and adopt or accept a record. The term includes, without limitation, an electronic signature as defined in NRS 719.100.

(j) "Stockholder of record" means a person whose name appears on the stock ledger of the corporation.

(k) "Street address" of a resident agent means the actual physical location in this State at which a resident agent is available for service of process.

2. General terms and powers given in this chapter are not restricted by the use of special terms, or by any grant of special powers contained in this chapter. [Part 47:177:1925; NCL § 1646] + [83:177:1925; A 1931, 415; 1931 NCL § 1682]—(NRS A 1965, 216; 1977, 184; 1989, 871; 1991, 1207; 1993, 944; 1995, 2093; 1997, 695; 1999, 1576; 2001, 101, 1358, 2722, 3199; 2003, 48, 3077)

### NRS 78.010 Definitions; construction. [Effective July 1, 2008.]

1. As used in this chapter:

(a) "Approval" and "vote" as describing action by the directors or stockholders mean the vote of directors in person or by written consent or of stockholders in person, by proxy or by written consent.

(b) "Articles," "articles of incorporation" and "certificate of incorporation" are synonymous terms and, unless the context otherwise requires, include all certificates filed pursuant to NRS 78.030, 78.180, 78.185, 78.1955, 78.209, 78.380, 78.385, 78.390, 78.725 and 78.730 and any articles of merger, conversion, exchange or domestication filed pursuant to NRS 92A.200 to 92A.240, inclusive, or 92A.270. Unless the context otherwise requires, these terms include restated articles and certificates of incorporation.

(c) "Directors" and "trustees" are synonymous terms.

(d) "Principal office" means the office, in or out of this State, where the principal executive offices of a domestic or foreign corporation are located.

(e) "Receiver" includes receivers and trustees appointed by a court as provided in this chapter or in chapter 32 of NRS.

(f) "Record" means information that is inscribed on a tangible medium or that is stored in an electronic or other medium and is retrievable in perceivable form.

(g) "Registered agent" has the meaning ascribed to it in NRS 77.230.

(h) "Registered office" means the office maintained at the street address of the registered agent.

(i) "Sign" means to affix a signature to a record.

(j) "Signature" means a name, word, symbol or mark executed or otherwise adopted, or a record encrypted or similarly processed in whole or in part, by a person with the present intent to identify himself and adopt or accept a record. The term includes, without limitation, an electronic signature as defined in NRS 719.100.

(k) "Stockholder of record" means a person whose name appears on the stock ledger of the corporation.

(l) "Street address" of a registered agent means the actual physical location in this State at which a registered agent is available for service of process.

2. General terms and powers given in this chapter are not restricted by the use of special terms, or by any grant of special powers contained in this chapter.
[Part 47:177:1925; NCL § 1646] + [83:177:1925; A 1931, 415; 1931 NCL § 1682]—(NRS A 1965, 216; 1977, 184; 1989, 871; 1991, 1207; 1993, 944; 1995, 2093; 1997, 695; 1999, 1576; 2001, 101, 1358, 2722, 3199; 2003, 48, 3077; 2007, 2639, effective July 1, 2008)

### NRS 78.015 Applicability of chapter; effect on corporations existing before April 1, 1925.

1. The provisions of this chapter apply to:

(a) Corporations organized in this State on or after October 1, 1991, except:

(1) Where the provisions of chapters 80, 84 and 89 of NRS are inconsistent with the provisions of this chapter;

(2) Corporations expressly excluded by the provisions of this chapter; and

(3) Corporations governed by the provisions of NRS 81.170 to 81.540, inclusive, and chapter 82 of NRS.

(b) Corporations whose charters are renewed or revived in the manner provided in NRS 78.730.

(c) Corporations organized and still existing under this chapter before October 1, 1991, or any prior act or any amendment thereto.

(d) Close corporations, unless otherwise provided in chapter 78A of NRS.

(e) All insurance companies, mutual fire insurance companies, surety companies, express companies, railroad companies, and public utility companies now existing and formed before October 1, 1991, under any other act or law of this State, subject to any special provisions concerning any class of corporations inconsistent with the provisions of this chapter, in which case the special provisions continue to apply.

2. Neither the existence of corporations formed or existing before April 1, 1925, nor any liability, cause of action, right, privilege or immunity validly existing in favor of or against any such corporation on April 1, 1925, are affected, abridged, taken away or impaired by this chapter, or by any change in the requirements for the formation of corporations provided by this chapter, nor by the amendment or repeal of any laws under which such prior existing corporations were formed or created. [1:177:1925; A 1935, 146; 1937, 4; 1945, 196; 1943 NCL § 1600]—(NRS A 1989, 948; 1991, 1207; 1995, 2094)

### NRS 78.020 Limitations on incorporation under chapter; compliance with other laws.

1. Insurance companies, mutual fire insurance companies, surety companies, express companies and railroad companies may be formed under this chapter, but such a corporation may not:

(a) Transact any such business within this State until it has first complied with all laws concerning or affecting the right to engage in such business.

(b) Infringe the laws of any other state or country in which it may intend to engage in business, by so incorporating under this chapter.

2. No trust company, savings and loan association, thrift company or corporation organized for the purpose of conducting a banking business may be organized under this chapter. [Part 4:177:1925; A 1929, 413; 1931, 415; 1949, 158; 1955, 402]—(NRS A 1975, 1; 1983, 117; 1997, 1014)

**NRS 78.025 Reserved power of State to amend or repeal chapter; chapter part of corporation's charter.** This chapter may be amended or repealed at the pleasure of the Legislature, and every corporation created under this chapter, or availing itself of any of the provisions of this chapter, and all stockholders of such corporation shall be bound by such amendment; but such amendment or repeal shall not take away or impair any remedy against any corporation, or its officers, for any liability which shall have been previously incurred. This chapter, and all amendments thereof, shall be a part of the charter of every corporation, except so far as the same are inapplicable and inappropriate to the objects of the corporation. [2:177:1925; NCL § 1601]

**NRS 78.026 Form required for filing of records.**

1. Each record filed with the Secretary of State pursuant to this chapter must be on or accompanied by a form prescribed by the Secretary of State.

2. The Secretary of State may refuse to file a record which does not comply with subsection 1 or which does not contain all of the information required by statute for filing the record.

3. If the provisions of the form prescribed by the Secretary of State conflict with the provisions of any record that is submitted for filing with the form:

(a) The provisions of the form control for all purposes with respect to the information that is required by statute to appear in the record in order for the record to be filed; and

(b) Unless otherwise provided in the record, the provisions of the record control in every other situation.

4. The Secretary of State may by regulation provide for the electronic filing of records with the Office of the Secretary of State. (Added to NRS by 2003, 20th Special Session, 26)

**NRS 78.027 Corporate records: Microfilming; imaging; return.** The Secretary of State may microfilm or image any record which is filed in his office with respect to a corporation pursuant to this chapter and

may return the original record to the corporation. (Added to NRS by 1977, 572; A 2003, 3077; 2003, 20th Special Session, 27)

**NRS 78.028 Filing of records written in language other than English.** No record which is written in a language other than English may be filed or submitted for filing in the Office of the Secretary of State pursuant to the provisions of this chapter unless it is accompanied by a verified translation of that record into the English language. (Added to NRS by 1995, 1112; A 2003, 3077)

**NRS 78.029 Procedure to submit replacement page to Secretary of State before actual filing of record.** Before the issuance of stock an incorporator, and after the issuance of stock an officer, of a corporation may authorize the Secretary of State in writing to replace any page of a record submitted for filing on an expedited basis, before the actual filing, and to accept the page as if it were part of the original record. (Added to NRS by 1997, 2807; A 1999, 1577; 2003, 3078)

**NRS 78.0295 Correction of inaccurate or defective record filed with Secretary of State.**

1. A corporation may correct a record filed in the Office of the Secretary of State with respect to the corporation if the record contains an inaccurate description of a corporate action or if the record was defectively signed, attested, sealed, verified or acknowledged.

2. To correct a record, the corporation must:

(a) Prepare a certificate of correction which:

(1) States the name of the corporation;

(2) Describes the record, including, without limitation, its filing date;

(3) Specifies the inaccuracy or defect;

(4) Sets forth the inaccurate or defective portion of the record in an accurate or corrected form; and

(5) Is signed by an officer of the corporation or, if no stock has been issued by the corporation, by the incorporator or a director of the corporation.

(b) Deliver the certificate to the Secretary of State for filing.

(c) Pay a filing fee of $175 to the Secretary of State.

3. A certificate of correction is effective on the effective date of the record it corrects except as to persons relying on the uncorrected record and adversely affected by the correction. As to those persons, the certificate is effective when filed. (Added to NRS by 1997, 693; A 2001, 1358, 3170, 3199; 2003, 3078; 2003, 20th Special Session, 27)

**NRS 78.0297 Corporate records: Manner of storage; conversion into clear and legible paper form; admissibility in evidence.**

1. Except as otherwise provided by federal or state law, any records maintained by a corporation in its regular course of business, including, without limitation, its stock ledger, books of account and minute books, may be kept on, by means of or be in the form of, any information processing system or other information storage device or medium.

2. A corporation shall convert within a reasonable time any records kept in the manner described in subsection 1 into clear and legible paper form upon the request of any person entitled to inspect the records maintained by the corporation pursuant to any provision of this chapter.

3. A clear and legible paper form produced from records kept in the manner described in subsection 1 is admissible in evidence and accepted for all other purposes to the same extent as an original paper record with the same information provided that the paper form portrays the record accurately. (Added to NRS by 2003, 3076)

### NRS 78.0298 Records or signatures maintained by corporation.

1. No record or signature maintained by a corporation is required to be created, generated, sent, communicated, received, stored or otherwise processed or used by electronic means or in electronic form.

2. The corporation may refuse to accept or conduct any transaction or create, generate, send, communicate, receive, store or otherwise process, use or accept any record or signature by electronic means or in electronic form. (Added to NRS by 2003, 3076)

## Formation

### NRS 78.030 Filing requirements. [Effective through June 30, 2008.]

1. One or more persons may establish a corporation for the transaction of any lawful business, or to promote or conduct any legitimate object or purpose, pursuant and subject to the requirements of this chapter, by:

(a) Signing and filing in the Office of the Secretary of State articles of incorporation; and

(b) Filing a certificate of acceptance of appointment, signed by the resident agent of the corporation, in the Office of the Secretary of State.

2. The articles of incorporation must be as provided in NRS 78.035, and the Secretary of State shall require them to be in the form prescribed. If any articles are defective in this respect, the Secretary of State shall return them for correction. [3:177:1925; A 1931, 415; 1931 NCL § 1602]—(NRS A 1963, 70; 1979, 394; 1981, 1888; 1989, 948; 1991, 1208; 1995, 2095; 1999, 1577; 2003, 3078)

### NRS 78.030 Filing requirements. [Effective July 1, 2008.]

1. One or more persons may establish a corporation for the transaction of any lawful business, or to promote or conduct any legitimate object or purpose, pursuant and subject to the requirements of this chapter, by signing and filing in the Office of the Secretary of State articles of incorporation.

2. The articles of incorporation must be as provided in NRS 78.035, and the Secretary of State shall require them to be in the form prescribed. If any articles are defective in this respect, the Secretary of State shall return them for correction. [3:177:1925; A 1931, 415; 1931 NCL § 1602]—(NRS A 1963, 70; 1979, 394; 1981, 1888; 1989, 948; 1991, 1208; 1995, 2095; 1999, 1577; 2003, 3078; 2007, 2640, effective July 1, 2008)

### NRS 78.035 Articles of incorporation: Required provisions. [Effective through June 30, 2008.] The articles of incorporation must set forth:

1. The name of the corporation. A name appearing to be that of a natural person and containing a given name or initials must not be used as a corporate name except with an additional word or words such as "Incorporated," "Limited," "Inc.," "Ltd.," "Company," "Co.," "Corporation," "Corp.," or other word which identifies it as not being a natural person.

2. The name of the person designated as the corporation's resident agent, the street address of the resident agent where process may be served upon the corporation, and the mailing address of the resident agent if different from the street address.

3. The number of shares the corporation is authorized to issue and, if more than one class or series of stock is authorized, the classes, the series and the number of shares of each class or series which the corporation is authorized to issue, unless the articles authorize the board of directors to fix and determine in a resolution the classes, series and numbers of each class or series as provided in NRS 78.195 and 78.196.

4. The names and addresses, either residence or business, of the first board of directors or trustees, together with any desired provisions relative to the right to change the number of directors as provided in NRS 78.115.

5. The name and address, either residence or business, of each of the incorporators signing the articles of incorporation. [Part 4:177:1925; A 1929, 413; 1931, 415; 1949, 158; 1955, 402]—(NRS A 1957, 75; 1967, 769; 1981, 1888; 1985, 1785; 1987, 81, 574, 1054; 1991, 1208; 1993, 945; 1995, 2095; 1999, 1577; 2003, 3078; 2003, 20th Special Session, 27)

**NRS 78.035 Articles of incorporation: Required provisions. [Effective July 1, 2008.]** The articles of incorporation must set forth:

1. The name of the corporation. A name appearing to be that of a natural person and containing a given name or initials must not be used as a corporate name except with an additional word or words such as "Incorporated," "Limited," "Inc.," "Ltd.," "Company," "Co.," "Corporation," "Corp.," or other word which identifies it as not being a natural person.

2. The information required pursuant to NRS 77.310.

3. The number of shares the corporation is authorized to issue and, if more than one class or series of stock is authorized, the classes, the series and the number of shares of each class or series which the corporation is authorized to issue, unless the articles authorize the board of directors to fix and determine in a resolution the classes, series and numbers of each class or series as provided in NRS 78.195 and 78.196.

4. The names and addresses, either residence or business, of the first board of directors or trustees, together with any desired provisions relative to the right to change the number of directors as provided in NRS 78.115.

5. The name and address, either residence or business, of each of the incorporators signing the articles of incorporation. [Part 4:177:1925; A 1929, 413; 1931, 415; 1949, 158; 1955, 402]—(NRS A 1957, 75; 1967, 769; 1981, 1888; 1985, 1785; 1987, 81, 574, 1054; 1991, 1208; 1993, 945; 1995, 2095; 1999, 1577; 2003, 3078; 2003, 20th Special Session, 27; 2007, 2640, effective July 1, 2008)

**NRS 78.037 Articles of incorporation: Optional provisions.** The articles of incorporation may also contain any provision, not contrary to the laws of this State:

1. For the management of the business and for the conduct of the affairs of the corporation;

2. Creating, defining, limiting or regulating the powers of the corporation or the rights, powers or duties of the directors, the officers or the stockholders, or any class of the stockholders, or the holders of bonds or other obligations of the corporation; or

3. Governing the distribution or division of the profits of the corporation. (Added to NRS by 1987, 80; A 1991, 1210; 1993, 945; 2001, 3171)

**NRS 78.039 Name of corporation: Distinguishable name required; availability of name of revoked, merged or otherwise terminated corporation; regulations.**

1. The name proposed for a corporation must be distinguishable on the records of the Secretary of State from the names of all other artificial persons formed, organized, registered or qualified pursuant to the provisions of this title that are on file in the Office of the Secretary of State and all names that are reserved in the Office of the Secretary of State pursuant to the provisions of this title. If a proposed name is not so distinguishable, the Secretary of State shall return the articles of incorporation containing the proposed name to the incorporator, unless the written, acknowledged consent of the holder of the name on file or reserved name to use the same name or the requested similar name accompanies the articles of incorporation.

2. For the purposes of this section and NRS 78.040, a proposed name is not distinguishable from a name on file or reserved name solely because one or the other contains distinctive lettering, a distinctive mark, a trademark or a trade name, or any combination of these.

3. The name of a corporation whose charter has been revoked, which has merged and is not the surviving entity or whose existence has otherwise terminated is available for use by any other artificial person.

4. The Secretary of State may adopt regulations that interpret the requirements of this section. (Added to NRS by 1975, 477; A 1987, 1056; 1991, 1210; 1993, 945; 1997, 2807; 1999, 1578)

**NRS 78.040 Name of corporation: Reservation; injunctive relief.**

1. The Secretary of State, when requested so to do, shall reserve, for a period of 90 days, the right to use any name available under NRS 78.039, for the use of any proposed corporation. During the period, a name so reserved is not available for use or reservation by any other artificial person forming, organizing, registering or qualifying in the Office of the Secretary of State pursuant to the provisions of this title without the written, acknowledged consent of the person at whose request the reservation was made.

2. The use by any other artificial person of a name in violation of subsection 1 or NRS 78.039 may be enjoined, even if the record under which the artificial person is formed, organized, registered or qualified has been filed by the Secretary of State. [4a:177:1925; added 1931, 415; 1931 NCL § 1603.01] + [4b:177:1925; added 1931, 415; 1931 NCL § 1603.02]—(NRS A 1963, 64; 1979, 395; 1981, 472; 1987, 1056; 1993, 946; 1999, 1578; 2003, 3079)

**NRS 78.045 Articles of incorporation: Approval or certification required before filing of certain articles or amendments. [Effective through December 31, 2007.]**

1. The Secretary of State shall not accept for filing any articles of incorporation or any certificate of amendment of articles of incorporation of any corporation formed pursuant to the laws of this State which

provides that the name of the corporation contains the word "bank" or "trust," unless:

(a) It appears from the articles or the certificate of amendment that the corporation proposes to carry on business as a banking or trust company, exclusively or in connection with its business as a bank, savings and loan association or thrift company; and

(b) The articles or certificate of amendment is first approved by the Commissioner of Financial Institutions.

2. The Secretary of State shall not accept for filing any articles of incorporation or any certificate of amendment of articles of incorporation of any corporation formed pursuant to the provisions of this chapter if it appears from the articles or the certificate of amendment that the business to be carried on by the corporation is subject to supervision by the Commissioner of Insurance or by the Commissioner of Financial Institutions, unless the articles or certificate of amendment is approved by the Commissioner who will supervise the business of the corporation.

3. Except as otherwise provided in subsection 7, the Secretary of State shall not accept for filing any articles of incorporation or any certificate of amendment of articles of incorporation of any corporation formed pursuant to the laws of this State if the name of the corporation contains the words "engineer," "engineered," "engineering," "professional engineer," "registered engineer" or "licensed engineer" unless:

(a) The State Board of Professional Engineers and Land Surveyors certifies that the principals of the corporation are licensed to practice engineering pursuant to the laws of this State; or

(b) The State Board of Professional Engineers and Land Surveyors certifies that the corporation is exempt from the prohibitions of NRS 625.520.

4. Except as otherwise provided in subsection 7, the Secretary of State shall not accept for filing any articles of incorporation or any certificate of amendment of articles of incorporation of any corporation formed pursuant to the laws of this State if the name of the corporation contains the words "architect," "architecture," "registered architect," "licensed architect," "registered interior designer," "registered interior design," "residential designer," "registered residential designer," "licensed residential designer" or "residential design" unless the State Board of Architecture, Interior Design and Residential Design certifies that:

(a) The principals of the corporation are holders of a certificate of registration to practice architecture or residential design or to practice as a registered interior designer, as applicable, pursuant to the laws of this State; or

(b) The corporation is qualified to do business in this State pursuant to NRS 623.349.

5. The Secretary of State shall not accept for filing any articles of incorporation or any certificate of amendment of articles of incorporation of any corporation formed pursuant to the laws of this State which provides that the name of the corporation contains the word "accountant," "accounting," "accountancy," "auditor" or "auditing" unless the Nevada State Board of Accountancy certifies that the corporation:

(a) Is registered pursuant to the provisions of chapter 628 of NRS; or

(b) Has filed with the Nevada State Board of Accountancy under penalty of perjury a written statement that the corporation is not engaged in the practice of accounting and is not offering to practice accounting in this State.

6. The Secretary of State shall not accept for filing any articles of incorporation or any certificate of amendment of articles of incorporation of any corporation formed or existing pursuant to the laws of this State which provides that the name of the corporation contains the words "common-interest community," "community association," "master association," "unit-owners' association" or "homeowners' association" or if it appears in the articles of incorporation or certificate of amendment that the purpose of the corporation is to operate as a unit-owners' association pursuant to chapter 116 of NRS unless the Administrator of the Real Estate Division of the Department of Business and Industry certifies that the corporation has:

(a) Registered with the Ombudsman for Owners in Common-Interest Communities pursuant to NRS 116.31158; and

(b) Paid to the Administrator of the Real Estate Division the fees required pursuant to NRS 116.31155.

7. The provisions of subsections 3 and 4 do not apply to any corporation, whose securities are publicly traded and regulated by the Securities Exchange Act of 1934, which does not engage in the practice of professional engineering, architecture or residential design or interior design, as applicable.

8. The Commissioner of Financial Institutions and the Commissioner of Insurance may approve or disapprove the articles or amendments referred to them pursuant to the provisions of this section. [4.5:177:1925; added 1949, 520; 1943 NCL § 1603.1]—(NRS A 1977, 1056; 1979, 1102; 1983, 467, 1696; 1987, 1873; 1993, 128; 1995, 1112; 1997, 1058; 1999, 1706, 2441; 2001, 111; 2003, 20th Special Session, 28; 2005, 2623; 2007, 2)

**NRS 78.045 Articles of incorporation: Approval or certification required before filing of certain articles or amendments. [Effective January 1, 2008.]**

1. The Secretary of State shall not accept for filing any articles of incorporation or any certificate of

amendment of articles of incorporation of any corporation formed pursuant to the laws of this State which provides that the name of the corporation contains the word "bank" or "trust," unless:

(a) It appears from the articles or the certificate of amendment that the corporation proposes to carry on business as a banking or trust company, exclusively or in connection with its business as a bank, savings and loan association or thrift company; and

(b) The articles or certificate of amendment is first approved by the Commissioner of Financial Institutions.

2. The Secretary of State shall not accept for filing any articles of incorporation or any certificate of amendment of articles of incorporation of any corporation formed pursuant to the provisions of this chapter if it appears from the articles or the certificate of amendment that the business to be carried on by the corporation is subject to supervision by the Commissioner of Insurance or by the Commissioner of Financial Institutions, unless the articles or certificate of amendment is approved by the Commissioner who will supervise the business of the corporation.

3. Except as otherwise provided in subsection 7, the Secretary of State shall not accept for filing any articles of incorporation or any certificate of amendment of articles of incorporation of any corporation formed pursuant to the laws of this State if the name of the corporation contains the words "engineer," "engineered," "engineering," "professional engineer," "registered engineer" or "licensed engineer" unless:

(a) The State Board of Professional Engineers and Land Surveyors certifies that the principals of the corporation are licensed to practice engineering pursuant to the laws of this State; or

(b) The State Board of Professional Engineers and Land Surveyors certifies that the corporation is exempt from the prohibitions of NRS 625.520.

4. Except as otherwise provided in subsection 7, the Secretary of State shall not accept for filing any articles of incorporation or any certificate of amendment of articles of incorporation of any corporation formed pursuant to the laws of this State if the name of the corporation contains the words "architect," "architecture," "registered architect," "licensed architect," "registered interior designer," "registered interior design," "residential designer," "registered residential designer," "licensed residential designer" or "residential design" unless the State Board of Architecture, Interior Design and Residential Design certifies that:

(a) The principals of the corporation are holders of a certificate of registration to practice architecture or residential design or to practice as a registered interior designer, as applicable, pursuant to the laws of this State; or

(b) The corporation is qualified to do business in this State pursuant to NRS 623.349.

5. The Secretary of State shall not accept for filing any articles of incorporation or any certificate of amendment of articles of incorporation of any corporation formed pursuant to the laws of this State which provides that the name of the corporation contains the word "accountant," "accounting," "accountancy," "auditor" or "auditing" unless the Nevada State Board of Accountancy certifies that the corporation:

(a) Is registered pursuant to the provisions of chapter 628 of NRS; or

(b) Has filed with the Nevada State Board of Accountancy under penalty of perjury a written statement that the corporation is not engaged in the practice of accounting and is not offering to practice accounting in this State.

6. The Secretary of State shall not accept for filing any articles of incorporation or any certificate of amendment of articles of incorporation of any corporation formed or existing pursuant to the laws of this State which provides that the name of the corporation contains the words "common-interest community," "community association," "master association," "unit-owners' association" or "homeowners' association" or if it appears in the articles of incorporation or certificate of amendment that the purpose of the corporation is to operate as a unit-owners' association pursuant to chapter 116 or 116B of NRS unless the Administrator of the Real Estate Division of the Department of Business and Industry certifies that the corporation has:

(a) Registered with the Ombudsman for Owners in Common-Interest Communities and Condominium Hotels pursuant to NRS 116.31158 or 116B.625; and

(b) Paid to the Administrator of the Real Estate Division the fees required pursuant to NRS 116.31155 or 116B.620.

7. The provisions of subsections 3 and 4 do not apply to any corporation, whose securities are publicly traded and regulated by the Securities Exchange Act of 1934, which does not engage in the practice of professional engineering, architecture or residential design or interior design, as applicable.

8. The Commissioner of Financial Institutions and the Commissioner of Insurance may approve or disapprove the articles or amendments referred to them pursuant to the provisions of this section. [4.5:177:1925; added 1949, 520; 1943 NCL § 1603.1]—(NRS A 1977, 1056; 1979, 1102; 1983, 467, 1696; 1987, 1873; 1993, 128; 1995, 1112; 1997, 1058; 1999, 1706, 2441; 2001, 111; 2003, 20th Special Session, 28; 2005, 2623; 2007, 2, 2279, effective January 1, 2008)

**NRS 78.050 Commencement of corporate existence. [Effective through June 30, 2008.]**

1. Upon the filing of the articles of incorporation and the certificate of acceptance pursuant to NRS 78.030, and the payment of the filing fees, the Secretary of State shall issue to the corporation a certificate that the articles, containing the required statement of facts, have been filed. From the date the articles are filed, the corporation is a body corporate, by the name set forth in the articles of incorporation, subject to the forfeiture of its charter or dissolution as provided in this chapter.

2. Neither an incorporator nor a director designated in the articles of incorporation thereby becomes a subscriber or stockholder of the corporation.

3. The filing of the articles of incorporation does not, by itself, constitute commencement of business by the corporation. [Part 5:177:1925; NCL § 1604]—(NRS A 1989, 948; 1991, 1211; 1993, 946)

### NRS 78.050 Commencement of corporate existence. [Effective July 1, 2008.]

1. Upon the filing of the articles of incorporation pursuant to NRS 78.030 and the payment of the filing fees, the Secretary of State shall issue to the corporation a certificate that the articles, containing the required statement of facts, have been filed. From the date the articles are filed, the corporation is a body corporate, by the name set forth in the articles of incorporation, subject to the forfeiture of its charter or dissolution as provided in this chapter.

2. Neither an incorporator nor a director designated in the articles of incorporation thereby becomes a subscriber or stockholder of the corporation.

3. The filing of the articles of incorporation does not, by itself, constitute commencement of business by the corporation. [Part 5:177:1925; NCL § 1604]—(NRS A 1989, 948; 1991, 1211; 1993, 946; 2007, 2641, effective July 1, 2008)

### NRS 78.055 Acceptable evidence of incorporation.

A copy of any articles of incorporation filed pursuant to this chapter, and certified by the Secretary of State under his official seal, or, with respect to a corporation organized before October 1, 1991, a copy of the copy thereof, filed with the county clerk, or microfilmed by the county clerk, under the county seal, certified by the clerk, must be received in all courts and places as prima facie evidence of the facts therein stated, and of the existence and incorporation of the corporation therein named. [Part 5:177:1925; NCL § 1604]—(NRS A 1963, 70; 1991, 1211)

## Powers

### NRS 78.060 General powers.

1. Any corporation organized under the provisions of this chapter:

(a) Has all the rights, privileges and powers conferred by this chapter.

(b) Has such rights, privileges and powers as may be conferred upon corporations by any other existing law.

(c) May at any time exercise those rights, privileges and powers, when not inconsistent with the provisions of this chapter, or with the purposes and objects for which the corporation is organized.

(d) Unless otherwise provided in its articles, has perpetual existence.

2. Every corporation, by virtue of its existence as such, is entitled:

(a) To have succession by its corporate name until dissolved and its affairs are wound up according to law.

(b) To sue and be sued in any court of law or equity.

(c) To make contracts.

(d) To appoint such officers and agents as the affairs of the corporation require, and to allow them suitable compensation.

(e) To make bylaws not inconsistent with the Constitution or laws of the United States, or of this State, for the management, regulation and government of its affairs and property, the transfer of its stock, the transaction of its business, and the calling and holding of meetings of its stockholders.

(f) To wind up and dissolve itself, or be wound up or dissolved, in the manner mentioned in this chapter.

(g) Unless otherwise provided in the articles, to engage in any lawful activity. [Part 8:177:1925; NCL § 1607] + [91:177:1925; NCL § 1690]—(NRS A 1969, 99; 1991, 1211; 2003, 3079)

### NRS 78.065 Adoption and use of corporate seal or stamp.

1. Every corporation, by virtue of its existence as such, shall have power to adopt and use a common seal or stamp, and alter the same at pleasure.

2. The use of a seal or stamp by a corporation on any corporate record is not necessary. The corporation may use a seal or stamp, if it desires, but such use or nonuse must not in any way affect the legality of the record. [Part 8:177:1925; NCL § 1607] + [85:177:1925; A 1953, 180]—(NRS A 1967, 102; 1971, 1100; 2003, 3080)

### NRS 78.070 Specific powers. Subject to such limitations, if any, as may be contained in its articles of incorporation, every corporation has the following powers:

1. To borrow money and contract debts when necessary for the transaction of its business, or for the exercise of its corporate rights, privileges or franchises, or for any other lawful purpose of its incorporation and to issue bonds, promissory notes, bills of exchange, debentures, and other obligations and evidences of indebtedness,

payable at a specified time or times, or payable upon the happening of a specified event or events, whether secured by mortgage, pledge or other security, or unsecured, for money borrowed, or in payment for property purchased or acquired, or for any other lawful object.

2. To guarantee, purchase, hold, take, obtain, receive, subscribe for, own, use, dispose of, sell, exchange, lease, lend, assign, mortgage, pledge, or otherwise acquire, transfer or deal in or with bonds or obligations of, or shares, securities or interests in or issued by, any person, government, governmental agency or political subdivision of government, and to exercise all the rights, powers and privileges of ownership of such an interest, including the right to vote, if any.

3. To purchase, hold, sell, pledge and transfer shares of its own stock, and use therefor its property or money.

4. To conduct business, have one or more offices, and hold, purchase, lease, mortgage, convey and take by devise or bequest real and personal property in this State, and in any of the several states, territories, possessions and dependencies of the United States, the District of Columbia, Puerto Rico and any foreign countries.

5. To do everything necessary and proper for the accomplishment of the objects enumerated in its articles of incorporation or necessary or incidental to the protection and benefit of the corporation, and, in general, to carry on any lawful business necessary or incidental to the attainment of the objects of the corporation, whether or not the business is similar in nature to the objects set forth in the articles of incorporation, except that:

(a) A corporation created under the provisions of this chapter does not possess the power of issuing bills, notes or other evidences of debt for circulation of money; and

(b) This chapter does not authorize the formation of banking corporations to issue or circulate money or currency within this State, or outside of this State, or at all, except the federal currency, or the notes of banks authorized under the laws of the United States.

6. To make donations for the public welfare or for charitable, scientific or educational purposes.

7. To enter into any relationship with another person in connection with any lawful activities.

8. To renounce in its articles of incorporation or by action by the board of directors any interest or expectancy to participate in specified business opportunities or specified classes or categories of business opportunities that are presented to the corporation or one or more of its officers, directors or stockholders. [9:177:1925; A 1931, 415; 1949, 158; 1953, 180]—(NRS A 1959, 690; 1963, 1146; 1969, 117; 1987, 576; 1991, 1212; 1993, 947; 1997, 696; 2003, 3080; 2007, 2414)

**NRS 78.075 Railroad companies: Powers.** In furtherance of and in addition to the powers which railroad companies organized under this chapter are entitled to exercise, but not in limitation of any of the powers granted by this chapter, every railroad company may:

1. Cause such examination and surveys for the proposed railroad to be made as may be necessary to the selection of the most advantageous route for the railroad, and for such purposes, by their officers, agents and employees, to enter upon the lands or waters of any persons, but subject to responsibility for all damages which they do thereto.

2. Receive, hold, take and convey, by deed or otherwise, as a natural person might or could do, such voluntary grants and donations of real estate, and other property of every description, as may be made to it to aid and encourage the construction, maintenance and accommodation of the railroad.

3. Purchase, and by voluntary grants and donations receive and take, and by its officers, engineers, surveyors and agents, enter upon and take possession of, and hold and use, in any manner they may deem proper, all such lands and real estate, and other property as the directors may deem necessary and proper for the construction and maintenance of the railroad, and for the stations, depots and other accommodations and purposes, deemed necessary to accomplish the object for which the corporation is formed.

4. Lay out its road or roads, not exceeding 200 feet wide, and construct and maintain the road with such tracks and with such appendages as may be deemed necessary for the convenient use of it. The company may make embankments, excavations, ditches, drains, culverts or otherwise, and procure timber, stone and gravel, or other materials, and may take as much more land, whenever they may think proper, as may be necessary for the purposes aforesaid, in the manner hereinafter provided, for the proper construction and security of the road.

5. Construct their road across, along or upon any stream of water, watercourse, roadstead, bay, navigable stream, street, avenue or highway, or across any railway, canal, ditch or flume which the route of its road intersects, crosses or runs along, in such manner as to afford security for life and property. The corporation shall restore the stream or watercourse, road, street, avenue, highway, railroad, canal, ditch or flume thus intersected to its former state, as near as may be, or in a sufficient manner not to have impaired unnecessarily its usefulness or injured its franchises.

6. Cross, intersect, join and unite its railroad with any other railroad, either before or after constructed, at any point upon its route, and upon the grounds of such other railroad company, with the necessary turnouts, sidings

and switches, and other conveniences, in furtherance of the objects of its connections; and every company whose railroad is, or will be hereafter, intersected by any new railroad in forming such intersections and connection, and grant the facilities aforesaid. If the two corporations cannot agree upon the amount of compensation to be made therefor, or the points or the manner of such crossings, intersections and connections, the same must be ascertained and determined by commissioners, to be appointed as is provided hereinafter in respect to the taking of lands, but this section is not to affect the rights and franchises heretofore granted.

7. Purchase lands, timber, stone, gravel or other materials to be used in the construction and maintenance of its road, or take them in the manner provided by this chapter. The railroad company may change the line of its road, in whole or in part, whenever a majority of the directors determine, as is provided hereinafter, but no such change may vary the general route of a road, as contemplated in the articles of incorporation of the company.

8. Receive by purchase, donation or otherwise, any lands, or other property, of any description, and hold and convey it in any manner the directors may think proper, the same as natural persons might or could do, that may be necessary for the construction and maintenance of its road, or for the erection of depots, turnouts, workshops, warehouses or for any other purposes necessary for the convenience of railroad companies, in order to transact the business usual for railroad companies.

9. Take, transport, carry and convey persons and property on their railroad, by the force and power of steam, of animals, or any mechanical power, or by any combinations of them, and receive tolls or compensation therefor.

10. Erect and maintain all necessary and convenient buildings, stations, depots and fixtures and machinery for the accommodation and use of their passengers, freight and business, obtain and hold the lands and other property necessary therefor, and acquire additional lands and rights-of-way and build and operate extensions or branches of its line of railroad.

11. Regulate the time and manner in which passengers and property are transported, and the tolls and compensation to be paid therefor, within the limits prescribed by law.

12. Regulate the force and speed of their locomotives, cars, trains or other machinery used and employed on their road, and establish, execute and enforce all needful and proper rules and regulations fully and completely for the management of its business transactions usual and proper for railroad companies.

13. Purchase, hold, sell and transfer shares of its own stock, bonds, debentures, or other securities issued by it, except that:

(a) No corporation may use its funds or property for the purchase of its own shares of stock when such use would cause any impairment of the capital of the corporation; and

(b) Shares of its own stock belonging to the corporation must not be voted upon, directly or indirectly, nor counted as outstanding for the purpose of any stockholders' quorum or vote.

14. Acquire, own, and operate motor vehicles, and air transportation facilities, and transport persons and property along and over the streets and highways of this State, for the transportation, for hire, of passengers, property and freight, either directly or through a subsidiary company or companies, subject to all relevant provisions of law concerning permits, licenses, franchises and the regulation of such form of transportation by motor vehicles or other agencies. Whenever the track of a railroad crosses a railroad or highway, such railroad or highway may be carried under, over or on a level with the track, as may be most expedient, and in cases where an embankment or cutting makes a change in the line of such railroad or highway desirable, with a view to a more easy ascent or descent, the company may take such additional lands and materials, if needed for the construction of such road or highway, on such new line, as may be deemed requisite by the railroad. Unless the lands and materials so taken are purchased, or voluntarily given for the purpose aforesaid, compensation therefor must be ascertained in the manner provided by law. [9(a):177:1925; added 1945, 196; 1943 NCL § 1608.01]— (NRS A 1993, 2762)

**NRS 78.080 Railroad companies: Rights-of-way granted by the State, counties and municipalities; limitations; reversion on abandonment; duties of companies.**

1. The right-of-way is hereby given and granted to all railroad companies that are now organized, or may be organized under the provisions of this chapter, or under the laws of any other state or territory, or under any act of Congress, to locate, construct and maintain their roads, or any part or parcel thereof, over and through any of the swamp or overflowed lands belonging to this State, or any other public lands which are now or may be the property of the State, at the time of constructing the railroad.

2. Such railroad companies are hereby authorized to survey and mark through the lands of the State, to be held by them for the track of their respective railroads, 200 feet in width, for the whole length the roads may be located over the lands of the State; and the right is hereby further given and granted to the companies to locate, occupy and hold all necessary sites and grounds for watering places, depots or other buildings, for the convenient use of the same, along the line of the road or

roads, so far as the places convenient for the same may fall upon the lands belonging to the State, except within the limits of any incorporated city or town, or within 3 miles where the same shall be taken, on paying to the State the value of the same.

3. No one depot, watering place, machine or workshop, or other buildings for the convenient use of such roads, shall cover over 6 acres each, and the sites or places on the lands of this State shall not be nearer to each other than 5 miles along the line of the roads.

4. The right is hereby further given and granted to the companies to take from any of the lands belonging to this State all such materials of earth, wood, stone or other materials whatever, as may be necessary or convenient, from time to time, for the first construction or equipment of the road or roads, or any part thereof.

5. If any road, at any time after its location, shall be discontinued or abandoned by the company or companies, or the location of any part thereof be so changed as not to cover the lands of the State thus previously occupied, then the lands so abandoned or left shall revert to this State.

6. When the location of the route of either of the railroads, or sites or places for depots, watering places, machine or workshops or other buildings for the convenient use of the same, shall be selected, the secretary of the company shall transmit to the Director of the State Department of Conservation and Natural Resources, and to the State Controller, and to the recorder of the county in which the lands so selected are situated, to each of the officers, a correct plot of the location of the railroad, or sites or places, before such selection shall become operative.

7. When any such company shall, for its purposes aforesaid, require any of the lands belonging to any of the counties, cities or towns in this State, the county, city and town officers, respectively, having charge of such lands, may grant and convey such land to such company, for a compensation which shall be agreed upon between them, or may donate and convey the same without any compensation; and if they shall not agree upon the sale and price, the same may be taken by the company as is provided in other cases of taking lands by condemnation.

8. Before any corporation incorporated or organized otherwise than under the laws of this State shall be entitled to any of the rights granted by this chapter, it shall file in the office of the county recorder of each county in which the railroad, or any part, extension or branch thereof shall be situate, a copy of its certificate or articles of incorporation, or of the act or law by which it was created, with the certified list of its officers, in the manner and form required by law. [9(b):177:1925; added 1945, 196; 1943 NCL § 1608.02]—(NRS A 1957, 653)

## NRS 78.085 Railroad companies: Filing and recording of certified maps and profiles.

1. Every railroad company in this State shall, within 90 days after its road is finally located:

(a) Cause to be made a map and profile thereof, and of the land taken and obtained for the use thereof, and the boundaries of the several counties through which the road may run;

(b) File the map and profile thereof in the Office of the Secretary of State and a duplicate thereof with the Public Utilities Commission of Nevada; and

(c) Cause to be made like maps of the parts thereof located in different counties, and record such maps in the office of the recorder of the county in which those parts of the road are located.

2. The maps and profiles must be certified by the chief engineer, the acting president and secretary of the company, and copies of the maps and profiles so certified and recorded as required by subsection 1 must be kept in the office of the company, subject to examination by all interested persons. [9(d):177:1925; added 1945, 196; 1943 NCL § 1608.04]—(NRS A 1997, 1963; 2001, 1751)

## Registered Office and Resident Agent

## NRS 78.090 Resident agent required; address of registered office; powers of bank or corporation who is resident agent; penalty for noncompliance; service upon resident agent in lieu of corporation. [Effective through June 30, 2008.]

1. Except during any period of vacancy described in NRS 78.097, every corporation must have a resident agent who resides or is located in this State. Every resident agent must have a street address for the service of process, and may have a separate mailing address such as a post office box, which may be different from the street address. The street address of the resident agent is the registered office of the corporation in this State.

2. If the resident agent is a bank or corporation, it may:

(a) Act as the fiscal or transfer agent of any state, municipality, body politic or corporation and in that capacity may receive and disburse money.

(b) Transfer, register and countersign certificates of stock, bonds or other evidences of indebtedness and act as agent of any corporation, foreign or domestic, for any purpose required by statute, or otherwise.

(c) Act as trustee under any mortgage or bond issued by any municipality, body politic or corporation, and accept and execute any other municipal or corporate trust not inconsistent with the laws of this State.

(d) Receive and manage any sinking fund of any corporation, upon such terms as may be agreed upon between the corporation and those dealing with it.

3. Every corporation organized pursuant to this chapter which fails or refuses to comply with the requirements of this section is subject to a fine of not less than $100 nor more than $500, to be recovered with costs by the State, before any court of competent jurisdiction, by action at law prosecuted by the Attorney General or by the district attorney of the county in which the action or proceeding to recover the fine is prosecuted.

4. All legal process and any demand or notice authorized by law to be served upon a corporation may be served upon the resident agent of the corporation in the manner provided in subsection 2 of NRS 14.020. If any demand, notice or legal process, other than a summons and complaint, cannot be served upon the resident agent, it may be served in the manner provided in NRS 14.030. These manners and modes of service are in addition to any other service authorized by law. [78:177:1925; A 1929, 413; NCL § 1677] + [Part 79:177:1925; NCL § 1678]—(NRS A 1959, 682; 1969, 571; 1987, 1057; 1989, 949, 975, 1971; 1991, 1213; 1993, 948; 1995, 2095)

**NRS 78.090 Registered agent required; address of registered office; powers of bank or corporation who is registered agent; penalty for noncompliance; service upon registered agent in lieu of corporation. [Effective July 1, 2008.]**

1. Every corporation must have a registered agent who resides or is located in this State. Notwithstanding the provisions of NRS 77.300, each registered agent must have a street address for receiving service of process, which is the registered office of the corporation in this State. If the registered agent is in the business of acting as a registered agent for more than one business entity, the physical street address of the registered office must be in a location for which such use is not prohibited by any local ordinance. The registered agent may have a separate mailing address such as a post office box, which may be different from the street address.

2. If the registered agent is a bank or corporation, it may:

(a) Act as the fiscal or transfer agent of any state, municipality, body politic or corporation and in that capacity may receive and disburse money.

(b) Transfer, register and countersign certificates of stock, bonds or other evidences of indebtedness and act as agent of any corporation, foreign or domestic, for any purpose required by statute, or otherwise.

(c) Act as trustee under any mortgage or bond issued by any municipality, body politic or corporation, and accept and execute any other municipal or corporate trust not inconsistent with the laws of this State.

(d) Receive and manage any sinking fund of any corporation, upon such terms as may be agreed upon between the corporation and those dealing with it.

3. Every corporation organized pursuant to this chapter which fails or refuses to comply with the requirements of this section is subject to a fine of not less than $100 nor more than $500, to be recovered with costs by the State, before any court of competent jurisdiction, by action at law prosecuted by the Attorney General or by the district attorney of the county in which the action or proceeding to recover the fine is prosecuted.

4. All legal process and any demand or notice authorized by law to be served upon a corporation may be served upon the registered agent of the corporation in the manner provided in subsection 2 of NRS 14.020. If any demand, notice or legal process, other than a summons and complaint, cannot be served upon the registered agent, it may be served in the manner provided in NRS 14.030. These manners and modes of service are in addition to any other service authorized by law. [78:177:1925; A 1929, 413; NCL § 1677] + [Part 79:177:1925; NCL § 1678]—(NRS A 1959, 682; 1969, 571; 1987, 1057; 1989, 949, 975, 1971; 1991, 1213; 1993, 948; 1995, 2095; 2007, 2641, effective July 1, 2008)

**NRS 78.095 Change of address of resident agent and registered office. [Effective through June 30, 2008.]**

1. Within 30 days after changing the location of his office from one address to another in this State, a resident agent shall sign a certificate setting forth:

(a) The names of all the corporations represented by the resident agent;

(b) The address at which the resident agent has maintained the registered office for each of such corporations; and

(c) The new address to which the resident agency will be transferred and at which the resident agent will thereafter maintain the registered office for each of the corporations recited in the certificate.

2. Upon the filing of the certificate in the Office of the Secretary of State, the registered office in this State of each of the corporations recited in the certificate is located at the new address of the resident agent thereof as set forth in the certificate. [1:17:1931; 1931 NCL § 1677.01]—(NRS A 1983, 261; 1989, 871; 1991, 1214; 1993, 948; 1995, 1112; 2003, 3081; R 2007, 2727, effective July 1, 2008)

**NRS 78.097 Resident agent: Resignation; designation of successor after death, resignation or removal from State. [Effective through June 30, 2008.]**

1. A resident agent who desires to resign shall file with the Secretary of State a signed statement, on a form provided by the Secretary of State, for each artificial person formed, organized, registered or qualified pursuant to the provisions of this title that he is unwilling to continue to act as the resident agent of the

artificial person for the service of process. The fee for filing a statement of resignation is $100 for the first artificial person for whom the resident agent is unwilling to continue to act as the agent and $1 for each additional artificial person listed on the statement of resignation. A resignation is not effective until the signed statement is filed with the Secretary of State.

2. The statement of resignation may contain a statement of the affected corporation appointing a successor resident agent for that corporation. A certificate of acceptance signed by the new resident agent, stating the full name, complete street address and, if different from the street address, mailing address of the new resident agent, must accompany the statement appointing a successor resident agent.

3. Upon the filing of the statement of resignation with the Secretary of State the capacity of the resigning person as resident agent terminates. If the statement of resignation contains no statement by the corporation appointing a successor resident agent, the resigning resident agent shall immediately give written notice, by mail, to the corporation of the filing of the statement and its effect. The notice must be addressed to any officer of the corporation other than the resident agent.

4. If a resident agent dies, resigns or removes from the State, the corporation, within 30 days thereafter, shall file with the Secretary of State a certificate of acceptance signed by the new resident agent. The certificate must set forth the full name and complete street address of the new resident agent for the service of process, and may have a separate mailing address, such as a post office box, which may be different from the street address.

5. A corporation that fails to file a certificate of acceptance signed by the new resident agent within 30 days after the death, resignation or removal of its former resident agent shall be deemed in default and is subject to the provisions of NRS 78.170 and 78.175. (Added to NRS by 1959, 681; A 1967, 89; 1969, 11; 1989, 949; 1991, 1214; 1993, 949; 1999, 1579; 2003, 3081; 2003, 20th Special Session, 29)

### NRS 78.097 Resignation of registered agent or termination of commercial registered agent. [Effective July 1, 2008.]

1. If a registered agent resigns pursuant to NRS 77.370 or if a commercial registered agent terminates its listing as a commercial registered agent pursuant to NRS 77.330, the corporation, before the effective date of the resignation or termination, shall file with the Secretary of State a statement of change of registered agent pursuant to NRS 77.340.

2. A corporation that fails to comply with subsection 1 shall be deemed in default and is subject to the provisions of NRS 78.170 and 78.175.

3. As used in this section, "commercial registered agent" has the meaning ascribed to it in NRS 77.040. (Added to NRS by 1959, 681; A 1967, 89; 1969, 11; 1989, 949; 1991, 1214; 1993, 949; 1999, 1579; 2003, 3081; 2003, 20th Special Session, 29; 2007, 2642, effective July 1, 2008)

### NRS 78.105 Maintenance of records at registered office; inspection and copying of records; civil liability; penalties. [Effective through June 30, 2008.]

1. A corporation shall keep a copy of the following records at its registered office:

(a) A copy certified by the Secretary of State of its articles of incorporation, and all amendments thereto;

(b) A copy certified by an officer of the corporation of its bylaws and all amendments thereto; and

(c) A stock ledger or a duplicate stock ledger, revised annually, containing the names, alphabetically arranged, of all persons who are stockholders of the corporation, showing their places of residence, if known, and the number of shares held by them respectively. In lieu of the stock ledger or duplicate stock ledger, the corporation may keep a statement setting out the name of the custodian of the stock ledger or duplicate stock ledger, and the present and complete mailing or street address where the stock ledger or duplicate stock ledger specified in this section is kept.

2. A stock ledger, duplicate stock ledger or statement setting out the name of the custodian of the stock ledger or duplicate stock ledger described in paragraph (c) of subsection 1 must be maintained by the resident agent of the corporation for 3 years following the resignation or termination of the resident agent or the dissolution of the corporation by the Secretary of State.

3. Any person who has been a stockholder of record of a corporation for at least 6 months immediately preceding his demand, or any person holding, or thereunto authorized in writing by the holders of, at least 5 percent of all of its outstanding shares, upon at least 5 days' written demand is entitled to inspect in person or by agent or attorney, during usual business hours, the records required by subsection 1 and make copies therefrom. Holders of voting trust certificates representing shares of the corporation must be regarded as stockholders for the purpose of this subsection. Every corporation that neglects or refuses to keep the records required by subsection 1 open for inspection, as required in this subsection, shall forfeit to the State the sum of $25 for every day of such neglect or refusal.

4. If any corporation willfully neglects or refuses to make any proper entry in the stock ledger or duplicate copy thereof, or neglects or refuses to permit an inspection of the records required by subsection 1 upon demand by a person entitled to inspect them, or refuses

to permit copies to be made therefrom, as provided in subsection 3, the corporation is liable to the person injured for all damages resulting to him therefrom.

5. When the corporation keeps a statement in the manner provided for in paragraph (c) of subsection 1, the information contained thereon must be given to any stockholder of the corporation demanding the information, when the demand is made during business hours. Every corporation that neglects or refuses to keep a statement available, as in this subsection required, shall forfeit to the State the sum of $25 for every day of such neglect or refusal.

6. In every instance where an attorney or other agent of the stockholder seeks the right of inspection, the demand must be accompanied by a power of attorney signed by the stockholder authorizing the attorney or other agent to inspect on behalf of the stockholder.

7. The right to copy records under subsection 3 includes, if reasonable, the right to make copies by photographic, xerographic or other means.

8. The corporation may impose a reasonable charge to recover the costs of labor and materials and the cost of copies of any records provided to the stockholder. [80:177:1925; A 1951, 332]—(NRS A 1959, 29; 1963, 217; 1965, 978; 1991, 1214; 1997, 697; 2003, 3082; 2007, 2642)

**NRS 78.105 Maintenance of records at registered office; inspection and copying of records; civil liability; penalties. [Effective July 1, 2008.]**

1. A corporation shall keep a copy of the following records at its registered office:

(a) A copy certified by the Secretary of State of its articles of incorporation, and all amendments thereto;

(b) A copy certified by an officer of the corporation of its bylaws and all amendments thereto; and

(c) A stock ledger or a duplicate stock ledger, revised annually, containing the names, alphabetically arranged, of all persons who are stockholders of the corporation, showing their places of residence, if known, and the number of shares held by them respectively. In lieu of the stock ledger or duplicate stock ledger, the corporation may keep a statement setting out the name of the custodian of the stock ledger or duplicate stock ledger, and the present and complete mailing or street address where the stock ledger or duplicate stock ledger specified in this section is kept.

2. A stock ledger, duplicate stock ledger or statement setting out the name of the custodian of the stock ledger or duplicate stock ledger described in paragraph (c) of subsection 1 must be maintained by the registered agent of the corporation for 3 years following the resignation or termination of the registered agent or the dissolution of the corporation by the Secretary of State.

3. Any person who has been a stockholder of record of a corporation for at least 6 months immediately preceding his demand, or any person holding, or thereunto authorized in writing by the holders of, at least 5 percent of all of its outstanding shares, upon at least 5 days' written demand is entitled to inspect in person or by agent or attorney, during usual business hours, the records required by subsection 1 and make copies therefrom. Holders of voting trust certificates representing shares of the corporation must be regarded as stockholders for the purpose of this subsection. Every corporation that neglects or refuses to keep the records required by subsection 1 open for inspection, as required in this subsection, shall forfeit to the State the sum of $25 for every day of such neglect or refusal.

4. If any corporation willfully neglects or refuses to make any proper entry in the stock ledger or duplicate copy thereof, or neglects or refuses to permit an inspection of the records required by subsection 1 upon demand by a person entitled to inspect them, or refuses to permit copies to be made therefrom, as provided in subsection 3, the corporation is liable to the person injured for all damages resulting to him therefrom.

5. When the corporation keeps a statement in the manner provided for in paragraph (c) of subsection 1, the information contained thereon must be given to any stockholder of the corporation demanding the information, when the demand is made during business hours. Every corporation that neglects or refuses to keep a statement available, as in this subsection required, shall forfeit to the State the sum of $25 for every day of such neglect or refusal.

6. In every instance where an attorney or other agent of the stockholder seeks the right of inspection, the demand must be accompanied by a power of attorney signed by the stockholder authorizing the attorney or other agent to inspect on behalf of the stockholder.

7. The right to copy records under subsection 3 includes, if reasonable, the right to make copies by photographic, xerographic or other means.

8. The corporation may impose a reasonable charge to recover the costs of labor and materials and the cost of copies of any records provided to the stockholder. [80:177:1925; A 1951, 332]—(NRS A 1959, 29; 1963, 217; 1965, 978; 1991, 1214; 1997, 697; 2003, 3082; 2007, 2642, effective July 1, 2008)

**NRS 78.107 Denial of request for inspection of records; defense to action for penalties or damages; authority of court to compel production of records.**

1. An inspection authorized by NRS 78.105 may be denied to a stockholder or other person upon his refusal to furnish to the corporation an affidavit that the inspection is not desired for a purpose which is in the

interest of a business or object other than the business of the corporation and that he has not at any time sold or offered for sale any list of stockholders of any domestic or foreign corporation or aided or abetted any person in procuring any such record of stockholders for any such purpose.

2. It is a defense to any action for penalties or damages under NRS 78.105 that the person suing has at any time sold, or offered for sale, any list of stockholders of the corporation, or any other corporation, or has aided or abetted any person in procuring any such stock list for any such purpose, or that the person suing desired inspection for a purpose which is in the interest of a business or object other than the business of the corporation.

3. This section does not impair the power or jurisdiction of any court to compel the production for examination of the books of a corporation in any proper case. (Added to NRS by 1997, 693)

### NRS 78.110 Resident agent: Revocation of appointment; change of name. [Effective through June 30, 2008.]

1. If a corporation created pursuant to this chapter desires to change its resident agent, the change may be effected by filing with the Secretary of State a certificate of change of resident agent signed by an officer of the corporation which sets forth:

(a) The name of the corporation;

(b) The name and street address of its present resident agent; and

(c) The name and street address of the new resident agent.

2. The new resident agent's certificate of acceptance must be a part of or attached to the certificate of change of resident agent.

3. If the name of a resident agent is changed as a result of a merger, conversion, exchange, sale, reorganization or amendment, the resident agent shall:

(a) File with the Secretary of State a certificate of name change of resident agent that includes:

(1) The current name of the resident agent as filed with the Secretary of State;

(2) The new name of the resident agent; and

(3) The name and file number of each artificial person formed, organized, registered or qualified pursuant to the provisions of this title that the resident agent represents; and

(b) Pay to the Secretary of State a filing fee of $100.

4. A change authorized by this section becomes effective upon the filing of the proper certificate of change. [89:177:1925; NCL § 1688]—(NRS A 1959, 683; 1989, 950; 1991, 1216; 1995, 2096; 1999, 1579; 2003, 20th Special Session, 30; R 2007, 2727, effective July 1, 2008)

## Directors and Officers

### NRS 78.115 Board of directors: Number and qualifications. The business of every corporation must be managed under the direction of a board of directors or trustees, all of whom must be natural persons who are at least 18 years of age. A corporation must have at least one director, and may provide in its articles of incorporation or in its bylaws for a fixed number of directors or a variable number of directors, and for the manner in which the number of directors may be increased or decreased. Unless otherwise provided in the articles of incorporation, directors need not be stockholders. [Part 31:177:1925; NCL § 1630]—(NRS A 1965, 1012; 1981, 384; 1987, 577; 1993, 949; 1995, 1113; 2003, 3083)

### NRS 78.120 Board of directors: General powers.

1. Subject only to such limitations as may be provided by this chapter, or the articles of incorporation of the corporation, the board of directors has full control over the affairs of the corporation.

2. Except as otherwise provided in this subsection and subject to the bylaws, if any, adopted by the stockholders, the directors may make the bylaws of the corporation. Unless otherwise prohibited by any bylaw adopted by the stockholders, the directors may adopt, amend or repeal any bylaw, including any bylaw adopted by the stockholders. The articles of incorporation may grant the authority to adopt, amend or repeal bylaws exclusively to the directors.

3. The selection of a period for the achievement of corporate goals is the responsibility of the directors. [Part 31:177:1925; NCL § 1630]—(NRS A 1991, 1217; 2003, 3083; 2005, 2176)

### NRS 78.125 Committees of board of directors: Designation; powers; membership.

1. Unless it is otherwise provided in the articles of incorporation, the board of directors may designate one or more committees which, to the extent provided in the resolution or resolutions or in the bylaws of the corporation, have and may exercise the powers of the board of directors in the management of the business and affairs of the corporation.

2. Each committee must include at least one director. Unless the articles of incorporation or the bylaws provide otherwise, the board of directors may appoint natural persons who are not directors to serve on committees.

3. The board of directors may designate one or more directors as alternate members of a committee to replace any member who is disqualified or absent from a meeting of the committee. The bylaws of the corporation may provide that, unless the board of directors appoints alternate members pursuant to this

subsection, the member or members of a committee present at a meeting and not disqualified from voting, whether or not the member or members constitute a quorum, may unanimously appoint another member of the board of directors to act at the meeting in the place of an absent or disqualified member of the committee. [32:177:1925; A 1929, 413; NCL § 1631]—(NRS A 1971, 1100; 1991, 1217; 1993, 949; 2001, 1359, 3199; 2003, 3083)

**NRS 78.130 Officers of corporation: Selection; qualifications; terms; powers and duties; filling of vacancies.**

1. Every corporation must have a president, a secretary and a treasurer.

2. Every corporation may also have one or more vice presidents, assistant secretaries and assistant treasurers, and such other officers and agents as may be deemed necessary.

3. All officers must be natural persons and must be chosen in such manner, hold their offices for such terms and have such powers and duties as may be prescribed by the bylaws or determined by the board of directors. Any natural person may hold two or more offices.

4. An officer holds office after the expiration of his term until a successor is chosen or until his resignation or removal before the expiration of his term. A failure to elect officers does not require the corporation to be dissolved. Any vacancy occurring in an office of the corporation by death, resignation, removal or otherwise, must be filled as the bylaws provide, or in the absence of such a provision, by the board of directors. [36:177:1925; A 1937, 291; 1931 NCL § 1635]—(NRS A 1960, 152; 1991, 1217; 1993, 950)

**NRS 78.135 Authority of directors and representatives of corporation.**

1. The statement in the articles of incorporation of the objects, purposes, powers and authorized business of the corporation constitutes, as between the corporation and its directors, officers or stockholders, an authorization to the directors and a limitation upon the actual authority of the representatives of the corporation. Such limitations may be asserted in a proceeding by a stockholder or the State to enjoin the doing or continuation of unauthorized business by the corporation or its officers, or both, in cases where third parties have not acquired rights thereby, or to dissolve the corporation, or in a proceeding by the corporation or by the stockholders suing in a representative suit against the officers or directors of the corporation for violation of their authority.

2. No limitation upon the business, purposes or powers of the corporation or upon the powers of the stockholders, officers or directors, or the manner of exercise of such powers, contained in or implied by the articles may be asserted as between the corporation or any stockholder and any third person.

3. Any contract or conveyance, otherwise lawful, made in the name of a corporation, which is authorized or ratified by the directors, or is done within the scope of the authority, actual or apparent, given by the directors, binds the corporation, and the corporation acquires rights thereunder, whether the contract is signed or is wholly or in part executory. [Part 31(a):177:1925; added 1949, 158; 1943 NCL § 1630.01]—(NRS A 1961, 94; 1993, 950; 2003, 3083)

**NRS 78.138 Directors and officers: Exercise of powers; performance of duties; presumptions and considerations; liability to corporation and stockholders.**

1. Directors and officers shall exercise their powers in good faith and with a view to the interests of the corporation.

2. In performing their respective duties, directors and officers are entitled to rely on information, opinions, reports, books of account or statements, including financial statements and other financial data, that are prepared or presented by:

(a) One or more directors, officers or employees of the corporation reasonably believed to be reliable and competent in the matters prepared or presented;

(b) Counsel, public accountants, financial advisers, valuation advisers, investment bankers or other persons as to matters reasonably believed to be within the preparer's or presenter's professional or expert competence; or

(c) A committee on which the director or officer relying thereon does not serve, established in accordance with NRS 78.125, as to matters within the committee's designated authority and matters on which the committee is reasonably believed to merit confidence, but a director or officer is not entitled to rely on such information, opinions, reports, books of account or statements if he has knowledge concerning the matter in question that would cause reliance thereon to be unwarranted.

3. Directors and officers, in deciding upon matters of business, are presumed to act in good faith, on an informed basis and with a view to the interests of the corporation.

4. Directors and officers, in exercising their respective powers with a view to the interests of the corporation, may consider:

(a) The interests of the corporation's employees, suppliers, creditors and customers;

(b) The economy of the State and Nation;

(c) The interests of the community and of society; and

(d) The long-term as well as short-term interests of the corporation and its stockholders, including the possibility that these interests may be best served by the continued independence of the corporation.

5. Directors and officers are not required to consider the effect of a proposed corporate action upon any particular group having an interest in the corporation as a dominant factor.

6. The provisions of subsections 4 and 5 do not create or authorize any causes of action against the corporation or its directors or officers.

7. Except as otherwise provided in NRS 35.230, 90.660, 91.250, 452.200, 452.270, 668.045 and 694A.030, or unless the articles of incorporation or an amendment thereto, in each case filed on or after October 1, 2003, provide for greater individual liability, a director or officer is not individually liable to the corporation or its stockholders or creditors for any damages as a result of any act or failure to act in his capacity as a director or officer unless it is proven that:

(a) His act or failure to act constituted a breach of his fiduciary duties as a director or officer; and

(b) His breach of those duties involved intentional misconduct, fraud or a knowing violation of law. (Added to NRS by 1991, 1184; A 1993, 951; 1999, 1580; 2001, 3171; 2003, 3084)

**NRS 78.139 Directors and officers: Duties, presumptions and powers when confronted with change or potential change in control of corporation.**

1. Except as otherwise provided in subsection 2 or the articles of incorporation, directors and officers confronted with a change or potential change in control of the corporation have:

(a) The duties imposed upon them by subsection 1 of NRS 78.138; and

(b) The benefit of the presumptions established by subsection 3 of that section.

2. If directors and officers take action to resist a change or potential change in control of a corporation which impedes the exercise of the right of stockholders to vote for or remove directors:

(a) The directors must have reasonable grounds to believe that a threat to corporate policy and effectiveness exists; and

(b) The action taken which impedes the exercise of the stockholders' rights must be reasonable in relation to that threat. If those facts are found, the directors and officers have the benefit of the presumption established by subsection 3 of NRS 78.138.

3. The provisions of subsection 2 do not apply to:

(a) Actions that only affect the time of the exercise of stockholders' voting rights; or

(b) The adoption or execution of plans, arrangements or instruments that deny rights, privileges, power or authority to a holder of a specified number or fraction of shares or fraction of voting power.

4. The provisions of subsections 2 and 3 do not permit directors or officers to abrogate any right conferred by statute or the articles of incorporation.

5. Directors may resist a change or potential change in control of the corporation if the directors by a majority vote of a quorum determine that the change or potential change is opposed to or not in the best interest of the corporation:

(a) Upon consideration of the interests of the corporation's stockholders and any of the matters set forth in subsection 4 of NRS 78.138; or

(b) Because the amount or nature of the indebtedness and other obligations to which the corporation or any successor to the property of either may become subject, in connection with the change or potential change in control, provides reasonable grounds to believe that, within a reasonable time:

(1) The assets of the corporation or any successor would be or become less than its liabilities;

(2) The corporation or any successor would be or become insolvent; or

(3) Any voluntary or involuntary proceeding pursuant to the federal bankruptcy laws concerning the corporation or any successor would be commenced by any person. (Added to NRS by 1999, 1575)

**NRS 78.140 Restrictions on transactions involving interested directors or officers; compensation of directors.**

1. A contract or other transaction is not void or voidable solely because:

(a) The contract or transaction is between a corporation and:

(1) One or more of its directors or officers; or

(2) Another corporation, firm or association in which one or more of its directors or officers are directors or officers or are financially interested;

(b) A common or interested director or officer:

(1) Is present at the meeting of the board of directors or a committee thereof which authorizes or approves the contract or transaction; or

(2) Joins in the signing of a written consent which authorizes or approves the contract or transaction pursuant to subsection 2 of NRS 78.315; or

(c) The vote or votes of a common or interested director are counted for the purpose of authorizing or approving the contract or transaction, if one of the circumstances specified in subsection 2 exists.

2. The circumstances in which a contract or other transaction is not void or voidable pursuant to subsection 1 are:

(a) The fact of the common directorship, office or financial interest is known to the board of directors or committee, and the board or committee authorizes, approves or ratifies the contract or transaction in good faith by a vote sufficient for the purpose without counting the vote or votes of the common or interested director or directors.

(b) The fact of the common directorship, office or financial interest is known to the stockholders, and they approve or ratify the contract or transaction in good faith by a majority vote of stockholders holding a majority of the voting power. The votes of the common or interested directors or officers must be counted in any such vote of stockholders.

(c) The fact of the common directorship, office or financial interest is not known to the director or officer at the time the transaction is brought before the board of directors of the corporation for action.

(d) The contract or transaction is fair as to the corporation at the time it is authorized or approved.

3. Common or interested directors may be counted in determining the presence of a quorum at a meeting of the board of directors or a committee thereof which authorizes, approves or ratifies a contract or transaction, and if the votes of the common or interested directors are not counted at the meeting, then a majority of the disinterested directors may authorize, approve or ratify a contract or transaction.

4. The fact that the vote or votes of the common or interested director or directors are not counted for purposes of subsection 2 does not prohibit any authorization, approval or ratification of a contract or transaction to be given by written consent pursuant to subsection 2 of NRS 78.315, regardless of whether the common or interested director signs such written consent or abstains in writing from providing consent.

5. Unless otherwise provided in the articles of incorporation or the bylaws, the board of directors, without regard to personal interest, may establish the compensation of directors for services in any capacity. If the board of directors establishes the compensation of directors pursuant to this subsection, such compensation is presumed to be fair to the corporation unless proven unfair by a preponderance of the evidence. [31(b):177:1925; added 1951, 328]—(NRS A 1959, 683; 1969, 113; 1989, 872; 1991, 1218; 1993, 952; 1997, 698; 2003, 3085; 2007, 2415)

## Annual List and Other Requirements; Defaulting Corporations

### NRS 78.150 Filing requirements; fees; powers and duties of Secretary of State. [Effective through June 30, 2008.]

1. A corporation organized pursuant to the laws of this State shall, on or before the last day of the first month after the filing of its articles of incorporation with the Secretary of State, file with the Secretary of State a list, on a form furnished by him, containing:

(a) The name of the corporation;

(b) The file number of the corporation, if known;

(c) The names and titles of the president, secretary and treasurer, or the equivalent thereof, and of all the directors of the corporation;

(d) The address, either residence or business, of each officer and director listed, following the name of the officer or director;

(e) The name and address of the lawfully designated resident agent of the corporation in this State; and

(f) The signature of an officer of the corporation certifying that the list is true, complete and accurate.

2. The corporation shall annually thereafter, on or before the last day of the month in which the anniversary date of incorporation occurs in each year, file with the Secretary of State, on a form furnished by him, an annual list containing all of the information required in subsection 1.

3. Each list required by subsection 1 or 2 must be accompanied by:

(a) A declaration under penalty of perjury that the corporation:

(1) Has complied with the provisions of NRS 360.780; and

(2) Acknowledges that pursuant to NRS 239.330, it is a category C felony to knowingly offer any false or forged instrument for filing with the Office of the Secretary of State.

(b) A statement as to whether the corporation is a publicly traded company. If the corporation is a publicly traded company, the corporation must list its Central Index Key. The Secretary of State shall include on his Internet website the Central Index Key of a corporation provided pursuant to this paragraph and instructions describing the manner in which a member of the public may obtain information concerning the corporation from the Securities and Exchange Commission.

4. Upon filing the list required by:

(a) Subsection 1, the corporation shall pay to the Secretary of State a fee of $125.

(b) Subsection 2, the corporation shall pay to the Secretary of State, if the amount represented by the total number of shares provided for in the articles is:

$75,000 or less...........................................................$125

Over $75,000 and not over $200,000 ........................175

Over $200,000 and not over $500,000 ......................275

Over $500,000 and not over $1,000,000 ...................375

Over $1,000,000:

For the first $1,000,000........................................375

For each additional $500,000 or fraction thereof...275 The maximum fee which may be charged pursuant to paragraph (b) for filing the annual list is $11,100.

5. If a director or officer of a corporation resigns and the resignation is not reflected on the annual or amended list of directors and officers, the corporation or the resigning director or officer shall pay to the Secretary of State a fee of $75 to file the resignation.

6. The Secretary of State shall, 90 days before the last day for filing each annual list required by subsection 2, cause to be mailed to each corporation which is required to comply with the provisions of NRS 78.150 to 78.185, inclusive, and which has not become delinquent, a notice of the fee due pursuant to subsection 4 and a reminder to file the annual list required by subsection 2. Failure of any corporation to receive a notice or form does not excuse it from the penalty imposed by law.

7. If the list to be filed pursuant to the provisions of subsection 1 or 2 is defective in any respect or the fee required by subsection 4 is not paid, the Secretary of State may return the list for correction or payment.

8. An annual list for a corporation not in default which is received by the Secretary of State more than 90 days before its due date shall be deemed an amended list for the previous year and must be accompanied by the appropriate fee as provided in subsection 4 for filing. A payment submitted pursuant to this subsection does not satisfy the requirements of subsection 2 for the year to which the due date is applicable. [Part 1:180:1925; A 1929, 122; 1931, 408; 1931 NCL § 1804]—(NRS A 1957, 315; 1959, 684; 1977, 401; 1979, 185; 1983, 689; 1985, 233; 1989, 976; 1991, 2460; 1993, 952; 1995, 2096; 1997, 2808, 3126; 1999, 639, 1581, 3018; 2001, 215, 1359, 3172, 3199; 2003, 928, 2253; 2003, 20th Special Session, 30, 182; 2005, 2249)

### NRS 78.150 Filing requirements; fees; powers and duties of Secretary of State. [Effective July 1, 2008.]

1. A corporation organized pursuant to the laws of this State shall, on or before the last day of the first month after the filing of its articles of incorporation with the Secretary of State, file with the Secretary of State a list, on a form furnished by him, containing:

(a) The name of the corporation;

(b) The file number of the corporation, if known;

(c) The names and titles of the president, secretary and treasurer, or the equivalent thereof, and of all the directors of the corporation;

(d) The address, either residence or business, of each officer and director listed, following the name of the officer or director;

(e) The information required pursuant to NRS 77.310; and

(f) The signature of an officer of the corporation certifying that the list is true, complete and accurate.

2. The corporation shall annually thereafter, on or before the last day of the month in which the anniversary date of incorporation occurs in each year, file with the Secretary of State, on a form furnished by him, an annual list containing all of the information required in subsection 1.

3. Each list required by subsection 1 or 2 must be accompanied by:

(a) A declaration under penalty of perjury that the corporation:

(1) Has complied with the provisions of NRS 360.780; and

(2) Acknowledges that pursuant to NRS 239.330, it is a category C felony to knowingly offer any false or forged instrument for filing with the Office of the Secretary of State.

(b) A statement as to whether the corporation is a publicly traded company. If the corporation is a publicly traded company, the corporation must list its Central Index Key. The Secretary of State shall include on his Internet website the Central Index Key of a corporation provided pursuant to this paragraph and instructions describing the manner in which a member of the public may obtain information concerning the corporation from the Securities and Exchange Commission.

4. Upon filing the list required by:

(a) Subsection 1, the corporation shall pay to the Secretary of State a fee of $125.

(b) Subsection 2, the corporation shall pay to the Secretary of State, if the amount represented by the total number of shares provided for in the articles is:

$75,000 or less............................................................$125
Over $75,000 and not over $200,000 .........................175
Over $200,000 and not over $500,000 .......................275
Over $500,000 and not over $1,000,000 ....................375
Over $1,000,000:
    For the first $1,000,000............................................375
    For each additional $500,000 or fraction thereof..275

The maximum fee which may be charged pursuant to paragraph (b) for filing the annual list is $11,100.

5. If a director or officer of a corporation resigns and the resignation is not reflected on the annual or amended list of directors and officers, the corporation or the resigning director or officer shall pay to the Secretary of State a fee of $75 to file the resignation.

6. The Secretary of State shall, 90 days before the last day for filing each annual list required by subsection 2, cause to be mailed to each corporation which is required to comply with the provisions of NRS 78.150 to 78.185, inclusive, and which has not become delinquent, a notice of the fee due pursuant to subsection 4 and a

reminder to file the annual list required by subsection 2. Failure of any corporation to receive a notice or form does not excuse it from the penalty imposed by law.

7. If the list to be filed pursuant to the provisions of subsection 1 or 2 is defective in any respect or the fee required by subsection 4 is not paid, the Secretary of State may return the list for correction or payment.

8. An annual list for a corporation not in default which is received by the Secretary of State more than 90 days before its due date shall be deemed an amended list for the previous year and must be accompanied by the appropriate fee as provided in subsection 4 for filing. A payment submitted pursuant to this subsection does not satisfy the requirements of subsection 2 for the year to which the due date is applicable. [Part 1:180:1925; A 1929, 122; 1931, 408; 1931 NCL § 1804]—(NRS A 1957, 315; 1959, 684; 1977, 401; 1979, 185; 1983, 689; 1985, 233; 1989, 976; 1991, 2460; 1993, 952; 1995, 2096; 1997, 2808, 3126; 1999, 639, 1581, 3018; 2001, 215, 1359, 3172, 3199; 2003, 928, 2253; 2003, 20th Special Session, 30, 182; 2005, 2249; 2007, 2643, effective July 1, 2008)

### NRS 78.152 List or statement to be maintained at registered office or principal place of business; requirement to assist in criminal investigation; failure to comply; regulations.

1. In addition to any records required to be kept at the registered office pursuant to NRS 78.105, a corporation that is not a publicly traded corporation shall maintain at its registered office or principal place of business in this State:

(a) A current list of its owners of record; or

(b) A statement indicating where such a list is maintained.

2. The corporation shall:

(a) Provide the Secretary of State with the name and contact information of the custodian of the list described in subsection 1. The information required pursuant to this paragraph shall be kept confidential by the Secretary of State.

(b) Provide written notice to the Secretary of State within 10 days after any change in the information contained in the list described in subsection 1.

3. Upon the request of any law enforcement agency in the course of a criminal investigation, the Secretary of State may require a corporation to:

(a) Submit to the Secretary of State, within 3 business days, a copy of the list required to be maintained pursuant to subsection 1; or

(b) Answer any interrogatory submitted by the Secretary of State that will assist in the criminal investigation.

4. If a corporation fails to comply with any requirement pursuant to subsection 3, the Secretary of State may take any action necessary, including, without limitation, the suspension or revocation of the corporate charter.

5. The Secretary of State shall not reinstate or revive a charter that was revoked or suspended pursuant to subsection 4 unless:

(a) The corporation complies with the requirements of subsection 3; or

(b) The law enforcement agency conducting the investigation advises the Secretary of State to reinstate or revive the corporate charter.

6. The Secretary of State may adopt regulations to administer the provisions of this section. (Added to NRS by 2007, 1315)

### NRS 78.153 Additional filing requirements for certain corporations: Criteria; statement; fees.

1. At the time of submitting any list required pursuant to NRS 78.150, a corporation that meets the criteria set forth in subsection 2 must submit:

(a) The statement required pursuant to subsection 3, accompanied by a declaration under penalty of perjury attesting that the statement does not contain any material misrepresentation of fact; and

(b) A fee of $100,000, to be distributed in the manner provided pursuant to subsection 4.

2. A corporation must submit a statement pursuant to this section if the corporation, including its parent and all subsidiaries:

(a) Holds 25 percent or more of the share of the market within this State for any product sold or distributed by the corporation within this State; and

(b) Has had, during the previous 5-year period, a total of five or more investigations commenced against the corporation, its parent or its subsidiaries in any jurisdiction within the United States, including all state and federal investigations:

(1) Which concern any alleged contract, combination or conspiracy in restraint of trade, as described in subsection 1 of NRS 598A.060, or which concern similar activities prohibited by a substantially similar law of another jurisdiction; and

(2) Which resulted in the corporation being fined or otherwise penalized or which resulted in the corporation being required to divest any holdings or being unable to acquire any holdings as a condition for the settlement, dismissal or resolution of those investigations.

3. A corporation that meets the criteria set forth in subsection 2 shall submit a statement which includes the following information with respect to each investigation:

(a) The jurisdiction in which the investigation was commenced.

(b) A summary of the nature of the investigation and the facts and circumstances surrounding the investigation.

(c) If the investigation resulted in criminal or civil litigation, a copy of all pleadings filed in the investigation by any party to the litigation.

(d) A summary of the outcome of the investigation, including specific information concerning whether any fine or penalty was imposed against the corporation and whether the corporation was required to divest any holdings or was unable to acquire any holdings as a condition for the settlement, dismissal or resolution of the investigation.

4. The fee collected pursuant to subsection 1 must be deposited in the Attorney General's Administration Budget Account and used solely for the purpose of investigating any alleged contract, combination or conspiracy in restraint of trade, as described in subsection 1 of NRS 598A.060. (Added to NRS by 2003, 927)

**NRS 78.155 Certificate of authorization to transact business.** If a corporation has filed the initial or annual list in compliance with NRS 78.150 and has paid the appropriate fee for the filing, the cancelled check or other proof of payment received by the corporation constitutes a certificate authorizing it to transact its business within this State until the last day of the month in which the anniversary of its incorporation occurs in the next succeeding calendar year. [2:180:1925; A 1931, 408; 1931 NCL § 1805]—(NRS A 1959, 684; 1981, 62; 1983, 689; 1993, 953; 1999, 1582; 2001, 3173; 2003, 20th Special Session, 31)

**NRS 78.165 Addresses of officers and directors required; failure to file. [Effective through June 30, 2008.]**

1. Each list required to be filed under the provisions of NRS 78.150 to 78.185, inclusive, must, after the name of each officer and director listed thereon, set forth the address, either residence or business, of each officer and director.

2. If the addresses are not stated for each person on any list offered for filing, the Secretary of State may refuse to file the list, and the corporation for which the list has been offered for filing is subject to all the provisions of NRS 78.150 to 78.185, inclusive, relating to failure to file the list within or at the times therein specified, unless a list is subsequently submitted for filing which conforms to the provisions of NRS 78.150 to 78.185, inclusive.

[3(a):180:1925; added 1951, 280]—(NRS A 1959, 685; 1985, 233; 1991, 1219; 2003, 3086; 2003, 20th Special Session, 31; R 2007, 2727, effective July 1, 2008)

**NRS 78.170 Defaulting corporations: Identification; reinstatement of corporation which is unit-owners' association; penalty. [Effective through December 31, 2007.]**

1. Each corporation which is required to make a filing and pay the fee prescribed in NRS 78.150 to 78.185,

inclusive, and which refuses or neglects to do so within the time provided shall be deemed in default.

2. Upon notification from the Administrator of the Real Estate Division of the Department of Business and Industry that a corporation which is a unit-owners' association as defined in NRS 116.011 has failed to register pursuant to NRS 116.31158 or failed to pay the fees pursuant to NRS 116.31155, the Secretary of State shall deem the corporation to be in default. If, after the corporation is deemed to be in default, the Administrator notifies the Secretary of State that the corporation has registered pursuant to NRS 116.31158 and paid the fees pursuant to NRS 116.31155, the Secretary of State shall reinstate the corporation if the corporation complies with the requirements for reinstatement as provided in this section and NRS 78.180 and 78.185.

3. For default there must be added to the amount of the fee a penalty of $75. The fee and penalty must be collected as provided in this chapter. [4:180:1925; A 1931, 408; 1931 NCL § 1807]—(NRS A 1977, 401, 606; 1979, 185; 1983, 690; 1985, 233; 1989, 976; 1991, 1219; 1995, 1113; 2001, 3173; 2003, 929; 2003, 20th Special Session, 32)

**NRS 78.170 Defaulting corporations: Identification; reinstatement of corporation which is unit-owners' association; penalty. [Effective January 1, 2008.]**

1. Each corporation which is required to make a filing and pay the fee prescribed in NRS 78.150 to 78.185, inclusive, and which refuses or neglects to do so within the time provided shall be deemed in default.

2. Upon notification from the Administrator of the Real Estate Division of the Department of Business and Industry that a corporation which is a unit-owners' association as defined in NRS 116.011 or 116B.030 has failed to register pursuant to NRS 116.31158 or 116B.625 or failed to pay the fees pursuant to NRS 116.31155 or 116B.620, the Secretary of State shall deem the corporation to be in default. If, after the corporation is deemed to be in default, the Administrator notifies the Secretary of State that the corporation has registered pursuant to NRS 116.31158 or 116B.625 and paid the fees pursuant to NRS 116.31155 or 116B.620, the Secretary of State shall reinstate the corporation if the corporation complies with the requirements for reinstatement as provided in this section and NRS 78.180 and 78.185.

3. For default there must be added to the amount of the fee a penalty of $75. The fee and penalty must be collected as provided in this chapter. [4:180:1925; A 1931, 408; 1931 NCL § 1807]—(NRS A 1977, 401, 606; 1979, 185; 1983, 690; 1985, 233; 1989, 976; 1991, 1219; 1995, 1113; 2001, 3173; 2003, 929; 2003, 20th Special Session, 32; 2007, 2281, effective January 1, 2008)

**NRS 78.175 Defaulting corporations: Duties of Secretary of State; revocation of charter and forfeiture of right to transact business; distribution of assets. [Effective through June 30, 2008.]**

1. The Secretary of State shall notify, by providing written notice to its resident agent, each corporation deemed in default pursuant to NRS 78.170. The written notice:

(a) Must include a statement indicating the amount of the filing fee, penalties incurred and costs remaining unpaid.

(b) At the request of the resident agent, may be provided electronically.

2. On the first day of the first anniversary of the month following the month in which the filing was required, the charter of the corporation is revoked and its right to transact business is forfeited.

3. The Secretary of State shall compile a complete list containing the names of all corporations whose right to transact business has been forfeited.

4. The Secretary of State shall forthwith notify, by providing written notice to its resident agent, each corporation specified in subsection 3 of the forfeiture of its charter. The written notice:

(a) Must include a statement indicating the amount of the filing fee, penalties incurred and costs remaining unpaid.

(b) At the request of the resident agent, may be provided electronically.

5. If the charter of a corporation is revoked and the right to transact business is forfeited as provided in subsection 2, all the property and assets of the defaulting domestic corporation must be held in trust by the directors of the corporation as for insolvent corporations, and the same proceedings may be had with respect thereto as are applicable to insolvent corporations. Any person interested may institute proceedings at any time after a forfeiture has been declared, but, if the Secretary of State reinstates the charter, the proceedings must at once be dismissed and all property restored to the officers of the corporation.

6. Where the assets are distributed, they must be applied in the following manner:

(a) To the payment of the filing fee, penalties incurred and costs due the State;

(b) To the payment of the creditors of the corporation; and

(c) Any balance remaining, to distribution among the stockholders. [Part 5:180:1925; NCL § 1808]—(NRS A 1957, 152; 1959, 59; 1973, 1026; 1977, 606; 1979, 185; 1991, 1219; 1995, 1113; 2001, 1360, 3199; 2003, 20th Special Session, 32)

**NRS 78.175 Defaulting corporations: Duties of Secretary of State; revocation of charter and forfeiture of right to transact business; distribution of assets. [Effective July 1, 2008.]**

1. The Secretary of State shall notify, by providing written notice to its registered agent, each corporation deemed in default pursuant to NRS 78.170. The written notice:

(a) Must include a statement indicating the amount of the filing fee, penalties incurred and costs remaining unpaid.

(b) At the request of the registered agent, may be provided electronically.

2. On the first day of the first anniversary of the month following the month in which the filing was required, the charter of the corporation is revoked and its right to transact business is forfeited.

3. The Secretary of State shall compile a complete list containing the names of all corporations whose right to transact business has been forfeited.

4. The Secretary of State shall forthwith notify, by providing written notice to its registered agent, each corporation specified in subsection 3 of the forfeiture of its charter. The written notice:

(a) Must include a statement indicating the amount of the filing fee, penalties incurred and costs remaining unpaid.

(b) At the request of the registered agent, may be provided electronically.

5. If the charter of a corporation is revoked and the right to transact business is forfeited as provided in subsection 2, all the property and assets of the defaulting domestic corporation must be held in trust by the directors of the corporation as for insolvent corporations, and the same proceedings may be had with respect thereto as are applicable to insolvent corporations. Any person interested may institute proceedings at any time after a forfeiture has been declared, but, if the Secretary of State reinstates the charter, the proceedings must at once be dismissed and all property restored to the officers of the corporation.

6. Where the assets are distributed, they must be applied in the following manner:

(a) To the payment of the filing fee, penalties incurred and costs due the State;

(b) To the payment of the creditors of the corporation; and

(c) Any balance remaining, to distribution among the stockholders. [Part 5:180:1925; NCL § 1808]—(NRS A 1957, 152; 1959, 59; 1973, 1026; 1977, 606; 1979, 185; 1991, 1219; 1995, 1113; 2001, 1360, 3199; 2003, 20th Special Session, 32; 2007, 2645, effective July 1, 2008)

**NRS 78.180 Defaulting corporations: Conditions and procedure for reinstatement. [Effective through June 30, 2008.]**

1. Except as otherwise provided in subsections 3 and 4 and NRS 78.152, the Secretary of State shall reinstate a corporation which has forfeited or which forfeits its right to transact business pursuant to the provisions of this chapter and shall restore to the corporation its right to carry on business in this State, and to exercise its corporate privileges and immunities, if it:

(a) Files with the Secretary of State:

(1) The list required by NRS 78.150;

(2) The statement required by NRS 78.153, if applicable; and

(3) A certificate of acceptance of appointment signed by its resident agent; and

(b) Pays to the Secretary of State:

(1) The filing fee and penalty set forth in NRS 78.150 and 78.170 for each year or portion thereof during which it failed to file each required annual list in a timely manner;

(2) The fee set forth in NRS 78.153, if applicable; and

(3) A fee of $300 for reinstatement.

2. When the Secretary of State reinstates the corporation, he shall issue to the corporation a certificate of reinstatement if the corporation:

(a) Requests a certificate of reinstatement; and

(b) Pays the required fees pursuant to subsection 8 of NRS 78.785.

3. The Secretary of State shall not order a reinstatement unless all delinquent fees and penalties have been paid, and the revocation of the charter occurred only by reason of failure to pay the fees and penalties.

4. If a corporate charter has been revoked pursuant to the provisions of this chapter and has remained revoked for a period of 5 consecutive years, the charter must not be reinstated.

5. Except as otherwise provided in NRS 78.185, a reinstatement pursuant to this section relates back to the date on which the corporation forfeited its right to transact business under the provisions of this chapter and reinstates the corporation's right to transact business as if such right had at all times remained in full force and effect. [6:180:1925; A 1927, 42; NCL § 1809]— (NRS A 1959, 60; 1973, 1027; 1975, 477; 1977, 402; 1985, 234, 1871; 1991, 1220; 1993, 953; 1995, 1114; 1997, 2808; 2001, 1360, 3173, 3199; 2003, 20th Special Session, 33; 2007, 1316, 2416)

**NRS 78.180 Defaulting corporations: Conditions and procedure for reinstatement. [Effective July 1, 2008.]**

1. Except as otherwise provided in subsections 3 and 4 and NRS 78.152, the Secretary of State shall reinstate a corporation which has forfeited or which forfeits its right to transact business pursuant to the provisions of this chapter and shall restore to the corporation its right to carry on business in this State, and to exercise its corporate privileges and immunities, if it:

(a) Files with the Secretary of State:

(1) The list required by NRS 78.150;

(2) The statement required by NRS 78.153, if applicable; and

(3) The information required pursuant to NRS 77.310; and

(b) Pays to the Secretary of State:

(1) The filing fee and penalty set forth in NRS 78.150 and 78.170 for each year or portion thereof during which it failed to file each required annual list in a timely manner;

(2) The fee set forth in NRS 78.153, if applicable; and

(3) A fee of $300 for reinstatement.

2. When the Secretary of State reinstates the corporation, he shall issue to the corporation a certificate of reinstatement if the corporation:

(a) Requests a certificate of reinstatement; and

(b) Pays the required fees pursuant to subsection 7 of NRS 78.785.

3. The Secretary of State shall not order a reinstatement unless all delinquent fees and penalties have been paid, and the revocation of the charter occurred only by reason of failure to pay the fees and penalties.

4. If a corporate charter has been revoked pursuant to the provisions of this chapter and has remained revoked for a period of 5 consecutive years, the charter must not be reinstated.

5. Except as otherwise provided in NRS 78.185, a reinstatement pursuant to this section relates back to the date on which the corporation forfeited its right to transact business under the provisions of this chapter and reinstates the corporation's right to transact business as if such right had at all times remained in full force and effect. [6:180:1925; A 1927, 42; NCL § 1809]— (NRS A 1959, 60; 1973, 1027; 1975, 477; 1977, 402; 1985, 234, 1871; 1991, 1220; 1993, 953; 1995, 1114; 1997, 2808; 2001, 1360, 3173, 3199; 2003, 20th Special Session, 33; 2007, 1316, 2416, 2645, effective July 1, 2008)

**NRS 78.185 Defaulting corporations: Reinstatement under old or new name; regulations.**

1. Except as otherwise provided in subsection 2, if a corporation applies to reinstate or revive its charter but its name has been legally reserved or acquired by another artificial person formed, organized, registered or qualified pursuant to the provisions of this title whose name is on file with the Office of the Secretary of State or reserved in the Office of the Secretary of State

pursuant to the provisions of this title, the corporation shall in its application for reinstatement submit in writing to the Secretary of State some other name under which it desires its corporate existence to be reinstated or revived. If that name is distinguishable from all other names reserved or otherwise on file, the Secretary of State shall reinstate the corporation under that new name. Upon the issuance of a certificate of reinstatement or revival under that new name, the articles of incorporation of the applying corporation shall be deemed to reflect the new name without the corporation having to comply with the provisions of NRS 78.385, 78.390 or 78.403.

2. If the applying corporation submits the written, acknowledged consent of the artificial person having a name, or the person who has reserved a name, which is not distinguishable from the old name of the applying corporation or a new name it has submitted, it may be reinstated or revived under that name.

3. For the purposes of this section, a proposed name is not distinguishable from a name on file or reserved name solely because one or the other contains distinctive lettering, a distinctive mark, a trademark or a trade name, or any combination of these.

4. The Secretary of State may adopt regulations that interpret the requirements of this section. [7:180:1925; NCL § 1810]—(NRS A 1961, 94; 1987, 1057; 1991, 1221; 1993, 953; 1997, 2809; 1999, 1582; 2003, 3086; 2003, 20th Special Session, 33; 2007, 1317, 2417)

## Stock and Other Securities; Distributions

**NRS 78.191 "Distribution" defined.** As used in NRS 78.191 to 78.307, inclusive, unless the context otherwise requires, the word "distribution" means a direct or indirect transfer of money or other property other than its own shares or the incurrence of indebtedness by a corporation to or for the benefit of its stockholders with respect to any of its shares. A distribution may be in the form of a declaration or payment of a dividend, a purchase, redemption or other acquisition of shares, a distribution of indebtedness, or otherwise. (Added to NRS by 1991, 1185)

**NRS 78.195 Issuance of more than one class or series of stock; rights of stockholders.**

1. If a corporation desires to have more than one class or series of stock, the articles of incorporation must prescribe, or vest authority in the board of directors to prescribe, the classes, series and the number of each class or series of stock and the voting powers, designations, preferences, limitations, restrictions and relative rights of each class or series of stock. If more than one class or series of stock is authorized, the articles of incorporation or the resolution of the board of directors passed pursuant to a provision of the articles must prescribe a distinguishing designation for each class and series. The voting powers, designations, preferences, limitations, restrictions, relative rights and distinguishing designation of each class or series of stock must be described in the articles of incorporation or the resolution of the board of directors before the issuance of shares of that class or series.

2. All shares of a series must have voting powers, designations, preferences, limitations, restrictions and relative rights identical with those of other shares of the same series and, except to the extent otherwise provided in the description of the series, with those of other series of the same class.

3. Unless otherwise provided in the articles of incorporation, no stock issued as fully paid up may ever be assessed and the articles of incorporation must not be amended in this particular.

4. Any rate, condition or time for payment of distributions on any class or series of stock may be made dependent upon any fact or event which may be ascertained outside the articles of incorporation or the resolution providing for the distributions adopted by the board of directors if the manner in which a fact or event may operate upon the rate, condition or time of payment for the distributions is stated in the articles of incorporation or the resolution. As used in this subsection, "fact or event" includes, without limitation, the existence of a fact or occurrence of an event, including, without limitation, a determination or action by a person, the corporation itself or any government, governmental agency or political subdivision of a government.

5. The provisions of this section do not restrict the directors of a corporation from taking action to protect the interests of the corporation and its stockholders, including, but not limited to, adopting or signing plans, arrangements or instruments that grant rights to stockholders or that deny rights, privileges, power or authority to a holder of a specified number of shares or percentage of share ownership or voting power. [11:177:1925; A 1929, 413; 1941, 374; 1931 NCL § 1610]—(NRS A 1961, 195; 1985, 1787; 1987, 577; 1989, 873; 1991, 1221; 1993, 954; 1995, 2097; 1999, 1582; 2001, 1361, 3199; 2003, 3086)

**NRS 78.1955 Establishment of matters regarding class or series of stock by resolution of board of directors.**

1. If the voting powers, designations, preferences, limitations, restrictions and relative rights of any class or series of stock have been established by a resolution of the board of directors pursuant to a provision in the articles of incorporation, a certificate of designation setting forth the resolution and stating the number of shares for each designation must be signed by an officer of the corporation and filed with the Secretary of State.

A certificate of designation signed and filed pursuant to this section must become effective before the issuance of any shares of the class or series.

2. Unless otherwise provided in the articles of incorporation or the certificate of designation being amended, if no shares of a class or series of stock established by a resolution of the board of directors have been issued, the designation of the class or series, the number of the class or series and the voting powers, designations, preferences, limitations, restrictions and relative rights of the class or series may be amended by a resolution of the board of directors pursuant to a certificate of amendment filed in the manner provided in subsection 4.

3. Unless otherwise provided in the articles of incorporation or the certificate of designation, if shares of a class or series of stock established by a resolution of the board of directors have been issued, the designation of the class or series, the number of the class or series and the voting powers, designations, preferences, limitations, restrictions and relative rights of the class or series may be amended by a resolution of the board of directors only if the amendment is approved as provided in this subsection. Unless otherwise provided in the articles of incorporation or the certificate of designation, the proposed amendment adopted by the board of directors must be approved by the vote of stockholders holding shares in the corporation entitling them to exercise a majority of the voting power, or such greater proportion of the voting power as may be required by the articles of incorporation or the certificate of designation, of:

(a) The class or series of stock being amended; and

(b) Each class and each series of stock which, before amendment, is senior to the class or series being amended as to the payment of distributions upon dissolution of the corporation, regardless of any limitations or restrictions on the voting power of that class or series.

4. A certificate of amendment to a certificate of designation must be signed by an officer of the corporation and filed with the Secretary of State and must:

(a) Set forth the original designation and the new designation, if the designation of the class or series is being amended;

(b) State that no shares of the class or series have been issued or state that the approval of the stockholders required pursuant to subsection 3 has been obtained; and

(c) Set forth the amendment to the class or series or set forth the designation of the class or series, the number of the class or series and the voting powers, designations, preferences, limitations, restrictions and relative rights of the class or series, as amended.

5. A certificate filed pursuant to subsection 1 or 4 is effective upon filing the certificate with the Secretary of State or upon a later date specified in the certificate, which must not be more than 90 days after the certificate is filed.

6. If shares of a class or series of stock established by a certificate of designation are not outstanding, the corporation may file a certificate which states that no shares of the class or series are outstanding and which contains the resolution of the board of directors authorizing the withdrawal of the certificate of designation establishing the class or series of stock. The certificate must identify the date and certificate of designation being withdrawn and must be signed by an officer of the corporation and filed with the Secretary of State. Upon filing the certificate and payment of the fee required pursuant to NRS 78.765, all matters contained in the certificate of designation regarding the class or series of stock are eliminated from the articles of incorporation.

7. NRS 78.380, 78.385 and 78.390 do not apply to certificates of amendment filed pursuant to this section. (Added to NRS by 1995, 2092; A 2001, 1362, 3199; 2005, 2177, 2250)

**NRS 78.196 Required and authorized classes or series of stock; shares called for redemption.**

1. Each corporation must have:

(a) One or more classes or series of shares that together have unlimited voting rights; and

(b) One or more classes or series of shares that together are entitled to receive the net assets of the corporation upon dissolution. If the articles of incorporation provide for only one class of stock, that class of stock has unlimited voting rights and is entitled to receive the net assets of the corporation upon dissolution.

2. The articles of incorporation, or a resolution of the board of directors pursuant thereto, may authorize one or more classes or series of stock that:

(a) Have special, conditional or limited voting powers, or no right to vote, except to the extent otherwise provided by this title;

(b) Are redeemable or convertible:

(1) At the option of the corporation, the stockholders or another person, or upon the occurrence of a designated event;

(2) For cash, indebtedness, securities or other property; or

(3) In a designated amount or in an amount determined in accordance with a designated formula or by reference to extrinsic data or events;

(c) Entitle the stockholders to distributions calculated in any manner, including dividends that may be cumulative, noncumulative or partially cumulative;

(d) Have preference over any other class or series of shares with respect to distributions, including dividends and distributions upon the dissolution of the corporation;

(e) Have par value; or

(f) Have powers, designations, preferences, limitations, restrictions and relative rights dependent upon any fact or event which may be ascertained outside of the articles of incorporation or the resolution if the manner in which the fact or event may operate on such class or series of stock is stated in the articles of incorporation or the resolution. As used in this paragraph, "fact or event" includes, without limitation, the existence of a fact or occurrence of an event, including, without limitation, a determination or action by a person, the corporation itself or any government, governmental agency or political subdivision of a government.

3. Unless otherwise provided in the articles of incorporation or in a resolution of the board of directors establishing a class or series of stock, shares which are subject to redemption and which have been called for redemption are not deemed to be outstanding shares for purposes of voting or determining the total number of shares entitled to vote on a matter on and after the date on which:

(a) Written notice of redemption has been sent to the holders of such shares; and

(b) A sum sufficient to redeem the shares has been irrevocably deposited or set aside to pay the redemption price to the holders of the shares upon surrender of any certificates.

4. The description of voting powers, designations, preferences, limitations, restrictions and relative rights of the classes or series of shares contained in this section is not exclusive. (Added to NRS by 1991, 1185; A 1999, 1583; 2001, 1363, 3199; 2003, 3087)

**NRS 78.197 Rights of persons holding obligations of corporation.** A corporation may provide in its articles of incorporation that the holder of a bond, debenture or other obligation of the corporation may have any of the rights of a stockholder in the corporation. (Added to NRS by 1987, 574; A 1993, 955)

**NRS 78.200 Rights or options to purchase stock.**

1. A corporation may create and issue rights or options entitling the holders thereof to purchase from the corporation any shares of its stock of any class or classes to be evidenced by or in such instrument or instruments as are approved by the board of directors.

2. The terms upon which, the time or times, which may be limited or unlimited in duration, at or within which, and the price or prices, including a formula by which such price or prices may be determined, at which any such shares may be purchased from the corporation upon the exercise of any such right or option may be fixed and stated in the articles of incorporation or in a resolution or resolutions adopted by the board of directors providing for the creation and issue of the rights or options, and, in every case, set forth or incorporated by reference in the instrument or instruments evidencing the rights or options. The judgment of the board of directors as to the consideration for such rights or options issued is conclusive in the absence of actual fraud in the transaction.

3. The board of directors may authorize one or more officers of the corporation to:

(a) Designate the persons to be recipients of rights or options created by the corporation; and

(b) Determine the number of rights or options to be received by the persons designated pursuant to paragraph (a).

4. The authorization pursuant to subsection 3 must specify the maximum number of rights or options the officer or officers may award. The board of directors may not authorize an officer to designate himself as a recipient of the rights or options. [11(a):177:1925; added 1949, 158; 1943 NCL § 1610.01]—(NRS A 1991, 1223; 1993, 955; 2003, 3088)

**NRS 78.205 Fractions of shares: Issuance; alternatives to issuance.**

1. A corporation is not obligated to but may sign and deliver a certificate for or including a fraction of a share.

2. In lieu of signing and delivering a certificate for a fraction of a share, a corporation may:

(a) Pay to any person otherwise entitled to become a holder of a fraction of a share an amount in cash based on a per share value, and that value or the method of determining that value must be specified in the articles, plan of reorganization, plan of merger or exchange, resolution of the board of directors, or other instrument pursuant to which the fractional share would otherwise be issued;

(b) Issue such additional fraction of a share as is necessary to increase the fractional share to a full share; or

(c) Sign and deliver registered or bearer scrip over the manual or facsimile signature of an officer of the corporation or of its agent for that purpose, exchangeable as provided on the scrip for full share certificates, but the scrip does not entitle the holder to any rights as a stockholder except as provided on the scrip. The scrip may provide that it becomes void unless the rights of the holders are exercised within a specified period and may contain any other provisions or conditions that the corporation deems advisable. Whenever any scrip ceases to be exchangeable for full share certificates, the shares that would otherwise have been issuable as provided on the scrip are deemed to be treasury shares unless the scrip contains other provisions for their disposition.

3. Any proposed corporate action that would result in money or scrip being delivered instead of fractional shares to stockholders who:

(a) Before the proposed corporate action becomes effective, hold 1 percent or more of the outstanding shares of the affected class or series; and

(b) Would otherwise be entitled to receive fractions of shares in exchange for the cancellation of all their outstanding shares, is subject to the provisions of NRS 92A.300 to 92A.500, inclusive. If the proposed corporate action is subject to those provisions, any stockholder who is obligated to accept money or scrip rather than receive a fraction of a share resulting from the action taken pursuant to this section may dissent in accordance with the provisions of NRS 92A.300 to 92A.500, inclusive, and obtain payment of the fair value of the fraction of a share to which the stockholder would otherwise be entitled. [11(b):177:1925; added 1953, 180]—(NRS A 1979, 1160; 1993, 956; 2001, 1364, 3199; 2003, 3089; 2005, 2178)

### NRS 78.2055 Decrease in number of issued and outstanding shares of class or series: Resolution by board of directors; approval by stockholders; rights of stockholders.

1. Unless otherwise provided in the articles of incorporation, a corporation that desires to decrease the number of issued and outstanding shares of a class or series held by each stockholder of record at the effective date and time of the change without correspondingly decreasing the number of authorized shares of the same class or series may do so if:

(a) The board of directors adopts a resolution setting forth the proposal to decrease the number of issued and outstanding shares of a class or series; and

(b) The proposal is approved by the vote of stockholders holding a majority of the voting power of the affected class or series, or such greater proportion as may be provided in the articles of incorporation, regardless of limitations or restrictions on the voting power of the affected class or series.

2. If the proposal required by subsection 1 is approved by the stockholders entitled to vote, the corporation may reissue its stock in accordance with the proposal after the effective date and time of the change.

3. Except as otherwise provided in this subsection, if a proposed decrease in the number of issued and outstanding shares of any class or series would adversely alter or change any preference, or any relative or other right given to any other class or series of outstanding shares, then the decrease must be approved by the vote, in addition to any vote otherwise required, of the holders of shares representing a majority of the voting power of each class or series whose preference or rights are adversely affected by the decrease, or such greater proportion as may be provided in the articles of incorporation, regardless of limitations or restrictions on the voting power of the adversely

affected class or series. The decrease does not have to be approved by the vote of the holders of shares representing a majority of the voting power of each class or series whose preference or rights are adversely affected by the decrease if the articles of incorporation specifically deny the right to vote on such a decrease.

4. Any proposal to decrease the number of issued and outstanding shares of any class or series, if any, that includes provisions pursuant to which only money will be paid or scrip will be issued to stockholders who:

(a) Before the decrease in the number of shares becomes effective, hold 1 percent or more of the outstanding shares of the affected class or series; and

(b) Would otherwise be entitled to receive fractions of shares in exchange for the cancellation of all their outstanding shares, is subject to the provisions of NRS 92A.300 to 92A.500, inclusive. If the proposal is subject to those provisions, any stockholder who is obligated to accept money or scrip rather than receive a fraction of a share resulting from the action taken pursuant to this section may dissent in accordance with the provisions of NRS 92A.300 to 92A.500, inclusive, and obtain payment of the fair value of the fraction of a share to which the stockholder would otherwise be entitled. (Added to NRS by 2001, 1357; A 2001, 3199; 2003, 3089)

### NRS 78.207 Change in number of authorized shares of class or series: Resolution by board of directors; approval by stockholders; rights of stockholders.

1. Unless otherwise provided in the articles of incorporation, a corporation that desires to change the number of shares of a class or series, if any, of its authorized stock by increasing or decreasing the number of authorized shares of the class or series and correspondingly increasing or decreasing the number of issued and outstanding shares of the same class or series held by each stockholder of record at the effective date and time of the change, may, except as otherwise provided in subsections 2 and 3, do so by a resolution adopted by the board of directors, without obtaining the approval of the stockholders. The resolution may also provide for a change of the par value, if any, of the same class or series of the shares increased or decreased. After the effective date and time of the change, the corporation may issue its stock in accordance therewith.

2. A proposal to increase or decrease the number of authorized shares of any class or series, if any, that includes provisions pursuant to which only money will be paid or scrip will be issued to stockholders who:

(a) Before the increase or decrease in the number of shares becomes effective, in the aggregate hold 10 percent or more of the outstanding shares of the affected class or series; and

(b) Would otherwise be entitled to receive fractions of shares in exchange for the cancellation of all of their outstanding shares, must be approved by the vote of stockholders holding a majority of the voting power of the affected class or series, or such greater proportion as may be provided in the articles of incorporation, regardless of limitations or restrictions on the voting power thereof.

3. Except as otherwise provided in this subsection, if a proposed increase or decrease in the number of authorized shares of any class or series would adversely alter or change any preference or any relative or other right given to any other class or series of outstanding shares, then the increase or decrease must be approved by the vote, in addition to any vote otherwise required, of the holders of shares representing a majority of the voting power of each class or series whose preference or rights are adversely affected by the increase or decrease, regardless of limitations or restrictions on the voting power thereof. The increase or decrease does not have to be approved by the vote of the holders of shares representing a majority of the voting power in each class or series whose preference or rights are adversely affected by the increase or decrease if the articles of incorporation specifically deny the right to vote on such an increase or decrease.

4. Any proposal to increase or decrease the number of authorized shares of any class or series, if any, that includes provisions pursuant to which only money will be paid or scrip will be issued to stockholders who:

(a) Before the increase or decrease in the number of shares becomes effective, hold 1 percent or more of the outstanding shares of the affected class or series; and

(b) Would otherwise be entitled to receive a fraction of a share in exchange for the cancellation of all of their outstanding shares, is subject to the provisions of NRS 92A.300 to 92A.500, inclusive. If the proposal is subject to those provisions, any stockholder who is obligated to accept money or scrip rather than receive a fraction of a share resulting from the action taken pursuant to this section may dissent in accordance with those provisions and obtain payment of the fair value of the fraction of a share to which the stockholder would otherwise be entitled. [Part 6:177:1925; A 1951, 28]—(NRS A 1959, 688; 1991, 1224; 1993, 956; 1995, 2098; 1997, 699; 2001, 1364, 3199; 2003, 3090)

**NRS 78.209 Change in number of authorized shares of class or series: Filing and effectiveness of certificate of change; amendment of articles of incorporation.**

1. A change pursuant to NRS 78.207 is not effective until after the filing in the Office of the Secretary of State of a certificate, signed by an officer of the corporation, setting forth:

(a) The current number of authorized shares and the par value, if any, of each class or series, if any, of shares before the change;

(b) The number of authorized shares and the par value, if any, of each class or series, if any, of shares after the change;

(c) The number of shares of each affected class or series, if any, to be issued after the change in exchange for each issued share of the same class or series;

(d) The provisions, if any, for the issuance of fractional shares, or for the payment of money or the issuance of scrip to stockholders otherwise entitled to a fraction of a share and the percentage of outstanding shares affected thereby; and

(e) That any required approval of the stockholders has been obtained. The provisions in the articles of incorporation of the corporation regarding the authorized number and par value, if any, of the changed class or series, if any, of shares shall be deemed amended as provided in the certificate at the effective date and time of the change.

2. Unless an increase or decrease of the number of authorized shares pursuant to NRS 78.207 is accomplished by an action that otherwise requires an amendment to the articles of incorporation of the corporation, such an amendment is not required by that section.

3. A certificate filed pursuant to subsection 1 is effective upon filing the certificate with the Secretary of State or upon a later date specified in the certificate, which must not be more than 90 days after the certificate is filed.

4. If a certificate filed pursuant to subsection 1 specifies an effective date, the board of directors may terminate the effectiveness of the certificate by resolution. A certificate of termination must:

(a) Be filed with the Secretary of State before the effective date specified in the certificate filed pursuant to subsection 1;

(b) Identify the certificate being terminated;

(c) State that the effectiveness of the certificate has been terminated;

(d) Be signed by an officer of the corporation; and

(e) Be accompanied by the fee required pursuant to NRS 78.765. (Added to NRS by 1997, 694; A 2001, 1365, 3199; 2005, 2179)

**NRS 78.211 Consideration for shares: Authority of board of directors; effect of receipt; corporate action pending receipt in future.**

1. The board of directors may authorize shares to be issued for consideration consisting of any tangible or intangible property or benefit to the corporation, including, but not limited to, cash, promissory notes,

services performed, contracts for services to be performed or other securities of the corporation. The judgment of the board of directors as to the consideration received for the shares issued is conclusive in the absence of actual fraud in the transaction.

2. When the corporation receives the consideration for which the board of directors authorized the issuance of shares, the shares issued therefor are fully paid.

3. The corporation may place in escrow shares issued for a contract for future services or benefits or a promissory note, or make any other arrangements to restrict the transfer of the shares. The corporation may credit distributions made for the shares against their purchase price, until the services are performed, the benefits are received or the promissory note is paid. If the services are not performed, the benefits are not received or the promissory note is not paid, the shares escrowed or restricted and the distributions credited may be cancelled in whole or in part.

4. For the purposes of this section, "benefit to the corporation" includes, without limitation, the authorization of the issuance of shares to up to 100 persons without consideration for the sole purpose of qualifying the corporation as a real estate investment trust pursuant to 26 U.S.C. §§ 856 et seq., as amended, or any successor provision, and any regulations adopted pursuant thereto. (Added to NRS by 1991, 1186; A 1993, 958; 2001, 1366, 3199; 2005, 2179)

## NRS 78.215 Issuance of shares for consideration or as share dividend.

1. A corporation may issue and dispose of its authorized shares for such consideration as may be prescribed in the articles of incorporation or, if no consideration is so prescribed, then for such consideration as may be fixed by the board of directors.

2. If a consideration is prescribed for shares without par value, that consideration must not be used to determine the fees required for filing articles of incorporation pursuant to NRS 78.760.

3. Unless the articles of incorporation provide otherwise, shares may be issued pro rata and without consideration to the corporation's stockholders or to the stockholders of one or more classes or series. An issuance of shares under this subsection is a share dividend.

4. Shares of one class or series may not be issued as a share dividend in respect of shares of another class or series unless:

(a) The articles of incorporation so authorize;

(b) A majority of the votes entitled to be cast by the class or series to be issued approve the issue; or

(c) There are no outstanding shares of the class or series to be issued.

5. If the board of directors does not fix the record date for determining stockholders entitled to a share dividend, it is the date the board of directors authorizes the share dividend. [13:177:1925; NCL § 1612]—(NRS A 1975, 478; 1991, 1225; 1993, 958)

## NRS 78.220 Subscriptions for corporate shares: Payment; default; irrevocability.

1. Subscriptions to the shares of a corporation, whether made before or after its organization, must be paid in full at such time or in such installments at such times as determined by the board of directors. Any call made by the board of directors for payment on subscriptions must be uniform as to all shares of the same class or series.

2. If default is made in the payment of any installment or call, the corporation may proceed to collect the amount due in the same manner as any debt due the corporation. In addition, the corporation may sell a sufficient number of the subscriber's shares at public auction to pay for the installment or call and any incidental charges incurred as a result of the sale. No penalty causing a forfeiture of a subscription, of stock for which a subscription has been signed, or of amounts paid thereon, may be declared against any subscriber unless the amount due remains unpaid for 30 days after written demand. Such written demand shall be deemed made when it is mailed by registered or certified mail, return receipt requested, to the subscriber's last known address. If any of the subscriber's shares are sold at public auction, any excess of the proceeds over the total of the amount due plus any incidental charges of the sale must be paid to the subscriber or his legal representative. If an action is brought to recover the amount due on a subscription or call, any judgment in favor of the corporation must be reduced by the amount of the net proceeds of any sale by the corporation of the subscriber's stock.

3. All stock subject to a delinquent installment or call and all amounts previously paid by a delinquent subscriber for the stock must be forfeited to the corporation if an amount due from a subscriber remains unpaid, the corporation has complied with the requirements of subsection 2 and:

(a) A bidder does not purchase the subscriber's shares at public auction; or

(b) The corporation does not collect the defaulted amount by an action at law.

4. If a receiver of a corporation has been appointed, all unpaid subscriptions must be paid at such times and in such installments as the receiver or the court may direct, subject, however, to the provisions of the subscription contract.

5. A subscription for shares of a corporation to be organized is irrevocable for 6 months unless otherwise provided by the subscription agreement or unless all of the subscribers consent to the revocation of the

subscription. [14:177:1925; NCL § 1613]—(NRS A 1977, 651; 2001, 1367, 3199; 2003, 3091)

**NRS 78.225 Stockholder's liability: No individual liability except for payment for which shares were authorized to be issued or which was specified in subscription agreement.** Unless otherwise provided in the articles of incorporation, no stockholder of any corporation formed under the laws of this State is individually liable for the debts or liabilities of the corporation. A purchaser of shares of stock from the corporation is not liable to the corporation or its creditors with respect to the shares, except to pay the consideration for which the shares were authorized to be issued or which was specified in the written subscription agreement. [15:177:1925; A 1929, 413; NCL § 1614]—(NRS A 1991, 1225)

**NRS 78.230 Liability of holder of stock as collateral security; liability of executors, administrators, guardians and trustees.**

1. No person holding shares in any corporation as collateral security shall be personally liable as a stockholder.

2. No executor, administrator, guardian or trustee, unless he, without authorization, shall have voluntarily invested the trust funds in such shares, shall be personally liable as a stockholder, but the estate and funds in the hands of such executor, administrator, guardian or trustee shall be liable. [16:177:1925; NCL § 1615]

**NRS 78.235 Stock certificates: Validation; facsimile signatures; uncertificated shares and informational statements; replacement.**

1. Except as otherwise provided in subsection 4, every stockholder is entitled to have a certificate, signed by officers or agents designated by the corporation for the purpose, certifying the number of shares in the corporation owned by the stockholder. A corporation has no power to issue a certificate in bearer form, and any such certificate that is issued is void and of no force or effect.

2. Whenever any certificate is countersigned or otherwise authenticated by a transfer agent or transfer clerk, and by a registrar, then a facsimile of the signatures of the officers or agents, the transfer agent or transfer clerk or the registrar of the corporation may be printed or lithographed upon the certificate in lieu of the actual signatures. If a corporation uses facsimile signatures of its officers and agents on its stock certificates, it cannot act as registrar of its own stock, but its transfer agent and registrar may be identical if the institution acting in those dual capacities countersigns or otherwise authenticates any stock certificates in both capacities.

3. If any officer or officers who have signed, or whose facsimile signature or signatures have been used on, any certificate or certificates for stock cease to be an officer or officers of the corporation, whether because of death, resignation or other reason, before the certificate or certificates have been delivered by the corporation, the certificate or certificates may nevertheless be adopted by the corporation and be issued and delivered as though the person or persons who signed the certificate or certificates, or whose facsimile signature or signatures have been used thereon, had not ceased to be an officer or officers of the corporation.

4. Unless otherwise provided in the articles of incorporation or bylaws, the board of directors may authorize the issuance of uncertificated shares of some or all of the shares of any or all of its classes or series. The issuance of uncertificated shares has no effect on existing certificates for shares until surrendered to the corporation, or on the respective rights and obligations of the stockholders. Unless otherwise provided by a specific statute, the rights and obligations of stockholders are identical whether or not their shares of stock are represented by certificates.

5. Within a reasonable time after the issuance or transfer of shares without certificates, the corporation shall send the stockholder a written statement containing the information required on the certificates pursuant to subsection 1. At least annually thereafter, the corporation shall provide to its stockholders of record, a written statement confirming the information contained in the informational statement previously sent pursuant to this subsection.

6. Unless otherwise provided in the articles of incorporation or bylaws, a corporation may issue a new certificate of stock or, if authorized by the board of directors pursuant to subsection 4, uncertificated shares in place of a certificate previously issued by it and alleged to have been lost, stolen or destroyed. A corporation may require an owner or legal representative of an owner of a lost, stolen or destroyed certificate to give the corporation a bond or other security sufficient to indemnify it against any claim that may be made against it for the alleged loss, theft or destruction of a certificate, or the issuance of a new certificate or uncertificated shares. [Part 18:177:1925; A 1929, 413; 1937, 8; 1931 NCL § 1617]—(NRS A 1965, 1012; 1987, 579; 1991, 1226; 1993, 959; 2001, 1367, 3199; 2007, 2417)

**NRS 78.240 Shares of stock are personal property; transfers.** The shares of stock in every corporation shall be personal property and shall be transferable on the books of the corporation, in such manner and under such regulations as may be provided in the bylaws, and as provided in chapter 104 of NRS. [Part 18:177:1925; A 1929, 413; 1937, 8; 1931 NCL § 1617]—(NRS A 1965, 917)

**NRS 78.242 Restrictions on transfer of stock.**

1. Subject to the limitation imposed by NRS 104.8204, a written restriction on the transfer or registration of transfer of the stock of a corporation, if permitted by this section, may be enforced against the holder of the restricted stock or any successor or transferee of the holder, including an executor, administrator, trustee, guardian or other fiduciary entrusted with like responsibility for the person or estate of the holder.

2. A restriction on the transfer or registration of transfer of the stock of a corporation may be imposed by the articles of incorporation or by the bylaws or by an agreement among any number of stockholders or between one or more stockholders and the corporation. No restriction so imposed is binding with respect to stocks issued before the adoption of the restriction unless the stockholders are parties to an agreement or voted in favor of the restriction.

3. A restriction on the transfer or the registration of transfer of shares is valid and enforceable against the transferee of the stockholder if the restriction is not prohibited by other law and its existence is noted conspicuously on the front or back of the stock certificate or is contained in the statement of information required by NRS 78.235. Unless so noted, a restriction is not enforceable against a person without knowledge of the restriction.

4. A restriction on the transfer or registration of transfer of stock of a corporation is permitted, without limitation by this enumeration, if it:

(a) Obligates the stockholder first to offer to the corporation or to any other stockholder or stockholders of the corporation or to any other person or persons or to any combination of the foregoing a prior opportunity, to be exercised within a reasonable time, to acquire the stock;

(b) Obligates the corporation or any holder of stock of the corporation or any other person or any combination of the foregoing to purchase stock which is the subject of an agreement respecting the purchase and sale of the stock;

(c) Requires the corporation or any stockholder or stockholders to consent to any proposed transfer of the stock or to approve the proposed transferee of stock;

(d) Prohibits the transfer of the stock to designated persons or classes of persons, and such designation is not manifestly unreasonable; or

(e) Prohibits the transfer of stock:

(1) To maintain the corporation's status when it is dependent on the number or identity of its stockholders;

(2) To preserve exemptions under federal or state laws governing taxes or securities, including, without limitation, the qualification of the corporation as a real estate investment trust pursuant to 26 U.S.C. §§ 856 et seq., as amended, or any successor provision, and any regulations adopted pursuant thereto; or

(3) For any other reasonable purpose.

5. For the purposes of this section, "stock" includes a security convertible into or carrying a right to subscribe for or to acquire stock. (Added to NRS by 1969, 112; A 1991, 1226; 2005, 2180)

**NRS 78.245 Corporate stocks, bonds and securities not taxed when owned by nonresidents or foreign corporations.** No stocks, bonds or other securities issued by any corporation organized under this chapter, nor the income or profits therefrom, nor the transfer thereof by assignment, descent, testamentary disposition or otherwise, shall be taxed by this State when such stocks, bonds or other securities shall be owned by nonresidents of this State or by foreign corporations. [87:177:1925; A 1929, 413; NCL § 1686]

**NRS 78.250 Cancellation of outstanding certificates or change in informational statements: Issuance of new certificates or statements; order for surrender of certificates; penalties for failure to comply.**

1. When the articles of incorporation are amended in any way affecting the statements contained in certificates for outstanding shares or informational statements sent pursuant to NRS 78.235, or it becomes desirable for any reason, in the discretion of the board of directors, to cancel any outstanding certificate for shares and issue a new certificate therefor conforming to the rights of the holder, the board of directors may send additional informational statements as provided in NRS 78.235 and order any holders of outstanding certificates for shares to surrender and exchange them for new certificates within a reasonable time to be fixed by the board of directors.

2. Such an order may provide that the holder of any certificate so ordered to be surrendered is not entitled to vote or to receive distributions or exercise any of the other rights of stockholders of record until he has complied with the order, but the order operates to suspend such rights only after notice and until compliance.

3. The duty to surrender any outstanding certificates may also be enforced by action at law. [18a:177:1925; added 1937, 8; 1931 NCL § 1617.01]—(NRS A 1987, 580; 1993, 960)

**NRS 78.257 Right of stockholders to inspect, copy and audit financial records; exceptions; civil and criminal liability; penalty.**

1. Any person who has been a stockholder of record of any corporation and owns not less than 15 percent of all of the issued and outstanding shares of the stock of such corporation or has been authorized in writing by

the holders of at least 15 percent of all its issued and outstanding shares, upon at least 5 days' written demand, is entitled to inspect in person or by agent or attorney, during normal business hours, the books of account and all financial records of the corporation, to make copies of records, and to conduct an audit of such records. Holders of voting trust certificates representing 15 percent of the issued and outstanding shares of the corporation are regarded as stockholders for the purpose of this subsection. The right of stockholders to inspect the corporate records may not be limited in the articles or bylaws of any corporation.

2. All costs for making copies of records or conducting an audit must be borne by the person exercising his rights set forth in subsection 1.

3. The rights authorized by subsection 1 may be denied to any stockholder upon his refusal to furnish the corporation an affidavit that such inspection, copies or audit is not desired for any purpose not related to his interest in the corporation as a stockholder. Any stockholder or other person, exercising rights set forth in subsection 1, who uses or attempts to use information, records or other data obtained from the corporation, for any purpose not related to the stockholder's interest in the corporation as a stockholder, is guilty of a gross misdemeanor.

4. If any officer or agent of any corporation keeping records in this State willfully neglects or refuses to permit an inspection of the books of account and financial records upon demand by a person entitled to inspect them, or refuses to permit an audit to be conducted, as provided in subsection 1, the corporation shall forfeit to the State the sum of $100 for every day of such neglect or refusal, and the corporation, officer or agent thereof is jointly and severally liable to the person injured for all damages resulting to him.

5. A stockholder who brings an action or proceeding to enforce any right set forth in this section or to recover damages resulting from its denial:

(a) Is entitled to costs and reasonable attorney's fees, if he prevails; or

(b) Is liable for such costs and fees, if he does not prevail, in the action or proceeding.

6. Except as otherwise provided in this subsection, the provisions of this section do not apply to any corporation that furnishes to its stockholders a detailed, annual financial statement or any corporation that has filed during the preceding 12 months all reports required to be filed pursuant to section 13 or section 15(d) of the Securities Exchange Act of 1934. A person who owns, or is authorized in writing by the owners of, at least 15 percent of the issued and outstanding shares of the stock of a corporation that has elected to be governed by subchapter S of the Internal Revenue Code and whose shares are not listed or traded on any recognized stock exchange is entitled to inspect the books of the corporation pursuant to subsection 1 and has the rights, duties and liabilities provided in subsections 2 to 5, inclusive. (Added to NRS by 1971, 863; A 1977, 659; 1997, 3092; 2001, 1368, 3199; 2003, 3092)

**NRS 78.265 Preemptive rights of stockholders in corporations organized before October 1, 1991.**

1. The provisions of this section apply to corporations organized in this State before October 1, 1991.

2. Except to the extent limited or denied by this section or the articles of incorporation, shareholders have a preemptive right to acquire unissued shares, treasury shares or securities convertible into such shares.

3. Unless otherwise provided in the articles of incorporation:

(a) A preemptive right does not exist:

(1) To acquire any shares issued to directors, officers or employees pursuant to approval by the affirmative vote of the holders of a majority of the shares entitled to vote or when authorized by a plan approved by such a vote of shareholders;

(2) To acquire any shares sold for a consideration other than cash;

(3) To acquire any shares issued at the same time that the shareholder who claims a preemptive right acquired his shares;

(4) To acquire any shares issued as part of the same offering in which the shareholder who claims a preemptive right acquired his shares; or

(5) To acquire any shares, treasury shares or securities convertible into such shares, if the shares or the shares into which the convertible securities may be converted are upon issuance registered pursuant to section 12 of the Securities Exchange Act of 1934, 15 U.S.C. § 78l.

(b) Holders of shares of any class that is preferred or limited as to dividends or assets are not entitled to any preemptive right.

(c) Holders of common stock are not entitled to any preemptive right to shares of any class that is preferred or limited as to dividends or assets or to any obligations, unless convertible into shares of common stock or carrying a right to subscribe to or acquire shares of common stock.

(d) Holders of common stock without voting power have no preemptive right to shares of common stock with voting power.

(e) The preemptive right is only an opportunity to acquire shares or other securities upon such terms as the board of directors fixes for the purpose of providing a fair and reasonable opportunity for the exercise of such right. [23:177:1925; NCL § 1622]—(NRS A 1977, 909; 1987, 581; 1991, 1227)

**NRS 78.267 Preemptive rights of stockholders in corporations organized on or after October 1, 1991.**

1. The provisions of this section apply to corporations organized in this State on or after October 1, 1991.

2. The stockholders of a corporation do not have a preemptive right to acquire the corporation's unissued shares except to the extent the articles of incorporation so provide.

3. A statement included in the articles of incorporation that "the corporation elects to have preemptive rights" or words of similar import have the following effects unless the articles of incorporation otherwise provide:

(a) The stockholders of the corporation have a preemptive right, granted on uniform terms and conditions prescribed by the board of directors to provide a fair and reasonable opportunity to exercise the right, to acquire proportional amounts of the corporation's unissued shares upon the decision of the board of directors to issue them.

(b) A stockholder may waive his preemptive right. A waiver evidenced by a writing is irrevocable even though it is not supported by consideration.

(c) There is no preemptive right with respect to:

(1) Shares issued as compensation to directors, officers, agents or employees of the corporation, its subsidiaries or affiliates;

(2) Shares issued to satisfy rights of conversion or options created to provide compensation to directors, officers, agents or employees of the corporation, its subsidiaries or affiliates;

(3) Shares authorized in articles of incorporation which are issued within 6 months from the effective date of incorporation; or

(4) Shares sold otherwise than for money.

(d) Holders of shares of any class without general voting rights but with preferential rights to distributions or assets have no preemptive rights with respect to shares of any class.

(e) Holders of shares of any class with general voting rights but without preferential rights to distributions or assets have no preemptive rights with respect to shares of any class with preferential rights to distributions or assets unless the shares with preferential rights are convertible into or carry a right to subscribe for or acquire shares without preferential rights.

(f) Shares subject to preemptive rights that are not acquired by stockholders may be issued to any person for 1 year after being offered to stockholders at a consideration set by the board of directors that is not lower than the consideration set for the exercise of preemptive rights. An offer at a lower consideration or after the expiration of one year is subject to the stockholders' preemptive rights.

4. As used in this section, "shares" includes a security convertible into or carrying a right to subscribe for or acquire shares. (Added to NRS by 1991, 1187)

**NRS 78.275 Assessments on stock: Levy and collection; sale after default in payment. [Effective through June 30, 2008.]**

1. The directors may at such times and in such amount, as they may from time to time deem the interest of the corporation to require, levy and collect assessments upon the assessable stock of the corporation in the manner provided in this section.

2. Notice of each assessment must be given to the stockholders personally, or by publication once a week for at least 4 weeks, in some newspaper published in the county in which the registered office or place of business of the corporation is located, and in a newspaper published in the county wherein the property of the corporation is situated if in this State, and if no paper is published in either of those counties, then the newspaper published nearest to the registered office in the State.

3. If after the notice has been given, any stockholder defaults in the payment of the assessment upon the shares held by him, so many of those shares may be sold as will be necessary for the payment of the assessment upon all the shares held by him, together with all costs of advertising and expenses of sale. The sale of the shares must be made at the office of the corporation at public auction to the highest bidder, after a notice thereof published for 4 weeks as directed in this section, and a copy of the notice mailed to each delinquent stockholder if his address is known 4 weeks before the sale. At the sale the person who offers to pay the assessment so due, together with the expenses of advertising and sale, for the smallest number of shares, or portion of a share, as the case may be, shall be deemed the highest bidder. [Part 74:177:1925; NCL § 1673]—(NRS A 1993, 960)

**NRS 78.275 Assessments on stock: Levy and collection; sale after default in payment. [Effective July 1, 2008.]**

1. The directors may at such times and in such amount, as they may from time to time deem the interest of the corporation to require, levy and collect assessments upon the assessable stock of the corporation in the manner provided in this section.

2. Notice of each assessment must be given to the stockholders personally, or by publication once a week for at least 4 weeks, in some newspaper published in the county in which the principal office of the corporation is located or, if the principal office of the corporation is not located in this State, in Carson City, and in a newspaper published in the county wherein the property of the corporation is situated if in this State.

3. If, after the notice has been given, any stockholder defaults in the payment of the assessment upon the shares held by him, so many of those shares may be sold as will be necessary for the payment of the assessment upon all the shares held by him, together with all costs of advertising and expenses of sale. The sale of the shares must be made at the office of the corporation at public auction to the highest bidder, after a notice thereof published for 4 weeks as directed in this section, and a copy of the notice mailed to each delinquent stockholder if his address is known 4 weeks before the sale. At the sale the person who offers to pay the assessment so due, together with the expenses of advertising and sale, for the smallest number of shares, or portion of a share, as the case may be, shall be deemed the highest bidder. [Part 74:177:1925; NCL § 1673]—(NRS A 1993, 960; 2007, 2646, effective July 1, 2008)

**NRS 78.280 Purchase by corporation of its own stock at assessment sale when no other available purchaser.**

1. Every corporation in this State may, whenever at any assessment sale of the stock of the corporation no person will take the stock and pay the assessment, or amount unpaid and due thereon and costs, purchase such stock and hold the stock for the benefit of the corporation.

2. All purchases of its own stock by any corporation in this State which have been previously made at assessment sales whereat outside persons have failed to bid, and which purchases were for the amount of assessments due, and costs or otherwise, are valid, and vest the legal title to the stock in the corporation.

3. The stock so purchased is subject to the control of the remaining stockholders, who may dispose of the stock as they may deem fit.

4. Whenever any portion of the stock of any corporation is held by the corporation by purchase or otherwise, a majority of the remaining shares of stock in the corporation is a majority of the shares of the stock in the incorporated company, for all purposes of election or voting on any question before a stockholders' meeting. [Part 74:177:1925; NCL § 1673]—(NRS A 1993, 2764)

**NRS 78.283 Treasury shares: Definition; limitations; retirement and disposal.**

1. As used in this section, "treasury shares" means shares of a corporation issued and thereafter acquired by the corporation or another entity, the majority of whose outstanding voting power to elect its general partner, directors, managers or members of the governing body is beneficially held, directly or indirectly, by the corporation, which have not been retired or restored to the status of unissued shares.

2. Treasury shares held by the corporation do not carry voting rights or participate in distributions, may not be counted as outstanding shares for any purpose and may not be counted as assets of the corporation for the purpose of computing the amount available for distributions.

3. Treasury shares held by another entity, the majority of whose outstanding voting power to elect its general partner, directors, managers or members of the governing body is beneficially held, directly or indirectly, by the corporation, do not carry voting rights and, unless otherwise determined by the board of directors of the corporation, do not participate in distributions, may not be counted as outstanding shares for any purpose and may not be counted as assets of the entity.

4. Unless the articles of incorporation provide otherwise, treasury shares may be retired and restored to the status of authorized and unissued shares without an amendment to the articles of incorporation or may be disposed of for such consideration as the board of directors may determine.

5. This section does not limit the right of a corporation to vote its shares held by it in a fiduciary capacity. (Added to NRS by 1959, 682; A 1981, 1890; 1991, 1228; 1997, 701; 2005, 2181)

**NRS 78.288 Distributions to stockholders.**

1. Except as otherwise provided in subsection 2 and the articles of incorporation, a board of directors may authorize and the corporation may make distributions to its stockholders, including distributions on shares that are partially paid.

2. No distribution may be made if, after giving it effect:

(a) The corporation would not be able to pay its debts as they become due in the usual course of business; or

(b) Except as otherwise specifically allowed by the articles of incorporation, the corporation's total assets would be less than the sum of its total liabilities plus the amount that would be needed, if the corporation were to be dissolved at the time of distribution, to satisfy the preferential rights upon dissolution of stockholders whose preferential rights are superior to those receiving the distribution.

3. The board of directors may base a determination that a distribution is not prohibited pursuant to subsection 2 on:

(a) Financial statements prepared on the basis of accounting practices that are reasonable in the circumstances;

(b) A fair valuation, including, but not limited to, unrealized appreciation and depreciation; or

(c) Any other method that is reasonable in the circumstances.

4. The effect of a distribution pursuant to subsection 2 must be measured:

(a) In the case of a distribution by purchase, redemption or other acquisition of the corporation's shares, as of the earlier of:

(1) The date money or other property is transferred or debt incurred by the corporation; or

(2) The date upon which the stockholder ceases to be a stockholder with respect to the acquired shares.

(b) In the case of any other distribution of indebtedness, as of the date the indebtedness is distributed.

(c) In all other cases, as of:

(1) The date the distribution is authorized if the payment occurs within 120 days after the date of authorization; or

(2) The date the payment is made if it occurs more than 120 days after the date of authorization.

5. A corporation's indebtedness to a stockholder incurred by reason of a distribution made in accordance with this section is at parity with the corporation's indebtedness to its general unsecured creditors except to the extent subordinated by agreement.

6. Indebtedness of a corporation, including indebtedness issued as a distribution, is not considered a liability for purposes of determinations pursuant to subsection 2 if its terms provide that payment of principal and interest are made only if and to the extent that payment of a distribution to stockholders could then be made pursuant to this section. If the indebtedness is issued as a distribution, each payment of principal or interest must be treated as a distribution, the effect of which must be measured on the date the payment is actually made. (Added to NRS by 1991, 1187; A 2001, 1369, 3199)

### NRS 78.300 Liability of directors for unlawful distributions.

1. The directors of a corporation shall not make distributions to stockholders except as provided by this chapter.

2. Except as otherwise provided in subsection 3 and NRS 78.138, in case of any violation of the provisions of this section, the directors under whose administration the violation occurred are jointly and severally liable, at any time within 3 years after each violation, to the corporation, and, in the event of its dissolution or insolvency, to its creditors at the time of the violation, or any of them, to the lesser of the full amount of the distribution made or of any loss sustained by the corporation by reason of the distribution to stockholders.

3. The liability imposed pursuant to subsection 2 does not apply to a director who caused his dissent to be entered upon the minutes of the meeting of the directors at the time the action was taken or who was not present at the meeting and caused his dissent to be entered on learning of the action. [75:177:1925; A 1931, 415; 1949, 158; 1943 NCL § 1674]—(NRS A 1987, 83; 1991, 1229; 2001, 3174)

### NRS 78.307 "Investment company" and "open-end investment company" defined; redemption of shares by open-end investment company.

1. As used in this section, unless the context requires otherwise:

(a) "Investment company" means any corporation, trust, association or fund which is engaged or proposes to engage in the business of investing, reinvesting, owning, holding or trading in securities, and whose assets are invested principally in cash or in securities of other issuers.

(b) "Open-end investment company" means any investment company which issues one or more series or classes of securities under the terms of which the holder of the security, upon presentation thereof to the issuer, is entitled to receive approximately his proportionate share of the current net assets of the issuer applicable to such series or class, or the cash equivalent thereof.

2. An open-end investment company may, from time to time, redeem its shares, in accordance with their terms, at approximately the proportionate share of the current net assets of the issuer applicable to such shares, or the cash equivalent thereof. (Added to NRS by 1961, 174)

## Meetings, Elections, Voting and Notice

### NRS 78.310 Stockholders' and directors' meetings: Location; authority to call.

1. Meetings of stockholders and directors of any corporation organized pursuant to the provisions of this chapter may be held within or without this State, in the manner provided by the bylaws of the corporation. The articles of incorporation may designate any place or places where such stockholders' or directors' meetings may be held, but in the absence of any provision therefor in the articles of incorporation, then the meetings must be held within or without this State, as directed from time to time by the bylaws of the corporation.

2. Unless otherwise provided in the articles of incorporation or bylaws, the entire board of directors, any two directors or the president may call annual and special meetings of the stockholders and directors. [Part 31:177:1925; NCL § 1630]—(NRS A 1993, 961; 2001, 1370, 3199)

### NRS 78.315 Directors' meetings: Quorum; consent for actions taken without meeting; participation by telephone or similar method.

1. Unless the articles of incorporation or the bylaws provide for a greater or lesser proportion, a majority of the board of directors of the corporation then in office, at a meeting duly assembled, is necessary to constitute a quorum for the transaction of business, and the act of directors holding a majority of the voting power of the directors, present at a meeting at which a quorum is present, is the act of the board of directors.

2. Unless otherwise restricted by the articles of incorporation or bylaws, any action required or permitted to be taken at a meeting of the board of directors or of a committee thereof may be taken without a meeting if, before or after the action, a written consent thereto is signed by all the members of the board or of the committee, except that such written consent is not required to be signed by:

(a) A common or interested director who abstains in writing from providing consent to the action. If a common or interested director abstains in writing from providing consent:

(1) The fact of the common directorship, office or financial interest must be known to the board of directors or committee before a written consent is signed by all the members of the board of the committee.

(2) Such fact must be described in the written consent.

(3) The board of directors or committee must approve, authorize or ratify the action in good faith by unanimous consent without counting the abstention of the common or interested director.

(b) A director who is a party to an action, suit or proceeding who abstains in writing from providing consent to the action of the board of directors or committee. If a director who is a party to an action, suit or proceeding abstains in writing from providing consent on the basis that he is a party to an action, suit or proceeding, the board of directors or committee must:

(1) Make a determination pursuant to NRS 78.751 that indemnification of the director is proper under the circumstances.

(2) Approve, authorize or ratify the action of the board of directors or committee in good faith by unanimous consent without counting the abstention of the director who is a party to an action, suit or proceeding.

3. Unless otherwise restricted by the articles of incorporation or bylaws, members of the board of directors or the governing body of any corporation, or of any committee designated by such board or body, may participate in a meeting of the board, body or committee by means of a telephone conference or similar methods of communication by which all persons participating in the meeting can hear each other. Participation in a meeting pursuant to this subsection constitutes presence in person at the meeting. [Part 31:177:1925; NCL § 1630]—(NRS A 1957, 75; 1959, 685; 1977, 412; 1991, 1229; 1993, 961; 1997, 701; 2001, 1370, 3199; 2007, 2418)

### NRS 78.320 Stockholders' meetings: Quorum; consent for actions taken without meeting; participation by telephone or similar method.

1. Unless this chapter, the articles of incorporation or the bylaws provide for different proportions:

(a) A majority of the voting power, which includes the voting power that is present in person or by proxy, regardless of whether the proxy has authority to vote on all matters, constitutes a quorum for the transaction of business; and

(b) Action by the stockholders on a matter other than the election of directors is approved if the number of votes cast in favor of the action exceeds the number of votes cast in opposition to the action.

2. Unless otherwise provided in the articles of incorporation or the bylaws, any action required or permitted to be taken at a meeting of the stockholders may be taken without a meeting if, before or after the action, a written consent thereto is signed by stockholders holding at least a majority of the voting power, except that if a different proportion of voting power is required for such an action at a meeting, then that proportion of written consents is required.

3. In no instance where action is authorized by written consent need a meeting of stockholders be called or notice given.

4. Unless otherwise restricted by the articles of incorporation or bylaws, stockholders may participate in a meeting of stockholders by means of a telephone conference or similar methods of communication by which all persons participating in the meeting can hear each other. Participation in a meeting pursuant to this subsection constitutes presence in person at the meeting.

5. Unless this chapter, the articles of incorporation or the bylaws provide for different proportions, if voting by a class or series of stockholders is permitted or required:

(a) A majority of the voting power of the class or series that is present in person or by proxy, regardless of whether the proxy has authority to vote on all matters, constitutes a quorum for the transaction of business; and

(b) An act by the stockholders of each class or series is approved if a majority of the voting power of a quorum of the class or series votes for the action. [29(a):177:1925; added 1949, 158; 1943 NCL § 1628.01]—(NRS A 1959, 686; 1987, 581; 1989, 875; 1991, 1229; 1993, 961; 1997, 702; 1999, 1584; 2001, 1371, 3199; 2007, 2419)

### NRS 78.325 Actions at meetings not regularly called: Ratification and approval.

1. Whenever all persons entitled to vote at any meeting, whether of directors, trustees or stockholders, consent, either by:

(a) A writing on the records of the meeting or filed with the secretary;

(b) Presence at such meeting and oral consent entered on the minutes; or

(c) Taking part in the deliberations at such meeting without objection, the doings of such meeting shall be as valid as if had at a meeting regularly called and noticed.

2. At such meeting any business may be transacted which is not excepted from the written consent or to the consideration of which no objection for want of notice is made at the time.

3. If any meeting be irregular for want of notice or of such consent, provided a quorum was present at such meeting, the proceedings of the meeting may be ratified and approved and rendered likewise valid and the irregularity or defect therein waived by a writing signed by all parties having the right to vote at such meeting.

4. Such consent or approval of stockholders or creditors may be by proxy or attorney, but all such proxies and powers of attorney must be in writing. [Part 92:177:1925; A 1929, 413; NCL § 1691]

## NRS 78.330 Directors: Election; terms; classification; voting power.

1. Unless elected pursuant to NRS 78.320, or unless the articles of incorporation or the bylaws require more than a plurality of the votes cast, directors of every corporation must be elected at the annual meeting of the stockholders by a plurality of the votes cast at the election. Unless otherwise provided in this chapter or in the bylaws, the board of directors has the authority to set the date, time and place for the annual meeting of the stockholders. If for any reason directors are not elected pursuant to NRS 78.320 or at the annual meeting of the stockholders, they may be elected at any special meeting of the stockholders which is called and held for that purpose. Unless otherwise provided in the articles of incorporation or bylaws, each director holds office after the expiration of his term until his successor is elected and qualified, or until he resigns or is removed.

2. The articles of incorporation or the bylaws may provide for the classification of directors as to the duration of their respective terms of office or as to their election by one or more authorized classes or series of shares, but at least one-fourth in number of the directors of every corporation must be elected annually. If an amendment reclassifying the directors would otherwise increase the term of a director, unless the amendment is to the articles of incorporation and otherwise provides, the term of each incumbent director on the effective date of the amendment terminates on the date it would have terminated had there been no reclassification.

3. The articles of incorporation may provide that the voting power of individual directors or classes of directors may be greater than or less than that of any other individual directors or classes of directors, and the different voting powers may be stated in the articles of incorporation or may be dependent upon any fact or event that may be ascertained outside the articles of incorporation if the manner in which the fact or event may operate on those voting powers is stated in the articles of incorporation. If the articles of incorporation provide that any directors may have voting power greater than or less than other directors, every reference in this chapter to a majority or other proportion of directors shall be deemed to refer to a majority or other proportion of the voting power of all of the directors or classes of directors, as may be required by the articles of incorporation. [Part 33:177:1925; A 1929, 413; NCL § 1632]—(NRS A 1967, 267; 1979, 215; 1987, 582; 1989, 875; 1993, 962; 1999, 1585; 2001, 1371, 3199; 2007, 2420)

## NRS 78.335 Directors: Removal; filling of vacancies.

1. Except as otherwise provided in this section, any director or one or more of the incumbent directors may be removed from office by the vote of stockholders representing not less than two-thirds of the voting power of the issued and outstanding stock entitled to vote.

2. In the case of corporations which have provided in their articles of incorporation for the election of directors by cumulative voting, any director or directors who constitute fewer than all of the incumbent directors may not be removed from office at any one time or as the result of any one transaction under the provisions of this section except upon the vote of stockholders owning sufficient shares to prevent each director's election to office at the time of removal.

3. The articles of incorporation may require the concurrence of more than two-thirds of the voting power of the issued and outstanding stock entitled to vote in order to remove one or more directors from office.

4. Whenever the holders of any class or series of shares are entitled to elect one or more directors, unless otherwise provided in the articles of incorporation, removal of any such director requires only the proportion of votes, specified in subsection 1, of the holders of that class or series, and not the votes of the outstanding shares as a whole.

5. All vacancies, including those caused by an increase in the number of directors, may be filled by a majority of the remaining directors, though less than a quorum, unless it is otherwise provided in the articles of incorporation.

6. Unless otherwise provided in the articles of incorporation, when one or more directors give notice of his or their resignation to the board, effective at a future date, the board may fill the vacancy or vacancies to take effect when the resignation or resignations become

effective, each director so appointed to hold office during the remainder of the term of office of the resigning director or directors.

7. If the articles or bylaws provide that the holders of any class or series of shares are entitled to elect one or more directors under specified circumstances and that, upon termination of those specified circumstances, the right terminates and the directors elected by the holders of the class or series of shares are no longer directors, the termination of a director pursuant to such provisions in the articles or bylaws shall not be deemed a removal of the director pursuant to this section. [Part 33:177:1925; A 1929, 413; NCL § 1632]—(NRS A 1989, 875; 1991, 1230; 1993, 962; 1999, 1585; 2003, 3093)

**NRS 78.340 Failure to hold election of directors on regular day does not dissolve corporation.** If the directors shall not be elected on the day designated for the purpose, the corporation shall not for that reason be dissolved; but every director shall continue to hold his office and discharge his duties until his successor has been elected. [34:177:1925; NCL § 1633]

**NRS 78.345 Election of directors by order of court upon failure of regular election. [Effective through June 30, 2008.]**

1. If any corporation fails to elect directors within 18 months after the last election of directors required by NRS 78.330, the district court has jurisdiction in equity, upon application of any one or more stockholders holding stock entitling them to exercise at least 15 percent of the voting power, to order the election of directors in the manner required by NRS 78.330.

2. The application must be made by petition filed in the county where the registered office of the corporation is located and must be brought on behalf of all stockholders desiring to be joined therein. Such notice must be given to the corporation and the stockholders as the court may direct.

3. The directors elected pursuant to this section have the same rights, powers and duties and the same tenure of office as directors elected by the stockholders at the annual meeting held at the time prescribed therefor, next before the date of the election pursuant to this section, would have had. [35:177:1925; NCL § 1634]—(NRS A 1991, 1231)

**NRS 78.345 Election of directors by order of court upon failure of regular election. [Effective July 1, 2008.]**

1. If any corporation fails to elect directors within 18 months after the last election of directors required by NRS 78.330, the district court has jurisdiction in equity, upon application of any one or more stockholders holding stock entitling them to exercise at least 15

percent of the voting power, to order the election of directors in the manner required by NRS 78.330.

2. The application must be made by petition filed in the county where the principal office of the corporation is located or, if the principal office is not located in this State, in Carson City, and must be brought on behalf of all stockholders desiring to be joined therein. Such notice must be given to the corporation and the stockholders as the court may direct.

3. The directors elected pursuant to this section have the same rights, powers and duties and the same tenure of office as directors elected by the stockholders at the annual meeting held at the time prescribed therefor, next before the date of the election pursuant to this section, would have had. [35:177:1925; NCL § 1634]—(NRS A 1991, 1231; 2007, 2646, effective July 1, 2008)

**NRS 78.347 Application by stockholder for order of court appointing custodian or receiver; requirements of custodian; authority of custodian; adoption of regulations by Secretary of State.**

1. Any stockholder may apply to the district court to appoint one or more persons to be custodians of the corporation, and, if the corporation is insolvent, to be receivers of the corporation when:

(a) The business of the corporation is suffering or is threatened with irreparable injury because the directors are so divided respecting the management of the affairs of the corporation that a required vote for action by the board of directors cannot be obtained and the stockholders are unable to terminate this division; or

(b) The corporation has abandoned its business and has failed within a reasonable time to take steps to dissolve, liquidate or distribute its assets in accordance with this chapter.

2. An applicant on whose behalf a stockholder has applied to the district court for a custodianship pursuant to subsection 1 shall provide the following information, along with an affidavit attesting that such information is true and correct, to the district court:

(a) A detailed list of all previous applications to a court in any jurisdiction for a custodianship of a publicly traded corporation that were filed by the applicant or an affiliate or subsidiary of the applicant.

(b) If an application listed in paragraph (a) was approved, a detailed description of the activities performed during the custodianship by the applicant or the affiliate or subsidiary of the applicant.

(c) A description of the current corporate status and business operation of any publicly traded corporation for which the applicant and any affiliate or subsidiary of the applicant has held a custodianship.

(d) A full disclosure of any and all previous criminal, administrative, civil or National Association of Securities Dealers, Inc., or Securities and Exchange Commission investigations, violations or convictions concerning the applicant and any affiliate or subsidiary of the applicant.

(e) Evidence of reasonable efforts by the applicant to contact the officers and directors of the corporation for which the custodianship is sought.

(f) Evidence of a demand by the applicant to the officers and directors of the corporation for which the custodianship is sought that the corporation comply with the provisions of chapter 78 of NRS and that the applicant did not receive a response.

3. The district court shall order any applicant who is granted custodianship pursuant to this section to:

(a) Comply with the provisions of NRS 78.180 or 80.170, as applicable. The custodian shall submit evidence of compliance with this paragraph to the district court.

(b) Provide reasonable notice to all shareholders of record of a shareholder meeting to be held within a reasonable time after an application for custodianship or receivership has been granted. The custodian shall submit evidence of compliance with this paragraph to the district court.

(c) Provide the district court with a report of the actions taken at the shareholder meeting noticed by the custodian.

(d) Provide the district court with periodic reports, at intervals to be determined by the court, of the activities of the custodian and the board of directors and the progress of the corporation.

(e) Provide any other information deemed necessary by the court.

4. Within 10 days after being appointed custodian of a Nevada publicly traded corporation, the custodian shall file with the Secretary of State an amendment to the articles of incorporation containing the following information:

(a) Disclosures of any previous criminal, administrative, civil or National Association of Securities Dealers, Inc., or Securities and Exchange Commission investigations, violations or convictions concerning the custodian and any affiliate of the custodian.

(b) A statement indicating that:

(1) Reasonable attempts were made to contact the officers or directors of the corporation to request that the corporation comply with corporate formalities and to continue its business.

(2) The custodian is in fact continuing the business and attempting to further the interests of the shareholders.

(3) The custodian will reinstate or maintain the corporate charter.

(c) Any other information required by regulation to be submitted to the Secretary of State.

5. The Secretary of State may adopt regulations to administer the provisions of subsection 4.

6. A custodian appointed pursuant to this section has all the powers and title of a trustee appointed under NRS 78.590, 78.635 and 78.650, but the authority of the custodian is to continue the business of the corporation and not to liquidate its affairs or distribute its assets, except when the district court so orders and except in cases arising pursuant to paragraph (b) of subsection 1. (Added to NRS by 1991, 1188; A 2007, 1317)

**NRS 78.350 Voting rights of stockholders; determination of stockholders entitled to notice of and to vote at meeting.**

1. Unless otherwise provided in the articles of incorporation, or in the resolution providing for the issuance of the stock adopted by the board of directors pursuant to authority expressly vested in it by the provisions of the articles of incorporation, every stockholder of record of a corporation is entitled at each meeting of stockholders thereof to one vote for each share of stock standing in his name on the records of the corporation. If the articles of incorporation, or the resolution providing for the issuance of the stock adopted by the board of directors pursuant to authority expressly vested in it by the articles of incorporation, provides for more or less than one vote per share for any class or series of shares on any matter, every reference in this chapter to a majority or other proportion of stock shall be deemed to refer to a majority or other proportion of the voting power of all of the shares or those classes or series of shares, as may be required by the articles of incorporation, or in the resolution providing for the issuance of the stock adopted by the board of directors pursuant to authority expressly vested in it by the provisions of the articles of incorporation, or the provisions of this chapter.

2. Unless a period of more than 60 days or a period of less than 10 days is prescribed or fixed in the articles of incorporation, the directors may prescribe a period not exceeding 60 days before any meeting of the stockholders during which no transfer of stock on the books of the corporation may be made, or may fix, in advance, a record date not more than 60 or less than 10 days before the date of any such meeting as the date as of which stockholders entitled to notice of and to vote at such meetings must be determined. Only stockholders of record on that date are entitled to notice or to vote at such a meeting. If a record date is not fixed, the record date is at the close of business on the day before the day on which the first notice is given or, if notice is waived, at the close of business on the day before the meeting is held. A determination of stockholders of record entitled to notice of or to vote at a meeting of stockholders applies to an adjournment of the meeting unless the board of directors fixes a new record date for the adjourned meeting. The board of directors must fix a

new record date if the meeting is adjourned to a date more than 60 days later than the date set for the original meeting.

3. The board of directors may adopt a resolution prescribing a date upon which the stockholders of record entitled to give written consent pursuant to NRS 78.320 must be determined. The date prescribed by the board of directors may not precede or be more than 10 days after the date the resolution is adopted by the board of directors. If the board of directors does not adopt a resolution prescribing a date upon which the stockholders of record entitled to give written consent pursuant to NRS 78.320 must be determined and:

(a) No prior action by the board of directors is required by this chapter or chapter 92A of NRS before the matter is submitted for consideration by the stockholders, the date is the first date on which a valid, written consent is delivered in accordance with the provisions of NRS 78.320.

(b) Prior action by the board of directors is required by this chapter or chapter 92A of NRS before the matter is submitted for consideration by the stockholders, the date is at the close of business on the day the board of directors adopts the resolution.

4. The provisions of this section do not restrict the directors from taking action to protect the interests of the corporation and its stockholders, including, but not limited to, adopting or signing plans, arrangements or instruments that deny rights, privileges, power or authority to a holder or holders of a specified number of shares or percentage of share ownership or voting power. [28:177:1925; NCL § 1627]—(NRS A 1965, 1012; 1989, 876; 1991, 1231; 1993, 963; 1999, 1586; 2003, 3094; 2005, 2181)

**NRS 78.352 Voting rights: Persons holding stock in fiduciary capacity; persons whose stock is pledged; joint owners of stock.**

1. A person holding stock in a fiduciary capacity is entitled to vote the shares so held.

2. A person whose stock is pledged is entitled to vote, unless in the pledge the pledgor has expressly empowered the pledgee to vote the stock, in which case only the pledgee or the proxy of the pledgee may vote the stock.

3. If shares or other securities having voting power stand of record in the names of two or more persons, whether fiduciaries, joint tenants, tenants in common or otherwise, or if two or more persons have the same fiduciary relationship respecting the shares or securities, unless the secretary of the corporation is given written notice to the contrary and is furnished with a copy of the instrument or order appointing them or creating the relationship, their acts with respect to voting have the following effect:

(a) If only one votes, that person's act binds all;

(b) If more than one votes, the act chosen by a majority of votes binds all; or

(c) If more than one votes, but the vote is evenly split on any particular matter, each faction may vote the shares or securities in question proportionally. (Added to NRS by 2001, 1356; A 2001, 3199)

**NRS 78.355 Stockholders' proxies.**

1. At any meeting of the stockholders of any corporation any stockholder may designate another person or persons to act as a proxy or proxies. If any stockholder designates two or more persons to act as proxies, a majority of those persons present at the meeting, or, if only one is present, then that one has and may exercise all of the powers conferred by the stockholder upon all of the persons so designated unless the stockholder provides otherwise.

2. Without limiting the manner in which a stockholder may authorize another person or persons to act for him as proxy pursuant to subsection 1, the following constitute valid means by which a stockholder may grant such authority:

(a) A stockholder may sign a writing authorizing another person or persons to act for him as proxy. The proxy may be limited to action on designated matters.

(b) A stockholder may authorize another person or persons to act for him as proxy by transmitting or authorizing the transmission of an electronic record to the person who will be the holder of the proxy or to a firm which solicits proxies or like agent who is authorized by the person who will be the holder of the proxy to receive the transmission. Any such electronic record must either set forth or be submitted with information from which it can be determined that the electronic record was authorized by the stockholder.

If it is determined that the electronic record is valid, the persons appointed by the corporation to count the votes of stockholders and determine the validity of proxies and ballots or other persons making those determinations must specify the information upon which they relied.

3. Any copy, communication by electronic transmission or other reliable reproduction of the record created pursuant to subsection 2 may be substituted for the original record for any purpose for which the original record could be used, if the copy, communication by electronic transmission or other reproduction is a complete reproduction of the entire original record.

4. Except as otherwise provided in subsection 5, no such proxy is valid after the expiration of 6 months from the date of its creation unless the stockholder specifies in it the length of time for which it is to continue in force, which may not exceed 7 years from the date of its creation. Subject to these restrictions, any proxy

properly created is not revoked and continues in full force and effect until:

(a) Another instrument or transmission revoking it or a properly created proxy bearing a later date is filed with or transmitted to the secretary of the corporation or another person or persons appointed by the corporation to count the votes of stockholders and determine the validity of proxies and ballots; or

(b) The stockholder revokes the proxy by attending the meeting and voting the stockholder's shares in person, in which case, any vote cast by the person or persons designated by the stockholder to act as a proxy or proxies must be disregarded by the corporation when the votes are counted.

5. A proxy shall be deemed irrevocable if the written authorization states that the proxy is irrevocable, but is irrevocable only for as long as it is coupled with an interest sufficient in law to support an irrevocable power, including, without limitation, the appointment as proxy of a pledgee, a person who purchased or agreed to purchase the shares, a creditor of the corporation who extended it credit under terms requiring the appointment, an employee of the corporation whose employment contract requires the appointment or a party to a voting agreement created pursuant to subsection 3 of NRS 78.365. Unless otherwise provided in the proxy, a proxy made irrevocable pursuant to this subsection is revoked when the interest with which it is coupled is extinguished, but the corporation may honor the proxy until notice of the extinguishment of the proxy is received by the corporation. A transferee for value of shares subject to an irrevocable proxy may revoke the proxy if he did not know of its existence when he acquired the shares and the existence of the irrevocable appointment was not noted conspicuously on the certificate representing the shares or on the information statement for shares without certificates.

6. If any stockholder subject to a properly created irrevocable proxy attends any meeting of the stockholders for which the authorization grants authority to act on the stockholder's behalf at the meeting to a proxy or proxies, unless expressly otherwise provided in the written authorization or electronic record:

(a) Only the proxy or proxies may have and exercise all the powers of the stockholder at the meeting; and

(b) Only a vote of the proxy or proxies may be regarded by the corporation when the votes are counted. [29:177:1925; A 1953, 180]—(NRS A 1991, 1232; 1997, 702; 2003, 3095; 2005, 2182)

**NRS 78.360 Cumulative voting.**

1. The articles of incorporation of any corporation may provide that at all elections of directors of the corporation each holder of stock possessing voting power is entitled to as many votes as equal the number of his shares of stock multiplied by the number of directors to be elected, and that he may cast all of his votes for a single director or may distribute them among the number to be voted for or any two or more of them, as he may see fit. To exercise the right of cumulative voting, one or more of the stockholders requesting cumulative voting must give written notice to the president or secretary of the corporation that the stockholder desires that the voting for the election of directors be cumulative.

2. The notice must be given not less than 48 hours before the time fixed for holding the meeting, if notice of the meeting has been given at least 10 days before the date of the meeting, and otherwise not less than 24 hours before the meeting. At the meeting, before the commencement of voting for the election of directors, an announcement of the giving of the notice must be made by the chairman or the secretary of the meeting or by or on behalf of the stockholder giving the notice. Notice to stockholders of the requirement of this subsection must be contained in the notice calling the meeting or in the proxy material accompanying the notice. [30:177:1925; NCL § 1629]—(NRS A 1969, 101; 1991, 1233; 1993, 963)

**NRS 78.365 Voting trusts.**

1. A stockholder, by agreement in writing, may transfer his stock to a voting trustee or trustees for the purpose of conferring the right to vote the stock for a period not exceeding 15 years upon the terms and conditions therein stated. Any certificates of stock so transferred must be surrendered and cancelled and new certificates for the stock issued to the trustee or trustees in which it must appear that they are issued pursuant to the agreement, and in the entry of ownership in the proper books of the corporation that fact must also be noted, and thereupon the trustee or trustees may vote the stock so transferred during the terms of the agreement. A duplicate of every such agreement must be filed in the registered office of the corporation and at all times during its terms be open to inspection by any stockholder or his attorney.

2. At any time within the 2 years next preceding the expiration of an agreement entered into pursuant to the provisions of subsection 1, or the expiration of an extension of that agreement, any beneficiary of the trust may, by written agreement with the trustee or trustees, extend the duration of the trust for a time not to exceed 15 years after the scheduled expiration date of the original agreement or the latest extension. An extension is not effective unless the trustee, before the expiration date of the original agreement or the latest extension, files a duplicate of the agreement providing for the extension in the registered office of the corporation. An agreement providing for an extension does not affect the rights or obligations of any person not a party to that agreement.

3. An agreement between two or more stockholders, if in writing and signed by them, may provide that in exercising any voting rights the stock held by them must be voted:

(a) Pursuant to the provisions of the agreement;

(b) As they may subsequently agree; or

(c) In accordance with a procedure agreed upon.

4. An agreement entered into pursuant to the provisions of subsection 3 is not effective for a term of more than 15 years, but at any time within the 2 years next preceding the expiration of the agreement the parties thereto may extend its duration for as many additional periods, each not to exceed 15 years, as they wish.

5. An agreement entered into pursuant to the provisions of subsection 1 or 3 is not invalidated by the fact that by its terms its duration is more than 15 years, but its duration shall be deemed amended to conform with the provisions of this section. [22:177:1925; A 1929, 413; 1951, 328]—(NRS A 1987, 582; 1989, 976; 1991, 1234; 1993, 964)

**NRS 78.370 Notice to stockholders.**

1. If under the provisions of this chapter stockholders are required or authorized to take any action at a meeting, the notice of the meeting must be in writing and signed by the president or a vice president, or the secretary or an assistant secretary, or by such other natural person or persons as the bylaws may prescribe or permit or the directors may designate.

2. The notice must state the purpose or purposes for which the meeting is called, the time when, and the place, which may be within or without this State, where it is to be held, and the means of electronic communications, if any, by which stockholders and proxies shall be deemed to be present in person and vote.

3. A copy of the notice must be delivered personally, mailed postage prepaid or given as provided in subsection 8 to each stockholder of record entitled to vote at the meeting not less than 10 nor more than 60 days before the meeting. If mailed, it must be directed to the stockholder at his address as it appears upon the records of the corporation, and upon the mailing of any such notice the service thereof is complete, and the time of the notice begins to run from the date upon which the notice is deposited in the mail for transmission to the stockholder. Personal delivery of any such notice to any officer of a corporation or association, to any member of a limited-liability company managed by its members, to any manager of a limited-liability company managed by managers, to any general partner of a partnership or to any trustee of a trust constitutes delivery of the notice to the corporation, association, limited-liability company, partnership or trust.

4. The articles of incorporation or the bylaws may require that the notice be also published in one or more newspapers.

5. Notice delivered or mailed to a stockholder in accordance with the provisions of this section and the provisions, if any, of the articles of incorporation or the bylaws is sufficient, and in the event of the transfer of his stock after such delivery or mailing and before the holding of the meeting it is not necessary to deliver or mail notice of the meeting to the transferee.

6. Unless otherwise provided in the articles of incorporation or the bylaws, if notice is required to be given, under any provision of this chapter or the articles of incorporation or bylaws of any corporation, to any stockholder to whom:

(a) Notice of two consecutive annual meetings, and all notices of meetings or of the taking of action by written consent without a meeting to him during the period between those two consecutive annual meetings; or

(b) All, and at least two, payments sent by first-class mail of dividends or interest on securities during a 12-month period, have been mailed addressed to him at his address as shown on the records of the corporation and have been returned undeliverable, the giving of further notices to him is not required. Any action or meeting taken or held without notice to such a stockholder has the same effect as if the notice had been given. If any such stockholder delivers to the corporation a written notice setting forth his current address, the requirement that notice be given to him is reinstated. If the action taken by the corporation is such as to require the filing of a certificate under any of the other sections of this chapter, the certificate need not state that notice was not given to persons to whom notice was not required to be given pursuant to this subsection. The giving of further notices to a stockholder is still required for any notice returned as undeliverable if the notice was given by electronic transmission.

7. Unless the articles of incorporation or bylaws otherwise require, and except as otherwise provided in this subsection, if a stockholders' meeting is adjourned to another date, time or place, notice need not be given of the date, time or place of the adjourned meeting if they are announced at the meeting at which the adjournment is taken. If a new record date is fixed for the adjourned meeting, notice of the adjourned meeting must be given to each stockholder of record as of the new record date.

8. Any notice to stockholders given by the corporation pursuant to any provision of this chapter, chapter 92A of NRS, the articles of incorporation or the bylaws is effective if given by a form of electronic transmission consented to by the stockholder to whom the notice is given. The consent is revocable by the stockholder by

written notice to the corporation. The consent is revoked if:

(a) The corporation is unable to deliver by electronic transmission two consecutive notices given by the corporation in accordance with the consent; and

(b) The inability to deliver by electronic transmission becomes known to the secretary, assistant secretary, transfer agent or other agent of the corporation responsible for the giving of notice. However, the inadvertent failure to treat the inability to deliver a notice by electronic transmission as a revocation does not invalidate any meeting or other action. 9. Notice given pursuant to subsection 8 shall be deemed given if:

(a) By facsimile machine, when directed to a number at which the stockholder has consented to receive notice;

(b) By electronic mail, when directed to an electronic mail address at which the stockholder has consented to receive notice;

(c) By a posting on an electronic network together with separate notice to the stockholder of the specific posting, upon the later of:

(1) Such posting; and

(2) The giving of the separate notice; and

(d) By any other form of electronic transmission, when directed to the stockholder. In the absence of fraud, an affidavit of the secretary, assistant secretary, transfer agent or other agent of the corporation that the notice has been given by a form of electronic transmission is prima facie evidence of the facts stated in the affidavit.

10. As used in this section, "electronic transmission" means any form of communication not directly involving the physical transmission of paper that:

(a) Creates a record that may be retained, retrieved and reviewed by a recipient of the communication; and

(b) May be directly reproduced in paper form by the recipient through an automated process. [27:177:1925; A 1941, 110; 1931 NCL § 1626]—(NRS A 1991, 1235; 1993, 965; 1999, 1587; 2003, 3096)

**NRS 78.375 Waiver of notice.** Whenever any notice whatever is required to be given under the provisions of this chapter, a waiver thereof in a signed writing or by transmission of an electronic record by the person or persons entitled to the notice, whether before or after the time stated therein, shall be deemed equivalent thereto. [Part 92:177:1925; A 1929, 413; NCL § 1691]—(NRS A 2003, 3098)

## Acquisition of Controlling Interest

**NRS 78.378 Applicability; imposition of stricter requirements; protection of corporation and its stockholders.**

1. The provisions of NRS 78.378 to 78.3793, inclusive, apply to any acquisition of a controlling interest in an issuing corporation unless the articles of incorporation or bylaws of the corporation in effect on the 10th day following the acquisition of a controlling interest by an acquiring person provide that the provisions of those sections do not apply to the corporation or to an acquisition of a controlling interest specifically by types of existing or future stockholders, whether or not identified.

2. The articles of incorporation, the bylaws or a resolution adopted by the directors of the issuing corporation may impose stricter requirements on the acquisition of a controlling interest in the corporation than the provisions of NRS 78.378 to 78.3793, inclusive.

3. The provisions of NRS 78.378 to 78.3793, inclusive, do not restrict the directors of an issuing corporation from taking action to protect the interests of the corporation and its stockholders, including, but not limited to, adopting or signing plans, arrangements or instruments that deny rights, privileges, power or authority to a holder of a specified number of shares or percentage of share ownership or voting power. (Added to NRS by 1987, 755; A 1989, 877; 1999, 1588; 2003, 3098)

**NRS 78.3781 Definitions.** As used in NRS 78.378 to 78.3793, inclusive, unless the context otherwise requires, the words and terms defined in NRS 78.3782 to 78.3788, inclusive, have the meanings ascribed to them in those sections. (Added to NRS by 1987, 756)

**NRS 78.3782 "Acquiring person" defined.** "Acquiring person" means any person who, individually or in association with others, acquires or offers to acquire, directly or indirectly, a controlling interest in an issuing corporation. The term does not include any person who, in the ordinary course of business and without an intent to avoid the requirements of NRS 78.378 to 78.3793, inclusive, acquires voting shares for the benefit of others, in respect of which he is not specifically authorized to exercise or direct the exercise of voting rights. (Added to NRS by 1987, 756)

**NRS 78.3783 "Acquisition" defined.**

1. Except as otherwise provided in subsection 2, "acquisition" means the direct or indirect acquisition of a controlling interest.

2. "Acquisition" does not include any acquisition of shares in good faith, and without an intent to avoid the requirements of NRS 78.378 to 78.3793, inclusive:

(a) By an acquiring person authorized pursuant to NRS 78.378 to 78.3793, inclusive, to exercise voting rights, to the extent that the new acquisition does not result in the acquiring person obtaining a controlling interest greater than that previously authorized; or

(b) Pursuant to:

(1) The laws of descent and distribution;

(2) The enforcement of a judgment;

(3) The satisfaction of a pledge or other security interest; or

(4) A merger, exchange, conversion, domestication or reorganization effected in compliance with the provisions of NRS 78.622, 92A.200 to 92A.240, inclusive, or 92A.270 to which the issuing corporation is a party. (Added to NRS by 1987, 756; A 1991, 1236; 1995, 2099; 2001, 1372, 3199)

**NRS 78.3784 "Control shares" defined.** "Control shares" means those outstanding voting shares of an issuing corporation which an acquiring person and those persons acting in association with an acquiring person:

1. Acquire in an acquisition or offer to acquire in an acquisition; and

2. Acquire within 90 days immediately preceding the date when the acquiring person became an acquiring person. (Added to NRS by 1987, 756)

**NRS 78.3785 "Controlling interest" defined.** "Controlling interest" means the ownership of outstanding voting shares of an issuing corporation sufficient, but for the provisions of NRS 78.378 to 78.3793, inclusive, to enable the acquiring person, directly or indirectly and individually or in association with others, to exercise:

1. One-fifth or more but less than one-third;

2. One-third or more but less than a majority; or

3. A majority or more, of all the voting power of the corporation in the election of directors. (Added to NRS by 1987, 756)

**NRS 78.3786 "Fair value" defined.** "Fair value" means a value not less than the highest price per share paid by the acquiring person in an acquisition. (Added to NRS by 1987, 756)

**NRS 78.3787 "Interested stockholder" defined.** "Interested stockholder" means a person who directly or indirectly exercises voting rights in the shares of an issuing corporation and who is:

1. An acquiring person;

2. An officer or a director of the corporation; or

3. An employee of the corporation. (Added to NRS by 1987, 757; A 1999, 1588)

**NRS 78.3788 "Issuing corporation" defined.** "Issuing corporation" means a corporation which is organized in this State and which:

1. Has 200 or more stockholders of record, at least 100 of whom have addresses in this State appearing on the stock ledger of the corporation; and

2. Does business in this State directly or through an affiliated corporation. (Added to NRS by 1987, 757; A 1989, 877; 1999, 1588)

**NRS 78.3789 Delivery of offeror's statement by acquiring person; contents of statement.** An acquiring person who has made or offered to make an acquisition of a controlling interest in an issuing corporation may deliver an offeror's statement to the registered office of the corporation. The acquiring person may request in the statement that the directors of the corporation call a special meeting of the stockholders of the corporation, as provided in NRS 78.379. The statement must set forth:

1. A recital that the statement is given pursuant to this section;

2. The name of the acquiring person and of every person associated with him in the acquisition;

3. The number of shares in any class of voting securities owned, as of the date of the statement, by the acquiring person and each person with whom he is associated, or which the acquiring person intends to acquire;

4. The percentage of the voting securities of the corporation owned, as of the date of the statement, by the acquiring person and each person with whom he is associated, or which the acquiring person intends to acquire; and

5. If the acquiring person has not yet acquired the securities of the corporation, a detailed description of:

(a) The terms and conditions of the proposed acquisition; and

(b) The means by which any required consideration, and any indebtedness incurred to consummate the transaction, are to be paid. (Added to NRS by 1987, 757; A 1993, 966)

**NRS 78.379 Voting rights of acquiring person; meeting of stockholders; statements to accompany notice of meeting.**

1. An acquiring person and those acting in association with an acquiring person obtain only such voting rights in the control shares as are conferred by a resolution of the stockholders of the corporation, approved at a special or annual meeting of the stockholders.

2. If an acquiring person so requests in an offeror's statement delivered pursuant to NRS 78.3789, and if he gives an undertaking to pay the expenses of the meeting, the directors of the corporation shall, within 10 days after delivery of the statement, call a special meeting of the stockholders to determine the voting rights to be accorded the control shares.

3. A notice of any meeting of stockholders at which the question of voting rights is to be determined must be accompanied by:

(a) A complete copy of the offeror's statement; and

(b) A statement of the board of directors of the corporation setting forth the position of the board with respect to the acquisition or, if it is the case, stating that the board makes no recommendation concerning the matter.

4. A special meeting of stockholders called pursuant to this section:

(a) Must not be held before the expiration of 30 days after the delivery of the offeror's statement, unless the statement contains a request that the meeting be held sooner.

(b) Must be held within 50 days after the delivery of the statement, unless the acquiring person otherwise agrees in writing that the meeting may be held after that time.

5. If the offeror's statement does not include a request that a special meeting be called, the question of voting rights must be presented to the next special or annual meeting of the stockholders. (Added to NRS by 1987, 757)

**NRS 78.3791 Approval of voting rights of acquiring person.** Except as otherwise provided by the articles of incorporation of the issuing corporation, a resolution of the stockholders granting voting rights to the control shares acquired by an acquiring person must be approved by:

1. The holders of a majority of the voting power of the corporation; and

2. If the acquisition would adversely alter or change any preference or any relative or other right given to any other class or series of outstanding shares, the holders of a majority of each class or series affected, excluding those shares as to which any interested stockholder exercises voting rights. (Added to NRS by 1987, 758; A 1991, 1236; 1999, 1589; 2001, 1372, 3199; 2003, 3098)

**NRS 78.3792 Redemption of control shares.**

1. If so provided in the articles of incorporation or the bylaws of the issuing corporation in effect on the 10th day following the acquisition of a controlling interest by an acquiring person, the issuing corporation may call for redemption of not less than all the control shares at the average price paid for the control shares, if:

(a) An offeror's statement is not delivered with respect to the acquisition as provided in NRS 78.3789 on or before the 10th day after the acquisition of the control shares; or

(b) An offeror's statement is delivered, but the control shares are not accorded full voting rights by the stockholders.

2. The issuing corporation shall call for redemption within 30 days after the occurrence of the event prescribed in paragraph (a) or

(b) of subsection 1, and the shares must be redeemed within 60 days after the call. (Added to NRS by 1987, 758; A 1989, 877)

**NRS 78.3793 Rights of dissenting stockholders.** Unless otherwise provided in the articles of incorporation or the bylaws of the issuing corporation in effect on the 10th day following the acquisition of a controlling interest by an acquiring person, if the control shares are accorded full voting rights pursuant to NRS 78.378 to 78.3793, inclusive, and the acquiring person has acquired control shares with a majority or more of all the voting power, any stockholder, as that term is defined in NRS 92A.325, other than the acquiring person, whose shares are not voted in favor of authorizing voting rights for the control shares may dissent in accordance with the provisions of NRS 92A.300 to 92A.500, inclusive, and obtain payment of the fair value of his shares. (Added to NRS by 1987, 758; A 1989, 877; 1993, 966; 2001, 1373, 3199)

## Amendment and Restatement of Articles of Incorporation

**NRS 78.380 Amendment of articles before issuance of voting stock.**

1. At least two-thirds of the incorporators or of the board of directors of any corporation, if no voting stock of the corporation has been issued, may amend the articles of incorporation of the corporation by signing and filing with the Secretary of State a certificate amending, modifying, changing or altering the articles, in whole or in part. The certificate must state that:

(a) The signers thereof are at least two-thirds of the incorporators or of the board of directors of the corporation, and state the name of the corporation; and

(b) As of the date of the certificate, no voting stock of the corporation has been issued.

2. A certificate filed pursuant to this section is effective upon filing the certificate with the Secretary of State or upon a later date specified in the certificate, which must not be more than 90 days after the certificate is filed.

3. If a certificate specifies an effective date and if no voting stock of the corporation has been issued, the board of directors may terminate the effectiveness of a certificate by filing a certificate of termination with the Secretary of State that:

(a) Identifies the certificate being terminated;

(b) States that no voting stock of the corporation has been issued;

(c) States that the effectiveness of the certificate has been terminated;

(d) Is signed by at least two-thirds of the board of directors of the corporation; and

(e) Is accompanied by the fee required pursuant to NRS 78.765.

4. This section does not permit the insertion of any matter not in conformity with this chapter. [Part 6:177:1925; A 1951, 28]—(NRS A 1959, 686; 1991, 1236;

1993, 966; 1999, 1589; 2001, 1373, 3199; 2003, 3099; 2005, 2184)

**NRS 78.385 Scope of amendments.**

1. Any corporation may amend its articles of incorporation in any of the following respects:

(a) By addition to its corporate powers and purposes, or diminution thereof, or both.

(b) By substitution of other powers and purposes, in whole or in part, for those prescribed by its articles of incorporation.

(c) By increasing, decreasing or reclassifying its authorized stock, by changing the number, par value, preferences, or relative, participating, optional or other rights, or the qualifications, limitations or restrictions of such rights, of its shares, or of any class or series of any class thereof whether or not the shares are outstanding at the time of the amendment, or by changing shares with par value, whether or not the shares are outstanding at the time of the amendment, into shares without par value or by changing shares without par value, whether or not the shares are outstanding at the time of the amendment, into shares with par value, either with or without increasing or decreasing the number of shares, and upon such basis as may be set forth in the certificate of amendment.

(d) By changing the name of the corporation.

(e) By making any other change or alteration in its articles of incorporation that may be desired.

2. All such changes or alterations may be effected by one certificate of amendment, but any articles of incorporation so amended, changed or altered may contain only such provisions as it would be lawful and proper to insert in original articles of incorporation pursuant to NRS 78.035 and 78.037, if the original articles were signed and filed at the time of making the amendment. [Part 7:177:1925; A 1931, 415; 1937, 8; 1949, 158; 1943 NCL § 1606]—(NRS A 1989, 878; 1991, 1237; 1999, 1589; 2003, 3099)

**NRS 78.390 Amendment of articles after issuance of stock: Procedure. [Effective through June 30, 2008.]**

1. Every amendment to the articles of incorporation must be made in the following manner:

(a) The board of directors must adopt a resolution setting forth the amendment proposed and either call a special meeting of the stockholders entitled to vote on the amendment or direct that the proposed amendment be considered at the next annual meeting of the stockholders entitled to vote on the amendment.

(b) At the meeting, of which notice must be given to each stockholder entitled to vote pursuant to the provisions of this section, a vote of the stockholders entitled to vote in person or by proxy must be taken for and against the proposed amendment. If it appears upon the canvassing of the votes that stockholders holding shares in the corporation entitling them to exercise at least a majority of the voting power, or such greater proportion of the voting power as may be required in the case of a vote by classes or series, as provided in subsections 2 and 4, or as may be required by the provisions of the articles of incorporation, have voted in favor of the amendment, an officer of the corporation shall sign a certificate setting forth the amendment, or setting forth the articles of incorporation as amended, and the vote by which the amendment was adopted.

(c) The certificate so signed must be filed with the Secretary of State.

2. Except as otherwise provided in this subsection, if any proposed amendment would adversely alter or change any preference or any relative or other right given to any class or series of outstanding shares, then the amendment must be approved by the vote, in addition to the affirmative vote otherwise required, of the holders of shares representing a majority of the voting power of each class or series adversely affected by the amendment regardless of limitations or restrictions on the voting power thereof. The amendment does not have to be approved by the vote of the holders of shares representing a majority of the voting power of each class or series whose preference or rights are adversely affected by the amendment if the articles of incorporation specifically deny the right to vote on such an amendment.

3. Provision may be made in the articles of incorporation requiring, in the case of any specified amendments, a larger proportion of the voting power of stockholders than that required by this section.

4. Different series of the same class of shares do not constitute different classes of shares for the purpose of voting by classes except when the series is adversely affected by an amendment in a different manner than other series of the same class.

5. The resolution of the stockholders approving the proposed amendment may provide that at any time before the effective date of the amendment, notwithstanding approval of the proposed amendment by the stockholders, the board of directors may, by resolution, abandon the proposed amendment without further action by the stockholders.

6. A certificate filed pursuant to subsection 1 is effective upon filing the certificate with the Secretary of State or upon a later date specified in the certificate, which must not be more than 90 days after the certificate is filed.

7. If a certificate filed pursuant to subsection 1 specifies an effective date and if the resolution of the stockholders approving the proposed amendment provides that the board of directors may abandon the proposed

amendment pursuant to subsection 5, the board of directors may terminate the effectiveness of the certificate by resolution and by filing a certificate of termination with the Secretary of State that:

(a) Is filed before the effective date specified in the certificate filed pursuant to subsection 1;

(b) Identifies the certificate being terminated;

(c) States that, pursuant to the resolution of the stockholders, the board of directors is authorized to terminate the effectiveness of the certificate;

(d) States that the effectiveness of the certificate has been terminated;

(e) Is signed by an officer of the corporation; and

(f) Is accompanied by a filing fee of $175. [Part 7:177:1925; A 1931, 415; 1937, 8; 1949, 158; 1943 NCL § 1606]—(NRS A 1959, 686; 1971, 1101; 1979, 395; 1991, 1238; 1993, 967; 1997, 703; 1999, 1590; 2001, 1374, 3174, 3196, 3199; 2003, 225, 3100; 2003, 20th Special Session, 34; 2005, 2184)

**NRS 78.390 Amendment of articles after issuance of stock: Procedure. [Effective July 1, 2008.]**

1. Except as otherwise provided in NRS 77.340, every amendment to the articles of incorporation must be made in the following manner:

(a) The board of directors must adopt a resolution setting forth the amendment proposed and either call a special meeting of the stockholders entitled to vote on the amendment or direct that the proposed amendment be considered at the next annual meeting of the stockholders entitled to vote on the amendment.

(b) At the meeting, of which notice must be given to each stockholder entitled to vote pursuant to the provisions of this section, a vote of the stockholders entitled to vote in person or by proxy must be taken for and against the proposed amendment. If it appears upon the canvassing of the votes that stockholders holding shares in the corporation entitling them to exercise at least a majority of the voting power, or such greater proportion of the voting power as may be required in the case of a vote by classes or series, as provided in subsections 2 and 4, or as may be required by the provisions of the articles of incorporation, have voted in favor of the amendment, an officer of the corporation shall sign a certificate setting forth the amendment, or setting forth the articles of incorporation as amended, and the vote by which the amendment was adopted.

(c) The certificate so signed must be filed with the Secretary of State.

2. Except as otherwise provided in this subsection, if any proposed amendment would adversely alter or change any preference or any relative or other right given to any class or series of outstanding shares, then the amendment must be approved by the vote, in addition to the affirmative vote otherwise required, of the holders of shares representing a majority of the voting power of each class or series adversely affected by the amendment regardless of limitations or restrictions on the voting power thereof. The amendment does not have to be approved by the vote of the holders of shares representing a majority of the voting power of each class or series whose preference or rights are adversely affected by the amendment if the articles of incorporation specifically deny the right to vote on such an amendment.

3. Provision may be made in the articles of incorporation requiring, in the case of any specified amendments, a larger proportion of the voting power of stockholders than that required by this section.

4. Different series of the same class of shares do not constitute different classes of shares for the purpose of voting by classes except when the series is adversely affected by an amendment in a different manner than other series of the same class.

5. The resolution of the stockholders approving the proposed amendment may provide that at any time before the effective date of the amendment, notwithstanding approval of the proposed amendment by the stockholders, the board of directors may, by resolution, abandon the proposed amendment without further action by the stockholders.

6. A certificate filed pursuant to subsection 1 is effective upon filing the certificate with the Secretary of State or upon a later date specified in the certificate, which must not be more than 90 days after the certificate is filed.

7. If a certificate filed pursuant to subsection 1 specifies an effective date and if the resolution of the stockholders approving the proposed amendment provides that the board of directors may abandon the proposed amendment pursuant to subsection 5, the board of directors may terminate the effectiveness of the certificate by resolution and by filing a certificate of termination with the Secretary of State that:

(a) Is filed before the effective date specified in the certificate filed pursuant to subsection 1;

(b) Identifies the certificate being terminated;

(c) States that, pursuant to the resolution of the stockholders, the board of directors is authorized to terminate the effectiveness of the certificate;

(d) States that the effectiveness of the certificate has been terminated;

(e) Is signed by an officer of the corporation; and

(f) Is accompanied by a filing fee of $175. [Part 7:177:1925; A 1931, 415; 1937, 8; 1949, 158; 1943 NCL § 1606]—(NRS A 1959, 686; 1971, 1101; 1979, 395; 1991, 1238; 1993, 967; 1997, 703; 1999, 1590; 2001, 1374, 3174, 3196, 3199; 2003, 225, 3100; 2003, 20th Special

Session, 34; 2005, 2184; 2007, 2647, effective July 1, 2008)

## NRS 78.403 Restatement of articles. [Effective through June 30, 2008.]

1. A corporation may restate, or amend and restate, in a single certificate the entire text of its articles of incorporation as amended by filing with the Secretary of State a certificate in the manner provided in this section. If the certificate alters or amends the articles in any manner, it must comply with the provisions of NRS 78.380, 78.385 and 78.390, as applicable.

2. If the certificate does not alter or amend the articles, it must be signed by an officer of the corporation and state that he has been authorized to sign the certificate by resolution of the board of directors adopted on the date stated, and that the certificate correctly sets forth the text of the articles of incorporation as amended to the date of the certificate.

3. The following may be omitted from the restated articles:

(a) The names, addresses, signatures and acknowledgments of the incorporators;

(b) The names and addresses of the members of the past and present boards of directors; and

(c) The name and address of the resident agent.

4. Whenever a corporation is required to file a certified copy of its articles, in lieu thereof it may file a certified copy of the most recent certificate restating its articles as amended, subject to the provisions of subsection 2, together with certified copies of all certificates of amendment filed subsequent to the restated articles and certified copies of all certificates supplementary to the original articles.

5. A certificate filed pursuant to this section is effective upon filing the certificate with the Secretary of State or upon a later date specified in the certificate, which must not be more than 90 days after the certificate is filed. (Added to NRS by 1959, 682; A 1985, 1789; 1989, 977; 1995, 2100; 1997, 704; 2001, 1375, 3199; 2003, 3101; 2003, 20th Special Session, 35; 2005, 2186)

## NRS 78.403 Restatement of articles. [Effective July 1, 2008.]

1. A corporation may restate, or amend and restate, in a single certificate the entire text of its articles of incorporation as amended by filing with the Secretary of State a certificate in the manner provided in this section. If the certificate alters or amends the articles in any manner, it must comply with the provisions of NRS 78.380, 78.385 and 78.390, as applicable.

2. If the certificate does not alter or amend the articles, it must be signed by an officer of the corporation and state that he has been authorized to sign the certificate by resolution of the board of directors adopted on the date stated, and that the certificate correctly sets forth the text of the articles of incorporation as amended to the date of the certificate.

3. The following may be omitted from the restated articles:

(a) The names, addresses, signatures and acknowledgments of the incorporators;

(b) The names and addresses of the members of the past and present boards of directors; and

(c) The information required pursuant to NRS 77.310.

4. Whenever a corporation is required to file a certified copy of its articles, in lieu thereof it may file a certified copy of the most recent certificate restating its articles as amended, subject to the provisions of subsection 2, together with certified copies of all certificates of amendment filed subsequent to the restated articles and certified copies of all certificates supplementary to the original articles.

5. A certificate filed pursuant to this section is effective upon filing the certificate with the Secretary of State or upon a later date specified in the certificate, which must not be more than 90 days after the certificate is filed. (Added to NRS by 1959, 682; A 1985, 1789; 1989, 977; 1995, 2100; 1997, 704; 2001, 1375, 3199; 2003, 3101; 2003, 20th Special Session, 35; 2005, 2186; 2007, 2648, effective July 1, 2008)

## Combinations with Interested Stockholders

**NRS 78.411 Definitions.** As used in NRS 78.411 to 78.444, inclusive, unless the context otherwise requires, the words and terms defined in NRS 78.412 to 78.432, inclusive, have the meanings ascribed to them in those sections. (Added to NRS by 1991, 1200)

**NRS 78.412 "Affiliate" defined.** "Affiliate" means a person that directly, or indirectly through one or more intermediaries, is controlled by, or is under common control with, a specified person. (Added to NRS by 1991, 1200)

**NRS 78.413 "Associate" defined.** "Associate," when used to indicate a relationship with any person, means:

1. Any corporation or organization of which that person is an officer or partner or is, directly or indirectly, the beneficial owner of 10 percent or more of any class of voting shares;

2. Any trust or other estate in which that person has a substantial beneficial interest or as to which he serves as trustee or in a similar fiduciary capacity; and

3. Any relative or spouse of that person, or any relative of the spouse, who has the same home as that person. (Added to NRS by 1991, 1200)

**NRS 78.414 "Beneficial owner" defined.** "Beneficial owner," when used with respect to any shares, means a person that:

1. Individually or with or through any of its affiliates or associates, beneficially owns the shares, directly or indirectly;

2. Individually or with or through any of its affiliates or associates, has:

(a) The right to acquire the shares, whether the right is exercisable immediately or only after the passage of time, under any agreement, arrangement or understanding, whether or not in writing, or upon the exercise of rights to convert or exchange, warrants or options, or otherwise, but a person is not considered the beneficial owner of shares tendered under an offer for a tender or exchange made by the person or any of his affiliates or associates until the tendered shares are accepted for purchase or exchange; or

(b) The right to vote the shares under any agreement, arrangement or understanding, whether or not in writing, but a person is not considered the beneficial owner of any shares under this paragraph if the agreement, arrangement or understanding to vote the shares arises solely from a revocable proxy or consent given in response to a solicitation made in accordance with the applicable regulations under the Securities Exchange Act and is not then reportable on a Schedule 13D under the Securities Exchange Act, or any comparable or successor report; or

3. Has any agreement, arrangement or understanding, whether or not in writing, for the purpose of acquiring, holding, voting, except voting under a revocable proxy or consent as described in paragraph (b) of subsection 2, or disposing of the shares with any other person who beneficially owns, or whose affiliates or associates beneficially own, directly or indirectly, the shares. (Added to NRS by 1991, 1200)

**NRS 78.416 "Combination" defined.** "Combination," when used in reference to any resident domestic corporation and any interested stockholder of the resident domestic corporation, means any of the following:

1. Any merger or consolidation of the resident domestic corporation or any subsidiary of the resident domestic corporation with:

(a) The interested stockholder; or

(b) Any other corporation, whether or not itself an interested stockholder of the resident domestic corporation, which is, or after the merger or consolidation would be, an affiliate or associate of the interested stockholder.

2. Any sale, lease, exchange, mortgage, pledge, transfer or other disposition, in one transaction or a series of transactions, to or with the interested stockholder or any affiliate or associate of the interested stockholder of assets of the resident domestic corporation or any subsidiary of the resident domestic corporation:

(a) Having an aggregate market value equal to 5 percent or more of the aggregate market value of all the assets, determined on a consolidated basis, of the resident domestic corporation;

(b) Having an aggregate market value equal to 5 percent or more of the aggregate market value of all the outstanding shares of the resident domestic corporation; or

(c) Representing 10 percent or more of the earning power or net income, determined on a consolidated basis, of the resident domestic corporation.

3. The issuance or transfer by the resident domestic corporation or any subsidiary of the resident domestic corporation, in one transaction or a series of transactions, of any shares of the resident domestic corporation or any subsidiary of the resident domestic corporation that have an aggregate market value equal to 5 percent or more of the aggregate market value of all the outstanding shares of the resident domestic corporation to the interested stockholder or any affiliate or associate of the interested stockholder except under the exercise of warrants or rights to purchase shares offered, or a dividend or distribution paid or made, pro rata to all stockholders of the resident domestic corporation.

4. The adoption of any plan or proposal for the liquidation or dissolution of the resident domestic corporation proposed by, or under any agreement, arrangement or understanding, whether or not in writing, with, the interested stockholder or any affiliate or associate of the interested stockholder.

5. Any:

(a) Reclassification of securities, including, without limitation, any splitting of shares, dividend distributed in shares, or other distribution of shares with respect to other shares, or any issuance of new shares in exchange for a proportionately greater number of old shares;

(b) Recapitalization of the resident domestic corporation;

(c) Merger or consolidation of the resident domestic corporation with any subsidiary of the resident domestic corporation; or

(d) Other transaction, whether or not with or into or otherwise involving the interested stockholder, proposed by, or under any agreement, arrangement or understanding, whether or not in writing, with, the interested stockholder or any affiliate or associate of the interested stockholder, which has the effect, directly or indirectly, of increasing the proportionate share of the outstanding shares of any class or series of voting shares or securities convertible into voting shares of the resident domestic corporation or any subsidiary of the resident domestic corporation which is directly or indirectly owned by the interested stockholder or any affiliate or associate of the interested stockholder, except as a result of immaterial changes because of adjustments of fractional shares.

6. Any receipt by the interested stockholder or any affiliate or associate of the interested stockholder of the benefit, directly or indirectly, except proportionately as a stockholder of the resident domestic corporation, of any loan, advance, guarantee, pledge or other financial assistance or any tax credit or other tax advantage provided by or through the resident domestic corporation. (Added to NRS by 1991, 1200)

**NRS 78.417 "Common shares" defined.** "Common shares" means any shares other than preferred shares. (Added to NRS by 1991, 1202)

**NRS 78.418 "Control," "controlling," "controlled by" and "under common control with" defined; presumption of control.**

1. Except as otherwise provided in subsection 2:

(a) "Control," used alone or in the terms "controlling," "controlled by" and "under common control with," means the possession, directly or indirectly, of the power to direct or cause the direction of the management and policies of a person, whether through the ownership of voting securities, by contract or otherwise.

(b) A person's beneficial ownership of 10 percent or more of the voting power of a corporation's outstanding voting shares creates a presumption that the person has control of the corporation.

2. A person is not considered to have control of a corporation if he holds voting power, in good faith and not for the purpose of circumventing the provisions of this chapter, as an agent, bank, broker, nominee, custodian or trustee for one or more beneficial owners who do not individually or as a group have control of the corporation. (Added to NRS by 1991, 1202)

**NRS 78.421 "Date of announcement" defined.** "Date of announcement," when used in reference to any combination, means the date of the first public announcement of the final, definitive proposal for the combination. (Added to NRS by 1991, 1202)

**NRS 78.422 "Date of consummation" defined.** "Date of consummation," with respect to any combination, means the date of the consummation of the combination or, in the case of a combination as to which a vote of stockholders is taken, the later of:

1. The business day before the vote; or

2. Twenty days before the date of consummation of the combination. (Added to NRS by 1991, 1202)

**NRS 78.423 "Interested stockholder" defined.**

1. "Interested stockholder," when used in reference to any resident domestic corporation, means any person, other than the resident domestic corporation or any subsidiary of the resident domestic corporation, who is:

(a) The beneficial owner, directly or indirectly, of 10 percent or more of the voting power of the outstanding voting shares of the resident domestic corporation; or

(b) An affiliate or associate of the resident domestic corporation and at any time within 3 years immediately before the date in question was the beneficial owner, directly or indirectly, of 10 percent or more of the voting power of the then outstanding shares of the resident domestic corporation.

2. To determine whether a person is an interested stockholder, the number of voting shares of the resident domestic corporation considered to be outstanding includes shares considered to be beneficially owned by that person through the application of NRS 78.414, but does not include any other unissued shares of a class of voting shares of the resident domestic corporation which may be issuable under any agreement, arrangement or understanding, or upon exercise of rights to convert, warrants or options, or otherwise. (Added to NRS by 1991, 1202; A 1993, 968)

**NRS 78.424 "Market value" defined.** "Market value," when used in reference to the shares or property of any resident domestic corporation, means:

1. In the case of shares, the highest closing sale price of a share during the 30 days immediately preceding the date in question on the composite tape for shares listed on the New York Stock Exchange, or, if the shares are not quoted on the composite tape or not listed on the New York Stock Exchange, on the principal United States securities exchange registered under the Securities Exchange Act on which the shares are listed, or, if the shares are not listed on any such exchange, the highest closing bid quoted with respect to a share during the 30 days preceding the date in question on the National Association of Securities Dealers, Inc.'s, Automated Quotations System or any system then in use, or if no such quotation is available, the fair market value on the date in question of a share as determined by the board of directors of the resident domestic corporation in good faith.

2. In the case of property other than cash or shares, the fair market value of the property on the date in question as determined by the board of directors of the resident domestic corporation in good faith. (Added to NRS by 1991, 1203)

**NRS 78.426 "Preferred shares" defined.** "Preferred shares" means any class or series of shares of a resident domestic corporation that under the bylaws or articles of incorporation of the resident domestic corporation:

1. Is entitled to receive payment of dividends before any payment of dividends on some other class or series of shares; or

2. Is entitled in the event of any voluntary liquidation, dissolution or winding up of the corporation to receive

payment or distribution of a preferential amount before any payments or distributions are received by some other class or series of shares. (Added to NRS by 1991, 1203)

### NRS 78.427 "Resident domestic corporation" defined.

1. "Resident domestic corporation" is limited to a domestic corporation that has 200 or more stockholders of record.

2. A resident domestic corporation does not cease to be a resident domestic corporation by reason of events occurring or actions taken while the resident domestic corporation is subject to NRS 78.411 to 78.444, inclusive. (Added to NRS by 1991, 1203; A 1999, 1591)

### NRS 78.428 "Securities Exchange Act" defined.

"Securities Exchange Act" means the Act of Congress known as the Securities Exchange Act of 1934, as amended, 15 U.S.C. §§ 78a et seq. (Added to NRS by 1991, 1203)

### NRS 78.429 "Share" defined. "Share" means:

1. Any share or similar security, any certificate of interest, any participation in any profit-sharing agreement, any voting-trust certificate, or any certificate of deposit for a share; and

2. Any security convertible, with or without consideration, into shares, or any warrant, call or other option or privilege of buying shares without being bound to do so, or any other security carrying any right to acquire, subscribe to, or purchase shares. (Added to NRS by 1991, 1203)

### NRS 78.431 "Subsidiary" defined.

"Subsidiary" of any resident domestic corporation means any other corporation of which a majority of the outstanding voting shares whose votes are entitled to be cast are owned, directly or indirectly, by the resident domestic corporation. (Added to NRS by 1991, 1203)

### NRS 78.432 "Voting shares" defined.

"Voting shares" means shares of stock of a corporation entitled to vote generally in the election of directors. (Added to NRS by 1991, 1204)

### NRS 78.433 Applicability: Generally.

NRS 78.411 to 78.444, inclusive, do not apply to any combination of a resident domestic corporation:

1. Which does not, as of the date that the person first becomes an interested stockholder, have a class of voting shares registered with the Securities and Exchange Commission under section 12 of the Securities Exchange Act, unless the corporation's articles of incorporation provide otherwise.

2. Whose articles of incorporation have been amended to provide that the resident domestic corporation is subject to NRS 78.411 to 78.444, inclusive, and which did not have a class of voting shares registered with the Securities and Exchange Commission under section 12 of the Securities Exchange Act on the effective date of the amendment, if the combination is with a person who first became an interested stockholder before the effective date of the amendment. (Added to NRS by 1991, 1206; A 2003, 3101)

### NRS 78.434 Applicability: Election not to be governed by provisions.

NRS 78.411 to 78.444, inclusive, do not apply to any combination of a resident domestic corporation:

1. Whose original articles of incorporation contain a provision expressly electing not to be governed by NRS 78.411 to 78.444, inclusive, unless the articles of incorporation are subsequently amended to provide that the corporation is subject to NRS 78.411 to 78.444, inclusive;

2. Whose articles of incorporation have been amended pursuant to subsection 1 and the combination is with a person who first became an interested stockholder before the effective date of the amendment;

3. Which, within 30 days after October 1, 1991, adopts an amendment to its bylaws expressly electing not to be governed by NRS 78.411 to 78.444, inclusive, which may be rescinded by subsequent amendment of the bylaws;

4. Which adopts an amendment to its articles of incorporation, approved by the affirmative vote of the holders, other than interested stockholders and their affiliates and associates, of a majority of the outstanding voting power of the resident domestic corporation, excluding the voting shares of interested stockholders and their affiliates and associates, expressly electing not to be governed by NRS 78.411 to 78.444, inclusive, but the amendment to the articles of incorporation is not effective until 18 months after the vote of the resident domestic corporation's stockholders and does not apply to any combination of the resident domestic corporation with a person who first became an interested stockholder on or before the effective date of the amendment; or

5. Whose articles of incorporation were amended to contain a provision expressly electing not to be governed by NRS 78.411 to 78.444, inclusive, before the date the corporation first became a resident domestic corporation. (Added to NRS by 1991, 1206; A 2003, 3102)

### NRS 78.436 Applicability: Combination with inadvertent interested stockholder.

NRS 78.411 to 78.444, inclusive, do not apply to any combination of a resident domestic corporation with an interested stockholder of the resident domestic corporation who became an interested stockholder inadvertently, if he:

1. As soon as practicable, divests himself of a sufficient amount of the voting power of the corporation so that he no longer is the beneficial owner, directly or indirectly, of 10 percent or more of the outstanding voting power of the resident domestic corporation; and

2. Would not at any time within 3 years preceding the date of announcement with respect to the combination have been an interested stockholder but for the inadvertent acquisition. (Added to NRS by 1991, 1207; A 1993, 968)

**NRS 78.437 Applicability: Combination with interested stockholder as of certain date.** NRS 78.411 to 78.444, inclusive, do not apply to any combination with an interested stockholder who:

1. Was an interested stockholder on January 1, 1991; or

2. Who first became an interested stockholder on the date that the resident domestic corporation first became a resident domestic corporation solely as a result of the corporation becoming a resident domestic corporation. (Added to NRS by 1991, 1207; A 2003, 3102)

**NRS 78.438 Combination prohibited within 3 years after stockholder becomes interested; exception; action on proposal.**

1. Except as otherwise provided in NRS 78.433 to 78.437, inclusive, a resident domestic corporation may not engage in any combination with any interested stockholder of the resident domestic corporation for 3 years after the date that the person first became an interested stockholder unless the combination or the transaction by which the person first became an interested stockholder is approved by the board of directors of the resident domestic corporation before the person first became an interested stockholder.

2. If a proposal in good faith regarding a combination is made in writing to the board of directors of the resident domestic corporation, the board of directors shall respond, in writing, within 30 days or such shorter period, if any, as may be required by the Securities Exchange Act, setting forth its reasons for its decision regarding the proposal.

3. If a proposal in good faith to purchase shares is made in writing to the board of directors of the resident domestic corporation, the board of directors, unless it responds affirmatively in writing within 30 days or such shorter period, if any, as may be required by the Securities Exchange Act, is considered to have disapproved the purchase.(Added to NRS by 1991, 1204; A 1993, 968; 2003, 3102)

**NRS 78.439 Authorized combinations: General requirements.** A resident domestic corporation may not engage in any combination with an interested stockholder of the resident domestic corporation after the expiration of 3 years after the person first became an interested stockholder other than a combination meeting all of the requirements of the articles of incorporation of the resident domestic corporation and either the requirements specified in subsection 1, 2 or 3 or all of the requirements specified in NRS 78.441 to 78.444, inclusive:

1. A combination approved by the board of directors of the resident domestic corporation before the date that the person first became an interested stockholder.

2. A combination with an interested stockholder if the transaction by which the person became an interested stockholder was approved by the board of directors of the resident domestic corporation before the person became an interested stockholder.

3. A combination approved by the affirmative vote of the holders of stock representing a majority of the outstanding voting power not beneficially owned by the interested stockholder proposing the combination, or any affiliate or associate of the interested stockholder proposing the combination, at a meeting called for that purpose no earlier than 3 years after the date that the person first became an interested stockholder. (Added to NRS by 1991, 1204; A 1993, 969; 2003, 3103)

**NRS 78.441 Authorized combinations: Consideration to be received by disinterested holders of common shares.** A combination engaged in with an interested stockholder of the resident domestic corporation more than 3 years after the date that the person first became an interested stockholder may be permissible if the aggregate amount of the cash and the market value, as of the date of consummation, of consideration other than cash to be received per share by all of the holders of outstanding common shares of the resident domestic corporation not beneficially owned by the interested stockholder immediately before that date is at least equal to the higher of the following:

1. The highest price per share paid by the interested stockholder, at a time when he was the beneficial owner, directly or indirectly, of 5 percent or more of the outstanding voting shares of the corporation, for any common shares of the same class or series acquired by him within 3 years immediately before the date of announcement with respect to the combination or within 3 years immediately before, or in, the transaction in which he became an interested stockholder, whichever is higher, plus, in either case, interest compounded annually from the earliest date on which the highest price per share was paid through the date of consummation at the rate for one-year obligations of the United States Treasury from time to time in effect, less the aggregate amount of any dividends paid in cash and the market value of any dividends paid other than in cash, per common share since the earliest date, but

no more may be subtracted than the amount of the interest.

2. The market value per common share on the date of announcement with respect to the combination or on the date that the person first became an interested stockholder, whichever is higher, plus interest compounded annually from that date through the date of consummation at the rate for one-year obligations of the United States Treasury from time to time in effect, less the aggregate amount of any dividends paid in cash and the market value of any dividends paid other than in cash, per common share since that date, but no more may be subtracted than the amount of the interest. (Added to NRS by 1991, 1204; A 1993, 969; 2003, 3103)

**NRS 78.442 Authorized combinations: Consideration to be received by disinterested holders of class or series of shares other than common shares.** A combination engaged in with an interested stockholder of the resident domestic corporation more than 3 years after the date that the person first became an interested stockholder may be permissible if the aggregate amount of the cash and the market value, as of the date of consummation, of consideration other than cash to be received per share by all of the holders of outstanding shares of any class or series of shares, other than common shares, of the resident domestic corporation not beneficially owned by the interested stockholder immediately before that date is at least equal to the highest of the following, whether or not the interested stockholder has previously acquired any shares of the class or series of shares:

1. The highest price per share paid by the interested stockholder, at a time when he was the beneficial owner, directly or indirectly, of 5 percent or more of the outstanding voting shares of the corporation, for any shares of that class or series of shares acquired by him within 3 years immediately before the date of announcement with respect to the combination or within 3 years immediately before, or in, the transaction in which he became an interested stockholder, whichever is higher, plus, in either case, interest compounded annually from the earliest date on which the highest price per share was paid through the date of consummation at the rate for one-year obligations of the United States Treasury from time to time in effect, less the aggregate amount of any dividends paid in cash and the market value of any dividends paid other than in cash, per share of the class or series of shares since the earliest date, but no more may be subtracted than the amount of the interest.

2. The highest preferential amount per share to which the holders of shares of the class or series of shares are entitled in the event of any voluntary liquidation, dissolution or winding up of the resident domestic corporation, plus the aggregate amount of any dividends declared or due to which the holders are entitled before payment of the dividends on some other class or series of shares, unless the aggregate amount of the dividends is included in the preferential amount.

3. The market value per share of the class or series of shares on the date of announcement with respect to the combination or on the date that the person first became an interested stockholder, whichever is higher, plus interest compounded annually from that date through the date of consummation at the rate for one-year obligations of the United States Treasury from time to time in effect, less the aggregate amount of any dividends paid in cash and the market value of any dividends paid other than in cash, per share of the class or series of shares since that date, but no more may be subtracted than the amount of the interest. (Added to NRS by 1991, 1205; A 1993, 970; 2003, 3104)

**NRS 78.443 Authorized combinations: Required form and distribution of consideration.** The consideration to be received by holders of a particular class or series of outstanding shares, including common shares, of the resident domestic corporation in the combination pursuant to NRS 78.441 and 78.442, must be in cash or in the same form as the interested stockholder has used to acquire the largest number of shares of the class or series of shares previously acquired by it, and the consideration must be distributed promptly. (Added to NRS by 1991, 1206)

**NRS 78.444 Authorized combinations: Restrictions on beneficial ownership of additional voting shares by interested stockholder.** A combination may be permissible if after the date that the person first became an interested stockholder and before the date of consummation with respect to the combination, the interested stockholder has not become the beneficial owner of any additional voting shares of the resident domestic corporation except:

1. As part of the transaction that resulted in his becoming an interested stockholder;

2. By virtue of proportionate splitting of shares, dividends distributed in shares, or other distributions of shares in respect of shares not constituting a combination;

3. Through a combination meeting all of the conditions of NRS 78.439; or

4. Through a purchase at any price that, if the price had been paid in an otherwise permissible combination whose date of announcement and date of consummation were the date of the purchase, would have satisfied the requirements of NRS 78.441, 78.442 and 78.443. (Added to NRS by 1991, 1206; A 1993, 971; 2003, 3105)

## Sale of Assets; Dissolution and Winding Up

**NRS 78.565 Sale, lease or exchange of assets: Authority; vote of stockholders.**

1. Unless otherwise provided in the articles of incorporation, every corporation may, by action taken at any meeting of its board of directors, sell, lease or exchange all of its property and assets, including its goodwill and its corporate franchises, upon such terms and conditions as its board of directors may approve, when and as authorized by the affirmative vote of stockholders holding stock in the corporation entitling them to exercise at least a majority of the voting power.

2. Unless otherwise provided in the articles of incorporation, a vote of stockholders is not necessary:

(a) For a transfer of assets by way of mortgage, or in trust or in pledge to secure indebtedness of the corporation; or

(b) To abandon the sale, lease or exchange of assets. [37:177:1925; NCL § 1636]—(NRS A 1989, 886; 1993, 973; 2001, 1376, 3199; 2007, 2420)

**NRS 78.570 Sale of property and franchise under decree of court.** Sales of the property and franchises of corporations that may be sold under a decree of court shall be made after such notice of the time and place as the court may deem proper. If the sales are made in the foreclosure of one or more mortgages, the court may order the sale to be made for the whole amount of indebtedness secured by the mortgage or mortgages, or for the amount of interest due under the mortgage or mortgages, subject to the payment by the purchaser of the outstanding indebtedness and interest secured thereby as they become due. In the latter event the court may, by proper orders, secure the assumption thereof by the purchaser. When a sale shall be ordered to be made, subject as aforesaid, the court shall direct the officer making such sale, in the event that the property and franchises offered do not sell for enough to pay the amount aforesaid, to sell the same free from encumbrances. Sales under this section shall be made on such credits as the court may deem proper. [38:177:1925; NCL § 1637]

**NRS 78.575 Procedure for dissolution before payment of capital and beginning of business.** Before the payment of any part of the capital and before beginning the business for which the corporation was created, the incorporators or the board of directors named in the articles of incorporation may dissolve a corporation by filing in the Office of the Secretary of State a certificate, signed by a majority of the incorporators or of the board of directors named in the articles of incorporation, stating that no part of the capital has been paid and the business has not begun, and thereupon the corporation is dissolved. [73:177:1925; NCL § 1672]—(NRS A 1993, 973; 1995, 1114; 1999, 1591)

**NRS 78.580 Procedure for dissolution after issuance of stock or beginning of business.**

1. If the board of directors of any corporation organized under this chapter, after the issuance of stock or the beginning of business, decides that the corporation should be dissolved, the board may adopt a resolution to that effect. If the corporation has issued no stock, only the directors need to approve the dissolution. If the corporation has issued stock, the directors must recommend the dissolution to the stockholders. The corporation shall notify each stockholder entitled to vote on dissolution, and the stockholders entitled to vote must approve the dissolution.

2. If the dissolution is approved by the directors or both the directors and stockholders, as respectively provided in subsection 1, the corporation shall file with the Office of the Secretary of State a certificate signed by an officer of the corporation setting forth that the dissolution has been approved by the directors, or by the directors and the stockholders, and a list of the names and addresses, either residence or business, of the corporation's president, secretary and treasurer, or the equivalent thereof, and all of its directors.

3. The dissolution takes effect upon the filing of the certificate of dissolution or upon a later date specified in the certificate, which must be not more than 90 days after the date on which the certificate is filed. [64:177:1925; NCL § 1663]—(NRS A 1963, 1391; 1979, 397; 1991, 1239; 1993, 973; 2001, 1376, 3199; 2003, 3105; 2003, 20th Special Session, 36)

**NRS 78.585 Continuation of corporation after dissolution for winding up business; limitation on actions by or against dissolved corporation.** The dissolution of a corporation does not impair any remedy or cause of action available to or against it or its directors, officers or shareholders arising before its dissolution and commenced within 2 years after the date of the dissolution. It continues as a body corporate for the purpose of prosecuting and defending suits, actions, proceedings and claims of any kind or character by or against it and of enabling it gradually to settle and close its business, to collect and discharge its obligations, to dispose of and convey its property, and to distribute its assets, but not for the purpose of continuing the business for which it was established. [65:177:1925]—(NRS A 1949, 170; 1955, 165; 1985, 1793)

**NRS 78.590 Trustees of dissolved corporation: Powers of directors.**

1. Upon the dissolution of any corporation under the provisions of NRS 78.580, or upon the expiration of

the period of its corporate existence, limited by its articles of incorporation, the directors become trustees thereof, with full power to settle the affairs, collect the outstanding debts, sell and convey the property, real and personal, and divide the money and other property among the stockholders, after paying or adequately providing for the payment of its liabilities and obligations.

2. After paying or adequately providing for the liabilities and obligations of the corporation, the trustees, with the written consent of stockholders holding stock in the corporation entitling them to exercise at least a majority of the voting power, may sell the remaining assets or any part thereof to a corporation organized under the laws of this or any other state, and take in payment therefor the stock or bonds, or both, of that corporation and distribute them among the stockholders of the liquidated corporation, in proportion to their interest therein. No such sale is valid as against any stockholder who, within 30 days after the mailing of notice to him of the sale, applies to the district court for an appraisal of the value of his interest in the assets so sold, and unless within 30 days after the appraisal is confirmed by the court the stockholders consenting to the sale, or some of them, pay to the objecting stockholder or deposit for his account, in the manner directed by the court, the amount of the appraisal. Upon the payment or deposit the interest of the objecting stockholder vests in the person or persons making the payment or deposit. [66:177:1925; NCL § 1665]—(NRS A 1993, 974)

**NRS 78.595 Trustees of dissolved corporation: Authority to sue and be sued; joint and several responsibility.** The persons constituted trustees as provided in NRS 78.590 shall have authority to sue for and recover the debts and property therein mentioned, by the name of the trustees of the corporation, describing it by its corporate name, and shall be suable by the same name for the debts owing by the corporation at the time of its dissolution, and shall be jointly and severally responsible for such debts, to the amounts of the moneys and property of the corporation which shall come into their hands or possession. [67:177:1925; NCL § 1666]

**NRS 78.600 Trustees or receivers for dissolved corporations: Appointment; powers.** When any corporation organized under this chapter shall be dissolved or cease to exist in any manner whatever, the district court, on application of any creditor or stockholder of the corporation, at any time, may either continue the directors trustees as provided in NRS 78.590, or appoint one or more persons to be receivers of and for the corporation, to take charge of the estate and effects thereof, and to collect the debts and property due and belonging to the corporation, with power to

prosecute and defend, in the name of the corporation, or otherwise, all such suits as may be necessary or proper for the purposes aforesaid, and to appoint an agent or agents under them, and to do all other acts which might be done by the corporation, if in being, that may be necessary for the final settlement of the unfinished business of the corporation. The powers of the trustees or receivers may be continued as long as the district court shall think necessary for the purposes aforesaid. [68:177:1925; NCL § 1667]

**NRS 78.605 Jurisdiction of district court.** The district court shall have jurisdiction of the application prescribed in NRS 78.600 and of all questions arising in the proceedings thereon, and may make such orders and decrees and issue injunctions therein as justice and equity shall require. [69:177:1925; NCL § 1668]

**NRS 78.610 Duties of trustees or receivers; payment and distribution to creditors and stockholders.** The trustees or receivers, after payment of all allowances, expenses and costs, and the satisfaction of all special and general liens upon the funds of the corporation to the extent of their lawful priority, shall pay the other debts due from the corporation, if the funds in their hands shall be sufficient therefor, and if not, they shall distribute the same ratably among all the creditors who shall prove their debts in the manner that shall be directed by an order or decree of the court for that purpose. If there shall be any balance remaining after the payment of the debts and necessary expenses (or the making of adequate provision therefor), they shall distribute and pay the same to and among those who shall be justly entitled thereto, as having been stockholders of the corporation, or their legal representatives. [70:177: 1925; NCL § 1669]

**NRS 78.615 Abatement of pending actions; substitution of dissolution trustees or receivers.** If any corporation organized under this chapter becomes dissolved by the expiration of its charter or otherwise, before final judgment obtained in any action pending or commenced in any court of record of this State against the corporation, the action shall not abate by reason thereof, but the dissolution of the corporation being suggested upon the record, and the names of the trustees or receivers of the corporation being entered upon the record, and notice thereof served upon the trustees or receivers, or if such service be impracticable upon the counsel of record in such case, the action shall proceed to final judgment against the trustees or receivers by the name of the corporation. [71:177:1925; NCL § 1670]

**NRS 78.620 Dissolution or forfeiture of charter by decree of court; filing.** Whenever any corporation is dissolved or its charter forfeited by decree or judgment of the district court, the decree or judgment shall be forthwith filed by the clerk of the court in the Office of the Secretary of State. [72:177:1925; NCL § 1671]

## Insolvency; Receivers and Trustees

### NRS 78.622 Reorganization under federal law: Powers of corporation.

1. If a corporation is under reorganization in a federal court pursuant to Title 11 of U.S.C., it may take any action necessary to carry out any proceeding and do any act directed by the court relating to reorganization, without further action by its directors or stockholders. This authority may be exercised by:

(a) The trustee in bankruptcy appointed by the court;

(b) Officers of the corporation designated by the court; or

(c) Any other representative appointed by the court, with the same effect as if exercised by the directors and stockholders of the corporation.

2. By filing a confirmed plan or order of reorganization, certified by the bankruptcy court, with the Secretary of State, the corporation may:

(a) Alter, amend or repeal its bylaws;

(b) Constitute or reconstitute and classify or reclassify its board of directors;

(c) Name, constitute or appoint directors and officers in place of or in addition to all or some of the directors or officers then in office;

(d) Amend its articles of incorporation;

(e) Make any change in its authorized and issued stock;

(f) Make any other amendment, change, alteration or provision authorized by this chapter; and

(g) Be dissolved, transfer all or part of its assets, or merge or consolidate, or make any other change authorized by this chapter.

3. In any action taken pursuant to subsections 1 and 2, a stockholder has no right to demand payment for his stock.

4. Any amendment of the articles of incorporation made pursuant to subsection 2 must be signed under penalty of perjury by the person authorized by the court and filed with the Secretary of State. If the amendment is filed in accordance with the order of reorganization, it becomes effective when it is filed unless otherwise ordered by the court.

5. Any filing with the Secretary of State pursuant to this section must be accompanied by the appropriate fee, if any. (Added to NRS by 1985, 1042; A 1993, 2765; 2001, 1376, 3199; 2003, 20th Special Session, 36)

### NRS 78.630 Application of creditors or stockholders of insolvent corporation for injunction and appointment of receiver or trustee; hearing. [Effective through June 30, 2008.]

1. Whenever any corporation becomes insolvent or suspends its ordinary business for want of money to carry on the business, or if its business has been and is being conducted at a great loss and greatly prejudicial to the interest of its creditors or stockholders, any creditors holding 10 percent of the outstanding indebtedness, or stockholders owning 10 percent of the outstanding stock entitled to vote, may, by petition setting forth the facts and circumstances of the case, apply to the district court of the county in which the registered office of the corporation is located for a writ of injunction and the appointment of a receiver or receivers or trustee or trustees.

2. The court, being satisfied by affidavit or otherwise of the sufficiency of the application and of the truth of the allegations contained in the petition and upon hearing after such notice as the court by order may direct, shall proceed in a summary way to hear the affidavits, proofs and allegations which may be offered in behalf of the parties.

3. If upon such inquiry it appears to the court that the corporation has become insolvent and is not about to resume its business in a short time thereafter, or that its business has been and is being conducted at a great loss and greatly prejudicial to the interests of its creditors or stockholders, so that its business cannot be conducted with safety to the public, it may issue an injunction to restrain the corporation and its officers and agents from exercising any of its privileges or franchises and from collecting or receiving any debts or paying out, selling, assigning or transferring any of its estate, money, lands, tenements or effects, except to a receiver appointed by the court, until the court otherwise orders. [46:177:1925; NCL § 1645]—(NRS A 1993, 974, 2765, 2820)

### NRS 78.630 Application of creditors or stockholders of insolvent corporation for injunction and appointment of receiver or trustee; hearing. [Effective July 1, 2008.]

1. Whenever any corporation becomes insolvent or suspends its ordinary business for want of money to carry on the business, or if its business has been and is being conducted at a great loss and greatly prejudicial to the interest of its creditors or stockholders, any creditors holding 10 percent of the outstanding indebtedness, or stockholders owning 10 percent of the outstanding stock entitled to vote, may, by petition setting forth the facts and circumstances of the case, apply to the district court of the county in which the principal office of the corporation is located or, if the principal office is not located in this State, to the district court in Carson City for a writ of injunction and the appointment of a receiver or receivers or trustee or trustees.

2. The court, being satisfied by affidavit or otherwise of the sufficiency of the application and of the truth of the allegations contained in the petition and upon hearing after such notice as the court by order may direct, shall proceed in a summary way to hear the affidavits, proofs and allegations which may be offered in behalf of the parties.

3. If upon such inquiry it appears to the court that the corporation has become insolvent and is not about to resume its business in a short time thereafter, or that its business has been and is being conducted at a great loss and greatly prejudicial to the interests of its creditors or stockholders, so that its business cannot be conducted with safety to the public, it may issue an injunction to restrain the corporation and its officers and agents from exercising any of its privileges or franchises and from collecting or receiving any debts or paying out, selling, assigning or transferring any of its estate, money, lands, tenements or effects, except to a receiver appointed by the court, until the court otherwise orders. [46:177:1925; NCL § 1645]—(NRS A 1993, 974, 2765, 2820; 2007, 2649, effective July 1, 2008)

### NRS 78.635 Appointment of receiver or trustee of insolvent corporation: Powers.

1. The district court, at the time of ordering the injunction, or at any time afterwards, may appoint a receiver or receivers or a trustee or trustees for the creditors and stockholders of the corporation.

2. The receiver or receivers or trustee or trustees shall have full power and authority:

(a) To demand, sue for, collect, receive and take into his or their possession all the goods and chattels, rights and credits, moneys and effects, lands and tenements, books, papers, choses in action, bills, notes and property, of every description of the corporation;

(b) To institute suits at law or in equity for the recovery of any estate, property, damages or demands existing in favor of the corporation;

(c) In his or their discretion to compound and settle with any debtor or creditor of the corporation, or with persons having possession of its property or in any way responsible at law or in equity to the corporation at the time of its insolvency or suspension of business, or afterwards, upon such terms and in such manner as he or they shall deem just and beneficial to the corporation; and

(d) In case of mutual dealings between the corporation and any person to allow just setoffs in favor of such person in all cases in which the same ought to be allowed according to law and equity.

3. A debtor who shall have in good faith paid his debt to the corporation without notice of its insolvency or suspension of business, shall not be liable therefor, and the receiver or receivers or trustee or trustees shall

have power to sell, convey and assign all the estate, rights and interests, and shall hold and dispose of the proceeds thereof under the directions of the district court. [Part 47:177:1925; NCL § 1646]—(NRS A 1969, 93)

### NRS 78.640 Property and privileges of insolvent corporation vest in appointed receiver.
All real and personal property of an insolvent corporation, wheresoever situated, and all its franchises, rights, privileges and effects shall, upon the appointment of a receiver, forthwith vest in him, and the corporation shall be divested of the title thereto. [48:177:1925; NCL § 1647]

### NRS 78.645 Corporation may resume control upon payment of debts and receipt of capital to conduct business; order of court dissolving corporation and forfeiting charter.

1. Whenever a receiver shall have been appointed as provided in NRS 78.635 and it shall afterwards appear that the debts of the corporation have been paid or provided for, and that there remains or can be obtained by further contributions sufficient capital to enable it to resume its business, the district court may, in its discretion, a proper case being shown, direct the receiver to reconvey to the corporation all its property, franchises, rights and effects, and thereafter the corporation may resume control of and enjoy the same as fully as if the receiver had never been appointed.

2. In every case in which the district court shall not direct such reconveyance, the court may, in its discretion, make a decree dissolving the corporation and declaring its charter forfeited and void. [49:177:1925; NCL § 1648]

### NRS 78.650 Stockholders' application for injunction and appointment of receiver when corporation mismanaged.

1. Any holder or holders of one-tenth of the issued and outstanding stock may apply to the district court, held in the district where the corporation has its principal place of business, for an order dissolving the corporation and appointing a receiver to wind up its affairs, and by injunction restrain the corporation from exercising any of its powers or doing business whatsoever, except by and through a receiver appointed by the court, whenever:

(a) The corporation has willfully violated its charter;

(b) Its trustees or directors have been guilty of fraud or collusion or gross mismanagement in the conduct or control of its affairs;

(c) Its trustees or directors have been guilty of misfeasance, malfeasance or nonfeasance;

(d) The corporation is unable to conduct the business or conserve its assets by reason of the act, neglect or refusal to function of any of the directors or trustees;

(e) The assets of the corporation are in danger of waste, sacrifice or loss through attachment, foreclosure, litigation or otherwise;

(f) The corporation has abandoned its business;

(g) The corporation has not proceeded diligently to wind up its affairs, or to distribute its assets in a reasonable time;

(h) The corporation has become insolvent;

(i) The corporation, although not insolvent, is for any cause not able to pay its debts or other obligations as they mature; or

(j) The corporation is not about to resume its business with safety to the public.

2. The application may be for the appointment of a receiver, without at the same time applying for the dissolution of the corporation, and notwithstanding the absence, if any there be, of any action or other proceeding in the premises pending in such court.

3. In any such application for a receivership, it is sufficient for a temporary appointment if notice of the same is given to the corporation alone, by process as in the case of an application for a temporary restraining order or injunction, and the hearing thereon may be had after 5 days' notice unless the court directs a longer or different notice and different parties.

4. The court may, if good cause exists therefor, appoint one or more receivers for such purpose, but in all cases directors or trustees who have been guilty of no negligence nor active breach of duty must be preferred in making the appointment. The court may at any time for sufficient cause make a decree terminating the receivership, or dissolving the corporation and terminating its existence, or both, as may be proper.

5. Receivers so appointed have, among the usual powers, all the functions, powers, tenure and duties to be exercised under the direction of the court as are conferred on receivers and as provided in NRS 78.635, 78.640 and 78.645, whether the corporation is insolvent or not.

[49a:177:1925; added 1941, 405; 1931 NCL § 1648.01]—(NRS A 1993, 2766)

**NRS 78.655 Reorganization of corporation by majority of stockholders during receivership.** Whenever stockholders holding stock entitling them to exercise at least a majority of the voting power of the corporation shall have agreed upon a plan for the reorganization of the corporation and a resumption by it of the management and control of its property and business, the corporation may, with the consent of the district court:

1. Upon the reconveyance to it of its property and franchises, mortgage the same for such amount as may be necessary for the purposes of reorganization; and

2. Issue bonds or other evidences of indebtedness, or additional stock of one or more classes, with or without nominal or par value, or both, or both bonds and stock, or certificates of investment or participation certificates, and use the same for the full or partial payment of the creditors who will accept the same, or otherwise dispose of the same for the purposes of the reorganization. [50:177:1925; NCL § 1649]

**NRS 78.660 Powers of district court.**

1. The court shall have power to send for persons and papers and to examine any persons, including the creditors and claimants, and the president, directors and other officers and agents of the corporation, on oath or affirmation, respecting its affairs and transactions and its estate, money, goods, chattels, credits, notes, bills and choses in action, real and personal estate and effects of every kind, and also respecting its debts, obligations, contracts and liabilities, and the claims against it.

2. If any person shall refuse to be sworn or affirmed, or to make answers to such questions as shall be put to him, or refuse to declare the whole truth touching the subject matter of the examination, the district court may commit such person to a place of confinement, there to remain until he shall submit himself to be examined, and pay all the costs of the proceedings against him. [51:177:1925; NCL § 1650]

**NRS 78.665 Receiver to take possession of corporate assets upon court order.** The receiver, upon order of the court, with the assistance of a peace officer, may break open, in the daytime, the houses, shops, warehouses, doors, trunks, chests or other places of the corporation where any of its goods, chattels, choses in action, notes, bills, moneys, books, papers or other writings or effects have been usually kept, or shall be, and take possession of the same and of the lands and tenements belonging to the corporation. [52:177:1925; NCL § 1651]

**NRS 78.670 Inventory, list of debts and reports by receiver.** The receiver, as soon as convenient, shall lay before the district court a full and complete inventory of all the estate, property and effects of the corporation, its nature and probable value, and an account of all debts due from and to it, as nearly as the same can be ascertained, and make a report to the court of his proceedings at least every 3 months thereafter during the continuance of the trust, and whenever he shall be so ordered. [53:177:1925; NCL § 1652]

**NRS 78.675 Creditors' proofs of claims; when participation barred; notice.** All creditors shall present and make proof to the receiver of their respective claims against the corporation within 6 months from the date of appointment of the receiver or trustee for the corporation, or sooner if the court shall order and direct, and all creditors and claimants failing to do so within the time limited by this section, or the time prescribed by the order of the court, shall by the direction of the court be barred from participating in the distribution of the assets of the corporation. The court shall also prescribe what notice, by publication or otherwise, shall be given to creditors of such limitation of time. [54:177:1925; A 1949, 158; 1943 NCL § 1653]

**NRS 78.680 Creditors' claims to be in writing under oath; examination of claimants.** Every claim against any corporation for which a receiver has been appointed shall be presented to the receiver in writing and upon oath. The claimant, if required, shall submit himself to such examination in relation to the claim as the court shall direct, and shall produce such books and papers relating to the claim as shall be required. The court shall have power to authorize the receiver to examine, under oath or affirmation, all witnesses produced before him touching the claim or any part thereof. [55:177:1925; NCL § 1654]

**NRS 78.685 Action on creditors' claims; appeal of disallowed claims.**

1. The clerk of the district court, immediately upon the expiration of the time fixed for the filing of claims, shall notify the trustee or receiver of the filing of the claims. The trustee or receiver shall inspect the claims and within 30 days notify each claimant of his decision. The trustee or receiver may require all creditors whose claims are disputed to submit themselves to an examination in relation to their claims, and to produce such books and papers relating to their claims as the trustee or receiver requests. The trustee or receiver may examine, under oath or affirmation, all witnesses produced before him regarding the claims, and shall pass upon and allow or disallow the claims, or any part thereof, and notify the claimants of his determination.

2. Every creditor or claimant who has received notice from the receiver or trustee that his claim has been disallowed in whole or in part may appeal to the district court within 30 days thereafter. The court, after a hearing, shall determine the rights of the parties. [56:177:1925; NCL § 1655] + [Part 57:177:1925; NCL § 1656]—(NRS A 1991, 1239)

**NRS 78.695 Substitution of receiver as party; abatement of actions.**

1. A receiver, upon application by him, shall be substituted as party plaintiff or complainant in the place and stead of the corporation in any suit or proceeding at law or in equity which was pending at the time of his appointment.

2. No action against a receiver of a corporation shall abate by reason of his death, but, upon suggestion of the facts on the record, shall be continued against his successor, or against the corporation in case no new receiver be appointed. [58:177:1925; NCL § 1657] + [59:177:1925; NCL § 1658]

**NRS 78.700 Sales of encumbered or deteriorating property.** Where property of an insolvent corporation is at the time of the appointment of a receiver encumbered with mortgages or other liens, the legality of which is brought in question, or the property is of a character which will materially deteriorate in value pending the litigation, the district court may order the receiver to sell the same, clear of encumbrances, at public or private sale, for the best price that can be obtained, and pay the money into court, there to remain subject to the same liens and equities of all parties in interest as was the property before sale, to be disposed of as the court shall direct. [60:177:1925; NCL § 1659]

**NRS 78.705 Compensation, costs and expenses of receiver.** Before distribution of the assets of an insolvent corporation among the creditors or stockholders, the district court shall allow a reasonable compensation to the receiver for his services and the costs and expenses of the administration of the trust, and the cost of the proceedings in the court, to be first paid out of the assets. [61:177:1925; NCL § 1660]

**NRS 78.710 Distribution of money to creditors and stockholders.** After payment of all allowances, expenses and costs, and the satisfaction of all special and general liens upon the funds of the corporation to the extent of their lawful priority, the creditors shall be paid proportionately to the amount of their respective debts, excepting mortgage and judgment creditors when the judgment has not been by confession for the purpose of preferring creditors. The creditors shall be entitled to distribution on debts not due, making in such case a rebate of interest, when interest is not accruing on the same. The surplus funds, if any, after payment of the creditors and the costs, expenses and allowances, shall be distributed among the stockholders or their legal representatives in proportion to their interests. [62:177:1925; NCL § 1661]

**NRS 78.715 Acts of majority of receivers effectual; removal and vacancies.**

1. Every matter and thing by this chapter required to be done by receivers or trustees shall be good and effectual, to all intents and purposes, if performed by a majority of them.

2. The district court may remove any receiver or trustee and appoint another or others in his place to fill any vacancy which may occur. [63:177:1925; NCL § 1662]

**NRS 78.720 Employees' liens for wages when corporation insolvent.**

1. Whenever any corporation becomes insolvent or is dissolved in any way or for any cause, the employees doing labor or service, of whatever character, in the regular employ of the corporation, have a lien upon the assets thereof for the amount of wages due to them, not exceeding $1,000, which have been earned within 3 months before the date of the insolvency or dissolution, which must be paid before any other debt of the corporation.

2. The word "employees" does not include any of the officers of the corporation. [86:177:1925; NCL § 1685]—(NRS A 1959, 607; 1983, 1362)

## Reincorporation; Renewal and Revival of Charters

**NRS 78.725 Domestic corporations in existence on April 1, 1925, may reincorporate under this chapter.**

1. Any corporation organized and existing under the laws of this State on April 1, 1925, may reincorporate under this chapter, either under the same or a different name, by:

(a) Filing with the Secretary of State a certificate signed by its president and attested by its secretary and duly authorized by a meeting of the stockholders called for that purpose, setting forth the statements required in an original certificate of incorporation by NRS 78.035; and

(b) Surrendering the existing charter or certificate of incorporation of the corporation, and accepting the provisions of this chapter.

2. Upon the filing of the certificate, the corporation shall be deemed to be incorporated under this chapter and is entitled to and possesses all the privileges, franchises and powers as if originally incorporated under this chapter. All the properties, rights and privileges theretofore belonging to the corporation, which were acquired by gift, grant, conveyance, assignment or otherwise, are hereby ratified, approved and confirmed and assured to the corporation with like effect and to all intents and purposes as if the same had been originally acquired through incorporation under this chapter.

3. Any corporation reincorporating under this chapter is subject to all the contracts, duties and obligations theretofore resting upon the corporation whose charter or certificate of incorporation is thus surrendered or to which the corporation is then in any way liable. [82:177:1925; NCL § 1681]—(NRS A 1971, 1105; 2003, 3106)

**NRS 78.730 Renewal or revival: Procedure; fee; certificate as evidence. [Effective through June 30, 2008.]**

1. Except as otherwise provided in NRS 78.152, any corporation which did exist or is existing under the laws of this State may, upon complying with the provisions of NRS 78.180, procure a renewal or revival of its charter for any period, together with all the rights, franchises, privileges and immunities, and subject to all its existing and preexisting debts, duties and liabilities secured or imposed by its original charter and amendments thereto, or existing charter, by filing:

(a) A certificate with the Secretary of State, which must set forth:

(1) The name of the corporation, which must be the name of the corporation at the time of the renewal or revival, or its name at the time its original charter expired.

(2) The name of the person designated as the resident agent of the corporation, his street address for the service of process, and his mailing address if different from his street address.

(3) The date when the renewal or revival of the charter is to commence or be effective, which may be, in cases of a revival, before the date of the certificate.

(4) Whether or not the renewal or revival is to be perpetual, and, if not perpetual, the time for which the renewal or revival is to continue.

(5) That the corporation desiring to renew or revive its charter is, or has been, organized and carrying on the business authorized by its existing or original charter and amendments thereto, and desires to renew or continue through revival its existence pursuant to and subject to the provisions of this chapter.

(b) A list of its president, secretary and treasurer, or the equivalent thereof, and all of its directors and their addresses, either residence or business.

2. A corporation whose charter has not expired and is being renewed shall cause the certificate to be signed by an officer of the corporation. The certificate must be approved by a majority of the voting power of the shares.

3. A corporation seeking to revive its original or amended charter shall cause the certificate to be signed by a person or persons designated or appointed by the stockholders of the corporation. The signing and filing of the certificate must be approved by the written consent of stockholders of the corporation holding at least a majority of the voting power and must contain a recital that this consent was secured. If no stock has been issued, the certificate must contain a statement of that fact, and a majority of the directors then in office may designate the person to sign the certificate. The corporation shall pay to the Secretary of State the fee required to establish a new corporation pursuant to the provisions of this chapter.

4. The filed certificate, or a copy thereof which has been

required to establish a new corporation pursuant to the provisions of this chapter.

4. The filed certificate, or a copy thereof which has been certified under the hand and seal of the Secretary of State, must be received in all courts and places as prima facie evidence of the facts therein stated and of the existence and incorporation of the corporation therein named. [93:177:1925]—(NRS A 1937, 4; 1953, 314; 1985, 1872; 1993, 975; 1995, 2100; 1997, 705; 1999, 1591; 2003, 3106; 2003, 20th Special Session, 37; 2007, 1319)

### NRS 78.730 Renewal or revival: Procedure; fee; certificate as evidence. [Effective July 1, 2008.]

1. Except as otherwise provided in NRS 78.152, any corporation which did exist or is existing under the laws of this State may, upon complying with the provisions of NRS 78.180, procure a renewal or revival of its charter for any period, together with all the rights, franchises, privileges and immunities, and subject to all its existing and preexisting debts, duties and liabilities secured or imposed by its original charter and amendments thereto, or existing charter, by filing:

(a) A certificate with the Secretary of State, which must set forth:

(1) The name of the corporation, which must be the name of the corporation at the time of the renewal or revival, or its name at the time its original charter expired.

(2) The information required pursuant to NRS 77.310.

(3) The date when the renewal or revival of the charter is to commence or be effective, which may be, in cases of a revival, before the date of the certificate.

(4) Whether or not the renewal or revival is to be perpetual, and, if not perpetual, the time for which the renewal or revival is to continue.

(5) That the corporation desiring to renew or revive its charter is, or has been, organized and carrying on the business authorized by its existing or original charter and amendments thereto, and desires to renew or continue through revival its existence pursuant to and subject to the provisions of this chapter.

(b) A list of its president, secretary and treasurer, or the equivalent thereof, and all of its directors and their addresses, either residence or business.

2. A corporation whose charter has not expired and is being renewed shall cause the certificate to be signed by an officer of the corporation. The certificate must be approved by a majority of the voting power of the shares.

3. A corporation seeking to revive its original or amended charter shall cause the certificate to be signed by a person or persons designated or appointed by the stockholders of the corporation. The signing and filing of the certificate must be approved by the written consent of stockholders of the corporation holding at least a majority of the voting power and must contain a recital that this consent was secured. If no stock has been issued, the certificate must contain a statement of that fact, and a majority of the directors then in office may designate the person to sign the certificate. The corporation shall pay to the Secretary of State the fee required to establish a new corporation pursuant to the provisions of this chapter.

4. The filed certificate, or a copy thereof which has been certified under the hand and seal of the Secretary of State, must be received in all courts and places as prima facie evidence of the facts therein stated and of the existence and incorporation of the corporation therein named. [93:177:1925]—(NRS A 1937, 4; 1953, 314; 1985, 1872; 1993, 975; 1995, 2100; 1997, 705; 1999, 1591; 2003, 3106; 2003, 20th Special Session, 37; 2007, 1319, 2649, effective July 1, 2008)

### NRS 78.740 Renewal or revival: Status of corporation.

1. Any corporation existing on or incorporated after April 1, 1925, desiring to renew or revive its corporate existence, upon complying with the provisions of this chapter, is and continues for the time stated in its certificate of renewal to be a corporation, and in addition to the rights, privileges and immunities conferred by its original charter, possesses and enjoys all the benefits of this chapter that are applicable to the nature of its business, and is subject to the restrictions and liabilities by this chapter imposed on such corporations.

2. Except as otherwise provided in NRS 78.185, a renewal or revival pursuant to NRS 78.730 relates back to the date on which the corporation's charter expired or was revoked and renews or revives the corporation's charter and right to transact business as if such right had at all times remained in full force and effect. [95:177:1925; NCL § 1694]—(NRS A 1993, 976; 2007, 2421)

## Suits Against Corporations, Directors, Officers, Employees, Agents and Stockholders

### NRS 78.745 Action against stockholder for unpaid subscriptions; limitation of action. No action shall be brought by the corporation against any stockholder for any unpaid subscription unless within 2 years after the debt becomes due, and no action shall be brought against the stockholder after he shall cease to be the owner of the shares, unless brought within 2 years from the time he shall have ceased to be a stockholder. [17:177:1925; NCL § 1616]

### NRS 78.746 Action against stockholder by judgment creditor; limitations.

1. On application to a court of competent jurisdiction by a judgment creditor of a stockholder, the court may

charge the stockholder's stock with payment of the unsatisfied amount of the judgment with interest. To the extent so charged, the judgment creditor has only the rights of an assignee of the stockholder's stock.

2. This section:

(a) Applies only to a corporation that:

(1) Has more than 1 but fewer than 75 stockholders of record at any time.

(2) Is not a subsidiary of a publicly traded corporation, either in whole or in part.

(3) Is not a professional corporation as defined in NRS 89.020.

(b) Does not apply to any liability of a stockholder that exists as the result of an action filed before July 1, 2007.

(c) Provides the exclusive remedy by which a judgment creditor of a stockholder or an assignee of a stockholder may satisfy a judgment out of the stockholder's stock of the corporation.

(d) Does not deprive any stockholder of the benefit of any exemption applicable to the stockholder's stock.

(e) Does not supersede any private agreement between a stockholder and a creditor. (Added to NRS by 2007, 2639)

### NRS 78.747 Liability of stockholder, director or officer for debt or liability of corporation.

1. Except as otherwise provided by specific statute, no stockholder, director or officer of a corporation is individually liable for a debt or liability of the corporation, unless the stockholder, director or officer acts as the alter ego of the corporation.

2. A stockholder, director or officer acts as the alter ego of a corporation if:

(a) The corporation is influenced and governed by the stockholder, director or officer;

(b) There is such unity of interest and ownership that the corporation and the stockholder, director or officer are inseparable from each other; and

(c) Adherence to the corporate fiction of a separate entity would sanction fraud or promote a manifest injustice.

3. The question of whether a stockholder, director or officer acts as the alter ego of a corporation must be determined by the court as a matter of law. (Added to NRS by 2001, 3170)

### NRS 78.750 Service of process on corporations. [Effective through June 30, 2008.]

1. In any action commenced against any corporation in any court of this State, service of process may be made in the manner provided by law and rule of court for the service of civil process.

2. Service of process on a corporation whose charter has been revoked or which has been continued as a body corporate pursuant to NRS 78.585 may be made by mailing copies of the process and any associated records by certified mail, with return receipt requested, to:

(a) The resident agent of the corporation, if there is one; and

(b) Each officer and director of the corporation as named in the list last filed with the Secretary of State before the dissolution or expiration of the corporation or the forfeiture of its charter. The manner of serving process described in this subsection does not affect the validity of any other service authorized by law. [81:177:1925; NCL § 1680]—(NRS A 1979, 568; 1997, 474; 2001, 1377, 3199; 2003, 3107)

### NRS 78.750 Service of process on corporations. [Effective July 1, 2008.]

1. In any action commenced against any corporation in any court of this State, service of process may be made in the manner provided by law and rule of court for the service of civil process.

2. Service of process on a corporation whose charter has been revoked or which has been continued as a body corporate pursuant to NRS 78.585 may be made by mailing copies of the process and any associated records by certified mail, with return receipt requested, to:

(a) The registered agent of the corporation, if there is one; and

(b) Each officer and director of the corporation as named in the list last filed with the Secretary of State before the dissolution or expiration of the corporation or the forfeiture of its charter. The manner of serving process described in this subsection does not affect the validity of any other service authorized by law. [81:177:1925; NCL § 1680]—(NRS A 1979, 568; 1997, 474; 2001, 1377, 3199; 2003, 3107; 2007, 2650, effective July 1, 2008)

### NRS 78.7502 Discretionary and mandatory indemnification of officers, directors, employees and agents: General provisions.

1. A corporation may indemnify any person who was or is a party or is threatened to be made a party to any threatened, pending or completed action, suit or proceeding, whether civil, criminal, administrative or investigative, except an action by or in the right of the corporation, by reason of the fact that he is or was a director, officer, employee or agent of the corporation, or is or was serving at the request of the corporation as a director, officer, employee or agent of another corporation, partnership, joint venture, trust or other enterprise, against expenses, including attorneys' fees, judgments, fines and amounts paid in settlement actually and reasonably incurred by him in connection with the action, suit or proceeding if he:

(a) Is not liable pursuant to NRS 78.138; or

(b) Acted in good faith and in a manner which he reasonably believed to be in or not opposed to the best interests of the corporation, and, with respect to any criminal action or proceeding, had no reasonable cause to believe his conduct was unlawful. The termination of any action, suit or proceeding by judgment, order, settlement, conviction or upon a plea of nolo contendere or its equivalent, does not, of itself, create a presumption that the person is liable pursuant to NRS 78.138 or did not act in good faith and in a manner which he reasonably believed to be in or not opposed to the best interests of the corporation, or that, with respect to any criminal action or proceeding, he had reasonable cause to believe that his conduct was unlawful.

2. A corporation may indemnify any person who was or is a party or is threatened to be made a party to any threatened, pending or completed action or suit by or in the right of the corporation to procure a judgment in its favor by reason of the fact that he is or was a director, officer, employee or agent of the corporation, or is or was serving at the request of the corporation as a director, officer, employee or agent of another corporation, partnership, joint venture, trust or other enterprise against expenses, including amounts paid in settlement and attorneys' fees actually and reasonably incurred by him in connection with the defense or settlement of the action or suit if he:

(a) Is not liable pursuant to NRS 78.138; or

(b) Acted in good faith and in a manner which he reasonably believed to be in or not opposed to the best interests of the corporation. Indemnification may not be made for any claim, issue or matter as to which such a person has been adjudged by a court of competent jurisdiction, after exhaustion of all appeals therefrom, to be liable to the corporation or for amounts paid in settlement to the corporation, unless and only to the extent that the court in which the action or suit was brought or other court of competent jurisdiction determines upon application that in view of all the circumstances of the case, the person is fairly and reasonably entitled to indemnity for such expenses as the court deems proper.

3. To the extent that a director, officer, employee or agent of a corporation has been successful on the merits or otherwise in defense of any action, suit or proceeding referred to in subsections 1 and 2, or in defense of any claim, issue or matter therein, the corporation shall indemnify him against expenses, including attorneys' fees, actually and reasonably incurred by him in connection with the defense. (Added to NRS by 1997, 694; A 2001, 3175)

**NRS 78.751 Authorization required for discretionary indemnification; advancement of expenses; limitation on indemnification and advancement of expenses.**

1. Any discretionary indemnification pursuant to NRS 78.7502, unless ordered by a court or advanced pursuant to subsection 2, may be made by the corporation only as authorized in the specific case upon a determination that indemnification of the director, officer, employee or agent is proper in the circumstances. The determination must be made:

(a) By the stockholders;

(b) By the board of directors by majority vote of a quorum consisting of directors who were not parties to the action, suit or proceeding;

(c) If a majority vote of a quorum consisting of directors who were not parties to the action, suit or proceeding so orders, by independent legal counsel in a written opinion; or

(d) If a quorum consisting of directors who were not parties to the action, suit or proceeding cannot be obtained, by independent legal counsel in a written opinion.

2. The articles of incorporation, the bylaws or an agreement made by the corporation may provide that the expenses of officers and directors incurred in defending a civil or criminal action, suit or proceeding must be paid by the corporation as they are incurred and in advance of the final disposition of the action, suit or proceeding, upon receipt of an undertaking by or on behalf of the director or officer to repay the amount if it is ultimately determined by a court of competent jurisdiction that he is not entitled to be indemnified by the corporation. The provisions of this subsection do not affect any rights to advancement of expenses to which corporate personnel other than directors or officers may be entitled under any contract or otherwise by law.

3. The indemnification pursuant to NRS 78.7502 and advancement of expenses authorized in or ordered by a court pursuant to this section:

(a) Does not exclude any other rights to which a person seeking indemnification or advancement of expenses may be entitled under the articles of incorporation or any bylaw, agreement, vote of stockholders or disinterested directors or otherwise, for either an action in his official capacity or an action in another capacity while holding his office, except that indemnification, unless ordered by a court pursuant to NRS 78.7502 or for the advancement of expenses made pursuant to subsection 2, may not be made to or on behalf of any director or officer if a final adjudication establishes that his acts or omissions involved intentional misconduct, fraud or a knowing violation of the law and was material to the cause of action.

(b) Continues for a person who has ceased to be a director, officer, employee or agent and inures to the benefit of the heirs, executors and administrators of such a person. (Added to NRS by 1969, 118; A 1987, 83; 1993, 976; 1997, 706; 2001, 1377, 3199)

**NRS 78.752 Insurance and other financial arrangements against liability of directors, officers, employees and agents.**

1. A corporation may purchase and maintain insurance or make other financial arrangements on behalf of any person who is or was a director, officer, employee or agent of the corporation, or is or was serving at the request of the corporation as a director, officer, employee or agent of another corporation, partnership, joint venture, trust or other enterprise for any liability asserted against him and liability and expenses incurred by him in his capacity as a director, officer, employee or agent, or arising out of his status as such, whether or not the corporation has the authority to indemnify him against such liability and expenses.

2. The other financial arrangements made by the corporation pursuant to subsection 1 may include the following:

(a) The creation of a trust fund.

(b) The establishment of a program of self-insurance.

(c) The securing of its obligation of indemnification by granting a security interest or other lien on any assets of the corporation.

(d) The establishment of a letter of credit, guaranty or surety. No financial arrangement made pursuant to this subsection may provide protection for a person adjudged by a court of competent jurisdiction, after exhaustion of all appeals therefrom, to be liable for intentional misconduct, fraud or a knowing violation of law, except with respect to the advancement of expenses or indemnification ordered by a court.

3. Any insurance or other financial arrangement made on behalf of a person pursuant to this section may be provided by the corporation or any other person approved by the board of directors, even if all or part of the other person's stock or other securities is owned by the corporation.

4. In the absence of fraud:

(a) The decision of the board of directors as to the propriety of the terms and conditions of any insurance or other financial arrangement made pursuant to this section and the choice of the person to provide the insurance or other financial arrangement is conclusive; and

(b) The insurance or other financial arrangement:

(1) Is not void or voidable; and

(2) Does not subject any director approving it to personal liability for his action, even if a director approving the insurance or other financial arrangement is a beneficiary of the insurance or other financial arrangement.

5. A corporation or its subsidiary which provides self-insurance for itself or for another affiliated corporation pursuant to this section is not subject to the provisions of title 57 of NRS. (Added to NRS by 1987, 80)

## Secretary of State: Duties and Fees

**NRS 78.755 Duties: Collection of fees; employment of new technology to aid in performance.**

1. The Secretary of State, for services relating to his official duties and the records of his office, shall charge and collect the fees designated in NRS 78.760 to 78.785, inclusive.

2. The Secretary of State may accept the filing of records by facsimile machine and employ new technology, as it is developed, to aid in the performance of all duties required by law. The Secretary of State may establish rules, fee schedules and regulations not inconsistent with law, for filing records by facsimile machine and for the adoption, employment and use of new technology in the performance of his duties. [Part 1:52:1933; A 1949, 363; 1951, 393] + [Part 2:52:1933; A 1949, 409; 1943 NCL § 7421.02]—(NRS A 1979, 76; 1991, 1239; 1997, 2810; 2003, 3107)

**NRS 78.760 Filing fees: Articles of incorporation.**

1. The fee for filing articles of incorporation is prescribed in the following schedule:

If the amount represented by the total number of shares provided for in the articles is:

$75,000 or less ........................................................$75

Over $75,000 and not over $200,000 ........................175

Over $200,000 and not over $500,000 ......................275

Over $500,000 and not over $1,000,000 ...................375

Over $1,000,000:

    For the first $1,000,000 .........................................375

    For each additional $500,000 or fraction thereof ..275

2. The maximum fee which may be charged pursuant to this section is $35,000 for:

(a) The original filing of articles of incorporation.

(b) A subsequent filing of any instrument which authorizes an increase in stock.

3. For the purposes of computing the filing fees according to the schedule in subsection 1, the amount represented by the total number of shares provided for in the articles of incorporation is:

(a) The aggregate par value of the shares, if only shares with a par value are therein provided for;

(b) The product of the number of shares multiplied by $1, regardless of any lesser amount prescribed as the value or consideration for which shares may be issued and disposed of, if only shares without par value are therein provided for; or

(c) The aggregate par value of the shares with a par value plus the product of the number of shares without par value multiplied by $1, regardless of any lesser amount prescribed as the value or consideration for which the shares without par value may be issued and disposed of, if shares with and without par value are therein provided for. For the purposes of this subsection, shares with no prescribed par value shall be deemed shares without par value.

4. The Secretary of State shall calculate filing fees pursuant to this section with respect to shares with a par value of less than one tenth of a cent as if the par value were one-tenth of a cent. [Part 1:52:1933; A 1949, 363; 1951, 393]—(NRS A 1975, 478; 1977, 402; 1983, 690; 1989, 978; 1991, 1240; 1993, 555, 978; 1995, 1115; 2001, 1378, 3176, 3199; 2003, 20th Special Session, 37)

### NRS 78.765 Filing fees: Certificate changing number of authorized shares; certificate of amendment to articles; certificate of correction; certificate of designation; certificate of termination; certificate of withdrawal.

1. The fee for filing a certificate changing the number of authorized shares pursuant to NRS 78.209 or a certificate of amendment to articles of incorporation that increases the corporation's authorized stock or a certificate of correction that increases the corporation's authorized stock is the difference between the fee computed at the rates specified in NRS 78.760 upon the total authorized stock of the corporation, including the proposed increase, and the fee computed at the rates specified in NRS 78.760 upon the total authorized capital, excluding the proposed increase. In no case may the amount be less than $175.

2. The fee for filing a certificate of amendment to articles of incorporation that does not increase the corporation's authorized stock or a certificate of correction that does not increase the corporation's authorized stock is $175.

3. The fee for filing a certificate or an amended certificate pursuant to NRS 78.1955 is $175.

4. The fee for filing a certificate of termination pursuant to NRS 78.209, 78.380 or 78.390 or a certificate of withdrawal pursuant to NRS 78.1955 is $175. [Part 1:52:1933; A 1949, 363; 1951, 393]—(NRS A 1983, 691; 1989, 978; 1991, 1240; 1993, 979; 1995, 1115, 2101; 1997, 708; 1999, 1592; 2001, 1379, 3177, 3199; 2003, 20th Special Session, 38)

### NRS 78.767 Filing fees: Certificates of restated articles of incorporation.

1. The fee for filing a certificate of restated articles of incorporation that does not increase the corporation's authorized stock is $175.

2. The fee for filing a certificate of restated articles of incorporation that increases the corporation's authorized stock is the difference between the fee computed

pursuant to NRS 78.760 based upon the total authorized stock of the corporation, including the proposed increase, and the fee computed pursuant to NRS 78.760 based upon the total authorized stock of the corporation, excluding the proposed increase. In no case may the amount be less than $175. (Added to NRS by 1959, 682; A 1983, 691; 1989, 979; 1993, 979; 1995, 1116; 2001, 3177; 2003, 20th Special Session, 39)

### NRS 78.780 Filing fee: Certificate of dissolution.

The fee for filing a certificate of dissolution whether it occurs before or after payment of capital and beginning of business is $75. [Part 1:52:1933; A 1949, 363; 1951, 393]—(NRS A 1981, 1890; 1989, 979; 1993, 979; 2001, 3178; 2003, 20th Special Session, 39; 2005, 2252)

### NRS 78.785 Miscellaneous fees. [Effective through June 30, 2008.]

1. The fee for filing a certificate of change of location of a corporation's registered office and resident agent, or a new designation of resident agent, is $60.

2. The fee for certifying a copy of articles of incorporation is $30.

3. The fee for certifying a copy of an amendment to articles of incorporation, or to a copy of the articles as amended, is $30.

4. The fee for certifying an authorized printed copy of the general corporation law as compiled by the Secretary of State is $30.

5. The fee for reserving a corporate name is $25.

6. The fee for signing a certificate of corporate existence which does not list the previous records relating to the corporation, or a certificate of change in a corporate name, is $50.

7. The fee for signing a certificate of corporate existence which lists the previous records relating to the corporation is $50.

8. The fee for signing, certifying or filing any certificate or record not provided for in NRS 78.760 to 78.785, inclusive, is $50.

9. The fee for copies provided by the Office of the Secretary of State is $2 per page.

10. The fees for filing articles of incorporation, articles of merger, or certificates of amendment increasing the basic surplus of a mutual or reciprocal insurer must be computed pursuant to NRS 78.760, 78.765 and 92A.210, on the basis of the amount of basic surplus of the insurer.

11. The fee for examining and provisionally approving any record at any time before the record is presented for filing is $125. [Part 1:52:1933; A 1949, 363; 1951, 393]—(NRS A 1959, 689; 1975, 565; 1977, 403; 1979, 398; 1981, 141; 1983, 692; 1985, 1873; 1987, 1058; 1989, 979; 1991, 1241; 1993, 979; 1995, 1116; 2001, 1379,

3178, 3199; 2003, 225, 3107; 2003, 20th Special Session, 39; 2005, 2252)

## NRS 78.785 Miscellaneous fees. [Effective July 1, 2008.]

1. The fee for certifying a copy of articles of incorporation is $30.

2. The fee for certifying a copy of an amendment to articles of incorporation, or to a copy of the articles as amended, is $30.

3. The fee for certifying an authorized printed copy of the general corporation law as compiled by the Secretary of State is $30.

4. The fee for reserving a corporate name is $25.

5. The fee for signing a certificate of corporate existence which does not list the previous records relating to the corporation, or a certificate of change in a corporate name, is $50.

6. The fee for signing a certificate of corporate existence which lists the previous records relating to the corporation is $50.

7. The fee for signing, certifying or filing any certificate or record not provided for in NRS 78.760 to 78.785, inclusive, is $50.

8. The fee for copies provided by the Office of the Secretary of State is $2 per page.

9. The fees for filing articles of incorporation, articles of merger, or certificates of amendment increasing the basic surplus of a mutual or reciprocal insurer must be computed pursuant to NRS 78.760, 78.765 and 92A.210, on the basis of the amount of basic surplus of the insurer.

10. The fee for examining and provisionally approving any record at any time before the record is presented for filing is $125. [Part 1:52:1933; A 1949, 363; 1951, 393]—(NRS A 1959, 689; 1975, 565; 1977, 403; 1979, 398; 1981, 141; 1983, 692; 1985, 1873; 1987, 1058; 1989, 979; 1991, 1241; 1993, 979; 1995, 1116; 2001, 1379, 3178, 3199; 2003, 225, 3107; 2003, 20th Special Session, 39; 2005, 2252; 2007, 2650, effective July 1, 2008)

## Miscellaneous Provisions

## NRS 78.795 Registration of natural person or corporation willing to serve as resident agent for corporation, limited liability company or limited partnership. [Effective through June 30, 2008.]

1. Any natural person or corporation residing or located in this State may register for that calendar year his willingness to serve as the resident agent of a domestic or foreign corporation, limited-liability company or limited partnership with the Secretary of State. The registration must state the full, legal name of the person or corporation willing to serve as the resident

agent and be accompanied by a fee of $500 per office location of the resident agent.

2. The Secretary of State shall maintain a list of those persons who are registered pursuant to subsection 1 and make the list available to persons seeking to do business in this State.

3. The Secretary of State may amend any information provided in the list if a person who is included in the list:

(a) Requests the amendment; and

(b) Pays a fee of $50.

4. The Secretary of State may adopt regulations prescribing the content, maintenance and presentation of the list. (Added to NRS by 1995, 1111; A 1999, 1593; 2003, 20th Special Session, 39)

## NRS 78.795 Registration of natural person or corporation willing to serve as registered agent for corporation, limited liability company or limited partnership. [Effective July 1, 2008.]

1. Any natural person or corporation residing or located in this State may register for that calendar year his willingness to serve as the registered agent of a domestic or foreign corporation, limited-liability company or limited partnership with the Secretary of State. The registration must state the full, legal name of the person or corporation willing to serve as the registered agent and be accompanied by a fee of $500 per office location of the registered agent.

2. The Secretary of State shall maintain a list of those persons who are registered pursuant to subsection 1 and make the list available to persons seeking to do business in this State.

3. The Secretary of State may amend any information provided in the list if a person who is included in the list:

(a) Requests the amendment; and

(b) Pays a fee of $50.

4. The Secretary of State may adopt regulations prescribing the content, maintenance and presentation of the list. (Added to NRS by 1995, 1111; A 1999, 1593; 2003, 20th Special Session, 39; 2007, 2651, effective July 1, 2008)

## CHAPTER 78A CLOSE CORPORATIONS

### General Provisions

NRS 78A.001 Definitions.

NRS 78A.004 "Record" defined.

NRS 78A.006 "Sign" defined.

NRS 78A.008 "Signature" defined.

NRS 78A.010 Applicability of chapter.

NRS 78A.013 Form required for filing of records.

### Formation

### Shares of Stock

### Powers and Duties

### Termination of Status as Close Corporation

* * *

### General Provisions

**NRS 78A.001 Definitions.** As used in this chapter, unless the context otherwise requires, the words and terms defined in NRS 78A.004, 78A.006 and 78A.008 have the meanings ascribed to them in those sections. (Added to NRS by 2003, 3108)

**NRS 78A.004 "Record" defined.** "Record" means information that is inscribed on a tangible medium or that is stored in an electronic or other medium and is retrievable in perceivable form. (Added to NRS by 2003, 3108)

**NRS 78A.006 "Sign" defined.** "Sign" means to affix a signature to a record. (Added to NRS by 2003, 3108)

**NRS 78A.008 "Signature" defined.** "Signature" means a name, word, symbol or mark executed or otherwise adopted, or a record encrypted or similarly processed in whole or in part, by a person with the present intent to identify himself and adopt or accept a record. The term includes, without limitation, an electronic signature as defined in NRS 719.100. (Added to NRS by 2003, 3108)

**NRS 78A.010 Applicability of chapter.** The provisions of this chapter apply to all close corporations formed pursuant to NRS 78A.020. Unless otherwise provided by this chapter, the provisions of chapter 78 of NRS are applicable to all close corporations. (Added to NRS by 1989, 940)

**NRS 78A.013 Form required for filing of records.**

1. Each record filed with the Secretary of State pursuant to this chapter must be on or accompanied by a form prescribed by the Secretary of State.

2. The Secretary of State may refuse to file a record which does not comply with subsection 1 or which does not contain all the information required by statute for filing the record.

3. If the provisions of the form prescribed by the Secretary of State conflict with the provisions of any record that is submitted for filing with the form:

(a) The provisions of the form control for all purposes with respect to the information that is required by statute to appear in the record in order for the record to be filed; and

(b) Unless otherwise provided in the record, the provisions of the record control in every other situation.

4. The Secretary of State may by regulation provide for the electronic filing of records with the Office of the Secretary of State. (Added to NRS by 2003, 20th Special Session, 40)

**NRS 78A.015 Filing of records written in language other than English.** No record which is written in a language other than English may be filed or submitted for filing in the Office of the Secretary of State pursuant to the provisions of this chapter unless it is accompanied by a verified translation of that record into the English language. (Added to NRS by 1995, 1117; A 2003, 3108)

### Formation

**NRS 78A.020 Filing requirements; required and optional provisions of articles of incorporation.**

1. A close corporation must be formed in accordance with NRS 78.030 to 78.055, inclusive, subject to the following requirements:

(a) All of the issued stock of the corporation of all classes, exclusive of treasury shares, must be represented by certificates and must be held of record by a specified number of persons, not to exceed 30.

(b) All of the issued stock of all classes must be subject to one or more of the restrictions on transfer pursuant to NRS 78A.050.

(c) The corporation shall not offer any of its stock of any class that would constitute a public offering within the meaning of the Securities Act of 1933, 15 U.S.C. §§ 77 et seq.

2. The articles of incorporation of a close corporation must:

(a) Set forth the matters required by NRS 78.035 except that the articles must state that there will be no board of directors if so agreed pursuant to NRS 78A.070.

(b) Contain a heading stating the name of the corporation and that it is a close corporation.

3. The articles of incorporation of a close corporation may set forth the qualifications of stockholders by specifying the classes of persons who are entitled to be holders of record of stock of any class, the classes of persons who are not entitled to be holders of record of stock of any class, or both.

4. To determine the number of holders of record of the stock of a close corporation, stock that is held in joint or common tenancy or by community property must be treated as held by one stockholder. (Added to NRS by 1989, 941; A 1993, 980)

**NRS 78A.030 Procedure for existing corporation to become close corporation.**

1. Any corporation organized under chapter 78 of NRS may become a close corporation pursuant to this chapter by signing, filing and recording, in accordance with NRS 78.390, a certificate of amendment of the certificate of incorporation which must:

(a) Contain a statement that the corporation elects to become a close corporation; and

(b) Meet the requirements of paragraph (a) of subsection 2 of NRS 78A.020.

2. Except as otherwise provided in subsection 3, the amendment must be adopted in accordance with the requirements of NRS 78.380 or 78.390.

3. If an amendment is adopted in accordance with the requirements of NRS 78.390, it must be approved by a vote of the holders of record of at least two-thirds of the shares of each class of stock of the corporation that are outstanding and entitled to vote, unless the articles of incorporation or bylaws require approval by a greater

proportion. (Added to NRS by 1989, 941; A 1999, 1593; 2001, 1380, 3199; 2003, 3108)

## Shares of Stock

**NRS 78A.040 Notice required on share certificates; effect of notice and restrictions on transfer of shares; shareholders to be provided with copies of provisions restricting rights.**

1. The following statement must appear conspicuously on each share certificate issued by a close corporation:

The rights of stockholders in a close corporation may differ materially from the rights of shareholders in other corporations. Copies of the certificate of incorporation, bylaws, shareholders' agreements and other records, any of which may restrict transfers of stock and affect voting and other rights, may be obtained by a shareholder on written request to the corporation.

2. A person claiming an interest in the shares of a close corporation that has complied with the requirement of subsection 1 is bound by the records referred to in the notice. A person claiming an interest in the shares of a close corporation that has not complied with the requirement of subsection 1 is bound by any record that he or a person through whom he claims has knowledge or notice.

3. A close corporation shall provide to any shareholder upon his written request and without charge, copies of the provisions that restrict transfer or affect voting or other rights of shareholders appearing in the articles of incorporation, bylaws, shareholders' agreements or voting trust agreements filed with the corporations.

4. Except as otherwise provided in subsection 5, the close corporation may refuse to register the transfer of stock into the name of a person to whom the stock of a close corporation has been transferred if the person has, or is presumed to have, notice that the transfer of the stock is in violation of a restriction on the transfer of stock. If the close corporation refuses to register the transfer of stock into the name of the transferee, the close corporation must notify the transferee of its refusal and state the reasons therefor.

5. Subsection 4 does not apply if:

(a) The transfer of stock, even if contrary to the restrictions on transfer of stock, has been consented to by all the stockholders of the close corporation; or

(b) The close corporation has amended its certificate of incorporation in accordance with NRS 78A.180.

6. The provisions of this section do not impair any rights of a transferee to:

(a) Rescind the transaction by which he acquired the stock; or

(b) Recover under any applicable warranty.

7. As used in this section, "transfer" is not limited to a transfer for value. (Added to NRS by 1989, 941; A 2003, 3109)

### NRS 78A.050 Transfer of shares prohibited; exceptions.

1. An interest in the shares of a close corporation may not be transferred, except to the extent permitted by the certificate of incorporation, the bylaws, a shareholders' agreement or a voting trust agreement.

2. Except as otherwise provided by the certificate of incorporation, the provisions of this section do not apply to a transfer:

(a) To the corporation or to any other shareholder of the same class or series of shares.

(b) To heirs at law.

(c) That has been approved in writing by all of the holders of the shares of the corporation having voting rights.

(d) To an executor or administrator upon the death of a shareholder or to a trustee or receiver as a result of a bankruptcy, insolvency, dissolution or similar proceeding brought by or against a shareholder.

(e) By merger or share exchange or an exchange of existing shares for other shares of a different class or series in the corporation.

(f) By a pledge as collateral for a loan that does not grant the pledgee any voting rights possessed by the pledgor.

(g) Made after the termination of the status of the corporation as a close corporation. (Added to NRS by 1989, 942)

### NRS 78A.060 Effect of attempt to transfer shares in violation of prohibition.

1. An attempt to transfer shares in a close corporation in violation of a prohibition against such a transfer is ineffective.

2. An attempt to transfer shares in a close corporation in violation of a prohibition against transfer that is not binding on the transferee because:

(a) The notice required by NRS 78A.040 was not given; or

(b) The prohibition is held unenforceable by a court of competent jurisdiction, gives the corporation an option to purchase the shares from the transferee for the same price and on the same terms that he purchased them. To exercise the option, the corporation must give the transferee written notice within 30 days after they receive a share certificate for registration in the name of the transferee. (Added to NRS by 1989, 943)

### Powers and Duties

### NRS 78A.070 Shareholders' agreements: Authority to enter; effect; amendment.

1. All shareholders of a close corporation who are entitled to vote may agree in writing to regulate the exercise of the corporate powers and the management of the business and affairs of the corporation or the relationship among the shareholders of the corporation.

2. An agreement authorized by this section is effective even if the agreement:

(a) Eliminates a board of directors.

(b) Restricts the discretion or powers of the board of directors or authorizes director proxies or weighted voting rights.

(c) Treats the corporation as a partnership.

(d) Creates a relationship among the shareholders or between the shareholders and the corporation that would otherwise be appropriate among partners.

3. If the corporation has a board of directors, an agreement authorized by this section that restricts the discretion or powers of the board of directors:

(a) Relieves directors of liability imposed by law; and

(b) Imposes that liability on each person in whom the discretion or power of the board is vested, to the extent that the discretion or power of the board of directors is governed by the agreement.

4. A provision eliminating a board of directors in an agreement authorized by this section is not effective unless the articles of incorporation contain a statement to that effect.

5. A provision entitling one or more shareholders to dissolve the corporation under NRS 78A.160 is effective if a statement of this right is contained in the articles of incorporation.

6. To amend an agreement authorized by this section, all shareholders entitled to vote must approve the amendment in writing, unless the agreement provides otherwise.

7. Subscribers for shares may act as shareholders with respect to an agreement authorized by this section if shares are not issued when the agreement was made.

8. This section does not prohibit any other agreement between or among shareholders in a close corporation. (Added to NRS by 1989, 944)

### NRS 78A.080 Shareholders' agreements: Validity.

A written agreement among stockholders of a close corporation or any provision of the certificate of incorporation or of the bylaws of the corporation that relates to any phase of the affairs of the corporation, including, but not limited to, the management of its business, the declaration and payment of dividends or other division of profits, the election of directors or officers, the employment of stockholders by the corporation or the arbitration of disputes is not invalid on the ground that it is an attempt by the parties to the agreement or by the stockholders of the corporation to treat the corporation as if it were a partnership or to arrange relations among the stockholders or between the stockholders and the corporation in a manner that would be appropriate only among partners. (Added to NRS by 1989, 947)

**NRS 78A.090 Operation without board of directors; elimination and reinstatement of board.**

1. A close corporation may operate without a board of directors if the certificate of incorporation contains a statement to that effect.

2. An amendment to the certificate of incorporation eliminating a board of directors must be approved:

(a) By all the shareholders of the corporation, whether or not otherwise entitled to vote on amendments; or

(b) If no shares have been issued, by all subscribers for shares, if any, or if none, by the incorporators.

3. While a corporation is operating without a board of directors as authorized by subsection 1:

(a) All corporate powers must be exercised by or under the authority of, and the business and affairs of the corporation managed under the direction of, the shareholders.

(b) Unless the articles of incorporation provide otherwise:

(1) Action requiring the approval of the board of directors or of both the board of directors and the shareholders is authorized if approved by the shareholders; and

(2) Action requiring a majority or greater percentage vote of the board of directors is authorized if approved by the majority or greater percentage of votes of the shareholders entitled to vote on the action.

(c) A requirement by a state or the United States that a record delivered for filing contain a statement that specified action has been taken by the board of directors is satisfied by a statement that the corporation is a close corporation without a board of directors and that the action was approved by the shareholders.

(d) The shareholders by resolution may appoint one or more shareholders to sign records as designated directors.

4. An amendment to the articles of incorporation that deletes the provision which eliminates a board of directors must be approved by the holders of at least two-thirds of the votes of each class or series of shares of the corporation, voting as separate voting groups, whether or not otherwise entitled to vote on amendments. The amendment must specify the number, names and mailing addresses of the directors of the corporation or describe who will perform the duties of the board of directors. (Added to NRS by 1989, 944; A 1999, 1593; 2001, 101, 2723; 2003, 3109)

**NRS 78A.100 Annual meeting.** A close corporation shall hold an annual meeting if one or more shareholders delivers a written notice to the corporation requesting a meeting. Upon receipt of a notice, the close corporation must hold a meeting within 30 days. (Added to NRS by 1989, 945)

**NRS 78A.110 Records signed, acknowledged or verified by person acting in more than one capacity.** Notwithstanding any law to the contrary, a person who holds more than one office in a close corporation may sign, acknowledge or verify in more than one capacity any record required to be signed, acknowledged or verified by the holders of two or more offices. (Added to NRS by 1989, 945; A 2003, 3110)

**NRS 78A.120 Limitation on liability of shareholders.** Personal liability may not be imposed upon shareholders of a close corporation solely as a result of the failure of the close corporation to observe the usual corporate formalities or requirements relating to the exercise of corporate powers or management of its business and affairs, where such failure results from the distinct nature and permissible functioning of a close corporation. (Added to NRS by 1989, 945)

**NRS 78A.130 Merger or share exchange; sale, lease or exchange of assets.**

1. A plan of merger or share exchange that if effected would:

(a) Terminate the close corporation status must be approved by the holders of at least two-thirds of the votes of each class or series of shares of the close corporation, voting as separate voting groups, whether or not the holders are entitled to vote on the plan.

(b) Create the surviving corporation as a close corporation must be approved by the holders of at least two-thirds of the votes of each class or series of shares of the surviving corporation, voting as separate voting groups, whether or not the holders are entitled to vote on the plan.

2. If not made in the usual and regular course of business, a sale, lease, exchange or other disposition of all or substantially all of the property of a close corporation must be approved by the holders of at least two-thirds of the votes of each class or series of shares of the corporation, voting as separate voting groups, whether or not the holders are entitled to vote on the transaction. (Added to NRS by 1989, 945)

**NRS 78A.140 Appointment of custodian, receiver or provisional director.**

1. Upon application of a stockholder, the court may appoint one or more persons to be custodians and, if the

corporation is insolvent, to be receivers of any close corporation when:

(a) The business and affairs of the close corporation are managed by the stockholders who are so divided that the business of the corporation is suffering or is threatened with irreparable injury and any remedy with respect to such a deadlock provided in the certificate of incorporation or bylaws or in any written agreement of the stockholders has failed; or

(b) The petitioning stockholder has the right to the dissolution of the corporation under a provision of the certificate of incorporation permitted by NRS 78A.160.

2. If the court determines that it would be in the best interest of the corporation, the court may appoint a provisional director in lieu of appointing a custodian or receiver for a close corporation. Such an appointment does not preclude any subsequent order of the court appointing a custodian or receiver for the corporation. (Added to NRS by 1989, 946)

### NRS 78A.150 Provisional director: Requirements for appointment; qualifications, rights and powers; compensation.

1. Notwithstanding any contrary provision of the certificate of incorporation, the bylaws or an agreement of the stockholders, the court may appoint a provisional director for a close corporation if the shareholders or directors, if any, are so divided concerning the management of the business and affairs of the corporation that the votes required for action by the board of directors cannot be obtained, with the consequence that the business and affairs of the corporation cannot be conducted to the advantage of the stockholders generally.

2. An application for relief pursuant to this section must be filed:

(a) By at least one-half of the number of directors then in office;

(b) By the holders of at least one-third of all stock then entitled to elect directors; or

(c) If there is more than one class of stock then entitled to elect one or more directors, by the holders of two-thirds of the stock of each class. The certificate of incorporation of a close corporation may provide that a lesser proportion of the directors, the stockholders or a class of stockholders may apply for relief under this section.

3. A provisional director:

(a) Must be an impartial person who is not a stockholder or a creditor of the corporation or of any subsidiary or affiliate of the corporation and whose further qualifications, if any, may be determined by the court.

(b) Is not a custodian or receiver of the corporation and does not have the title and powers of a custodian or receiver appointed under NRS 78A.140.

(c) Has the rights and powers of an elected director of the corporation, including the right to notice of and to vote at meetings of directors, until such time as he may be removed by order of the court.

4. The compensation of a provisional director must be determined by agreement between the provisional director and the corporation subject to the approval of the court, which may fix his compensation in the absence of agreement or in the event of disagreement between the provisional director and the corporation. (Added to NRS by 1989, 946)

### NRS 78A.160 Option of stockholder to dissolve corporation: Inclusion in certificate of incorporation; exercise of option; notice on stock certificate.

1. The certificate of incorporation of any close corporation may include a provision granting to any stockholder or to the holder of any specified number or percentage of shares of any class of stock an option to have the corporation dissolved at will or upon the occurrence of any specified event or contingency. Whenever any option to dissolve is exercised, the stockholders who exercise the option shall give written notice thereof to all other stockholders. Thirty days after the notice is sent, the dissolution of the corporation must proceed as if the required number of stockholders having voting power consented in writing to dissolution of the corporation as provided by NRS 78.320.

2. If the certificate of incorporation as originally filed does not contain a provision authorized by subsection 1, the certificate may be amended to include such a provision if adopted by the affirmative vote of the holders of all the outstanding stock, whether or not otherwise entitled to vote, unless the certificate of incorporation specifically authorizes such an amendment by a vote which is not less than two-thirds of all the outstanding stock, whether or not otherwise entitled to vote.

3. Each stock certificate in any corporation whose certificate of incorporation authorizes dissolution as permitted by this section must conspicuously note on the face of the certificate the existence of the provision or the provision is ineffective. (Added to NRS by 1989, 947)

### Termination of Status as Close Corporation

### NRS 78A.170 Time of termination of status. A close corporation is subject to the provisions of this chapter until:

1. The corporation files with the Secretary of State a certificate of amendment deleting from the certificate of incorporation the provisions required or permitted by NRS 78A.020, to be stated in the certificate of incorporation; or

2. A provision or condition required or permitted by NRS 78A.020 to be stated in a certificate of incorpora-

tion has been breached and the corporation or any stockholder has not acted pursuant to NRS 78A.190 to prevent the loss of status or remedy the breach. (Added to NRS by 1989, 941)

**NRS 78A.180 Voluntary termination of status.**

1. A corporation may voluntarily terminate its status as a close corporation, and cease to be subject to the provisions of this chapter, by amending the certificate of incorporation to delete therefrom the additional provisions required or permitted by NRS 78A.020 to be stated in the certificate of incorporation of a close corporation. An amendment must be adopted and become effective in accordance with NRS 78.390, except that it must be approved by a vote of the holders of record of at least two-thirds of the voting shares of each class of stock of the corporation that are outstanding.

2. The certificate of incorporation of a close corporation may provide that on any amendment to terminate the status as a close corporation, a vote greater than two-thirds or a vote of all shares of any class may be required. If the certificate of incorporation contains such a provision, that provision may not be amended, repealed or modified by any vote less than that required to terminate the status of the corporation as a close corporation.

3. A certificate filed pursuant to this section is effective upon filing the certificate with the Secretary of State or upon a later date specified in the certificate, which must not be more than 90 days after the certificate is filed. (Added to NRS by 1989, 943; A 2005, 2186)

**NRS 78A.190 Involuntary termination of status; intervention by court.**

1. The status of a corporation as a close corporation terminates if one or more of the provisions or conditions of this chapter cease to exist or be fulfilled unless:

(a) Within 30 days after the occurrence of the event, or within 30 days after the event has been discovered by the corporation, whichever is later, the corporation files with the Secretary of State a signed certificate stating that a specified provision or condition included in the certificate of incorporation to qualify the corporation as a close corporation has ceased to be applicable and furnishes a copy of the certificate to each stockholder; and

(b) The corporation, concurrently with the filing of a certificate, takes such steps as are necessary to correct the situation that threatens the status as a close corporation, including the refusal to register the transfer of stock which has been wrongfully transferred as provided by NRS 78A.050 or commencing a proceeding under subsection 2.

2. Upon the suit of the close corporation or any stockholder, the court has jurisdiction to:

(a) Issue all orders necessary to prevent the corporation from losing its status as a close corporation.

(b) Restore the status of the corporation as a close corporation by enjoining or setting aside any act or threatened act on the part of the corporation or a stockholder that would be inconsistent with any of the provisions or conditions required or permitted by this chapter to be stated in the certificate of incorporation of a close corporation, unless it is an act approved in accordance with NRS 78A.050.

(c) Enjoin or set aside any transfer or threatened transfer of stock of a close corporation that is contrary to the terms of the certificate of incorporation or of any permitted restriction on transfer.

(d) Enjoin any public offering or threatened public offering of stock of the close corporation. (Added to NRS by 1989, 943; A 1999, 1594; 2003, 3110)

**NRS 78A.200 Effect of termination of status.**

1. A corporation that terminates its status as a close corporation is subject to the provisions of chapter 78 of NRS.

2. Termination of the status of a close corporation does not affect any right of a shareholder or of the corporation under an agreement or the articles of incorporation unless invalidated by law. (Added to NRS by 1989, 946)

**CHAPTER 86 LIMITED-LIABILITY COMPANIES**

**General Provisions**

NRS 86.011 Definitions.

NRS 86.022 "Articles" and "articles of organization" defined.

NRS 86.031 "Bankrupt" defined.

NRS 86.051 "Foreign limited-liability company" defined.

NRS 86.061 "Limited-liability company" and "company" defined.

NRS 86.065 "Majority in interest" defined.

NRS 86.071 "Manager" defined.

NRS 86.081 "Member" defined.

NRS 86.091 "Member's interest" defined.

NRS 86.095 "Noneconomic member" defined.

NRS 86.101 "Operating agreement" defined.

NRS 86.111 "Real property" defined.

NRS 86.116 "Record" defined.

NRS 86.118 "Registered agent" defined. [Effective July 1, 2008.]

NRS 86.121 "Registered office" defined. [Effective through June 30, 2008.]

NRS 86.121 "Registered office" defined. [Effective July 1, 2008.]

## Organization

## Resident Agent and Registered Office

## Annual List; Defaulting Companies

## Operation

## Liability, Indemnification and Insurance

## Derivative Actions

## Dissolution

## Foreign Limited-Liability Companies

NRS 86.5466 Defaulting companies: Duties of Secretary of State. [Effective through June 30, 2008.]

NRS 86.5466 Defaulting companies: Duties of Secretary of State. [Effective July 1, 2008.]

NRS 86.5467 Defaulting companies: Conditions and procedure for reinstatement. [Effective through June 30, 2008.]

NRS 86.5467 Defaulting companies: Conditions and procedure for reinstatement. [Effective July 1, 2008.]

NRS 86.5468 Defaulting companies: Reinstatement under old or new name; regulations.

NRS 86.547 Cancellation of registration.

NRS 86.548 Transaction of business without registration.

NRS 86.5483 Activities not constituting transaction of business.

NRS 86.5487 Determination of whether solicitation is made or accepted.

NRS 86.549 Action by Attorney General to restrain transaction of business.

## Miscellaneous Provisions

NRS 86.555 Issuance of occupational or professional license to limited-liability company by board or commission; regulations.

NRS 86.557 Form required for filing of records.

NRS 86.561 Fees. [Effective through June 30, 2008.]

NRS 86.561 Fees. [Effective July 1, 2008.]

NRS 86.563 Procedure to submit replacement page to Secretary of State before actual filing of record.

NRS 86.566 Filing of records written in language other than English.

NRS 86.568 Correction of inaccurate or defective record filed with Secretary of State.

NRS 86.571 Waiver of notice.

NRS 86.580 Renewal or revival of charter: Procedure; fee; certificate as evidence. [Effective through June 30, 2008.]

NRS 86.580 Renewal or revival of charter: Procedure; fee; certificate as evidence. [Effective July 1, 2008.]

NRS 86.590 Renewal or revival of charter: Status of company.

* * *

## General Provisions

**NRS 86.011 Definitions.** As used in this chapter, unless the context otherwise requires, the words and terms defined in NRS 86.022 to 86.128, inclusive, have the meanings ascribed to them in those sections. (Added to NRS by 1991, 1292; A 1993, 1012; 1995, 2107; 1999, 1611; 2001, 1388, 3199; 2003, 3136; 2005, 2190; 2007, 2669)

**NRS 86.022 "Articles" and "articles of organization" defined.** "Articles" and "articles of organization" are synonymous terms and, unless the context otherwise requires, include certificates and restated articles of organization filed pursuant to NRS 86.221 and articles of merger, conversion, exchange or domestication filed pursuant to NRS 92A.200 to 92A.240, inclusive, or 92A.270. (Added to NRS by 2001, 1384; A 2001, 3199)

**NRS 86.031 "Bankrupt" defined.** "Bankrupt" is limited to the effect of the federal statutes codified as Title 11 of the United States Code. (Added to NRS by 1991, 1292)

**NRS 86.051 "Foreign limited-liability company" defined.** "Foreign limited-liability company" means a limited-liability company formed under the laws of any jurisdiction other than this State. (Added to NRS by 1991, 1292)

**NRS 86.061 "Limited-liability company" and "company" defined.** "Limited-liability company" or "company" means a limited-liability company organized and existing under this chapter. (Added to NRS by 1991, 1292)

**NRS 86.065 "Majority in interest" defined.** "Majority in interest" means a majority of the interests in the current profits of a limited-liability company. (Added to NRS by 1995, 2106; A 1997, 715)

**NRS 86.071 "Manager" defined.** "Manager" means a person, or one of several persons, designated in or selected pursuant to the articles of organization or operating agreement of a limited-liability company to manage the company. (Added to NRS by 1991, 1293; A 1997, 715)

**NRS 86.081 "Member" defined.** "Member" means the owner of a member's interest in a limited-liability company or a noneconomic member. (Added to NRS by 1991, 1293; A 1997, 715; 2001, 1388, 3199)

**NRS 86.091 "Member's interest" defined.** "Member's interest" means his share of the economic interests in a limited-liability company, including profits, losses and distributions of assets. (Added to NRS by 1991, 1293; A 1997, 715)

**NRS 86.095 "Noneconomic member" defined.** "Noneconomic member" means a member of a limited-liability company who:

1. Does not own a member's interest in the company;

2. Does not have an obligation to contribute capital to the company;

3. Does not have a right to participate in or receive distributions of profits of the company or an obligation to contribute to the losses of the company; and

4. May have voting rights and other rights and privileges given to noneconomic members of the company by the articles of organization or operating agreement. (Added to NRS by 2001, 1384; A 2001, 3199)

**NRS 86.101 "Operating agreement" defined.** "Operating agreement" means any valid written agreement of the members as to the affairs of a limited-liability company and the conduct of its business. (Added to NRS by 1991, 1293)

**NRS 86.111 "Real property" defined.** "Real property" includes land, any interest, leasehold or estate in land, and any improvements on it. (Added to NRS by 1991, 1293)

**NRS 86.116 "Record" defined.** "Record" means information that is inscribed on a tangible medium or that is stored in an electronic or other medium and is retrievable in perceivable form. (Added to NRS by 2003, 3134)

**NRS 86.118 "Registered agent" defined. [Effective July 1, 2008.]** "Registered agent" has the meaning ascribed to it in NRS 77.230. (Added to NRS by 2007, 2669, effective July 1, 2008)

**NRS 86.121 "Registered office" defined. [Effective through June 30, 2008.]** "Registered office" of a limited-liability company means the office maintained at the street address of its resident agent. (Added to NRS by 1991, 1293; A 1993, 1012; 1995, 1126)

**NRS 86.121 "Registered office" defined. [Effective July 1, 2008.]** "Registered office" of a limited-liability company means the office maintained at the street address of its registered agent. (Added to NRS by 1991, 1293; A 1993, 1012; 1995, 1126; 2007, 2669, effective July 1, 2008)

**NRS 86.125 "Resident agent" defined. [Effective through June 30, 2008.]** "Resident agent" means the agent appointed by the company upon whom process or a notice or demand authorized by law to be served upon the company may be served. (Added to NRS by 1995, 2106; R 2007, 2727, effective July 1, 2008)

**NRS 86.1255 "Series" and "series of members" defined.** "Series" and "series of members" are synonymous terms and, unless the context otherwise requires, mean a series of members' interests having separate rights, powers or duties with respect to property, obligations or profits and losses associated with property or obligations, which are specified in the articles of organization or operating agreement or specified by one or more members or managers or other persons as provided in the articles of organization or operating agreement. (Added to NRS by 2005, 2189)

**NRS 86.126 "Sign" defined.** "Sign" means to affix a signature to a record. (Added to NRS by 1999, 1610; A 2003, 3136)

**NRS 86.127 "Signature" defined.** "Signature" means a name, word, symbol or mark executed or otherwise adopted, or a record encrypted or similarly processed in whole or in part, by a person with the present intent to identify himself and adopt or accept a record. The term includes, without limitation, an electronic signature as defined in NRS 719.100. (Added to NRS by 1999, 1610; A 2001, 101, 2724; 2003, 3136)

**NRS 86.128 "Street address" defined. [Effective through June 30, 2008.]** "Street address" of a resident agent means the actual physical location in this State at which a resident agent is available for service of process. (Added to NRS by 1999, 1610)

**NRS 86.128 "Street address" defined. [Effective July 1, 2008.]** "Street address" of a registered agent means the actual physical location in this State at which a registered agent is available for service of process. (Added to NRS by 1999, 1610; A 2007, 2669, effective July 1, 2008)

**NRS 86.131 Applicability of chapter to foreign and interstate commerce.** The provisions of this chapter apply to commerce with foreign nations and among the several states. It is the intention of the Legislature by enactment of this chapter that the legal existence of limited-liability companies formed under this chapter be recognized beyond the limits of this State and that, subject to any reasonable requirement of registration, any such company transacting business outside this State be granted protection of full faith and credit under Section 1 of Article IV of the Constitution of the United States. (Added to NRS by 1991, 1304)

**NRS 86.135 Amendment or repeal of provisions of chapter; chapter deemed part of articles of company.** The provisions of this chapter may be amended or repealed at the pleasure of the legislature. A limited-liability company created pursuant to the provisions of this chapter or availing itself of any of the provisions of this chapter and all members and managers of the limited-liability company are bound by the amendment. An amendment or repeal does not take away or impair any remedy against a limited-liability company or its managers or members for a liability that has been previously incurred. The provisions of this chapter and all amendments thereof are a part of the articles of every limited-liability company. (Added to NRS by 2001, 1385; A 2001, 3199)

## Organization

**NRS 86.141 Purpose for organization.**

1. Except as otherwise provided in subsection 2, a limited-liability company may be organized under this chapter for any lawful purpose.

2. A limited-liability company may not be organized for the purpose of insurance unless approved to do so by the Commissioner of Insurance. (Added to NRS by 1991, 1293; A 1995, 496; 2005, 2257)

**NRS 86.151 Filing requirements. [Effective through June 30, 2008.]**

1. One or more persons may form a limited-liability company by:

(a) Signing and filing with the Secretary of State articles of organization for the company; and

(b) Filing with the Secretary of State a certificate of acceptance of appointment, signed by the resident agent of the company.

2. Upon the filing of the articles of organization and the certificate of acceptance with the Secretary of State, and the payment to him of the required filing fees, the Secretary of State shall issue to the company a certificate that the articles, containing the required statement of facts, have been filed.

3. A signer of the articles of organization or a manager designated in the articles does not thereby become a member of the company. At all times after commencement of business by the company, the company must have one or more members. The filing of the articles does not, by itself, constitute commencement of business by the company. (Added to NRS by 1991, 1293; A 1993, 1012; 1995, 1126, 2107; 1997, 715; 1999, 1611; 2003, 3136)

**NRS 86.151 Filing requirements. [Effective July 1, 2008.]**

1. One or more persons may form a limited-liability company by signing and filing with the Secretary of State articles of organization for the company.

2. Upon the filing of the articles of organization with the Secretary of State and the payment to him of the required filing fees, the Secretary of State shall issue to the company a certificate that the articles, containing the required statement of facts, have been filed.

3. A signer of the articles of organization or a manager designated in the articles does not thereby become a member of the company. At all times after commencement of business by the company, the company must have one or more members. The filing of the articles does not, by itself, constitute commencement of business by the company. (Added to NRS by 1991, 1293; A 1993, 1012; 1995, 1126, 2107; 1997, 715; 1999, 1611; 2003, 3136; 2007, 2669, effective July 1, 2008)

**NRS 86.155 Perpetual existence of company.** Unless otherwise provided in its articles of organization or operating agreement, a limited-liability company has perpetual existence. (Added to NRS by 1997, 714)

**NRS 86.161 Articles of organization: Required and optional provisions. [Effective through June 30, 2008.]**

1. The articles of organization must set forth:

(a) The name of the limited-liability company;

(b) The name and complete street address of its resident agent, and the mailing address of the resident agent if different from the street address;

(c) The name and address, either residence or business, of each of the organizers signing the articles;

(d) If the company is to be managed by:

(1) One or more managers, the name and address, either residence or business, of each initial manager; or

(2) The members, the name and address, either residence or business, of each initial member; and

(e) If the company is to have one or more series of members and the debts or liabilities of any series are to be enforceable against the assets of that series only and not against the assets of another series or the company generally, a statement to that effect and a statement:

(1) Setting forth the relative rights, powers and duties of the series; or

(2) Indicating that the relative rights, powers and duties of the series will be set forth in the operating agreement or established as provided in the operating agreement.

2. The articles may set forth any other provision, not inconsistent with law, which the members elect to set out in the articles of organization for the regulation of the internal affairs of the company, including any provisions which under this chapter are required or permitted to be set out in the operating agreement of the company.

3. It is not necessary to set out in the articles of organization:

(a) The rights of the members to contract debts on behalf of the limited-liability company if the limited-liability company is managed by its members;

(b) The rights of the manager or managers to contract debts on behalf of the limited-liability company if the limited-liability company is managed by a manager or managers; or

(c) Any of the powers enumerated in this chapter. (Added to NRS by 1991, 1293; A 1993, 1012; 1995, 1126, 2107; 1997, 716; 1999, 1612; 2003, 3136; 2003, 20th Special Session, 63; 2005, 2190)

**NRS 86.161 Articles of organization: Required and optional provisions. [Effective July 1, 2008.]**

1. The articles of organization must set forth:

(a) The name of the limited-liability company;

(b) The information required pursuant to NRS 77.310;

(c) The name and address, either residence or business, of each of the organizers signing the articles;

(d) If the company is to be managed by:

(1) One or more managers, the name and address, either residence or business, of each initial manager; or

(2) The members, the name and address, either residence or business, of each initial member; and

(e) If the company is to have one or more series of members and the debts or liabilities of any series are to be enforceable against the assets of that series only and not against the assets of another series or the company generally, a statement to that effect and a statement:

(1) Setting forth the relative rights, powers and duties of the series; or

(2) Indicating that the relative rights, powers and duties of the series will be set forth in the operating agreement or established as provided in the operating agreement.

2. The articles may set forth any other provision, not inconsistent with law, which the members elect to set out in the articles of organization for the regulation of the internal affairs of the company, including any provisions which under this chapter are required or permitted to be set out in the operating agreement of the company.

3. It is not necessary to set out in the articles of organization:

(a) The rights of the members to contract debts on behalf of the limited-liability company if the limited-liability company is managed by its members;

(b) The rights of the manager or managers to contract debts on behalf of the limited-liability company if the limited-liability company is managed by a manager or managers; or

(c) Any of the powers enumerated in this chapter. (Added to NRS by 1991, 1293; A 1993, 1012; 1995, 1126, 2107; 1997, 716; 1999, 1612; 2003, 3136; 2003, 20th Special Session, 63; 2005, 2190; 2007, 2670, effective July 1, 2008)

**NRS 86.171 Name of company: Distinguishable name required; availability of name of revoked, merged or otherwise terminated company; limitations; regulations. [Effective through December 31, 2007.]**

1. The name of a limited-liability company formed under the provisions of this chapter must contain the words "Limited-Liability Company," "Limited Liability Company," "Limited Company," or "Limited" or the abbreviations "Ltd.," "L.L.C.," "L.C.," "LLC" or "LC." The word "Company" may be abbreviated as "Co."

2. The name proposed for a limited-liability company must be distinguishable on the records of the Secretary of State from the names of all other artificial persons formed, organized, registered or qualified pursuant to the provisions of this title that are on file in the Office of the Secretary of State and all names that are reserved in the Office of the Secretary of State pursuant to the provisions of this title. If a proposed name is not so distinguishable, the Secretary of State shall return the articles of organization to the organizer, unless the written, acknowledged consent of the holder of the name on file or reserved name to use the same name or the requested similar name accompanies the articles of organization.

3. For the purposes of this section and NRS 86.176, a proposed name is not distinguishable from a name on file or reserved name solely because one or the other contains distinctive lettering, a distinctive mark, a trademark or a trade name, or any combination thereof.

4. The name of a limited-liability company whose charter has been revoked, which has merged and is not the surviving entity or whose existence has otherwise terminated is available for use by any other artificial person.

5. The Secretary of State shall not accept for filing any articles of organization for any limited-liability company if the name of the limited-liability company contains the word "accountant," "accounting," "accountancy," "auditor" or "auditing" unless the Nevada State Board of Accountancy certifies that the limited-liability company:

(a) Is registered pursuant to the provisions of chapter 628 of NRS; or

(b) Has filed with the Nevada State Board of Accountancy under penalty of perjury a written statement that the limited-liability company is not engaged in the practice of accounting and is not offering to practice accounting in this State.

6. The Secretary of State shall not accept for filing any articles of organization or certificate of amendment of articles of organization of any limited-liability company formed or existing pursuant to the laws of this State which provides that the name of the limited-liability company contains the word "bank" or "trust" unless:

(a) It appears from the articles of organization or the certificate of amendment that the limited-liability company proposes to carry on business as a banking or trust company, exclusively or in connection with its business as a bank, savings and loan association or thrift company; and

(b) The articles of organization or certificate of amendment is first approved by the Commissioner of Financial Institutions.

7. The Secretary of State shall not accept for filing any articles of organization or certificate of amendment of articles of organization of any limited-liability company formed or existing pursuant to the provisions of this

chapter if it appears from the articles or the certificate of amendment that the business to be carried on by the limited-liability company is subject to supervision by the Commissioner of Insurance or by the Commissioner of Financial Institutions unless the articles or certificate of amendment is approved by the Commissioner who will supervise the business of the limited-liability company.

8. Except as otherwise provided in subsection 7, the Secretary of State shall not accept for filing any articles of organization or certificate of amendment of articles of organization of any limited-liability company formed or existing pursuant to the laws of this State which provides that the name of the limited-liability company contains the words "engineer," "engineered," "engineering," "professional engineer," "registered engineer" or "licensed engineer" unless:

(a) The State Board of Professional Engineers and Land Surveyors certifies that the principals of the limited-liability company are licensed to practice engineering pursuant to the laws of this State; or

(b) The State Board of Professional Engineers and Land Surveyors certifies that the limited-liability company is exempt from the prohibitions of NRS 625.520.

9. Except as otherwise provided in subsection 7, the Secretary of State shall not accept for filing any articles of organization or certificate of amendment of articles of organization of any limited-liability company formed or existing pursuant to the laws of this State which provides that the name of the limited-liability company contains the words "architect," "architecture," "registered architect," "licensed architect," "registered interior designer," "registered interior design," "residential designer," "registered residential designer," "licensed residential designer" or "residential design" unless the State Board of Architecture, Interior Design and Residential Design certifies that:

(a) The principals of the limited-liability company are holders of a certificate of registration to practice architecture or residential design or to practice as a registered interior designer, as applicable, pursuant to the laws of this State;

(b) The limited-liability company is qualified to do business in this State pursuant to NRS 623.349.

10. The Secretary of State shall not accept for filing any articles of organization or certificate of amendment of articles of organization of any limited-liability company formed or existing pursuant to the laws of this State which provides that the name of the limited-liability company contains the words "common-interest community," "community association," "master association," "unitowners' association" or "homeowners' association" or if it appears in the articles of organization or certificate of amendment of articles of organization that the purpose of the limited-liability company is to operate as a unit-owners' association pursuant to chapter 116 of

NRS unless the Administrator of the Real Estate Division of the Department of Business and Industry certifies that the limited liability company has:

(a) Registered with the Ombudsman for Owners in Common-Interest Communities pursuant to NRS 116.31158; and

(b) Paid to the Administrator of the Real Estate Division the fees required pursuant to NRS 116.31155.

11. The Secretary of State may adopt regulations that interpret the requirements of this section. (Added to NRS by 1991, 1294; A 1993, 1013; 1995, 2108; 1997, 2812; 1999, 1612, 1709; 2001, 101; 2003, 3137; 2003, 20th Special Session, 64; 2005, 2190, 2258, 2627; 2007, 6)

**NRS 86.171 Name of company: Distinguishable name required; availability of name of revoked, merged or otherwise terminated company; limitations; regulations. [Effective January 1, 2008.]**

1. The name of a limited-liability company formed under the provisions of this chapter must contain the words "Limited-Liability Company," "Limited Liability Company," "Limited Company," or "Limited" or the abbreviations "Ltd.," "L.L.C.," "L.C.," "LLC" or "LC." The word "Company" may be abbreviated as "Co."

2. The name proposed for a limited-liability company must be distinguishable on the records of the Secretary of State from the names of all other artificial persons formed, organized, registered or qualified pursuant to the provisions of this title that are on file in the Office of the Secretary of State and all names that are reserved in the Office of the Secretary of State pursuant to the provisions of this title. If a proposed name is not so distinguishable, the Secretary of State shall return the articles of organization to the organizer, unless the written, acknowledged consent of the holder of the name on file or reserved name to use the same name or the requested similar name accompanies the articles of organization.

3. For the purposes of this section and NRS 86.176, a proposed name is not distinguishable from a name on file or reserved name solely because one or the other contains distinctive lettering, a distinctive mark, a trademark or a trade name, or any combination thereof.

4. The name of a limited-liability company whose charter has been revoked, which has merged and is not the surviving entity or whose existence has otherwise terminated is available for use by any other artificial person.

5. The Secretary of State shall not accept for filing any articles of organization for any limited-liability company if the name of the limited-liability company contains the word "accountant," "accounting," "accountancy," "auditor" or "auditing" unless the Nevada State Board of Accountancy certifies that the limited-liability company:

(a) Is registered pursuant to the provisions of chapter 628 of NRS; or

(b) Has filed with the Nevada State Board of Accountancy under penalty of perjury a written statement that the limited-liability company is not engaged in the practice of accounting and is not offering to practice accounting in this State.

6. The Secretary of State shall not accept for filing any articles of organization or certificate of amendment of articles of organization of any limited-liability company formed or existing pursuant to the laws of this State which provides that the name of the limited-liability company contains the word "bank" or "trust" unless:

(a) It appears from the articles of organization or the certificate of amendment that the limited-liability company proposes to carry on business as a banking or trust company, exclusively or in connection with its business as a bank, savings and loan association or thrift company; and (b) The articles of organization or certificate of amendment is first approved by the Commissioner of Financial Institutions.

7. The Secretary of State shall not accept for filing any articles of organization or certificate of amendment of articles of organization of any limited-liability company formed or existing pursuant to the provisions of this chapter if it appears from the articles or the certificate of amendment that the business to be carried on by the limited-liability company is subject to supervision by the Commissioner of Insurance or by the Commissioner of Financial Institutions unless the articles or certificate of amendment is approved by the Commissioner who will supervise the business of the limited-liability company.

8. Except as otherwise provided in subsection 7, the Secretary of State shall not accept for filing any articles of organization or certificate of amendment of articles of organization of any limited-liability company formed or existing pursuant to the laws of this State which provides that the name of the limited-liability company contains the words "engineer," "engineered," "engineering," "professional engineer," "registered engineer" or "licensed engineer" unless:

(a) The State Board of Professional Engineers and Land Surveyors certifies that the principals of the limited-liability company are licensed to practice engineering pursuant to the laws of this State; or

(b) The State Board of Professional Engineers and Land Surveyors certifies that the limited-liability company is exempt from the prohibitions of NRS 625.520.

9. Except as otherwise provided in subsection 7, the Secretary of State shall not accept for filing any articles of organization or certificate of amendment of articles of organization of any limited-liability company formed or existing pursuant to the laws of this State which provides that the name of the limited-liability company contains the words "architect," "architecture," "registered architect," "licensed architect," "registered interior designer," "registered interior design," "residential designer," "registered residential designer," "licensed residential designer" or "residential design" unless the State Board of Architecture, Interior Design and Residential Design certifies that:

(a) The principals of the limited-liability company are holders of a certificate of registration to practice architecture or residential design or to practice as a registered interior designer, as applicable, pursuant to the laws of this State;

(b) The limited-liability company is qualified to do business in this State pursuant to NRS 623.349.

10. The Secretary of State shall not accept for filing any articles of organization or certificate of amendment of articles of organization of any limited-liability company formed or existing pursuant to the laws of this State which provides that the name of the limited-liability company contains the words "common-interest community," "community association," "master association," "unitowners'

association" or "homeowners' association" or if it appears in the articles of organization or certificate of amendment of articles of organization that the purpose of the limited-liability company is to operate as a unit-owners' association pursuant to chapter 116 or 116B of NRS unless the Administrator of the Real Estate Division of the Department of Business and Industry certifies that the limited-liability company has:

(a) Registered with the Ombudsman for Owners in Common-Interest Communities and Condominium Hotels pursuant to NRS 116.31158 or 116B.625; and

(b) Paid to the Administrator of the Real Estate Division the fees required pursuant to NRS 116.31155 or 116B.620.

11. The Secretary of State may adopt regulations that interpret the requirements of this section. (Added to NRS by 1991, 1294; A 1993, 1013; 1995, 2108; 1997, 2812; 1999, 1612, 1709; 2001, 101; 2003, 3137; 2003, 20th Special Session, 64; 2005, 2190, 2258, 2627; 2007, 6, 2284, effective January 1, 2008)

### NRS 86.176 Name of company: Reservation; injunctive relief.

1. The Secretary of State, when requested so to do, shall reserve, for a period of 90 days, the right to use any name available under NRS 86.171, for the use of any proposed limited-liability company. During the period, a name so reserved is not available for use or reservation by any other artificial person forming, organizing, registering or qualifying in the Office of the Secretary of State pursuant to the provisions of this title without the written, acknowledged consent of the person at whose request the reservation was made.

2. The use by any other artificial person of a name in violation of subsection 1 or NRS 86.171 may be enjoined, even if the record under which the artificial person is formed, organized, registered or qualified has been filed by the Secretary of State. (Added to NRS by 1993, 1009; A 1999, 1613; 2003, 3138)

### NRS 86.201 Commencement of organizational existence. [Effective through June 30, 2008.]

1. A limited-liability company is considered legally organized pursuant to this chapter upon:

(a) Filing the articles of organization with the Secretary of State or upon a later date specified in the articles of organization;

(b) Filing the certificate of acceptance of the resident agent with the Secretary of State; and

(c) Paying the required filing fees to the Secretary of State.

2. A limited-liability company must not transact business or incur indebtedness, except that which is incidental to its organization or to obtaining subscriptions for or payment of contributions, until the company is considered legally organized pursuant to subsection 1.

3. A limited-liability company is an entity distinct from its managers and members. (Added to NRS by 1991, 1294; A 1993, 1014; 1995, 1127, 2108; 2001, 1388, 3199; 2007, 2424)

### NRS 86.201 Commencement of organizational existence. [Effective July 1, 2008.]

1. A limited-liability company is considered legally organized pursuant to this chapter upon:

(a) Filing the articles of organization with the Secretary of State or upon a later date specified in the articles of organization; and

(b) Paying the required filing fees to the Secretary of State.

2. A limited-liability company must not transact business or incur indebtedness, except that which is incidental to its organization or to obtaining subscriptions for or payment of contributions, until the company is considered legally organized pursuant to subsection 1.

3. A limited-liability company is an entity distinct from its managers and members. (Added to NRS by 1991, 1294; A 1993, 1014; 1995, 1127, 2108; 2001, 1388, 3199; 2007, 2424, 2670, effective July 1, 2008)

### NRS 86.211 Articles of organization: Notice imparted by filing. The fact that the articles of organization are on file in the Office of the Secretary of State is notice that the limited-liability company is a limited-liability company and is notice of all other facts sets forth therein which are required to be set forth in the articles of organization, unless the existence and facts set forth have been rebutted and made a part of a record of any court of competent jurisdiction. (Added to NRS by 1991, 1294)

### NRS 86.216 Amendment of articles of organization before issuance of member's interest.

1. For any limited-liability company where management is vested in one or more managers and where no member's interest in the limited-liability company has been issued, at least two-thirds of the organizers or the managers of the limited-liability company may amend the articles of organization of the limited-liability company by signing and filing with the Secretary of State a certificate amending, modifying, changing or altering the articles, in whole or in part. The certificate must state that:

(a) The signers thereof are at least two-thirds of the organizers or the managers of the limited-liability company, and state the name of the limited-liability company; and

(b) As of the date of the certificate, no member's interest in the limited-liability company has been issued.

2. A certificate filed pursuant to this section is effective upon filing the certificate with the Secretary of State or upon a later date specified in the certificate, which must not be more than 90 days after the certificate is filed.

3. If a certificate filed pursuant to this section specifies an effective date and if no member's interest in the limited-liability company has been issued, the managers of the limited-liability company may terminate the effectiveness of the certificate by filing a certificate of termination with the Secretary of State that:

(a) Identifies the certificate being terminated;

(b) States that no member's interest in the limited-liability company has been issued;

(c) States that the effectiveness of the certificate has been terminated;

(d) Is signed by at least two-thirds of the managers; and

(e) Is accompanied by a filing fee of $175.

4. This section does not permit the insertion of any matter not in conformity with this chapter. (Added to NRS by 2005, 2189)

### NRS 86.221 Amendment and restatement of articles of organization. [Effective through June 30, 2008.]

1. The articles of organization of a limited-liability company may be amended for any purpose, not inconsistent with law, as determined by all of the members or permitted by the articles or an operating agreement.

2. An amendment must be made in the form of a certificate setting forth:

(a) The name of the limited-liability company;

(b) Whether the limited-liability company is managed by managers or members; and

(c) The amendment to the articles of organization.

3. The certificate of amendment must be signed by a manager of the company or, if management is not vested in a manager, by a member.

4. Restated articles of organization may be signed and filed in the same manner as a certificate of amendment. If the certificate alters or amends the articles in any manner, it must be accompanied by a form prescribed by the Secretary of State setting forth which provisions of the articles of organization on file with the Secretary of State are being altered or amended.

5. The following may be omitted from the restated articles of organization:

(a) The names, addresses, signatures and acknowledgments of the organizers;

(b) The names and addresses of the past and present members or managers; and

(c) The name and address of the resident agent. (Added to NRS by 1991, 1304; A 1993, 1014; 1995, 1127, 2108; 1997, 716; 1999, 1613; 2001, 1388, 3199; 2003, 3138; 2003, 20th Special Session, 65; 2005, 2192, 2259)

### NRS 86.221 Amendment and restatement of articles of organization. [Effective July 1, 2008.]

1. The articles of organization of a limited-liability company may be amended for any purpose, not inconsistent with law, as determined by all of the members or permitted by the articles or an operating agreement.

2. Except as otherwise provided in NRS 77.340, an amendment must be made in the form of a certificate setting forth:

(a) The name of the limited-liability company;

(b) Whether the limited-liability company is managed by managers or members; and

(c) The amendment to the articles of organization.

3. The certificate of amendment must be signed by a manager of the company or, if management is not vested in a manager, by a member.

4. Restated articles of organization may be signed and filed in the same manner as a certificate of amendment. If the certificate alters or amends the articles in any manner, it must be accompanied by a form prescribed by the Secretary of State setting forth which provisions of the articles of organization on file with the Secretary of State are being altered or amended.

5. The following may be omitted from the restated articles of organization:

(a) The names, addresses, signatures and acknowledgments of the organizers;

(b) The names and addresses of the past and present members or managers; and

(c) The information required pursuant to NRS 77.310. (Added to NRS by 1991, 1304; A 1993, 1014; 1995, 1127, 2108; 1997, 716; 1999, 1613; 2001, 1388, 3199; 2003, 3138; 2003, 20th Special Session, 65; 2005, 2192, 2259; 2007, 2671, effective July 1, 2008)

### NRS 86.226 Filing of certificate of amendment or judicial decree of amendment; effective date.

1. A signed certificate of amendment, or a certified copy of a judicial decree of amendment, must be filed with the Secretary of State. A person who signs a certificate as an agent, officer or fiduciary of the limited-liability company need not exhibit evidence of his authority as a prerequisite to filing. Unless the Secretary of State finds that a certificate does not conform to law, upon his receipt of all required filing fees he shall file the certificate.

2. A certificate of amendment or judicial decree of amendment is effective upon filing the certificate with the Secretary of State or upon a later date specified in the certificate or judicial decree, which must not be more than 90 days after the certificate or judicial decree is filed.

3. If a certificate specifies an effective date and if the resolution of the members approving the proposed amendment provides that one or more managers or, if management is not vested in a manager, one or more members may abandon the proposed amendment, then those managers or members may terminate the effectiveness of the certificate by filing a certificate of termination with the Secretary of State that:

(a) Is filed before the effective date specified in the certificate or judicial decree filed pursuant to subsection 1;

(b) Identifies the certificate being terminated;

(c) States that, pursuant to the resolution of the members, the manager of the company or, if management is not vested in a manager, a designated member is authorized to terminate the effectiveness of the certificate;

(d) States that the effectiveness of the certificate has been terminated;

(e) Is signed by a manager of the company or, if management is not vested in a manager, a designated member; and

(f) Is accompanied by a filing fee of $175.

(Added to NRS by 1993, 1009; A 1995, 2109; 1997, 717; 1999, 1613; 2001, 1388, 3180, 3199; 2003, 3138; 2003, 20th Special Session, 65; 2005, 2193)

## Resident Agent and Registered Office

### NRS 86.231 Resident agent required; address of registered office; change of address. [Effective through June 30, 2008.]

1. Except during any period of vacancy described in NRS 86.251, a limited-liability company shall have a resident agent who must have a street address for the service of process. The street address of the resident agent is the registered office of the limited-liability company in this State.

2. Within 30 days after changing the location of his office from one address to another in this State, a resident agent shall file a certificate with the Secretary of State setting forth the names of the limited-liability companies represented by him, the address at which he has maintained the office for each of the limited-liability companies, and the new address to which the office is transferred. (Added to NRS by 1991, 1295; A 1993, 1015; 1995, 1127, 2109)

## NRS 86.231 Registered agent required; address of registered office. [Effective July 1, 2008.]

A limited-liability company shall have a registered agent who must have a street address for the service of process. The street address of the registered agent is the registered office of the limited-liability company in this State. (Added to NRS by 1991, 1295; A 1993, 1015; 1995, 1127, 2109; 2007, 2671, effective July 1, 2008)

## NRS 86.235 Resident agent: Revocation of appointment; change of name. [Effective through June 30, 2008.]

1. If a limited-liability company formed pursuant to this chapter desires to change its resident agent, the change may be effected by filing with the Secretary of State a certificate of change of resident agent signed by a manager of the company or, if management is not vested in a manager, by a member, that sets forth:

(a) The name of the limited-liability company;

(b) The name and street address of its present resident agent; and

(c) The name and street address of the new resident agent.

2. The new resident agent's certificate of acceptance must be a part of or attached to the certificate of change of resident agent.

3. If the name of a resident agent is changed as a result of a merger, conversion, exchange, sale, reorganization or amendment, the resident agent shall:

(a) File with the Secretary of State a certificate of name change of resident agent that includes:

(1) The current name of the resident agent as filed with the Secretary of State;

(2) The new name of the resident agent; and

(3) The name and file number of each artificial person formed, organized, registered or qualified pursuant to the provisions of this title that the resident agent represents; and

(b) Pay to the Secretary of State a filing fee of $100.

4. A change authorized by this section becomes effective upon the filing of the proper certificate of change. (Added to NRS by 1995, 1125; A 1997, 717; 1999, 1614; 2003, 20th Special Session, 66; R 2007, 2727, effective July 1, 2008)

## NRS 86.241 Maintenance of records at office in State; inspection and copying of records.

1. Each limited-liability company shall continuously maintain in this State an office, which may but need not be a place of its business in this State, at which it shall keep, unless otherwise provided by an operating agreement:

(a) A current list of the full name and last known business address of each member and manager, separately identifying the members in alphabetical order and the managers, if any, in alphabetical order;

(b) A copy of the filed articles of organization and all amendments thereto, together with signed copies of any powers of attorney pursuant to which any record has been signed; and

(c) Copies of any then effective operating agreement of the company.

2. Records kept pursuant to this section are subject to inspection and copying at the reasonable request, and at the expense, of any member during ordinary business hours, unless otherwise provided in an operating agreement. (Added to NRS by 1991, 1295; A 1993, 1015; 1995, 2110; 2003, 3139)

## NRS 86.246 List or statement to be maintained at registered office or principal place of business; requirement to assist in criminal investigation; failure to comply; regulations.

1. In addition to any records required to be kept pursuant to NRS 86.241, a limited-liability company shall maintain at its registered office or principal place of business in this State:

(a) A current list of each member and manager; or

(b) A statement indicating where such a list is maintained.

2. A limited-liability company shall:

(a) Provide the Secretary of State with the name and contact information of the custodian of the list described in subsection 1. The information required pursuant to this paragraph shall be kept confidential by the Secretary of State.

(b) Provide written notice to the Secretary of State within 10 days after any change in the information contained in the list described in subsection 1.

3. Upon the request of any law enforcement agency in the course of a criminal investigation, the Secretary of State may require a limited-liability company to:

(a) Submit to the Secretary of State, within 3 business days, a copy of the list required to be maintained pursuant to subsection 1; or

(b) Answer any interrogatory submitted by the Secretary of State that will assist in the criminal investigation.

4. If a limited-liability company fails to comply with any requirement pursuant to subsection 3, the Secretary of State may take any action necessary, including, without limitation, the suspension or revocation of the charter of the limited-liability company.

5. The Secretary of State shall not reinstate or revive a charter that was revoked or suspended pursuant to subsection 4 unless:

(a) The limited-liability company complies with the requirements of subsection 3; or

(b) The law enforcement agency conducting the investigation advises the Secretary of State to reinstate or revive the charter.

6. The Secretary of State may adopt regulations to administer the provisions of this section. (Added to NRS by 2007, 1323)

**NRS 86.251 Resident agent: Resignation; designation of successor after death, resignation or movement from State. [Effective through June 30, 2008.]**

1. A resident agent who desires to resign shall:

(a) File with the Secretary of State a signed statement in the manner provided pursuant to subsection 1 of NRS 78.097 that he is unwilling to continue to act as the resident agent of the limited-liability company for the service of process; and

(b) Pay to the Secretary of State the filing fee set forth in subsection 1 of NRS 78.097. A resignation is not effective until the signed statement is filed with the Secretary of State.

2. The statement of resignation may contain a statement of the affected limited-liability company appointing a successor resident agent for that limited-liability company, giving the agent's full name, street address for the service of process, and mailing address if different from the street address. A certificate of acceptance signed by the new resident agent must accompany the statement appointing a successor resident agent.

3. Upon the filing of the statement of resignation with the Secretary of State, the capacity of the resigning person as resident agent terminates. If the statement of resignation contains no statement by the limited-liability company appointing a successor resident agent, the resigning agent shall immediately give written notice, by mail, to the limited-liability company of the filing of the statement and its effect. The notice must be addressed to any manager or, if none, to any member of the limited-liability company other than the resident agent.

4. If a resident agent dies, resigns or moves from the State, the limited-liability company, within 30 days thereafter, shall file with the Secretary of State a certificate of acceptance signed by the new resident agent. The certificate must set forth the name, complete street address and mailing address, if different from the street address, of the new resident agent.

5. Each limited-liability company which fails to file a certificate of acceptance signed by the new resident agent within 30 days after the death, resignation or removal of its resident agent as provided in subsection 4 shall be deemed in default and is subject to the provisions of NRS 86.272 and 86.274. (Added to NRS by 1991, 1296; A 1993, 1016; 1995, 1128; 1999, 1614; 2003, 3139; 2003, 20th Special Session, 66)

**NRS 86.251 Resignation of registered agent or termination of commercial registered agent. [Effective July 1, 2008.]**

1. If a registered agent resigns pursuant to NRS 77.370 or if a commercial registered agent terminates its listing as a commercial registered agent pursuant to NRS 77.330, the limited-liability company, before the effective date of the resignation or termination, shall file with the Secretary of State a statement of change of registered agent pursuant to NRS 77.340.

2. Each limited-liability company which fails to comply with subsection 1 shall be deemed in default and is subject to the provisions of NRS 86.272 and 86.274.

3. As used in this section, "commercial registered agent" has the meaning ascribed to it in NRS 77.040. (Added to NRS by 1991, 1296; A 1993, 1016; 1995, 1128; 1999, 1614; 2003, 3139; 2003, 20th Special Session, 66; 2007, 2671, effective July 1, 2008)

**NRS 86.261 Service of process, notice or demand upon resident agent. [Effective through June 30, 2008.]**

1. The resident agent appointed by a limited-liability company is an agent of the company upon whom any process, notice or demand required or permitted by law to be served upon the company may be served.

2. This section does not limit or affect the right to serve any process, notice or demand required or permitted by law to be served upon a limited-liability company in any other manner permitted by law. (Added to NRS by 1991, 1296; A 1995, 1128; 1997, 474)

**NRS 86.261 Service of process, notice or demand upon registered agent. [Effective July 1, 2008.]**

1. The registered agent appointed by a limited-liability company is an agent of the company upon whom any process, notice or demand required or permitted by law to be served upon the company may be served.

2. This section does not limit or affect the right to serve any process, notice or demand required or permitted by law to be served upon a limited-liability company in any other manner permitted by law. (Added to NRS by 1991, 1296; A 1995, 1128; 1997, 474; 2007, 2672, effective July 1, 2008)

## Annual List; Defaulting Companies

### NRS 86.263 Filing requirements; fees; notice. [Effective through June 30, 2008.]

1. A limited-liability company shall, on or before the last day of the first month after the filing of its articles of organization with the Secretary of State, file with the Secretary of State, on a form furnished by him, a list that contains:

(a) The name of the limited-liability company;

(b) The file number of the limited-liability company, if known;

(c) The names and titles of all of its managers or, if there is no manager, all of its managing members;

(d) The address, either residence or business, of each manager or managing member listed, following the name of the manager or managing member;

(e) The name and street address of its lawfully designated resident agent in this State; and

(f) The signature of a manager or managing member of the limited-liability company certifying that the list is true, complete and accurate.

2. The limited-liability company shall thereafter, on or before the last day of the month in which the anniversary date of its organization occurs, file with the Secretary of State, on a form furnished by him, an annual list containing all of the information required in subsection 1.

3. Each list required by subsections 1 and 2 must be accompanied by a declaration under penalty of perjury that the limited liability company:

(a) Has complied with the provisions of NRS 360.780; and

(b) Acknowledges that pursuant to NRS 239.330, it is a category C felony to knowingly offer any false or forged instrument for filing in the Office of the Secretary of State.

4. Upon filing:

(a) The initial list required by subsection 1, the limited-liability company shall pay to the Secretary of State a fee of $125.

(b) Each annual list required by subsection 2, the limited-liability company shall pay to the Secretary of State a fee of $125.

5. If a manager or managing member of a limited-liability company resigns and the resignation is not reflected on the annual or amended list of managers and managing members, the limited-liability company or the resigning manager or managing member shall pay to the Secretary of State a fee of $75 to file the resignation.

6. The Secretary of State shall, 90 days before the last day for filing each list required by subsection 2, cause to be mailed to each limited-liability company which is required to comply with the provisions of this section, and which has not become delinquent, a notice of the fee due under subsection 4 and a reminder to file a list required by subsection 2. Failure of any company to receive a notice or form does not excuse it from the penalty imposed by law.

7. If the list to be filed pursuant to the provisions of subsection 1 or 2 is defective or the fee required by subsection 4 is not paid, the Secretary of State may return the list for correction or payment.

8. An annual list for a limited-liability company not in default received by the Secretary of State more than 90 days before its due date shall be deemed an amended list for the previous year. (Added to NRS by 1993, 1010; A 1995, 1129, 2110; 1997, 2813; 2001, 3181; 2003, 20th Special Session, 67, 184; 2005, 2259; 2007, 1324)

### NRS 86.263 Filing requirements; fees; notice. [Effective July 1, 2008.]

1. A limited-liability company shall, on or before the last day of the first month after the filing of its articles of organization with the Secretary of State, file with the Secretary of State, on a form furnished by him, a list that contains:

(a) The name of the limited-liability company;

(b) The file number of the limited-liability company, if known;

(c) The names and titles of all of its managers or, if there is no manager, all of its managing members;

(d) The address, either residence or business, of each manager or managing member listed, following the name of the manager or managing member;

(e) The information required pursuant to NRS 77.310; and

(f) The signature of a manager or managing member of the limited-liability company certifying that the list is true, complete and accurate.

2. The limited-liability company shall thereafter, on or before the last day of the month in which the anniversary date of its organization occurs, file with the Secretary of State, on a form furnished by him, an annual list containing all of the information required in subsection 1.

3. Each list required by subsections 1 and 2 must be accompanied by a declaration under penalty of perjury that the limited liability company:

(a) Has complied with the provisions of NRS 360.780; and

(b) Acknowledges that pursuant to NRS 239.330, it is a category C felony to knowingly offer any false or forged instrument for filing in the Office of the Secretary of State.

4. Upon filing:

(a) The initial list required by subsection 1, the limited-liability company shall pay to the Secretary of State a fee of $125.

(b) Each annual list required by subsection 2, the limited-liability company shall pay to the Secretary of State a fee of $125.

5. If a manager or managing member of a limited-liability company resigns and the resignation is not reflected on the annual or amended list of managers and managing members, the limited-liability company or the resigning manager or managing member shall pay to the Secretary of State a fee of $75 to file the resignation.

6. The Secretary of State shall, 90 days before the last day for filing each list required by subsection 2, cause to be mailed to each limited-liability company which is required to comply with the provisions of this section, and which has not become delinquent, a notice of the fee due under subsection 4 and a reminder to file a list required by subsection 2. Failure of any company to receive a notice or form does not excuse it from the penalty imposed by law.

7. If the list to be filed pursuant to the provisions of subsection 1 or 2 is defective or the fee required by subsection 4 is not paid, the Secretary of State may return the list for correction or payment.

8. An annual list for a limited-liability company not in default received by the Secretary of State more than 90 days before its due date shall be deemed an amended list for the previous year. (Added to NRS by 1993, 1010; A 1995, 1129, 2110; 1997, 2813; 2001, 3181; 2003, 20th Special Session, 67, 184; 2005, 2259; 2007, 1324, 2672, effective July 1, 2008)

### NRS 86.264 Additional filing requirements for certain companies: Criteria; statement; fees.

1. At the time of submitting any list required pursuant to NRS 86.263, a limited-liability company that meets the criteria set forth in subsection 2 must submit:

(a) The statement required pursuant to subsection 3, accompanied by a declaration under penalty of perjury attesting that the statement does not contain any material misrepresentation of fact; and

(b) A fee of $100,000, to be distributed in the manner provided pursuant to subsection 4.

2. A limited-liability company must submit a statement pursuant to this section if the limited-liability company, including its parent and all subsidiaries:

(a) Holds 25 percent or more of the share of the market within this State for any product sold or distributed by the limited-liability company within this State; and

(b) Has had, during the previous 5-year period, a total of five or more investigations commenced against the limited-liability company, its parent or its subsidiaries in any jurisdiction within the United States, including all state and federal investigations:

(1) Which concern any alleged contract, combination or conspiracy in restraint of trade, as described in subsection 1 of NRS 598A.060, or which concern similar activities prohibited by a substantially similar law of another jurisdiction; and

(2) Which resulted in the limited-liability company being fined or otherwise penalized or which resulted in the limited-liability company being required to divest any holdings or being unable to acquire any holdings as a condition for the settlement, dismissal or resolution of those investigations.

3. A limited-liability company that meets the criteria set forth in subsection 2 shall submit a statement which includes the following information with respect to each investigation:

(a) The jurisdiction in which the investigation was commenced.

(b) A summary of the nature of the investigation and the facts and circumstances surrounding the investigation.

(c) If the investigation resulted in criminal or civil litigation, a copy of all pleadings filed in the investigation by any party to the litigation.

(d) A summary of the outcome of the investigation, including specific information concerning whether any fine or penalty was imposed against the limited-liability company and whether the limited-liability company was required to divest any holdings or was unable to acquire any holdings as a condition for the settlement, dismissal or resolution of the investigation.

4. The fee collected pursuant to subsection 1 must be deposited in the Attorney General's Administration Budget Account and used solely for the purpose of investigating any alleged contract, combination or conspiracy in restraint of trade, as described in subsection 1 of NRS 598A.060. (Added to NRS by 2003, 20th Special Session, 58)

### NRS 86.266 Certificate of authorization to transact business.
If a limited-liability company has filed the initial or annual list in compliance with NRS 86.263 and has paid the appropriate fee for the filing, the cancelled check or other proof of payment received by the limited-liability company constitutes a certificate authorizing it to transact its business within this State until the last day of the month in which the anniversary of its formation occurs in the next

succeeding calendar year. (Added to NRS by 1993, 1010; A 1995, 1129; 1999, 1615; 2001, 3182; 2003, 20th Special Session, 68)

### NRS 86.269 Addresses of managers and members required; failure to file.

1. Each list required to be filed under the provisions of NRS 86.263 must, after the name of each manager and member listed thereon, set forth the address, either residence or business, of each manager or member.

2. If the addresses are not stated for each person on any list offered for filing, the Secretary of State may refuse to file the list, and the limited-liability company for which the list has been offered for filing is subject to the provisions of NRS 86.272 and 86.274 relating to failure to file the list within or at the times therein specified, unless a list is subsequently submitted for filing which conforms to the provisions of this section. (Added to NRS by 1993, 1010; A 2003, 3140; 2003, 20th Special Session, 68)

### NRS 86.272 Defaulting companies: Identification; reinstatement; penalty. [Effective through December 31, 2007.]

1. Each limited-liability company which is required to make a filing and pay the fee prescribed in NRS 86.263 and 86.264 and which refuses or neglects to do so within the time provided is in default.

2. Upon notification from the Administrator of the Real Estate Division of the Department of Business and Industry that a limited liability company which is a unit-owners' association as defined in NRS 116.011 has failed to register pursuant to NRS 116.31158 or failed to pay the fees pursuant to NRS 116.31155, the Secretary of State shall deem the limited-liability company to be in default. If, after the limited-liability company is deemed to be in default, the Administrator notifies the Secretary of State that the limited-liability company has registered pursuant to NRS 116.31158 and paid the fees pursuant to NRS 116.31155, the Secretary of State shall reinstate the limited-liability company if the limited-liability company complies with the requirements for reinstatement as provided in this section and NRS 86.276.

3. For default there must be added to the amount of the fee a penalty of $75. The fee and penalty must be collected as provided in this chapter. (Added to NRS by 1993, 1010; A 1995, 1129; 2001, 3182; 2003, 20th Special Session, 69; 2005, 2629)

### NRS 86.272 Defaulting companies: Identification; reinstatement; penalty. [Effective January 1, 2008.]

1. Each limited-liability company which is required to make a filing and pay the fee prescribed in NRS 86.263

and 86.264 and which refuses or neglects to do so within the time provided is in default.

2. Upon notification from the Administrator of the Real Estate Division of the Department of Business and Industry that a limited liability company which is a unit-owners' association as defined in NRS 116.011 or 116B.030 has failed to register pursuant to NRS 116.31158 or 116B.625 or failed to pay the fees pursuant to NRS 116.31155 or 116B.620, the Secretary of State shall deem the limited-liability company to be in default. If, after the limited-liability company is deemed to be in default, the Administrator notifies the Secretary of State that the limited-liability company has registered pursuant to NRS 116.31158 or 116B.625 and paid the fees pursuant to NRS 116.31155 or 116B.620, the Secretary of State shall reinstate the limited-liability company if the limited-liability company complies with the requirements for reinstatement as provided in this section and NRS 86.276.

3. For default there must be added to the amount of the fee a penalty of $75. The fee and penalty must be collected as provided in this chapter. (Added to NRS by 1993, 1010; A 1995, 1129; 2001, 3182; 2003, 20th Special Session, 69; 2005, 2629; 2007, 2286, effective January 1, 2008)

### NRS 86.274 Defaulting companies: Duties of Secretary of State; forfeiture; distribution of assets. [Effective through June 30, 2008.]

1. The Secretary of State shall notify, by providing written notice to its resident agent, each limited-liability company deemed in default pursuant to the provisions of this chapter. The written notice:

(a) Must include a statement indicating the amount of the filing fee, penalties incurred and costs remaining unpaid.

(b) At the request of the resident agent, may be provided electronically.

2. On the first day of the first anniversary of the month following the month in which the filing was required, the charter of the company is revoked and its right to transact business is forfeited.

3. The Secretary of State shall compile a complete list containing the names of all limited-liability companies whose right to transact business has been forfeited.

4. The Secretary of State shall forthwith notify, by providing written notice to its resident agent, each limited-liability company specified in subsection 3 of the forfeiture of its charter. The written notice:

(a) Must include a statement indicating the amount of the filing fee, penalties incurred and costs remaining unpaid.

(b) At the request of the resident agent, may be provided electronically.

5. If the charter of a limited-liability company is revoked and the right to transact business is forfeited, all of the property and assets of the defaulting company must be held in trust by the managers or, if none, by the members of the company, and the same proceedings may be had with respect to its property and assets as apply to the dissolution of a limited-liability company pursuant to NRS 86.505 and 86.521. Any person interested may institute proceedings at any time after a forfeiture has been declared, but, if the Secretary of State reinstates the charter, the proceedings must be dismissed and all property restored to the company.

6. If the assets are distributed, they must be applied in the following manner:

(a) To the payment of the filing fee, penalties incurred and costs due to the State; and

(b) To the payment of the creditors of the company. Any balance remaining must be distributed among the members as provided in subsection 1 of NRS 86.521. (Added to NRS by 1993, 1011; A 1995, 1130; 2001, 1389, 3199; 2003, 48; 2003, 20th Special Session, 69)

**NRS 86.274 Defaulting companies: Duties of Secretary of State; forfeiture; distribution of assets. [Effective July 1, 2008.]**

1. The Secretary of State shall notify, by providing written notice to its registered agent, each limited-liability company deemed in default pursuant to the provisions of this chapter. The written notice:

(a) Must include a statement indicating the amount of the filing fee, penalties incurred and costs remaining unpaid.

(b) At the request of the registered agent, may be provided electronically.

2. On the first day of the first anniversary of the month following the month in which the filing was required, the charter of the company is revoked and its right to transact business is forfeited.

3. The Secretary of State shall compile a complete list containing the names of all limited-liability companies whose right to transact business has been forfeited.

4. The Secretary of State shall forthwith notify, by providing written notice to its registered agent, each limited-liability company specified in subsection 3 of the forfeiture of its charter. The written notice:

(a) Must include a statement indicating the amount of the filing fee, penalties incurred and costs remaining unpaid.

(b) At the request of the registered agent, may be provided electronically.

5. If the charter of a limited-liability company is revoked and the right to transact business is forfeited, all of the property and assets of the defaulting company must be held in trust by the managers or, if none, by the members of the company, and the same proceedings may be had with respect to its property and assets as apply to the dissolution of a limited-liability company pursuant to NRS 86.505 and 86.521. Any person interested may institute proceedings at any time after a forfeiture has been declared, but, if the Secretary of State reinstates the charter, the proceedings must be dismissed and all property restored to the company.

6. If the assets are distributed, they must be applied in the following manner:

(a) To the payment of the filing fee, penalties incurred and costs due to the State; and

(b) To the payment of the creditors of the company. Any balance remaining must be distributed among the members as provided in subsection 1 of NRS 86.521. (Added to NRS by 1993, 1011; A 1995, 1130; 2001, 1389, 3199; 2003, 48; 2003, 20th Special Session, 69; 2007, 2673, effective July 1, 2008)

**NRS 86.276 Defaulting companies: Conditions and procedure for reinstatement. [Effective through June 30, 2008.]**

1. Except as otherwise provided in subsections 3 and 4 and NRS 86.246, the Secretary of State shall reinstate any limited-liability company which has forfeited or which forfeits its right to transact business pursuant to the provisions of this chapter and shall restore to the company its right to carry on business in this State, and to exercise its privileges and immunities, if it:

(a) Files with the Secretary of State:

(1) The list required by NRS 86.263;

(2) The statement required by NRS 86.264, if applicable; and

(3) A certificate of acceptance of appointment signed by its resident agent; and

(b) Pays to the Secretary of State:

(1) The filing fee and penalty set forth in NRS 86.263 and 86.272 for each year or portion thereof during which it failed to file in a timely manner each required annual list;

(2) The fee set forth in NRS 86.264, if applicable; and

(3) A fee of $300 for reinstatement.

2. When the Secretary of State reinstates the limited-liability company, he shall issue to the company a certificate of reinstatement if the limited-liability company:

(a) Requests a certificate of reinstatement; and

(b) Pays the required fees pursuant to NRS 86.561.

3. The Secretary of State shall not order a reinstatement unless all delinquent fees and penalties have been paid, and the revocation of the charter occurred only by reason of failure to pay the fees and penalties.

4. If a company's charter has been revoked pursuant to the provisions of this chapter and has remained revoked for a period of 5 consecutive years, the charter must not be reinstated.

5. Except as otherwise provided in NRS 86.278, a reinstatement pursuant to this section relates back to the date on which the company forfeited its right to transact business under the provisions of this chapter and reinstates the company's right to transact business as if such right had at all times remained in full force and effect. (Added to NRS by 1993, 1011; A 1995, 1130; 1997, 2814; 2001, 1390, 3182, 3199; 2003, 20th Special Session, 70; 2007, 1325, 2424)

**NRS 86.276 Defaulting companies: Conditions and procedure for reinstatement. [Effective July 1, 2008.]**

1. Except as otherwise provided in subsections 3 and 4 and NRS 86.246, the Secretary of State shall reinstate any limited-liability company which has forfeited or which forfeits its right to transact business pursuant to the provisions of this chapter and shall restore to the company its right to carry on business in this State, and to exercise its privileges and immunities, if it:

(a) Files with the Secretary of State:

(1) The list required by NRS 86.263;

(2) The statement required by NRS 86.264, if applicable; and

(3) The information required pursuant to NRS 77.310; and

(b) Pays to the Secretary of State:

(1) The filing fee and penalty set forth in NRS 86.263 and 86.272 for each year or portion thereof during which it failed to file in a timely manner each required annual list;

(2) The fee set forth in NRS 86.264, if applicable; and

(3) A fee of $300 for reinstatement.

2. When the Secretary of State reinstates the limited-liability company, he shall issue to the company a certificate of reinstatement if the limited-liability company:

(a) Requests a certificate of reinstatement; and

(b) Pays the required fees pursuant to NRS 86.561.

3. The Secretary of State shall not order a reinstatement unless all delinquent fees and penalties have been paid, and the revocation of the charter occurred only by reason of failure to pay the fees and penalties.

4. If a company's charter has been revoked pursuant to the provisions of this chapter and has remained revoked for a period of 5 consecutive years, the charter must not be reinstated.

5. Except as otherwise provided in NRS 86.278, a reinstatement pursuant to this section relates back to the date on which the company forfeited its right to transact business under the provisions of this chapter and reinstates the company's right to transact business as if such right had at all times remained in full force and effect. (Added to NRS by 1993, 1011; A 1995, 1130; 1997, 2814; 2001, 1390, 3182, 3199; 2003, 20th Special Session, 70; 2007, 1325, 2424, 2674, effective July 1, 2008)

**NRS 86.278 Defaulting companies: Reinstatement under old or new name; regulations.**

1. Except as otherwise provided in subsection 2, if a limited-liability company applies to reinstate its charter but its name has been legally acquired or reserved by any other artificial person formed, organized, registered or qualified pursuant to the provisions of this title whose name is on file with the Office of the Secretary of State or reserved in the Office of the Secretary of State pursuant to the provisions of this title, the company shall submit in writing to the Secretary of State some other name under which it desires its existence to be reinstated. If that name is distinguishable from all other names reserved or otherwise on file, the Secretary of State shall reinstate the limited-liability company under that new name.

2. If the applying limited-liability company submits the written, acknowledged consent of the artificial person having the name, or the person reserving the name, which is not distinguishable from the old name of the applying company or a new name it has submitted, it may be reinstated under that name.

3. For the purposes of this section, a proposed name is not distinguishable from a name on file or reserved name solely because one or the other contains distinctive lettering, a distinctive mark, a trademark or a trade name or any combination of these.

4. The Secretary of State may adopt regulations that interpret the requirements of this section. (Added to NRS by 1993, 1012; A 1997, 2814; 1999, 1615; 2003, 20th Special Session, 70)

## Operation

**NRS 86.281 General powers.** A limited-liability company organized and existing pursuant to this chapter may exercise the powers and privileges granted by this chapter and may:

1. Sue and be sued, complain and defend, in its name;

2. Purchase, take, receive, lease or otherwise acquire, own, hold, improve, use and otherwise deal in and with real or personal property, or an interest in it, wherever situated;

3. Sell, convey, mortgage, pledge, lease, exchange, transfer and otherwise dispose of all or any part of its property and assets;

4. Lend money to and otherwise assist its members;

5. Purchase, take, receive, subscribe for or otherwise acquire, own, hold, vote, use, employ, sell, mortgage, lend, pledge or otherwise dispose of, and otherwise use and deal in and with shares, member's interests or other interests in or obligations of domestic or foreign limited-liability companies, domestic or foreign corporations, joint ventures or similar associations, general or limited partnerships or natural persons, or direct or indirect obligations of the United States or of any government, state, territory, governmental district or municipality or of any instrumentality of it;

6. Make contracts and guarantees and incur liabilities, borrow money at such rates of interest as the company may determine, issue its notes, bonds and other obligations and secure any of its obligations by mortgage or pledge of all or any part of its property, franchises and income;

7. Lend, invest and reinvest its money and take and hold real property and personal property for the payment of money so loaned or invested;

8. Conduct its business, carry on its operations and have and exercise the powers granted by this chapter in any state, territory, district or possession of the United States, or in any foreign country;

9. Appoint managers and agents, define their duties and fix their compensation;

10. Cease its activities and surrender its articles of organization;

11. Exercise all powers necessary or convenient to effect any of the purposes for which the company is organized; and

12. Hold a license issued pursuant to the provisions of chapter 463 of NRS. (Added to NRS by 1991, 1297; A 1993, 2011; 1997, 718; 2001, 1390, 3199)

**NRS 86.286 Operating agreement.**

1. A limited-liability company may, but is not required to, adopt an operating agreement. An operating agreement may be adopted only by the unanimous vote or unanimous written consent of the members, or by the sole member, and the operating agreement must be in writing. Unless otherwise provided in the operating agreement, amendments to the agreement may be adopted only by the unanimous vote or unanimous written consent of the persons who are members at the time of amendment.

2. An operating agreement may be adopted before, after or at the time of the filing of the articles of organization and, whether entered into before, after or at the time of the filing, may become effective at the formation of the limited-liability company or at a later date specified in the operating agreement. If an operating agreement is adopted:

(a) Before the filing of the articles of organization or before the effective date of formation specified in the articles of organization, the operating agreement is not effective until the effective date of formation of the limited-liability company.

(b) After the filing of the articles of organization or after the effective date of formation specified in the articles of organization, the operating agreement binds the limited-liability company and may be enforced whether or not the limited-liability company assents to the operating agreement.

3. An operating agreement may provide that a certificate of limited-liability company interest issued by the limited-liability company may evidence a member's interest in a limited-liability company. (Added to NRS by 1995, 2106; A 1997, 718; 2001, 1391, 3199; 2007, 2425)

**NRS 86.291 Management.**

1. Except as otherwise provided in this section or the articles of organization, management of a limited-liability company is vested in its members in proportion to their contribution to its capital, as adjusted from time to time to reflect properly any additional contributions or withdrawals by the members.

2. Unless otherwise provided in the articles of organization or operating agreement, the management of a series is vested in the members associated with the series in proportion to their contribution to the capital of the series, as adjusted from time to time to reflect properly any additional contributions or withdrawals from the assets or income of the series by the members associated with the series.

3. If provision is made in the articles of organization, management of the company may be vested in a manager or managers, who may but need not be members, in the manner prescribed by the operating agreement of the company. The manager or managers also hold the offices and have the responsibilities accorded to them by the members and set out in the operating agreement. (Added to NRS by 1991, 1300; A 1993, 1017; 1995, 1131; 1997, 719; 2001, 1391, 3199; 2005, 2192)

**NRS 86.293 Noneconomic members.** The articles of organization or operating agreement of a limited-liability company may provide for one or more noneconomic members or classes of noneconomic members. (Added to NRS by 2001, 1387; A 2001, 3199)

**NRS 86.296 Classes of members or managers; series of members.**

1. The articles of organization or operating agreement of a limited-liability company may create classes of members or managers, define their relative rights, powers and duties, and may authorize the creation, in the manner provided in the operating agreement, of additional classes of members or managers with the relative rights, powers and duties as may from time to

time be established, including, without limitation, rights, powers and duties senior to existing classes of members or managers. The articles of organization or operating agreement may provide that any member, or class or group of members, has voting rights that differ from other classes or groups.

2. The articles of organization or operating agreement of a limited-liability company may create one or more series of members, or vest authority in one or more members or managers of the company or in other persons to create one or more series of members, including, without limitation, rights, powers and duties senior to existing series of members. The articles of organization or operating agreement may provide that any member associated with a series has voting rights that differ from other members or series, or no voting rights at all. A series may have separate powers, rights or duties with respect to specified property or obligations of the company or profits and losses associated with specified property or obligations, and any series may have a separate business purpose or investment objective.

3. The debts, liabilities, obligations and expenses incurred, contracted for or otherwise existing with respect to a particular series are enforceable against the assets of that series only, and not against the assets of the company generally or any other series, if:

(a) Separate and distinct records are maintained for the series and the assets associated with the series are held, directly or indirectly, including through a nominee or otherwise, and accounted for separately from the other assets of the company and any other series; and

(b) The articles of organization comply, or an amendment to the articles complies, with the provisions of paragraph (e) of subsection 1 of NRS 86.161. Unless otherwise provided in the articles of organization or operating agreement, no debts, liabilities, obligations and expenses incurred, contracted for or otherwise existing with respect to the company generally or any other series are enforceable against the assets of the series.

4. The articles of organization or operating agreement may provide that the debts, liabilities, obligations and expenses incurred, contracted for or otherwise existing with respect to a particular series are enforceable against the assets of that series only, and not against the assets of the company generally or any other series.

5. Unless otherwise provided in the articles of organization or operating agreement, any event described in this chapter or in the articles of organization or operating agreement that causes a manager to cease to be a manager with respect to a series does not, in itself, cause the manager to cease to be a manager with respect to the company or with respect to any other series. Unless otherwise provided in the articles of organization or operating agreement, any event described in

this chapter or in the articles of organization or operating agreement that causes a manager to cease to be associated with a series does not, in itself, cause the member to cease to be associated with any other series, terminate the continued membership of a member in the company or cause the termination of the series, regardless of whether the member was the last remaining member associated with the series. (Added to NRS by 2001, 1385; A 2001, 3199; 2005, 2193)

**NRS 86.301 Limitation on authority to contract debt or incur liability.** Except as otherwise provided in this chapter, its articles of organization or its operating agreement, no debt may be contracted or liability incurred by or on behalf of a limited-liability company, except by:

1. One or more managers of a company which is managed by a manager or managers;

2. Any member of a company which is managed by its members;

3. Any agent, officer, employee or other representative of the company authorized in the operating agreement or in another writing by a manager or managers, if the company is managed by a manager or managers; or

4. Any agent, officer, employee or other representative of the company authorized in the operating agreement or in another writing by a member, if the company is managed by its members. (Added to NRS by 1991, 1300; A 1997, 719; 1999, 1615; 2001, 1391, 3199; 2003, 3140)

**NRS 86.311 Acquisition, ownership and disposition of property.** Real and personal property owned or purchased by a company must be held and owned, and conveyance made, in the name of the company. Except as otherwise provided in the company's articles of organization or operating agreement, instruments and records providing for the acquisition, mortgage or disposition of property of the company are valid and binding upon the company if signed by:

1. One or more managers of a company which is managed by a manager or managers;

2. Any member of a company which is managed by its members;

3. Any agent, officer, employee or other representative of the company authorized in the operating agreement or in another writing by a manager or managers, if the company is managed by a manager or managers; or

4. Any agent, officer, employee or other representative of the company authorized in the operating agreement or in another writing by a member, if the company is managed by its members. (Added to NRS by 1991, 1300; A 1997, 719; 2003, 3140)

**NRS 86.321 Contributions to capital: Form.** The contributions to capital of a member to a limited-liability company may be in cash, property or services rendered, or a promissory note or other binding obligation to contribute cash or property or to perform services. (Added to NRS by 1991, 1300; A 1997, 719)

## NRS 86.331 Resignation or withdrawal of member: Limitation; payment to member who rightfully resigns or withdraws.

1. Except as otherwise provided in chapter 463 of NRS, other applicable law, the articles of organization or the operating agreement, a member may not resign or withdraw as a member from a limited-liability company before the dissolution and winding up of the company.

2. If a member has a right to resign or withdraw, the amount that a resigning or withdrawing member is entitled to receive from the company for his interest must be determined pursuant to the provisions of this chapter, chapter 463 of NRS, the articles of organization or the operating agreement. If not otherwise provided therein, a resigning or withdrawing member is entitled to receive, within a reasonable time after resignation or withdrawal, the fair market value of his interest on the date of resignation or withdrawal. (Added to NRS by 1991, 1301; A 1993, 2012; 1995, 2111; 1997, 719)

## NRS 86.335 Resignation or withdrawal of member in violation of operating agreement; loss of right to participate upon resignation or withdrawal. Except as otherwise provided in this chapter, chapter 463 of NRS, the articles of organization or the operating agreement:

1. If the resignation or withdrawal of a member violates the operating agreement:

(a) The amount payable to the member who has resigned or withdrawn is the fair market value of his interest reduced by the amount of all damages sustained by the company or its other members as a result of the violation; and

(b) The company may defer the payment for so long as necessary to prevent unreasonable hardship to the company.

2. Except as otherwise provided in chapter 463 of NRS, the articles of organization or the operating agreement, a member who resigns or withdraws ceases to be a member, has no voting rights and has no right to participate in the management of the company, even if under this section a payment due him from the company is deferred. (Added to NRS by 1997, 714)

## NRS 86.341 Distribution of profits. A limited-liability company may, from time to time, divide the profits of its business and distribute them to its members, and any transferee as his interest may appear, upon the basis stipulated in the operating agreement. If the operating agreement does not otherwise provide, profits and losses must be allocated proportionately to the value, as shown in the records of the company, of the contributions made by each

member and not returned. (Added to NRS by 1991, 1301; A 1997, 720)

## NRS 86.343 Distribution of profits and contributions: Prohibition; applicable determinations; liability of member for violation.

1. Except as otherwise provided in subsection 2, a distribution of the profits and contributions of a limited-liability company must not be made if, after giving it effect:

(a) The company would not be able to pay its debts as they become due in the usual course of business; or

(b) Except as otherwise specifically permitted by the articles of organization, the total assets of the company would be less than the sum of its total liabilities.

2. A distribution of the profits and contributions of a series of the company must not be made if, after giving it effect:

(a) The company would not be able to pay the debts of the series from assets of the series as debts of the series become due in the usual course of business; or

(b) Except as otherwise specifically permitted by the articles of organization, the total assets of the series would be less than the sum of the total liabilities of the series.

3. The manager or, if management of the company is not vested in a manager or managers, the members may base a determination that a distribution is not prohibited pursuant to this section on:

(a) Financial statements prepared on the basis of accounting practices that are reasonable in the circumstances;

(b) A fair valuation, including unrealized appreciation and depreciation; or

(c) Any other method that is reasonable in the circumstances.

4. The effect of a distribution pursuant to this section must be measured:

(a) In the case of a distribution by purchase, redemption or other acquisition by the company of member's interests, as of the earlier of:

(1) The date on which money or other property is transferred or debt incurred by the company; or

(2) The date on which the member ceases to be a member with respect to his acquired interest.

(b) In the case of any other distribution of indebtedness, as of the date on which the indebtedness is distributed.

(c) In all other cases, as of:

(1) The date on which the distribution is authorized if the payment occurs within 120 days after the date of authorization; or

(2) The date on which the payment is made if it occurs more than 120 days after the date of authorization.

5. Indebtedness of the company, or a series of the company, including indebtedness issued as a distribution, is not considered a liability for purposes of determinations pursuant to this section if its terms provide that payment of principal and interest are to be made only if and to the extent that payment of a distribution to the members could then be made pursuant to this section. If the indebtedness is issued as a distribution, each payment of principal or interest must be treated as a distribution, the effect of which must be measured as of the date of payment.

6. Except as otherwise provided in subsection 7, a member who receives a distribution in violation of this section is liable to the limited-liability company for the amount of the distribution. This subsection does not affect the validity of an obligation or liability of a member created by an agreement or other applicable law for the amount of a distribution.

7. A member who receives a distribution from a limited-liability company in violation of this section is not liable to the limited liability company and, in the event of its dissolution or insolvency, to its creditors, or any of them, for the amount of the distribution after the expiration of 3 years after the date of the distribution unless an action to recover the distribution from the member is commenced before the expiration of the 3-year period following the distribution. (Added to NRS by 1997, 713; A 2001, 1392, 3199; 2005, 2194)

### NRS 86.346 Distributions: Form; status of member or transferee.

1. Unless otherwise provided in the operating agreement, a member, regardless of the nature of his contributions, or a transferee, regardless of the nature of his predecessor's contributions, has no right to demand or receive any distribution from a limited-liability company in any form other than cash.

2. Except as otherwise provided in NRS 86.391 and 86.521, and unless otherwise provided in the operating agreement, at the time a member or transferee becomes entitled to receive a distribution he has the status of and is entitled to all remedies available to a creditor of the company with respect to the distribution. (Added to NRS by 1995, 2106; A 1997, 720)

### NRS 86.351 Nature and transfer of member's interest; rights of transferee; substituted members.

1. The interest of each member of a limited-liability company is personal property. The articles of organization or operating agreement may prohibit or regulate the transfer of a member's interest. Unless otherwise provided in the articles or operating agreement, a transferee of a member's interest has no right to participate in the management of the business and affairs of the company or to become a member unless a majority in interest of the other members approve the transfer.

If so approved, the transferee becomes a substituted member. The transferee is only entitled to receive the share of profits or other compensation by way of income, and the return of contributions, to which his transferor would otherwise be entitled.

2. A substituted member has all the rights and powers and is subject to all the restrictions and liabilities of his transferor, except that the substitution of the transferee does not release the transferor from any liability to the company. (Added to NRS by 1991, 1302; A 1995, 2112; 1997, 720; 2001, 1392, 3199)

## Liability, Indemnificatin and Insurance

### NRS 86.361 Liability of persons assuming to act as company without authority. All persons who assume to act as a limited liability company without authority to do so are jointly and severally liable for all debts and liabilities of the company. (Added to NRS by 1991, 1304)

### NRS 86.371 Liability of member or manager for debts or liabilities of company. Unless otherwise provided in the articles of organization or an agreement signed by the member or manager to be charged, no member or manager of any limited-liability company formed under the laws of this State is individually liable for the debts or liabilities of the company. (Added to NRS by 1991, 1300; A 1995, 2112)

### NRS 86.381 Member of company is not proper party in proceeding by or against company; exception. A member of a limited-liability company is not a proper party to proceedings by or against the company, except where the object is to enforce the member's right against or liability to the company. (Added to NRS by 1991, 1304)

### NRS 86.391 Liability of member to company.

1. A member is liable to a limited-liability company:

(a) For a difference between his contributions to capital as actually made and as stated in the articles of organization or operating agreement as having been made; and

(b) For any unpaid contribution to capital which he agreed in the articles of organization or operating agreement to make in the future at the time and on the conditions stated in the articles of organization or operating agreement.

2. A member holds as trustee for the company specific property stated in the articles of organization or operating agreement as contributed by him, but which was not so contributed.

3. The liabilities of a member as set out in this section can be waived or compromised only by the consent of all of the members, but a waiver or compromise does not affect the right of a creditor of the company to enforce the liabilities if he extended credit or his claim arose

before the effective date of an amendment of the articles of organization or operating agreement effecting the waiver or compromise. (Added to NRS by 1991, 1301; A 1997, 721; 2001, 1393, 3199)

### NRS 86.401 Rights and remedies of creditor of member.

1. On application to a court of competent jurisdiction by a judgment creditor of a member, the court may charge the member's interest with payment of the unsatisfied amount of the judgment with interest. To the extent so charged, the judgment creditor has only the rights of an assignee of the member's interest.

2. This section:

(a) Provides the exclusive remedy by which a judgment creditor of a member or an assignee of a member may satisfy a judgment out of the member's interest of the judgment debtor.

(b) Does not deprive any member of the benefit of any exemption applicable to his interest. (Added to NRS by 1991, 1302; A 2001, 1393, 3199; 2003, 20th Special Session, 71)

### NRS 86.411 Indemnification of manager, member, employee or agent: Proceeding other than by company.

A limited-liability company may indemnify any person who was or is a party or is threatened to be made a party to any threatened, pending or completed action, suit or proceeding, whether civil, criminal, administrative or investigative, except an action by or in the right of the company, by reason of the fact that he is or was a manager, member, employee or agent of the company, or is or was serving at the request of the company as a manager, member, employee or agent of another limited-liability company, corporation, partnership, joint venture, trust or other enterprise, against expenses, including attorney's fees, judgments, fines and amounts paid in settlement actually and reasonably incurred by him in connection with the action, suit or proceeding if he acted in good faith and in a manner which he reasonably believed to be in or not opposed to the best interests of the company, and, with respect to any criminal action or proceeding, had no reasonable cause to believe his conduct was unlawful. The termination of any action, suit or proceeding by judgment, order, settlement or conviction, or upon a plea of nolo contendere or its equivalent, does not, of itself, create a presumption that the person did not act in good faith and in a manner which he reasonably believed to be in or not opposed to the best interests of the limited-liability company, and that, with respect to any criminal action or proceeding, he had reasonable cause to believe that his conduct was unlawful. (Added to NRS by 1991, 1297; A 1997, 721)

### NRS 86.421 Indemnification of manager, member, employee or agent: Proceeding by company.

A limited-liability company may indemnify any person who was or is a party or is threatened to be made a party to any threatened, pending or completed action or suit by or in the right of the company to procure a judgment in its favor by reason of the fact that he is or was a manager, member, employee or agent of the company, or is or was serving at the request of the company as a manager, member, employee or agent of another limited-liability company, corporation, partnership, joint venture, trust or other enterprise against expenses, including amounts paid in settlement and attorneys' fees actually and reasonably incurred by him in connection with the defense or settlement of the action or suit if he acted in good faith and in a manner in which he reasonably believed to be in or not opposed to the best interests of the company. Indemnification may not be made for any claim, issue or matter as to which such a person has been adjudged by a court of competent jurisdiction, after exhaustion of all appeals therefrom, to be liable to the company or for amounts paid in settlement to the company, unless and only to the extent that the court in which the action or suit was brought or other court of competent jurisdiction determines upon application that in view of all the circumstances of the case, he is fairly and reasonably entitled to indemnity for such expenses as the court deems proper. (Added to NRS by 1991, 1298; A 1997, 722)

### NRS 86.431 Indemnification of manager, member, employee or agent: Scope; authorization.

1. To the extent that a manager, member, employee or agent of a limited-liability company has been successful on the merits or otherwise in defense of any action, suit or proceeding described in NRS 86.411 and 86.421, or in defense of any claim, issue or matter therein, the company shall indemnify him against expenses, including attorney's fees, actually and reasonably incurred by him in connection with the defense.

2. Any indemnification under NRS 86.411 and 86.421, unless ordered by a court or advanced pursuant to NRS 86.441, may be made by the limited-liability company only as authorized in the specific case upon a determination that indemnification of the manager, member, employee or agent is proper in the circumstances. The determination must be made:

(a) By the members or managers as provided in the articles of organization or the operating agreement;

(b) If there is no provision in the articles of organization or the operating agreement, by a majority in interest of the members who are not parties to the action, suit or proceeding;

(c) If a majority in interest of the members who are not parties to the action, suit or proceeding so order, by independent legal counsel in a written opinion; or

(d) If members who are not parties to the action, suit or proceeding cannot be obtained, by independent legal counsel in a written opinion. (Added to NRS by 1991, 1298; A 1993, 1017; 1997, 722)

**NRS 86.441 Indemnification of member or manager: Advancement of expenses.** The articles of organization, the operating agreement or a separate agreement made by a limited-liability company may provide that the expenses of members and managers incurred in defending a civil or criminal action, suit or proceeding must be paid by the company as they are incurred and in advance of the final disposition of the action, suit or proceeding, upon receipt of an undertaking by or on behalf of the manager or member to repay the amount if it is ultimately determined by a court of competent jurisdiction that he is not entitled to be indemnified by the company. The provisions of this section do not affect any rights to advancement of expenses to which personnel of the company other than managers or members may be entitled under any contract or otherwise by law. (Added to NRS by 1991, 1299; A 1997, 723)

**NRS 86.451 Indemnification of manager, member, employee or agent: Effect of provisions on other rights; continuation after cessation of status.** Indemnification or advancement of expenses authorized in or ordered by a court pursuant to NRS 86.411 to 86.441, inclusive:

1. Does not exclude any other rights to which a person seeking indemnification or advancement of expenses may be entitled under the articles of organization or any operating agreement, vote of members or disinterested managers, if any, or otherwise, for an action in his official capacity or an action in another capacity while holding his office, except that indemnification, unless ordered by a court pursuant to NRS 86.421 or for the advancement of expenses made pursuant to NRS 86.441, may not be made to or on behalf of any member or manager if a final adjudication establishes that his acts or omissions involved intentional misconduct, fraud or a knowing violation of the law and was material to the cause of action.

2. Continues for a person who has ceased to be a member, manager, employee or agent and inures to the benefit of his heirs, executors and administrators. (Added to NRS by 1991, 1299; A 1997, 723)

**NRS 86.461 Maintenance of insurance or other financial arrangements against liability of member, manager, employee or agent.**

1. A limited-liability company may purchase and maintain insurance or make other financial arrangements on behalf of any person who is or was a member, manager, employee or agent of the company, or is or was serving at the request of the company as a manager, member, employee or agent of another corporation, limited-liability company, partnership, joint venture, trust or other enterprise for any liability asserted against him and liability and expenses incurred by him in his capacity as a manager, member, employee or agent, or arising out of his status as such, whether or not the company has the authority to indemnify him against such liability and expenses.

2. The other financial arrangements made by the company pursuant to subsection 1 may include:

(a) The creation of a trust fund.

(b) The establishment of a program of self-insurance.

(c) The securing of its obligation of indemnification by granting a security interest or other lien on any assets of the company.

(d) The establishment of a letter of credit, guaranty or surety. No financial arrangement made pursuant to this subsection may provide protection for a person adjudged by a court of competent jurisdiction, after exhaustion of all appeals therefrom, to be liable for intentional misconduct, fraud or a knowing violation of law, except with respect to the advancement of expenses or indemnification ordered by a court.

3. Any insurance or other financial arrangement made on behalf of a person pursuant to this section may be provided by the company or any other person approved by the managers, if any, or by the members, if no managers exist, even if all or part of the other person's member's interest in the company is owned by the company. (Added to NRS by 1991, 1299)

**NRS 86.471 Effect of providing insurance or other financial arrangements against liability of member, manager, employee or agent.** In the absence of fraud:

1. The decision of a limited-liability company as to the propriety of the terms and conditions of any insurance or other financial arrangement made pursuant to NRS 86.461 and the choice of the person to provide the insurance or other financial arrangement is conclusive; and

2. The insurance or other financial arrangement:

(a) Is not void or voidable; and

(b) Does not subject any manager or member approving it to personal liability for his action, even if a manager or member approving the insurance or other financial arrangement is a beneficiary of the insurance or other financial arrangement. (Added to NRS by 1991, 1300)

**NRS 86.481 Exclusion of company which provides self-insurance from title 57 of NRS.** A limited-liability company or its subsidiary which provides self-insurance for itself or for an affiliated limited-liability company pursuant to NRS 86.461 is not subject to the provisions of title 57 of NRS. (Added to NRS by 1991, 1300)

## Derivative Actions

**NRS 86.483 Authority of member to bring action.** A member, including a noneconomic member unless otherwise prohibited by the terms of the articles of organization or operating agreement, may bring an action in the right of a limited-liability company to recover a judgment in its favor if managers or members with authority to do so have refused to bring the action or if an effort to cause those managers or members to bring the action is not likely to succeed. (Added to NRS by 2001, 1385; A 2001, 3199; 2003, 3141; 2007, 2425)

**NRS 86.485 Qualifications of plaintiff.** In a derivative action, the plaintiff must be a member at the time of the transaction of which he complains. (Added to NRS by 2001, 1386; A 2001, 3199; 2003, 3141)

**NRS 86.487 Pleading.** In a derivative action, the complaint must set forth with particularity:

1. The effort of the plaintiff to secure initiation of the action by a manager or member; or

2. The reasons for the plaintiff not making the effort to secure initiation of the action by a manager or member. (Added to NRS by 2001, 1386; A 2001, 3199)

**NRS 86.489 Expenses.** If a derivative action is successful, in whole or in part, or if anything is received by the plaintiff as a result of a judgment, compromise or settlement of an action or claim, the court may award the plaintiff reasonable expenses, including reasonable attorney's fees, and shall direct him to remit to the limited-liability company the remainder of those proceeds received by him. (Added to NRS by 2001, 1386; A 2001, 3199)

## Dissolution

**NRS 86.490 Dissolution before commencement of business; limitations.**

1. Before the commencement of business by any limited-liability company where management is vested in one or more managers and where no member's interest in the limited-liability company has been issued, at least two-thirds of the organizers or the managers of the limited-liability company may dissolve the limited-liability company by filing with the Secretary of State a certificate of dissolution to dissolve the limited-liability company.

2. A certificate of dissolution filed with the Secretary of State pursuant to subsection 1 must state that:

(a) The management of the limited-liability company is vested in one or more managers;

(b) The limited-liability company has not commenced business; and

(c) No member's interest in the limited-liability company has been issued. (Added to NRS by 2007, 2424)

**NRS 86.491 Events requiring dissolution and winding up of affairs; effect of certain events affecting member.**

1. A limited-liability company must be dissolved and its affairs wound up:

(a) At the time, if any, specified in the articles of organization;

(b) Upon the occurrence of an event specified in an operating agreement;

(c) Unless otherwise provided in the articles of organization or operating agreement, upon the affirmative vote or written agreement of all the members; or

(d) Upon entry of a decree of judicial dissolution pursuant to NRS 86.495.

2. The affairs of a series of a limited-liability company must be wound up:

(a) At the time, if any, specified in the articles of organization;

(b) Upon the occurrence of an event specified in the operating agreement;

(c) Unless otherwise provided in the articles of organization or operating agreement, upon the affirmative vote or written agreement of all the members associated with the series; or

(d) Upon entry of a decree of judicial termination of the series pursuant to NRS 86.495.

3. Unless otherwise provided in the articles of organization or operating agreement, upon the occurrence of an event requiring the affairs of a series to be wound up, a manager of the series who has not wrongfully terminated the series or, if none, the members associated with a series, or a person approved by all those members, may wind up the affairs of the series. Unless otherwise provided in the articles of organization or operating agreement, the person or persons winding up the affairs of the series:

(a) May take all actions necessary or proper to wind up the affairs of the series; and

(b) Shall distribute the assets of the series as provided in NRS 86.521 to the creditors of the series and the members associated with the series.

4. Except as otherwise provided in the articles of organization or operating agreement, the death, retirement, resignation, expulsion, bankruptcy, dissolution or disso-ciation of a member or any other event affecting a

member, including, without limitation, a sole member, does not:

(a) Terminate the status of the person as a member; or

(b) Cause the limited-liability company to be dissolved or its affairs to be wound up.

5. Except as otherwise provided in the articles of organization or operating agreement, upon the death of a natural person who is the sole member of a limited-liability company or the sole member associated with a series, the status of the member, including the member's interest, may pass to the heirs, successors and assigns of the member by will or applicable law. The heir, successor or assign of the member's interest becomes a substituted member pursuant to NRS 86.351, subject to administration as provided by applicable law, without the permission or consent of the heirs, successors or assigns or those administering the estate of the deceased member. (Added to NRS by 1991, 1302; A 1995, 2112; 1997, 723; 2001, 1394, 3199; 2005, 2195)

**NRS 86.495 Dissolution by decree of court; termination of series by decree of court.**

1. Upon application by or for a member, the district court may decree dissolution of a limited-liability company whenever it is not reasonably practicable to carry on the business of the company in conformity with the articles of organization or operating agreement.

2. Upon application by or for a member of a series, the district court may decree the termination of the series only, and not the dissolution of the company, whenever it is not reasonably practicable to carry on the business of the series in conformity with the articles of organization or operating agreement. (Added to NRS by 2001, 1385; A 2001, 3199; 2005, 2196)

**NRS 86.505 Continuation of company after dissolution for winding up of affairs; limitation on actions by or against dissolved company.** The dissolution of a limited-liability company does not impair any remedy or cause of action available to or against it or its managers or members arising before its dissolution and commenced within 2 years after the date of the dissolution. A dissolved company continues as a company for the purpose of prosecuting and defending suits, actions, proceedings and claims of any kind or nature by or against it and of enabling it gradually to settle and close its business, to collect and discharge its obligations, to dispose of and convey its property, and to distribute its assets, but not for the purpose of continuing the business for which it was established. (Added to NRS by 1995, 2106; A 1997, 724)

**NRS 86.521 Distribution of assets after dissolution.**

1. In settling accounts after dissolution, the liabilities of a limited-liability company are entitled to payment in the following order:

(a) Those to creditors, including members who are creditors, in the order of priority as provided and to the extent otherwise permitted by law, except those to members of the limited-liability company on account of their contributions;

(b) Those to members of the limited-liability company in respect of their share of the profits and other compensation by way of income on their contributions; and

(c) Those to members of the limited-liability company in respect of their contributions to capital.

2. Subject to any statement in the operating agreement, members share in the company's assets in respect to their claims for capital and in respect to their claims for profits or for compensation by way of income on their contributions, respectively, in proportion to the respective amounts of the claims. (Added to NRS by 1991, 1303; A 1995, 2113)

**NRS 86.531 Articles of dissolution: Required provisions.**

1. When all debts, liabilities and obligations have been paid and discharged or adequate provision has been made therefor and all of the remaining property and assets have been distributed to the members, articles of dissolution must be prepared and signed setting forth:

(a) The name of the limited-liability company;

(b) That all debts, obligations and liabilities have been paid and discharged or that adequate provision has been made therefor;

(c) That all the remaining property and assets have been distributed among its members in accordance with their respective rights and interests; and

(d) That there are no suits pending against the company in any court or that adequate provision has been made for the satisfaction of any judgment, order or decree which may be entered against it in any pending suit.

2. The articles must be signed by a manager, or if there is no manager by a member, of the company. (Added to NRS by 1991, 1303; A 1995, 2113; 1999, 1616)

**NRS 86.541 Articles of dissolution: Filing; effect of filing.**

1. The signed articles of dissolution must be filed with the Secretary of State. Articles of dissolution are effective upon filing the articles with the Secretary of State or upon a later date specified in the articles, which must not be more than 90 days after the articles are filed.

2. Upon the filing of the articles of dissolution or upon a later date specified in the articles, the existence of the

company ceases, except for the purpose of suits, other proceedings and appropriate action as provided in this chapter. The manager or managers in office at the time of dissolution, or the survivors of them, are thereafter trustees for the members and creditors of the dissolved company and as such have authority to distribute any property of the company discovered after dissolution, convey real estate and take such other action as may be necessary on behalf of and in the name of the dissolved company. (Added to NRS by 1991, 1303; A 1995, 2113; 1999, 1616; 2001, 1394, 3199; 2005, 2197)

## Foreign Limited-Liability Companies

**NRS 86.543 Law governing organization, internal affairs and liability of managers and members.** Subject to the Constitution of this State:

1. The laws of the state, pursuant to which a foreign limited-liability company is organized, govern its organization, internal affairs and the liability of its managers and members; and

2. A foreign limited-liability company may not be denied registration by reason of any difference between the laws of the state of organization and the laws of this State. (Added to NRS by 2001, 1386; A 2001, 3199)

**NRS 86.544 Filing requirements; required provisions of application for registration. [Effective through June 30, 2008.]** Before transacting business in this State, a foreign limited-liability company must register with the Secretary of State. In order to register, a foreign limited-liability company must submit to the Secretary of State an application for registration as a foreign limited liability company, signed by a manager of the company or, if management is not vested in a manager, a member of the company and a signed certificate of acceptance of a resident agent. The application for registration must set forth:

1. The name of the foreign limited-liability company and, if different, the name under which it proposes to register and transact business in this State;

2. The state and date of its formation;

3. The name and address of the resident agent in this State whom the foreign limited-liability company elects to appoint;

4. A statement that the Secretary of State is appointed the agent of the foreign limited-liability company for service of process if the authority of the resident agent has been revoked, or if the resident agent has resigned or cannot be found or served with the exercise of reasonable diligence;

5. The address of the office required to be maintained in the state of its organization by the laws of that state or, if not so required, of the principal office of the foreign limited-liability company;

6. The name and business address of each manager or, if management is not vested in a manager, each member;

7. The address of the office at which is kept a list of the names and addresses of the members and their capital contributions, together with an undertaking by the foreign limited-liability company to keep those records until the registration in this State of the foreign limited-liability company is cancelled or withdrawn; and

8. If the foreign limited-liability company has one or more series of members and if the debts or liabilities of a series are enforceable against the assets of that series only and not against the assets of the company generally or another series, a statement to that effect. (Added to NRS by 2001, 1386; A 2001, 3199; 2003, 3141; 2005, 2197)

**NRS 86.544 Filing requirements; required provisions of application for registration. [Effective July 1, 2008.]** Before transacting business in this State, a foreign limited-liability company must register with the Secretary of State. In order to register, a foreign limited-liability company must submit to the Secretary of State an application for registration as a foreign limited-liability company, signed by a manager of the company or, if management is not vested in a manager, a member of the company. The application for registration must set forth:

1. The name of the foreign limited-liability company and, if different, the name under which it proposes to register and transact business in this State;

2. The state and date of its formation;

3. The information required pursuant to NRS 77.310;

4. A statement that the Secretary of State is appointed the agent of the foreign limited-liability company for service of process if the authority of the registered agent has been revoked, or if the registered agent has resigned or cannot be found or served with the exercise of reasonable diligence;

5. The address of the office required to be maintained in the state of its organization by the laws of that state or, if not so required, of the principal office of the foreign limited-liability company;

6. The name and business address of each manager or, if management is not vested in a manager, each member;

7. The address of the office at which is kept a list of the names and addresses of the members and their capital contributions, together with an undertaking by the foreign limited-liability company to keep those records until the registration in this State of the foreign limited-liability company is cancelled or withdrawn; and

8. If the foreign limited-liability company has one or more series of members and if the debts or liabilities of a series are enforceable against the assets of that series only and not against the assets of the company generally or another series, a statement to that effect. (Added to NRS by 2001, 1386; A 2001, 3199; 2003, 3141; 2005, 2197; 2007, 2675, effective July 1, 2008)

**NRS 86.545 Issuance of certificate of registration by Secretary of State.** If the Secretary of State finds that an application for registration conforms to law and all requisite fees have been paid, he shall issue a certificate of registration to transact business in this State and mail it to the person who filed the application or his representative. (Added to NRS by 2001, 1387; A 2001, 3199)

**NRS 86.546 Name for registration.** A foreign limited-liability company may register with the Secretary of State under any name, whether or not it is the name under which it is registered in its state of organization, which contains the words required by NRS 86.171 and which could be registered by a domestic limited-liability company. (Added to NRS by 2001, 1387; A 2001, 3199)

**NRS 86.5461 Annual list: Filing requirements; fees; powers and duties of Secretary of State. [Effective through June 30, 2008.]**

1. Each foreign limited-liability company doing business in this State shall, on or before the last day of the first month after the filing of its application for registration as a foreign limited-liability company with the Secretary of State, and annually thereafter on or before the last day of the month in which the anniversary date of its qualification to do business in this State occurs in each year, file with the Secretary of State a list on a form furnished by him that contains:

(a) The name of the foreign limited-liability company;

(b) The file number of the foreign limited-liability company, if known;

(c) The names and titles of all its managers or, if there is no manager, all its managing members;

(d) The address, either residence or business, of each manager or managing member listed pursuant to paragraph (c);

(e) The name and street address of its lawfully designated resident agent in this State; and

(f) The signature of a manager or managing member of the foreign limited-liability company certifying that the list is true, complete and accurate.

2. Each list filed pursuant to this section must be accompanied by a declaration under penalty of perjury that the foreign limited liability company:

(a) Has complied with the provisions of NRS 360.780; and

(b) Acknowledges that pursuant to NRS 239.330, it is a category C felony to knowingly offer any false or forged instrument for filing with the Office of the Secretary of State.

3. Upon filing:

(a) The initial list required by this section, the foreign limited-liability company shall pay to the Secretary of State a fee of $125.

(b) Each annual list required by this section, the foreign limited-liability company shall pay to the Secretary of State a fee of $125.

4. If a manager or managing member of a foreign limited-liability company resigns and the resignation is not reflected on the annual or amended list of managers and managing members, the foreign limited-liability company or the resigning manager or managing member shall pay to the Secretary of State a fee of $75 to file the resignation.

5. The Secretary of State shall, 90 days before the last day for filing each annual list required by this section, cause to be mailed to each foreign limited-liability company which is required to comply with the provisions of NRS 86.5461 to 86.5468, inclusive, and which has not become delinquent, the blank forms to be completed and filed with him. Failure of any foreign limited-liability company to receive the forms does not excuse it from the penalty imposed by the provisions of NRS 86.5461 to 86.5468, inclusive.

6. If the list to be filed pursuant to the provisions of subsection 1 is defective or the fee required by subsection 3 is not paid, the Secretary of State may return the list for correction or payment.

7. An annual list for a foreign limited-liability company not in default which is received by the Secretary of State more than 90 days before its due date must be deemed an amended list for the previous year and does not satisfy the requirements of this section for the year to which the due date is applicable. (Added to NRS by 2003, 20th Special Session, 60; A 2005, 2260)

**NRS 86.5461 Annual list: Filing requirements; fees; powers and duties of Secretary of State. [Effective July 1, 2008.]**

1. Each foreign limited-liability company doing business in this State shall, on or before the last day of the first month after the filing of its application for registration as a foreign limited-liability company with the Secretary of State, and annually thereafter on or before the last day of the month in which the anniversary date of its qualification to do business in this State occurs in each year, file with the Secretary of State a list on a form furnished by him that contains:

(a) The name of the foreign limited-liability company;

(b) The file number of the foreign limited-liability company, if known;

(c) The names and titles of all its managers or, if there is no manager, all its managing members;

(d) The address, either residence or business, of each manager or managing member listed pursuant to paragraph (c);

(e) The information required pursuant to NRS 77.310; and

(f) The signature of a manager or managing member of the foreign limited-liability company certifying that the list is true, complete and accurate.

2. Each list filed pursuant to this section must be accompanied by a declaration under penalty of perjury that the foreign limited liability company:

(a) Has complied with the provisions of NRS 360.780; and

(b) Acknowledges that pursuant to NRS 239.330, it is a category C felony to knowingly offer any false or forged instrument for filing with the Office of the Secretary of State.

3. Upon filing:

(a) The initial list required by this section, the foreign limited-liability company shall pay to the Secretary of State a fee of $125.

(b) Each annual list required by this section, the foreign limited-liability company shall pay to the Secretary of State a fee of $125.

4. If a manager or managing member of a foreign limited-liability company resigns and the resignation is not reflected on the annual or amended list of managers and managing members, the foreign limited-liability company or the resigning manager or managing member shall pay to the Secretary of State a fee of $75 to file the resignation.

5. The Secretary of State shall, 90 days before the last day for filing each annual list required by this section, cause to be mailed to each foreign limited-liability company which is required to comply with the provisions of NRS 86.5461 to 86.5468, inclusive, and which has not become delinquent, the blank forms to be completed and filed with him. Failure of any foreign limited-liability company to receive the forms does not excuse it from the penalty imposed by the provisions of NRS 86.5461 to 86.5468, inclusive.

6. If the list to be filed pursuant to the provisions of subsection 1 is defective or the fee required by subsection 3 is not paid, the Secretary of State may return the list for correction or payment.

7. An annual list for a foreign limited-liability company not in default which is received by the Secretary of State more than 90 days before its due date shall be deemed an amended list for the previous year and does not satisfy the requirements of this section for the year to which the due date is applicable. (Added to NRS by

2003, 20th Special Session, 60; A 2005, 2260; 2007, 2675, effective July 1, 2008)

**NRS 86.54615 List or statement to be maintained at registered office or principal place of business; requirement to assist in criminal investigation; failure to comply; regulations.**

1. A foreign limited-liability company shall maintain at its registered office or principal place of business in this State:

(a) A current list of each member and manager; or

(b) A statement indicating where such a list is maintained.

2. The foreign limited-liability company shall:

(a) Provide the Secretary of State with the name and contact information of the custodian of the list described in subsection 1. The information required pursuant to this paragraph shall be kept confidential by the Secretary of State.

(b) Provide written notice to the Secretary of State within 10 days after any change in the information contained in the list described in subsection 1.

3. Upon the request of any law enforcement agency in the course of a criminal investigation, the Secretary of State may require a foreign limited-liability company to:

(a) Submit to the Secretary of State, within 3 business days, a copy of the list required to be maintained pursuant to subsection 1; or

(b) Answer any interrogatory submitted by the Secretary of State that will assist in the criminal investigation.

4. If a foreign limited-liability company fails to comply with any requirement pursuant to subsection 3, the Secretary of State may take any action necessary, including, without limitation, the suspension or revocation of the registration of the foreign limited-liability company.

5. The Secretary of State shall not reinstate or revive a registration that was revoked or suspended pursuant to subsection 4 unless:

(a) The foreign limited-liability company complies with the requirements of subsection 3; or

(b) The law enforcement agency conducting the investigation advises the Secretary of State to reinstate or revive the registration.

6. The Secretary of State may adopt regulations to administer the provisions of this section. (Added to NRS by 2007, 1323)

**NRS 86.5462 Additional filing requirements for certain companies: Criteria; statement; fees.**

1. At the time of submitting any list required pursuant to NRS 86.5461, a foreign limited-liability company

that meets the criteria set forth in subsection 2 must submit:

(a) The statement required pursuant to subsection 3, accompanied by a declaration under penalty of perjury attesting that the statement does not contain any material misrepresentation of fact; and

(b) A fee of $100,000, to be distributed in the manner provided pursuant to subsection 4.

2. A foreign limited-liability company must submit a statement pursuant to this section if the foreign limited-liability company, including its parent and all subsidiaries:

(a) Holds 25 percent or more of the share of the market within this State for any product sold or distributed by the foreign limited liability company within this State; and

(b) Has had, during the previous 5-year period, a total of five or more investigations commenced against the foreign limited liability company, its parent or its subsidiaries in any jurisdiction within the United States, including all state and federal investigations:

(1) Which concern any alleged contract, combination or conspiracy in restraint of trade, as described in subsection 1 of NRS 598A.060, or which concern similar activities prohibited by a substantially similar law of another jurisdiction; and

(2) Which resulted in the foreign limited-liability company being fined or otherwise penalized or which resulted in the foreign limited-liability company being required to divest any holdings or being unable to acquire any holdings as a condition for the settlement, dismissal or resolution of those investigations.

3. A foreign limited-liability company that meets the criteria set forth in subsection 2 shall submit a statement which includes the following information with respect to each investigation:

(a) The jurisdiction in which the investigation was commenced.

(b) A summary of the nature of the investigation and the facts and circumstances surrounding the investigation.

(c) If the investigation resulted in criminal or civil litigation, a copy of all pleadings filed in the investigation by any party to the litigation.

(d) A summary of the outcome of the investigation, including specific information concerning whether any fine or penalty was imposed against the foreign limited-liability company and whether the foreign limited-liability company was required to divest any holdings or was unable to acquire any holdings as a condition for the settlement, dismissal or resolution of the investigation.

4. The fee collected pursuant to subsection 1 must be deposited in the Attorney General's Administration Budget Account and used solely for the purpose of investigating any alleged contract, combination or conspiracy in restraint of trade, as described in subsection 1 of NRS 598A.060. (Added to NRS by 2003, 20th Special Session, 61)

**NRS 86.5463 Certificate of authorization to transact business.** If a foreign limited-liability company has filed the initial or annual list in compliance with NRS 86.5461 and has paid the appropriate fee for the filing, the cancelled check or other proof of payment received by the foreign limited-liability company constitutes a certificate authorizing it to transact its business within this State until the last day of the month in which the anniversary of its qualification to transact business occurs in the next succeeding calendar year. (Added to NRS by 2003, 20th Special Session, 61)

**NRS 86.5464 Addresses of managers or managing members required; failure to file.**

1. Each list required to be filed under the provisions of NRS 86.5461 to 86.5468, inclusive, must, after the name of each manager or, if there is no manager, each of its managing members listed thereon, set forth the address, either residence or business, of each manager or managing member.

2. If the addresses are not stated for each person on any list offered for filing, the Secretary of State may refuse to file the list, and the foreign limited-liability company for which the list has been offered for filing is subject to all the provisions of NRS 86.5461 to 86.5468, inclusive, relating to failure to file the list within or at the times therein specified, unless a list is subsequently submitted for filing which conforms to the provisions of this section. (Added to NRS by 2003, 20th Special Session, 62)

**NRS 86.5465 Defaulting companies: Identification; forfeiture of right to transact business; penalty.**

1. Each foreign limited-liability company which is required to make a filing and pay the fee prescribed in NRS 86.5461 to 86.5468, inclusive, and which refuses or neglects to do so within the time provided is in default.

2. For default there must be added to the amount of the fee a penalty of $75, and unless the filing is made and the fee and penalty are paid on or before the last day of the month in which the anniversary date of the foreign limited-liability company occurs, the defaulting foreign limited-liability company by reason of its default forfeits its right to transact any business within this State. The fee and penalty must be collected as provided in this chapter. (Added to NRS by 2003, 20th Special Session, 62)

**NRS 86.5466 Defaulting companies: Duties of Secretary of State. [Effective through June 30, 2008.]**

1. The Secretary of State shall notify, by providing written notice to its resident agent, each foreign limited-liability company deemed in default pursuant to NRS 86.5465. The written notice:

(a) Must include a statement indicating the amount of the filing fee, penalties incurred and costs remaining unpaid.

(b) At the request of the resident agent, may be provided electronically.

2. Immediately after the last day of the month in which the anniversary date of its organization occurs, the Secretary of State shall compile a complete list containing the names of all foreign limited-liability companies whose right to transact business has been forfeited.

3. The Secretary of State shall notify, by providing written notice to its resident agent, each foreign limited-liability company specified in subsection 2 of the forfeiture of its right to transact business. The written notice:

(a) Must include a statement indicating the amount of the filing fee, penalties incurred and costs remaining unpaid.

(b) At the request of the resident agent, may be provided electronically. (Added to NRS by 2003, 20th Special Session, 62)

**NRS 86.5466 Defaulting companies: Duties of Secretary of State. [Effective July 1, 2008.]**

1. The Secretary of State shall notify, by providing written notice to its registered agent, each foreign limited-liability company deemed in default pursuant to NRS 86.5465. The written notice:

(a) Must include a statement indicating the amount of the filing fee, penalties incurred and costs remaining unpaid.

(b) At the request of the registered agent, may be provided electronically.

2. Immediately after the last day of the month in which the anniversary date of its organization occurs, the Secretary of State shall compile a complete list containing the names of all foreign limited-liability companies whose right to transact business has been forfeited.

3. The Secretary of State shall notify, by providing written notice to its registered agent, each foreign limited-liability company specified in subsection 2 of the forfeiture of its right to transact business. The written notice:

(a) Must include a statement indicating the amount of the filing fee, penalties incurred and costs remaining unpaid.

(b) At the request of the registered agent, may be provided electronically. (Added to NRS by 2003, 20th Special Session, 62; A 2007, 2676, effective July 1, 2008)

**NRS 86.5467 Defaulting companies: Conditions and procedure for reinstatement. [Effective through June 30, 2008.]**

1. Except as otherwise provided in subsections 3 and 4 and NRS 86.54615, the Secretary of State shall reinstate a foreign limited liability company which has forfeited or which forfeits its right to transact business under the provisions of this chapter and shall restore to the foreign limited-liability company its right to transact business in this State, and to exercise its privileges and immunities, if it:

(a) Files with the Secretary of State:

(1) The list required by NRS 86.5461;

(2) The statement required by NRS 86.5462, if applicable; and

(3) A certificate of acceptance of appointment signed by its resident agent; and

(b) Pays to the Secretary of State:

(1) The filing fee and penalty set forth in NRS 86.5461 and 86.5465 for each year or portion thereof that its right to transact business was forfeited;

(2) The fee set forth in NRS 86.5462, if applicable; and

(3) A fee of $300 for reinstatement.

2. When the Secretary of State reinstates the foreign limited-liability company, he shall issue to the foreign limited-liability company a certificate of reinstatement if the foreign limited-liability company:

(a) Requests a certificate of reinstatement; and

(b) Pays the required fees pursuant to NRS 86.561.

3. The Secretary of State shall not order a reinstatement unless all delinquent fees and penalties have been paid and the revocation of the right to transact business occurred only by reason of failure to pay the fees and penalties.

4. If the right of a foreign limited-liability company to transact business in this State has been forfeited pursuant to the provisions of this chapter and has remained forfeited for a period of 5 consecutive years, the right must not be reinstated.

5. Except as otherwise provided in NRS 86.5468, a reinstatement pursuant to this section relates back to the date on which the foreign limited-liability company forfeited its right to transact business under the provisions of this chapter and reinstates the foreign limited-liability company's right to transact business as if such right had at all times remained in full force and

effect. (Added to NRS by 2003, 20th Special Session, 62; A 2007, 1325, 2426)

**NRS 86.5467 Defaulting companies: Conditions and procedure for reinstatement. [Effective July 1, 2008.]**

1. Except as otherwise provided in subsections 3 and 4 and NRS 86.54615, the Secretary of State shall reinstate a foreign limited liability company which has forfeited or which forfeits its right to transact business under the provisions of this chapter and shall restore to the foreign limited-liability company its right to transact business in this State, and to exercise its privileges and immunities, if it:

(a) Files with the Secretary of State:

(1) The list required by NRS 86.5461;

(2) The statement required by NRS 86.5462, if applicable; and

(3) The information required pursuant to NRS 77.310; and

(b) Pays to the Secretary of State:

(1) The filing fee and penalty set forth in NRS 86.5461 and 86.5465 for each year or portion thereof that its right to transact business was forfeited;

(2) The fee set forth in NRS 86.5462, if applicable; and

(3) A fee of $300 for reinstatement.

2. When the Secretary of State reinstates the foreign limited-liability company, he shall issue to the foreign limited-liability company a certificate of reinstatement if the foreign limited-liability company:

(a) Requests a certificate of reinstatement; and

(b) Pays the required fees pursuant to NRS 86.561.

3. The Secretary of State shall not order a reinstatement unless all delinquent fees and penalties have been paid and the revocation of the right to transact business occurred only by reason of failure to pay the fees and penalties.

4. If the right of a foreign limited-liability company to transact business in this State has been forfeited pursuant to the provisions of this chapter and has remained forfeited for a period of 5 consecutive years, the right must not be reinstated.

5. Except as otherwise provided in NRS 86.5468, a reinstatement pursuant to this section relates back to the date on which the foreign limited-liability company forfeited its right to transact business under the provisions of this chapter and reinstates the foreign limited-liability company's right to transact business as if such right had at all times remained in full force and effect. (Added to NRS by 2003, 20th Special Session, 62; A 2007, 1325, 2426, 2677, effective July 1, 2008)

**NRS 86.5468 Defaulting companies: Reinstatement under old or new name; regulations.**

1. Except as otherwise provided in subsection 2, if a foreign limited-liability company applies to reinstate its registration but its name has been legally reserved or acquired by another artificial person formed, organized, registered or qualified pursuant to the provisions of this title whose name is on file with the Office of the Secretary of State or reserved in the Office of the Secretary of State pursuant to the provisions of this title, the foreign limited-liability company must in its application for reinstatement submit in writing to the Secretary of State some other name under which it desires its existence to be reinstated. If that name is distinguishable from all other names reserved or otherwise on file, the Secretary of State shall reinstate the foreign limited-liability company under that new name.

2. If the applying foreign limited-liability company submits the written, acknowledged consent of the artificial person having a name, or the person who has reserved a name, which is not distinguishable from the old name of the applying foreign limited-liability company or a new name it has submitted, it may be reinstated under that name.

3. For the purposes of this section, a proposed name is not distinguishable from a name on file or reserved solely because one or the other contains distinctive lettering, a distinctive mark, a trademark or a trade name, or any combination thereof.

4. The Secretary of State may adopt regulations that interpret the requirements of this section. (Added to NRS by 2003, 20th Special Session, 63)

**NRS 86.547 Cancellation of registration.**

1. A foreign limited-liability company may cancel its registration by filing with the Secretary of State a certificate of cancellation signed by a manager of the company or, if management is not vested in a manager, a member of the company. The certificate, which must be accompanied by the required fees, must set forth:

(a) The name of the foreign limited-liability company;

(b) The effective date of the cancellation if other than the date of the filing of the certificate of cancellation, which must not be more than 90 days after the certificate is filed; and

(c) Any other information deemed necessary by the manager of the company or, if management is not vested in a manager, a member of the company.

2. A cancellation pursuant to this section does not terminate the authority of the Secretary of State to accept service of process on the foreign limited-liability company with respect to causes of action arising from the transaction of business in this State by the foreign limited-liability company. (Added to NRS by 2001, 1387; A 2001, 3199; 2003, 20th Special Session, 71; 2005, 2197)

**NRS 86.548 Transaction of business without registration.**

1. A foreign limited-liability company transacting business in this State may not maintain any action, suit or proceeding in any court of this State until it has registered in this State.

2. The failure of a foreign limited-liability company to register in this State does not impair the validity of any contract or act of the foreign limited-liability company, or prevent the foreign limited-liability company from defending any action, suit or proceeding in any court of this State.

3. A foreign limited-liability company, by transacting business in this State without registration, appoints the Secretary of State as its agent for service of process with respect to causes of action arising out of the transaction of business in this State by the foreign limited-liability company. (Added to NRS by 2001, 1387; A 2001, 3199)

**NRS 86.5483 Activities not constituting transaction of business.**

1. For the purposes of NRS 86.543 to 86.549, inclusive, the following activities do not constitute transacting business in this State:

(a) Maintaining, defending or settling any proceeding;

(b) Holding meetings of the managers or members or carrying on other activities concerning internal company affairs;

(c) Maintaining accounts in banks or credit unions;

(d) Maintaining offices or agencies for the transfer, exchange and registration of the company's own securities or maintaining trustees or depositaries with respect to those securities; (e) Making sales through independent contractors;

(f) Soliciting or receiving orders outside this State through or in response to letters, circulars, catalogs or other forms of advertising, accepting those orders outside this State and filling them by shipping goods into this State;

(g) Creating or acquiring indebtedness, mortgages and security interests in real or personal property;

(h) Securing or collecting debts or enforcing mortgages and security interests in property securing the debts;

(i) Owning, without more, real or personal property;

(j) Isolated transactions completed within 30 days and not a part of a series of similar transactions;

(k) The production of motion pictures as defined in NRS 231.020;

(l) Transacting business as an out-of-state depository institution pursuant to the provisions of title 55 of NRS; and

(m) Transacting business in interstate commerce.

2. The list of activities in subsection 1 is not exhaustive.

3. A person who is not transacting business in this State within the meaning of this section need not qualify or comply with any provision of this chapter, title 55 or 56 of NRS or chapter 645A, 645B or 645E of NRS unless he:

(a) Maintains an office in this State for the transaction of business; or

(b) Solicits or accepts deposits in the State, except pursuant to the provisions of chapter 666 or 666A of NRS.

4. The fact that a person is not transacting business in this State within the meaning of this section:

(a) Does not affect the determination of whether any court, administrative agency or regulatory body in this State may exercise personal jurisdiction over the person in any civil action, criminal action, administrative proceeding or regulatory proceeding; and

(b) Except as otherwise provided in subsection 3, does not affect the applicability of any other provision of law with respect to the person and may not be offered as a defense or introduced in evidence in any civil action, criminal action, administrative proceeding or regulatory proceeding to prove that the person is not transacting business in this State, including, without limitation, any civil action, criminal action, administrative proceeding or regulatory proceeding involving an alleged violation of chapter 597, 598 or 598A of NRS.

5. As used in this section, "deposits" means demand deposits, savings deposits and time deposits, as those terms are defined in chapter 657 of NRS. (Added to NRS by 2003, 3134)

**NRS 86.5487 Determination of whether solicitation is made or accepted.**

1. For the purposes of NRS 86.5483, a solicitation of a deposit is made in this State, whether or not either party is present in this State, if the solicitation:

(a) Originates in this State; or

(b) Is directed by the solicitor to a destination in this State and received where it is directed, or at a post office in this State if the solicitation is mailed.

2. A solicitation of a deposit is accepted in this State if acceptance:

(a) Is communicated to the solicitor in this State; and

(b) Has not previously been communicated to the solicitor, orally or in writing, outside this State. Acceptance is communicated to the solicitor in this State, whether or not either party is present in this State, if the depositor directs

it to the solicitor reasonably believing the solicitor to be in this State and it is received where it is directed, or at any post office in this State if the acceptance is mailed.

3. A solicitation made in a newspaper or other publication of general, regular and paid circulation is not made in this State if the publication:

(a) Is not published in this State; or

(b) Is published in this State but has had more than two-thirds of its circulation outside this State during the 12 months preceding the solicitation. If a publication is published in editions, each edition is a separate publication except for material common to all editions.

4. A solicitation made in a radio or television program or other electronic communication received in this State which originates outside this State is not made in this State. A radio or television program or other electronic communication shall be deemed to have originated in this State if the broadcast studio or origin of the source of transmission is located within the State, unless:

(a) The program or communication is syndicated and distributed from outside this State for redistribution to the general public in this State;

(b) The program is supplied by a radio, television or other electronic network whose electronic signal originates outside this State for redistribution to the general public in this State;

(c) The program or communication is an electronic signal that originates outside this State and is captured for redistribution to the general public in this State by a community antenna or cable, radio, cable television or other electronic system; or

(d) The program or communication consists of an electronic signal which originates within this State, but which is not intended for redistribution to the general public in this State. (Added to NRS by 2003, 3135)

**NRS 86.549 Action by Attorney General to restrain transaction of business.** The Attorney General may bring an action to restrain a foreign limited-liability company from transacting business in this State in violation of NRS 86.543 to 86.549, inclusive. (Added to NRS by 2001, 1387; A 2001, 3199; 2003, 3141)

## Miscellaneous Provisions

**NRS 86.555 Issuance of occupational or professional license to limited-liability company by board or commission; regulations.**

1. Except as otherwise provided by statute, an agency, board or commission that regulates an occupation or profession pursuant to title 54, 55 or 56 of NRS may grant a license to a limited-liability company or a foreign limited-liability company if the agency, board or commission is authorized to grant a license to a corporation formed pursuant to chapter 78 of NRS.

2. An agency, board or commission that makes a license available to a limited-liability company or foreign limited-liability company pursuant to subsection 1 shall adopt regulations:

(a) Listing the persons in the limited-liability company or foreign limited-liability company who must qualify for the license or indicating that the agency, board or commission will use other means to determine whether the limited-liability company or foreign limited-liability company qualifies for a license;

(b) Listing the persons who may engage in the activity for which the license is required on behalf of the limited-liability company or foreign limited-liability company;

(c) Indicating whether the limited-liability company or foreign limited-liability company may engage in a business other than the business for which the license is required;

(d) Listing the changes, if any, in the management or control of the limited-liability company or foreign limited-liability company that require notice, review, approval or other action by the agency, board or commission; and

(e) Setting forth the conditions under which a limited-liability company or foreign limited-liability company may obtain a license.

3. An agency, board or commission that adopts regulations pursuant to subsection 2 shall not impose a restriction or requirement on a limited-liability company or foreign limited-liability company which is significantly different from or more burdensome than the restrictions or requirements imposed on a partnership or corporation. (Added to NRS by 1997, 714)

**NRS 86.557 Form required for filing of records.**

1. Each record filed with the Secretary of State pursuant to this chapter must be on or accompanied by a form prescribed by the Secretary of State.

2. The Secretary of State may refuse to file a record which does not comply with subsection 1 or which does not contain all of the information required by statute for filing the record.

3. If the provisions of the form prescribed by the Secretary of State conflict with the provisions of any record that is submitted for filing with the form:

(a) The provisions of the form control for all purposes with respect to the information that is required by statute to appear in the record in order for the record to be filed; and

(b) Unless otherwise provided in the record, the provisions of the record control in every other situation.

4. The Secretary of State may by regulation provide for the electronic filing of records with the Office of the Secretary of State. (Added to NRS by 2003, 20th Special Session, 59)

**NRS 86.561 Fees. [Effective through June 30, 2008.]**

1. The Secretary of State shall charge and collect for:

(a) Filing the original articles of organization, or for registration of a foreign company, $75;

(b) Amending or restating the articles of organization, amending the registration of a foreign company or filing a certificate of correction, $175;

(c) Filing the articles of dissolution of a domestic or foreign company, $75;

(d) Filing a statement of change of address of a records or registered office, or change of the resident agent, $60;

(e) Certifying a copy of articles of organization or an amendment to the articles, $30;

(f) Certifying an authorized printed copy of this chapter, $30;

(g) Reserving a name for a limited-liability company, $25;

(h) Filing a certificate of cancellation, $75;

(i) Signing, filing or certifying any other record, $50; and

(j) Copies provided by the Office of the Secretary of State, $2 per page.

2. The Secretary of State shall charge and collect, at the time of any service of process on him as agent for service of process of a limited-liability company, $100 which may be recovered as taxable costs by the party to the action causing the service to be made if the party prevails in the action.

3. Except as otherwise provided in this section, the fees set forth in NRS 78.785 apply to this chapter. (Added to NRS by 1991, 1305; A 1993, 1017; 1995, 1131; 2001, 1395, 3182, 3199; 2003, 3141; 2003, 20th Special Session, 72; 2005, 2261)

**NRS 86.561 Fees. [Effective July 1, 2008.]**

1. The Secretary of State shall charge and collect for:

(a) Filing the original articles of organization, or for registration of a foreign company, $75;

(b) Amending or restating the articles of organization, amending the registration of a foreign company or filing a certificate of correction, $175;

(c) Filing the articles of dissolution of a domestic or foreign company, $75;

(d) Certifying a copy of articles of organization or an amendment to the articles, $30;

(e) Certifying an authorized printed copy of this chapter, $30;

(f) Reserving a name for a limited-liability company, $25;

(g) Filing a certificate of cancellation, $75;

(h) Signing, filing or certifying any other record, $50; and

(i) Copies provided by the Office of the Secretary of State, $2 per page.

2. The Secretary of State shall charge and collect, at the time of any service of process on him as agent for service of process of a limited-liability company, $100 which may be recovered as taxable costs by the party to the action causing the service to be made if the party prevails in the action.

3. Except as otherwise provided in this section, the fees set forth in NRS 78.785 apply to this chapter. (Added to NRS by 1991, 1305; A 1993, 1017; 1995, 1131; 2001, 1395, 3182, 3199; 2003, 3141; 2003, 20th Special Session, 72;

2005, 2261; 2007, 2677, effective July 1, 2008)

**NRS 86.563 Procedure to submit replacement page to Secretary of State before actual filing of record.** Before the issuance of members' interests an organizer, and after the issuance of members' interests, a manager, of a limited-liability company may authorize the Secretary of State in writing to replace any page of a record submitted for filing on an expedited basis, before the actual filing, and to accept the page as if it were part of the original record. The signed authorization of the organizer or manager to the Secretary of State permits, but does not require, the Secretary of State to alter the original record as requested. (Added to NRS by 1997, 2812; A 1999, 1611; 2001, 109; 2003, 3142)

**NRS 86.566 Filing of records written in language other than English.** No record which is written in a language other than English may be filed or submitted for filing in the Office of the Secretary of State pursuant to the provisions of this chapter unless it is accompanied by a verified translation of that record into the English language. (Added to NRS by 1995, 1126; A 2003, 3142)

**NRS 86.568 Correction of inaccurate or defective record filed with Secretary of State.**

1. A limited-liability company may correct a record filed in the Office of the Secretary of State with respect to the limited-liability company if the record contains an inaccurate description of a company action or was defectively signed, attested, sealed, verified or acknowledged.

2. To correct a record, the limited-liability company must:

(a) Prepare a certificate of correction that:

(1) States the name of the limited-liability company;

(2) Describes the record, including, without limitation, its filing date;

(3) Specifies the inaccuracy or defect;

(4) Sets forth the inaccurate or defective portion of the record in an accurate or corrected form; and

(5) Is signed by a manager of the company or, if management is not vested in a manager, by a member of the company.

(b) Deliver the certificate to the Secretary of State for filing.

(c) Pay a filing fee of $175 to the Secretary of State.

3. A certificate of correction is effective on the effective date of the record it corrects except as to persons relying on the uncorrected record and adversely affected by the correction. As to those persons, the certificate is effective when filed. (Added to NRS by 2001, 1385; A 2001, 3197, 3199; 2003, 3142; 2003, 20th Special Session, 72)

**NRS 86.571 Waiver of notice.** When, under the provisions of this chapter or under the provisions of the articles of organization or operating agreement of a limited-liability company, notice is required to be given to a member or to a manager of the company, if it has a manager or managers, a waiver in writing signed by the person or persons entitled to the notice, whether before or after the time stated in it, is equivalent to the giving of notice. (Added to NRS by 1991, 1304)

**NRS 86.580 Renewal or revival of charter: Procedure; fee; certificate as evidence. [Effective through June 30, 2008.]**

1. Except as otherwise provided in NRS 86.246, a limited-liability company which did exist or is existing pursuant to the laws of this State may, upon complying with the provisions of NRS 86.276, procure a renewal or revival of its charter for any period, together with all the rights, franchises, privileges and immunities, and subject to all its existing and preexisting debts, duties and liabilities secured or imposed by its original charter and amendments thereto, or existing charter, by filing:

(a) A certificate with the Secretary of State, which must set forth:

(1) The name of the limited-liability company, which must be the name of the limited-liability company at the time of the renewal or revival, or its name at the time its original charter expired.

(2) The name of the person lawfully designated as the resident agent of the limited-liability company, his street address for the service of process, and his mailing address if different from his street address.

(3) The date when the renewal or revival of the charter is to commence or be effective, which may be, in cases of a revival, before the date of the certificate.

(4) Whether or not the renewal or revival is to be perpetual, and, if not perpetual, the time for which the renewal or revival is to continue.

(5) That the limited-liability company desiring to renew or revive its charter is, or has been, organized and carrying on the business authorized by its existing or original charter and amendments thereto, and desires to renew or continue through revival its existence pursuant to and subject to the provisions of this chapter.

(b) A list of its managers, or if there are no managers, all its managing members and their mailing or street addresses, either residence or business.

2. A limited-liability company whose charter has not expired and is being renewed shall cause the certificate to be signed by its manager, or if there is no manager, by a person designated by its members. The certificate must be approved by a majority in interest.

3. A limited-liability company seeking to revive its original or amended charter shall cause the certificate to be signed by a person or persons designated or appointed by the members. The signing and filing of the certificate must be approved by the written consent of a majority in interest and must contain a recital that this consent was secured. The limited-liability company shall pay to the Secretary of State the fee required to establish a new limited-liability company pursuant to the provisions of this chapter.

4. The filed certificate, or a copy thereof which has been certified under the hand and seal of the Secretary of State, must be received in all courts and places as prima facie evidence of the facts therein stated and of the existence of the limited-liability company therein named.

5. Except as otherwise provided in NRS 86.278, a renewal or revival pursuant to this section relates back to the date on which the limited-liability company's charter expired or was revoked and renews or revives the limited-liability company's charter and right to transact business as if such right had at all times remained in full force and effect. (Added to NRS by 1999, 1610; A 2001, 1395, 3199; 2003, 3143; 2003, 20th Special Session, 73; 2007, 1326, 2426)

**NRS 86.580 Renewal or revival of charter: Procedure; fee; certificate as evidence. [Effective July 1, 2008.]**

1. Except as otherwise provided in NRS 86.246, a limited-liability company which did exist or is existing pursuant to the laws of this State may, upon complying with the provisions of NRS 86.276, procure a renewal or revival of its charter for any period, together with all the rights, franchises, privileges and immunities, and subject to all its existing and preexisting debts, duties and liabilities secured or imposed by its original charter and amendments thereto, or existing charter, by filing:

(a) A certificate with the Secretary of State, which must set forth:

(1) The name of the limited-liability company, which must be the name of the limited-liability company at the time of the renewal or revival, or its name at the time its original charter expired.

(2) The information required pursuant to NRS 77.310.

(3) The date when the renewal or revival of the charter is to commence or be effective, which may be, in cases of a revival, before the date of the certificate.

(4) Whether or not the renewal or revival is to be perpetual, and, if not perpetual, the time for which the renewal or revival is to continue.

(5) That the limited-liability company desiring to renew or revive its charter is, or has been, organized and carrying on the business authorized by its existing or original charter and amendments thereto, and desires to renew or continue through revival its existence pursuant to and subject to the provisions of this chapter.

(b) A list of its managers or, if there are no managers, all its managing members and their mailing or street addresses, either residence or business.

2. A limited-liability company whose charter has not expired and is being renewed shall cause the certificate to be signed by its manager or, if there is no manager, by a person designated by its members. The certificate must be approved by a majority in interest.

3. A limited-liability company seeking to revive its original or amended charter shall cause the certificate to be signed by a person or persons designated or appointed by the members. The signing and filing of the certificate must be approved by the written consent of a majority in interest and must contain a recital that this consent was secured. The limited-liability company shall pay to the Secretary of State the fee required to establish a new limited-liability company pursuant to the provisions of this chapter.

4. The filed certificate, or a copy thereof which has been certified under the hand and seal of the Secretary of State, must be received in all courts and places as prima facie evidence of the facts therein stated and of the existence of the limited-liability company therein named.

5. Except as otherwise provided in NRS 86.278, a renewal or revival pursuant to this section relates back to the date on which the limited-liability company's charter expired or was revoked and renews or revives the limited-liability company's charter and right to transact business as if such right had at all times remained in full force and effect. (Added to NRS by 1999, 1610; A 2001, 1395, 3199; 2003, 3143; 2003, 20th Special Session, 73; 2007, 1326, 2426, 2678, effective July 1, 2008)

**NRS 86.590 Renewal or revival of charter: Status of company.** A limited-liability company that has revived or renewed its charter pursuant to the provisions of this chapter:

1. Is a limited-liability company and continues to be a limited-liability company for the time stated in the certificate of revival or renewal;

2. Possesses the rights, privileges and immunities conferred by the original charter and by this chapter; and

3. Is subject to the restrictions and liabilities set forth in this chapter. (Added to NRS by 1999, 1611; A 2001, 101)

**ROSS MILLER**
**Secretary of State**
**202 North Carson Street**
**Carson City, Nevada 89701-4201**
**Phone: (775) 684 5708**
**Website: secretaryofstate.biz**

---

# Profit Corporation Fee Schedule
# Effective 10-1-05
### Page 1

---

**PROFIT CORPORATIONS <u>INITIAL FILING</u> FEE :**   Pursuant to NRS 78, 80, 78A, and 89 Domestic and Foreign Corporations, Close Corporations and Professional Corporations.

Fees are based on the value of the total number of authorized shares stated in the Articles of Incorporation as prescribed by NRS 78.760:

| | |
|---|---|
| $75,000 or less | $75.00 |
| over $75,000 and not over $200,000 | $175.00 |
| over $200,000 and not over $500,000 | $275.00 |
| over $500,000 and not over $1,000,000 | $375.00 |
| **OVER $1,000,000** | |
| For the first $1,000,000 | $375.00 |
| For each additional $500,000 - or fraction thereof | $275.00 |
| Maximum fee | $35,000.00 |

For the purpose of computing the filing fee, the value (capital) represented by the total number of shares authorized in the Articles of Incorporation is determined by computing the:

A. total authorized shares multiplied by their par value or;
B. total authorized shares without par value multiplied by $1.00 or;
C. the sum of (a) and (b) above if both par and no par shares.

*Filing fees are calculated on a minimum par value of one-tenth of a cent (.001), regardless if the stated par value is less.*

**The 24-hour expedite fee for Articles of Incorporation for any of the above entities is $125.00 in addition to the filing fee based upon stock.**

**The 2-hour expedite fee is $500.00 in addition to the filing fee based upon stock.**

**The 1-hour expedite fee is $1000.00 in addition to the filing fee based upon stock.**

*PLEASE NOTE: the expedite fee is in addition to the standard filing fee charged on each filing and/or order.*

<u>**24-HOUR EXPEDITE TIME CONSTRAINTS:**</u>

Each filing submitted receives same day filing date and may be picked up within 24-hours.  Filings to be mailed the next business day if received by 2:00 pm of receipt date and no later than the 2nd business day if received after 2:00 pm.

Expedite period begins when filing or service request is received in this office in fileable form.

The Secretary of State reserves the right to extend the expedite period in times of extreme volume, staff shortages, or equipment malfunction.  These extensions are few and will rarely extend more than a few hours.

**ROSS MILLER**
Secretary of State
202 North Carson Street
Carson City, Nevada 89701-4201
Phone: (775) 684 5708
Website: secretaryofstate.biz

| Profit Corporation Fee Schedule |
| :---: |
| **Effective 10-1-05** |
| **Page 2** |

## OTHER PROFIT CORPORATION FEES:

| | |
|---|---|
| Articles of Association pursuant to NRS 89.210 (Professional Association) | $75.00 |
| Reinstatement Fee | $300.00 |
| Certificate of Amendment, minimum fee* | $175.00 |
| Certificate pursuant to NRS 78.209 (stock split), minimum fee* | $175.00 |
| Certificate pursuant to NRS 78.1955 (stock designation) | $175.00 |
| Amendment to Certificate pursuant NRS 78.1955 (stock designation) | $175.00 |
| Amendment of Modified Name | $175.00 |
| Restated Articles, minimum fee* | $175.00 |
| Certificate of Correction, minimum fee* | $175.00 |
| Certificate of Termination (includes filings pursuant to NRS 78.209, 78.380 and 78.390) | $175.00 |
| Termination Pursuant to NRS 92A | $350.00 |
| Articles of Merger* or Exchange | $350.00 |
| Dissolution of Corporation | $75.00 |
| Withdrawal of Foreign Corporation | $75.00 |
| Preclearance of any Document | $125.00 |
| Articles of Conversion – contact office for fee information | |
| Articles of Domestication – contact office for fee information | |
| Revival of Corporation – contact office for fee information | |
| **24-Hour Expedite fee for above filings** | **$125.00** |
| | |
| Change of Resident Agent/Address | $60.00 |
| Resident Agent Name Change | $100.00 |
| Resignation of Director or Officer | $75.00 |
| Resignation of Resident Agent   (plus $1.00 for each additional entity listed) | $100.00 |
| Name Reservation | $25.00 |
| **24-Hour Expedite fee for above filings** | **$25.00** |
| | |
| Apostille | $20.00 |
| Certificate of Good Standing | $50.00 |
| Initial List of Officers and Directors | $125.00 |
| Annual or Amended List of Officers and Directors | See Annual List Fee Schedule |
| Annual List of Officers and Directors (Professional Association) | $125.00 |
| **24-Hour Expedite fee for above filings** | **$75.00** |
| | |
| Certification of Documents – per certification | $30.00 |
| Copies – per page | $2.00 |
| Late Fee for List of Officers | $75.00 |

*Fee will be higher if stock is increased a significant amount, according to the initial filing fee schedule on page 1 of the profit corporation fee schedule.  Maximum fee for an increase in stock is $35,000.00.

**2-Hour Expedite is available on all of the above filings at the fee of $500.00 per item.**

**1-Hour Expedite is available on all of the above filings at the fee of $1000.00 per item.**

***PLEASE NOTE:*** *the expedite fee is in addition to the standard filing fee charged on each filing and/or order.*

**24-HOUR EXPEDITE TIME CONSTRAINTS:**  Each filing submitted receives same day filing date and may be picked up within 24-hours.  Filings to be mailed the next business day if received by 2:00 pm of receipt date and no later than the 2nd business day if received after 2:00 pm.  Expedite period begins when filing or service request is received in this office in fileable form.  The Secretary of State reserves the right to extend the expedite period in times of extreme volume, staff shortages, or equipment malfunction.  These extensions are few and will rarely extend more than a few hours.

Nevada Secretary of State Form Fee Schedule-Profit Page 2 2007
Revised on: 01/01/07

**ROSS MILLER**
**Secretary of State**
**202 North Carson Street**
**Carson City, Nevada 89701-4201**
**Phone: (775) 684 5708**
**Website: secretaryofstate.biz**

## Limited-Liability Company Fee Schedule Effective 10-1-05

**LIMITED-LIABILITY COMPANY FEES:** Pursuant to NRS 86 for both Domestic and Foreign Limited-Liability Companies.

| | |
|---|---|
| Articles of Organization | $75.00 |
| Registration of Foreign Limited-Liability Company | $75.00 |
| Reinstatement Fee | $300.00 |
| Certificate of Amendment | $175.00 |
| Restated Articles | $175.00 |
| Certificate of Correction | $175.00 |
| Certificate of Termination  (pursuant to NRS 86.226) | $175.00 |
| Merger | $350.00 |
| Termination Pursuant to NRS 92A | $350.00 |
| Dissolution of Domestic Limited-Liability Company | $75.00 |
| Dissolution of Foreign Limited-Liability Company | $75.00 |
| Preclearance of any Document | $125.00 |
| Articles of Conversion – contact office for fee information | |
| Articles of Domestication – contact office for fee information | |
| Revival of Limited-Liability Company – contact office for fee information | |
| **24-Hour Expedite fee for above filings** | **$125.00** |
| | |
| Change of Resident Agent/Address | $60.00 |
| Resident Agent Name Change | $100.00 |
| Resignation of Manager or Managing Member | $75.00 |
| Resignation of Resident Agent     (plus $1.00 for each additional entity listed) | $100.00 |
| Name Reservation | $25.00 |
| **24-Hour Expedite fee for above filings** | **$25.00** |
| | |
| Apostille | $20.00 |
| Certificate of Good Standing | $50.00 |
| Initial List of Managers or Members | $125.00 |
| Annual or Amended List of Managers or Members | $125.00 |
| **24-Hour Expedite fee for above filings** | **$75.00** |
| | |
| Certification of Documents – per certification | $30.00 |
| Copies – per page | $2.00 |
| Late Fee for List of Managers or Members | $75.00 |

**2-Hour Expedite is available on all of the above filings at the fee of $500.00 per item.**

**1-Hour Expedite is available on all of the above filings at the fee of $1000.00 per item.**

*PLEASE NOTE: the expedite fee is in addition to the standard filing fee charged on each filing and/or order.*

**24-HOUR EXPEDITE TIME CONSTRAINTS:**

Each filing submitted receives same day filing date and may be picked up within 24 hours.  Filings to be mailed the next business day if received by 2:00 pm of receipt date and no later than the 2nd business day if received after 2:00 pm. Expedite period begins when filing or service request is received in this office in fileable form.  The Secretary of State reserves the right to extend the expedite period in times of extreme volume, staff shortages, or equipment malfunction. These extensions are few and will rarely extend more than a few hours.

Nevada Secretary of State Form Fee Schedule-LLC 2007
Revised on: 01/01/07

# State Addresses

Included in this appendix are the addresses, phone numbers, and websites of the state offices in which a corporation must be registered. Once you have formed your Nevada corporation, you will need to register it as a foreign corporation doing business in your home state.

You should contact the office in your state for the latest forms and fee schedule.

## ALABAMA

Secretary of State
Corporations Division
P.O. Box 5616
Montgomery, AL 36103
Phone: 334-242-5324
Fax: 334-240-3138
www.sos.state.al.us

## ALASKA

Division of Corporations, Business,
and Professional Licensing
Corporations Section
P.O. Box 110808
Juneau, AK 99811
Phone: 907-465-2530
Fax: 907-465-3257
www.commerce.state.ak.us/occ/
home.htm

## ARIZONA

Arizona Corporation Commission
1300 West Washington Street, 1st
Floor
Phoenix, AZ 85007
Phone: 602-542-3026
or
400 West Congress, Suite 221
Tucson, AZ 85701
Phone: 520-628-6560
www.azcc.gov/divisions/corporations

## ARKANSAS

Secretary of State
Business and Commercial (UCC)
Services
State Capitol, Room 256
Little Rock, AR 72201
Phone: 501-682-1010
www.sos.arkansas.gov/corp_ucc.html

## CALIFORNIA

Department of Corporations
320 West 4th Street, Suite 750
Los Angeles, CA 90013
Phone: 866-275-2677
www.corp.ca.gov/index.html

## COLORADO

Secretary of State
Business Center
1700 Broadway, Suite 200
Denver, CO 80290
Phone: 303-894-2200
Fax: 303-869-4864
www.sos.state.co.us/pubs/business/main.htm

## CONNECTICUT

Secretary of State
Commercial Recording Division
30 Trinity Street
Hartford, CT 06106
Phone: 860-509-6002
www.sots.ct.gov/commercialrecording/
crdforms.html

## DELAWARE

State of Delaware
Division of Corporations
John G. Townsend Building
401 Federal Street, Suite 4
Dover, DE 19901
Phone: 302-739-3073
Fax: 302-739-3812
www.corp.delaware.gov

## DISTRICT OF COLUMBIA

Department of Consumer and Regulatory Affairs
Corporations Division
941 North Capitol Street, Room 1100
Washington, DC 20002
Phone: 202-442-4432
Fax: 202-442-4523
http://mblr.dc.gov/corp/index.shtm

## FLORIDA

Department of State
Division of Corporations
Clifton Building
2661 Executive Center Circle
Tallahassee, FL 32301
Phone: 850-245-6939
www.sunbiz.org

## GEORGIA

Secretary of State
Corporations Division
2 MLK Jr. Drive SE
Suite 1104, West Tower
Atlanta, GA 30334
Phone: 404-656-2817
Fax: 404-657-2248
http://sos.georgia.gov/corporations

## HAWAII

Department of Commerce and Consumer Affairs
Business Registration Division
King Kalakaua Building
335 Merchant Street, Room 201
Honolulu, HI 96813
Phone: 808-586-2744
Fax: 808-586-2733
http://hawaii.gov/dcca/areas/breg/registration

## IDAHO

Secretary of State
Business Entities
450 North 4th Street
Boise, ID 83720
Phone: 208-334-2301
Fax: 208-334-2080
www.idsos.state.id.us/corp/corpindex.htm

## ILLINOIS

Secretary of State
Business Services
501 South 2nd Street, Room 328
Springfield, IL 62756
Phone: 217-782-6961
www.cyberdriveillinois.com/departments/business
  _services/home.html

## INDIANA

Secretary of State
Business Services Division
302 West Washington, Room E-018
Indianapolis, IN 46204
Phone: 317-232-6531
Fax: 317-233-3283
www.in.gov/sos/business

## IOWA

Secretary of State
Business Services
Lucas Building, First Floor
Des Moines, IA 50319
Phone: 515-281-5204
Fax: 515-242-5953
www.sos.state.ia.us/business/index.html

## KANSAS

Secretary of State
Business Filing Center
Memorial Hall, 1st Floor
120 SW 10th Avenue
Topeka, KS 66612
Phone: 785-296-4564
www.kssos.org/business/business.html

## KENTUCKY

Office of the Secretary of State
Business Filings
700 Capital Avenue, Suite 154
Frankfort, KY 40602
Phone: 502-564-2848
Fax: 502-564-4075
http://sos.ky.gov/business/filings

## LOUISIANA

Secretary of State
Corporations Division
8549 United Plaza Boulevard
Baton Rouge, LA 70804
Phone: 225-925-4704
www.sos.louisiana.gov

## MAINE

Bureau of Corporations, Elections, and
Commissions
Corporations Division
101 State House Station
Augusta, ME 04333
Phone: 207-624-7736
Fax: 207-287-5874
http://maine.gov/sos/cec/corp/

## MARYLAND

Secretary of State
State Department of Assessments and Taxation
301 West Preston Street, Room 809
Baltimore, MD 21201
Phone: 410-767-1350
Fax: 410-333-7097
www.dat.state.md.us

## MASSACHUSETTS

Secretary of the Commonwealth
Corporations Division
One Ashburton Place, 17th Floor
Boston, MA 02108
Phone: 617-727-9640
Fax: 617-742-4538
www.sec.state.ma.us/COR/coridx.htm

## MICHIGAN

Michigan Department of Labor and Economic
Growth
Corporation Division
P.O. Box 30054
Lansing, MI 48909
Phone: 517-241-6470
Fax: 517-241-0538
www.michigan.gov/corporations

## MINNESOTA

Secretary of State
Business Center
60 Empire Drive, Suite 100
St. Paul, MN 55103
Phone: 612-296-2803
Fax: 651-297-7067
www.sos.state.mn.us/home/index.asp?page=3

## MISSISSIPPI

Secretary of State
Business Services Division
700 North Street
Jackson, MS 39202
Phone: 800-256-3494
Fax: 601-359-1607
www.sos.state.ms.us/busserv/corp/
corporations.asp

## MISSOURI

Secretary of State
Corporations Division
600 West Main Street, Room 322
Jefferson City, MO 65101
Phone: 866-223-6535
www.sos.mo.gov/business/corporations

## MONTANA

Secretary of State
Business Services Division
State Capitol, Room 260
1301 6th Avenue
Helena, MT 59620
Phone: 406-444-3665
Fax: 406-444-3976
http://sos.mt.gov/BSB/index.asp

## NEBRASKA

Secretary of State
Corporations Division
State Capitol, Room 1301
Lincoln, NE 68509
Phone: 402-471-4079
Fax: 402-471-3666
www.sos.ne.gov/business/corp_serv/index.html

## NEVADA

Secretary of State
Business Center
101 North Carson Street, Suite 3
Carson City, NV 89701
Phone: 775-684-5708
Fax: 775-684-5725
http://sos.state.nv.us/business

## NEW HAMPSHIRE

Department of State
Corporate Division
107 North Main Street
Concord, NH 03301
Phone: 603-271-3246
www.sos.nh.gov/corporate

## NEW JERSEY

Division of Revenue
P.O. Box 628
Trenton, NJ 08646
Phone: 609-292-9292
www.state.nj.us/treasury/revenue

## NEW MEXICO

Public Regulation Commission
Corporation Bureau
P.O. Box 1269
Santa Fe, NM 87504
Phone: 800-947-4722
Fax: 505-827-4387
www.nmprc.state.nm.us/cb.htm

## NEW YORK

Department of State
Division of Corporations
One Commerce Plaza
99 Washington Avenue, Suite 600
Albany, NY 12231
Phone: 518-473-2492
Fax: 518-474-1418
www.dos.state.ny.us/corp/corpwww.html

## NORTH CAROLINA

Department of Secretary of State
2 South Salisbury Street
Raleigh, NC 27601
Phone: 919-807-2225
Fax: 919-807-2039
www.secretary.state.nc.us/corporations

## NORTH DAKOTA

Secretary of State
Business Services
600 East Boulevard Avenue
Bismarck, ND 58505
Phone: 800-352-0867
Fax: 701-328-2992
www.nd.gov/sos/businessserv

## OHIO

Secretary of State
Business Services
180 East Broad Street
Columbus, OH 43215
Phone: 877-767-6446
www.sos.state.oh.us/sos/businessservices/
   corp.aspx

## OKLAHOMA

Secretary of State
Business Filing Department
2300 North Lincoln Boulevard, Room 101
Oklahoma City, OK 73105
Phone: 405-521-3912
Fax: 405-521-3771
www.sos.state.ok.us/business/business_
filing.htm

## OREGON

Secretary of State
Corporation Division
255 Capitol Street, NE, Suite 151
Salem, OR 97310
Phone: 503-986-2200
Fax: 503-378-4381
www.sos.state.or.us/corporation

## PENNSYLVANIA

Department of State
Corporation Bureau
206 North Office Building
Harrisburg, PA 17120
Phone: 888-659-9962
www.dos.state.pa.us/corps

## RHODE ISLAND

Secretary of State
Corporations Division
148 West River Street
Providence, RI 02904
Phone: 401-222-3040
www.sec.state.ri.us/corps

## SOUTH CAROLINA

Secretary of State
Corporations Division
1205 Pendleton Street, Suite 525
Columbia, SC 29201
Phone: 803-734-2158
Fax: 803-734-1614
www.scsos.com

## SOUTH DAKOTA

Secretary of State
Business Services
500 East Capital Avenue, Suite 204
Pierre, SD 57501
Phone: 605-773-4845
Fax: 605-773-4550
www.sdsos.gov/businessservices/
   corporations.shtm

## TENNESSEE

Department of State
Division of Business Services
312 8th Avenue North, 6th Floor
Nashville, TN 37243
Phone: 615-741-2286
www.state.tn.us/sos/bus_svc/corporations.htm

## TEXAS

Secretary of State
Corporations Section
1019 Brazos
Austin, TX 78701
Phone: 512-463-5555
Fax: 512-463-5709
www.sos.state.tx.us/corp/index.shtml

## UTAH

Division of Corporations and Commercial Code
160 East 300 South, 2nd Floor
Salt Lake City, UT 84111
Phone: 877-526-3994
Fax: 801-530-6438
http://corporations.utah.gov

## VERMONT

Secretary of State
Corporations Division
81 River Street
Montpelier, VT 05609
Phone: 802-828-2386
Fax: 802-828-2853
www.sec.state.vt.us/corps

## VIRGINIA

State Corporation Commission
1300 East Main Street
Richmond, VA 23219
Phone: 800-552-7945
www.scc.virginia.gov

## WASHINGTON

Secretary of State
Corporations Division
80 Capitol Way South
Olympia, WA 98504
360-753-7115
www.secstate.wa.gov/corps

## WEST VIRGINIA

Secretary of State
Business Organizations
1900 Kanawha Boulevard East
Charleston, WV 25305
Phone: 304-558-8000
Fax: 304-558-8381
www.wvsos.com/business/main.htm

## WISCONSIN

Department of Financial Institutions
Corporations Bureau
P.O. Box 7846
Madison, WI 53707
Phone: 608-261-7577
Fax: 608-267-6813
www.wdfi.org/corporations

## WYOMING

Secretary of State
Corporations Division
200 West 24th Street, Room 110
Cheyenne, WY 82002
Phone: 307-777-7311
Fax: 307-777-5339
http://soswy.state.wy.us/corporat/corporat.htm

# Nevada Resident Agents

The following is a list of companies that can serve as a resident agent for your Nevada corporation or LLC.

This list evolves as new companies open for business and other companies merge or close. For the most up-to-date list, see the Nevada Secretary of State's website at:

http://sos.state.nv.us/business/comm_rec/ralist

**1st Nevada Agents**
Kirk S. Schumacher
5605 Riggins Court, Suite 270
Reno, NV 89502
Phone: 775-823-9494
Fax: 775-829-9400
Email: kschumacher@1stnevada.com
www.1stnevadaagents.com

**1st Nevada Incorporating Network**
1802 North Carson Street, #240E
Carson City, NV 89701
Phone: 866-399-1992
Fax: 866-399-4909
Email: 1stnvincorp@pyramid.net

**A-1 Corp Services**
Maria Calvano
800 East Charleston Boulevard
Las Vegas, NV 89104
Phone: 800-701-5364
Fax: 702-214-9499
Email: mcalvano@csanv.com
www.csanv.com

**AAAAA Incorporating Services, Inc.**
Jeneale Carlson
823 South Sixth Street, Suite 100
Las Vegas, NV 89191
Phone: 877-786-8500
Fax: 877-786-9500
Email: residentagents@aol.com
www.corporateplace.com

**Acorn Corporate Services, Inc.**
3224 McLeod Drive, Suite 110
Las Vegas, NV 89121
Phone: 800-266-1296
Fax: 702-310-9911
Email: acorninfo@bossoffice.com
www.acorncorp.com

**Advantage Corporation Services, Inc.**
Brian Morgan
12 West Mesquite Boulevard #108
Mesquite, NV 89027
Phone: 866-289-6920
Fax: 702-345-3473
Email: bmorgan@acsnevada.com
www.acsnevada.com

**Agency Services of Nevada**
Kelly L. Turner, Esq.
c/o Turner Law Ltd.
245 East Liberty Street, Suite 200
Reno, NV 89501
Phone: 888-828-8208
Fax: 775-786-6755
www.nevadabusinessentities.com

**Amcorp LLC**
Denise Man and Julie Leftwich
723 South Casino Center Boulevard
Las Vegas, NV 89101
Phone: 888-310-3330
Fax: 702-384-2529
Email: amcorp@lvcm.com
www.amcorpllc.com

**American Corporate Register, Inc.**
Phil Herr
711 South Carson Street, Suite 6
Carson City, NV 89701
Phone: 800-944-1120
Fax: 800-775-2705
Email: phil@incnevada.com
www.incnevada.com

**An Attorney as Resident Agent**
Christopher R. Grobl, Esq.
4625 West Nevso Drive, Suites 2 & 3
Las Vegas, NV 89103
Phone: 800-923-7870
Fax: 702-253-9240
Email: chris@silverstatelegal.com
www.silverstatelegal.com

**Brent Parker & Associates, Ltd.**
Brent Parker
4625 West Nevso Drive, Suites 2 & 3
Las Vegas, NV 89103
Phone: 800-923-7870
Fax: 702-253-9240
Email: bparker@silverstatelegal.com
www.silverstatelegal.com

**Budget Corp.**
Tracey Padilla
2050 Russett Way
Carson City, NV 89703
Phone: 888-274-1130
Fax: 775-884-9383
Email: tracey@budgetcorp.com
www.budgetcorp.com

**Budget Corporate Renewals, Inc.**
Janet Carriger
3132 West Post Road
Las Vegas, NV 89118
Phone: 702-870-5351
Fax: 702-880-7044
Email: janet@budgetcorporationservices.com
www.budgetcorporationservices.com

**Business Filings Incorporated**
6100 Neil Road, Suite 500
Reno, NV 89511
Phone: 800-981-7183
Fax: 608-827-5100
Email: info@bizfilings.com
www.bizfilings.com

**CATS—Corporation Services of Nevada, Inc.**
Stephen J. Herlihy
4560 South Decatur Boulevard, Suite 202
Las Vegas, NV 89103
Phone: 702-367-1931
Fax: 702-871-4086
Email: catsnevada@cs.com

**Complete Contractor Services**
Norman Huddleson
826 East Charleston Boulevard
Las Vegas, NV 89104
Phone: 888-762-3926
Fax: 702-384-2601
Email: norm@contractorassistance.com
www.contractorassistance.com

**Corporate Advisory Service, Inc.**
Michael D. Taylor
251 Jeanell Drive, Suite 3
Carson City, NV 89703
Phone: 800-533-2677
Fax: 775-882-5121
Email: info@corpadvise.com
www.corpadvise.com

**Corporate Capital Formation, Inc.**
Roger Coleman and Cynthia Taylor
2724 Otter Creek Court, 101
Las Vegas, NV 89117
Phone: 866-320-5913
Fax: 702-320-5914
Email: rcole_1@yahoo.com
www.nevada-business-corporation.com

**Corporate Place, Inc., The**
Oliver K. Meservy, CPA
Corporate Place
823 South Sixth Street, Suite 100
Las Vegas, NV 89101
Phone: 877-786-8500
Fax: 877-786-9500
Email: residentagents@aol.com
www.corporateplace.com

**Corporate Service Center, Inc.**
Trevor C. Rowley
5190 Neil Road, Suite 430
Reno, NV 89502
Phone: 800-638-2320
Fax: 775-329-0852
Email: trowley@corporateservicecenter.com
www.corporateservicecenter.com

**Corporate Services of Nevada**
Don Harmer
502 North Division Street
Carson City, NV 89703
Phone: 800-655-0538
Fax: 775-883-2723
Email: corpsvcs@msn.com
www.incorporationsolutions.com

**Corporation Makers, Inc.**
Joel Schnur
1100 Salem Rose
Las Vegas, NV 89144
Phone: 800-267-7657
Fax: 702-243-5159
Email: corpmakers@aol.com
www.corpmakers.com

**Crome, Teresa**
1651 Nevada Hwy.
Boulder City, NV 89005
Phone: 702-294-0552
Fax: 702-294-0996
Email: teresa@gibsonair.com

**Drinkwater Law Offices**
Bonnie Drinkwater
5421 Kietzke Lane, Suite 100
Reno, NV 89511
Phone: 775-828-0800
Fax: 775-828-0858
Email: bdrinkwater@drinkwaterlaw.com
www.drinkwaterlaw.com

**Forward Nevada**
Lisa Nosz
2880 West Sahara Avenue
Las Vegas, NV 89102
Phone: 888-377-6245
Fax: 702-220-6244
Email: lisa@forwardnevada.com
www.forwardnevada.com

**Fountainhead Associates, Inc.**
Gwen Currie
312 West Fourth Street
Carson City, NV 89703
Phone: 800-574-0255
Fax: 775-884-0187
Email: gwen@corpkeeper.com
www.corpkeeper.com

**GKL Resident Agents/Filings, Inc.**
Gregory K. Lee
1000 East William Street, Suite 204
Carson City, NV 89701
Phone: 888-682-4368
Fax: 775-841-2065
Email: info@gklnv.com
www.gklnv.com

**Hilbrecht & Associates**
Norman Hilbrecht
723 South Casino Center Boulevard
Las Vegas, NV 89101
Phone: 702-384-1036
Fax: 702-384-2529
Email: hilbrecht@lvcm.com
www.lawyers.com/hilbrecht

**Hill, Douglas R.**
440 Ridge Street #2
Reno, NV 89501
Phone: 775-786-1155
Fax: 775-786-0230

**Incorp Services, Inc.**
3155 East Patrick Lane, Suite 1
Las Vegas, NV 89120
Phone: 800-246-2677
Fax: 702-866-2689
www.incorp.com

**Incorporate-Us.com, LLC**
Jodi Farmer
1285 Baring Boulevard #205
Sparks, NV 89434
Phone: 877-446-2677
Fax: 775-626-8435
Email: customerservice@incorporate-us.com
www.incorporate-us.com

**Incorporating Solutions Group, Inc.**
Lissa Mitchell
10120 South Eastern Avenue, Suite 200
Henderson, NV 89052
Phone: 888-537-5581
Fax: 714-242-0444
Email: infor@incsolgroup.com
www.incsolgroup.com

**ISL, Inc.**
Kim Sharpe
10 Bodie Drive
Carson City, NV 89706
Phone: 800-346-4646
Email: orders@incserv.com
www.incserv.com

**Laughlin Associates, Inc.**
Brent Buscay
2533 North Carson Street
Carson City, NV 89706
Phone: 800-648-0966
Fax: 775-883-4874
Email: bbuscay@laughlinusa.com
www.laughlinusa.com

**Mail Link, LLC**
Eric Ruecker
848 North Rainbow Boulevard
Las Vegas, NV 89107
Phone: 888-267-1109
Fax: 702-258-3357
Email: info@maillinkplus.com
www.maillinkplus.com

**National Registered Agents of Nevada, Inc.**
Paul J. Hagan and Gabe Hughes
1000 East Williams Street, Suite 204
Carson City, NV 89701
Phone: 800-562-6429
Fax: 800-562-6504
Email: nvinfo@nrai.com

**Nevada Corporate Filings Plus, Inc.**
William Levine
3036 Donnegal Bay Drive
Las Vegas, NV 89117
Phone: 702-362-4616
Fax: 702-362-4616
Email: pro1040@aol.com
www.corpfilingsplus.com

**Nevada Corporate Formations, Inc.**
Jere Dougherty
1500 East Tropicana Avenue, Suite 100
Las Vegas, NV 89119
Phone: 866-734-7400
Fax: 702-734-7455
Email: ncfinc@lvcoxmail.com

**Nevada Corporate Headquarters, Inc.**
Dianna Temple
101 Convention Center Drive, Suite 700
Las Vegas, NV 89109
Phone: 800-398-1077
Fax: 702-221-0904
Email: dtemple@nchinc.com
www.nchinc.com

**Nevada Corporate Planners, Inc.**
Scott Letourneau
7477 North Lake Mead Boulevard, Suite 170
Las Vegas, NV 89128
Phone: 888-627-7007
Fax: 702-220-6444
Email: scott@nvinc.com
www.nvinc.com

**Nevada Registrations, Inc.**
Irene B. McMillan and Todd J. McMillan
5795 South Sandhill Road, Suite F
Las Vegas, NV 89120
Phone: 800-454-9674
Fax: 702-435-1477
Email: todd@nevadaregistrations.com
www.nevadaregistrations.com

**O'Connor, Lawrence J.**
10220 Hawkeye Circle
Reno, NV 89523
Phone: 775-345-6747
Fax: 775-345-6749
Email: terraborlarry@aol.com

**Paracorp Incorporated**
Nancy Gaches
318 North Carson Street #208
Carson City, NV 89701
Phone: 888-972-7273
Fax: 888-886-7168
Email: nv@parasec.com
www.parasec.com

**Professional Legal Assistors**
Dottie Randazzo
500 North Rainbow Boulevard, Suite 300
Las Vegas, NV 89107
Phone: 800-621-7008
Fax: 888-232-9022
Email: dottie@biz-usa.com
www.biz-usa.com

**Registered Agent Solutions, Inc.**
James J. Governor
726 South Casino Center Boulevard, Suite 207
Las Vegas, NV 89101
Phone: 888-705-7274
Fax: 888-706-7274
Email: jgovernor@rasi.com
www.rasi.com

**Resident Agency National, Inc.**
Catherine A. Mead
377 South Nevada Street
Carson City, NV 89703
Phone: 775-882-7549
Fax: 775-882-4283
Email: ran1977@sbcglobal.net

**Resident Agents of Nevada, Inc.**
Diane Kalinowski and Sandra Miller
711 South Carson Street, Suite 4
Carson City, NV 89701
Phone: 888-663-8232
Fax: 775-882-6818
Email: agents@nevada.org
www.nevada.org

**Sage International, Inc.**
Cheri S. Hill
1135 Terminal Way, Suite 209
Reno, NV 89502
Phone: 800-254-5779
Fax: 775-786-2013
Email: corpinfo@sageintl.com
www.sageintl.com

**Silver Shield Services, Inc.**
Samara Noser
2840 Hwy 95 Alt S #7
Silver Springs, NV 89429
Phone: 775-577-4822
Fax: 775-577-4429
Email: staff@shieldcorp.net
www.shieldcorp.net

**State Agent & Transfer Syndicate, Inc.**
Jed Block and Tristin Alishio
112 North Curry Street
Carson City, NV 89703
Phone: 800-253-1013
Fax: 775-882-8628
Email: info@nevadacorpfilings.com
www.nevadacorpfilings.com

**Sutton Law Center, P.C.**
Lyn Millard and Garrett Sutton
348 Mill Street
Reno, NV 89501
Phone: 800-700-1430
Fax: 775-824-0105
Email: info@sutlaw.com
www.sutlaw.com

**United Trade Network**
Artis Parker
7975 West Sahara Avenue, Suite 104
Las Vegas, NV 89117
Phone: 866-702-2677
Fax: 702-974-0723
Email: aparker@unitedtradenetwork.com
www.unitedtradenetwork.com

**UPS Store 135, The**
Barbara and Richard Ferrante
3540 West Sahara Avenue #e-6
Las Vegas, NV 89102
Phone: 702-367-6252
Fax: 702-367-6421
Email: store0135@theupsstore.com

**UPS Store, 1650, The**
Donna M. Stanton
3395 South Jones Boulevard
Las Vegas, NV 89146
Phone: 800-221-9175
Fax: 702-221-9341
Email: store1650@theupsstore.com

**UPS Store, The**
Barbara Stoll-Frank
1350 East Flamingo Road
Las Vegas, NV 89119
Phone: 702-732-0024
Fax: 702-796-0913
Email: store0097@theupsstore.com
www.theupsstorenv.com

**Val-U-Corp Services, Inc.**
Phillip Patton and Daniel Kramer
1802 North Carson Street, Suite 212
Carson City, NV 89701
Phone: 800-555-9141
Fax: 775-887-0738
Email: val-u-corp@val-u-corp.com
www.val-u-corp.com

**Windmill Realty Advisors, Inc.**
Faramarz Yousefzadeh
101 Convention Center Drive
Las Vegas, NV 89101
Phone: 702-650-5504
Fax: 702-650-5509

# Blank Forms

appendix d

This appendix contains the blank forms that can be used to form a Nevada corporation or LLC. Be sure to read the text before using any of these forms. If you do not understand any of the forms, you should consult an attorney. Although the forms can be torn out for use, you may want to copy them first in case you make a mistake or want to use them again.

## FORMS USED FOR BOTH CORPORATIONS AND LLCS

## FORMS USED ONLY FOR CORPORATIONS

## FORMS USED ONLY FOR LLCS

**ROSS MILLER**
Secretary of State
202 North Carson Street
Carson City, Nevada 89701-4201
(775) 684 5708
Website: secretaryofstate.biz

## Credit Card Checklist
### (For Counter, Telephone, Fax and Mail Requests)

USE BLACK INK ONLY - DO NOT HIGHLIGHT

Service Type:    Counter ☐    Telephone ☐    Mail ☐    Fax ☐

Expedite Service: *(Requires additional fees)*

PLEASE EXPEDITE:    **24-HOUR** SERVICE ☐    **2-HOUR** SERVICE ☐    **1-HOUR** SERVICE ☐

Card Type: (Mark one box)

VISA ☐    MasterCard ☐    Discover ☐    American Express ☐

Customer Credit Card Number:                                                          V CODE*

☐☐☐☐☐☐☐☐☐☐☐☐☐☐☐☐    ☐☐☐☐

\* 3-digit number found on the far right of the backside of VISA, MasterCard and Discover cards
4-digit number found on the front right side of American Express card.

**NOTICE:** *For security and verification purposes, all credit card payments must include the 3 or 4-digit CVV2 code (VCode) number located on the credit card. Failure to include this code will result in the rejection of your filing or service request.*

Expiration Date:    Month ☐    Year ☐

Amount:    $ ☐

Cardholder Information:

Entity Name ☐

Name ☐

Billing Address ☐

City, State, Zip ☐

Telephone ☐

AUTHORIZATION:    CUSTOMER AUTHORIZES THE SECRETARY OF STATE TO BILL AN AMOUNT NOT TO
EXCEED $ ☐ TO BE CHARGED TO THE ABOVE CREDIT CARD
NUMBER.

X_____
### CARDHOLDER SIGNATURE

Nevada Secretary of State Form Credit Card 2007
Revised on: 06/05/07

*This page intentionally blank.*

# REQUEST FOR CORPORATE FORMS

To: Department of Corporate Filings

Please send us any of the following that are available without charge and advise of the cost of any for which there is a charge.

Form for registering a foreign ☐ corporation ☐ LLC to do business in this state.

Copy of statutes applicable to foreign businesses doing business in this state.

Please send to: _____
                         Name (Printed or typed)

                _____
                                 Address

                _____
                              City, State, & Zip

*This page intentionally blank.*

| Form **SS-4** | **Application for Employer Identification Number** | OMB No. 1545-0003 |
|---|---|---|

Form **SS-4**
(Rev. July 2007)
Department of the Treasury
Internal Revenue Service

(For use by employers, corporations, partnerships, trusts, estates, churches, government agencies, Indian tribal entities, certain individuals, and others.)
▶ See separate instructions for each line.    ▶ Keep a copy for your records.

EIN

**Type or print clearly.**

**1** Legal name of entity (or individual) for whom the EIN is being requested

**2** Trade name of business (if different from name on line 1)

**3** Executor, administrator, trustee, "care of" name

**4a** Mailing address (room, apt., suite no. and street, or P.O. box)

**5a** Street address (if different) (Do not enter a P.O. box.)

**4b** City, state, and ZIP code (if foreign, see instructions)

**5b** City, state, and ZIP code (if foreign, see instructions)

**6** County and state where principal business is located

**7a** Name of principal officer, general partner, grantor, owner, or trustor

**7b** SSN, ITIN, or EIN

**8a** Is this application for a limited liability company (LLC) (or a foreign equivalent)?    ☐ Yes    ☐ No

**8b** If 8a is "Yes," enter the number of LLC members    ▶

**8c** If 8a is "Yes," was the LLC organized in the United States?    ☐ Yes    ☐ No

**9a** Type of entity (check only one box). **Caution.** If 8a is "Yes," see the instructions for the correct box to check.

☐ Sole proprietor (SSN) _____
☐ Partnership
☐ Corporation (enter form number to be filed) ▶ _____
☐ Personal service corporation
☐ Church or church-controlled organization
☐ Other nonprofit organization (specify) ▶ _____
☐ Other (specify) ▶

☐ Estate (SSN of decedent) _____
☐ Plan administrator (TIN) _____
☐ Trust (TIN of grantor) _____
☐ National Guard    ☐ State/local government
☐ Farmers' cooperative    ☐ Federal government/military
☐ REMIC    ☐ Indian tribal governments/enterprises
Group Exemption Number (GEN) if any ▶

**9b** If a corporation, name the state or foreign country (if applicable) where incorporated

State

Foreign country

**10** **Reason for applying** (check only one box)

☐ Started new business (specify type) ▶ _____
☐ Hired employees (Check the box and see line 13.)
☐ Compliance with IRS withholding regulations
☐ Other (specify) ▶

☐ Banking purpose (specify purpose) ▶ _____
☐ Changed type of organization (specify new type) ▶ _____
☐ Purchased going business
☐ Created a trust (specify type) ▶ _____
☐ Created a pension plan (specify type) ▶ _____

**11** Date business started or acquired (month, day, year). See instructions.

**12** Closing month of accounting year

**13** Highest number of employees expected in the next 12 months (enter -0- if none).

| Agricultural | Household | Other |
|---|---|---|
| | | |

**14** Do you expect your employment tax liability to be $1,000 or less in a full calendar year? ☐ Yes ☐ No (If you expect to pay $4,000 or less in total wages in a full calendar year, you can mark "Yes.")

**15** First date wages or annuities were paid (month, day, year). **Note.** If applicant is a withholding agent, enter date income will first be paid to nonresident alien (month, day, year) ▶

**16** Check **one** box that best describes the principal activity of your business.
☐ Construction    ☐ Rental & leasing    ☐ Transportation & warehousing    ☐ Health care & social assistance    ☐ Wholesale-agent/broker
☐ Real estate    ☐ Manufacturing    ☐ Finance & insurance    ☐ Accommodation & food service    ☐ Wholesale-other    ☐ Retail
☐ Other (specify)

**17** Indicate principal line of merchandise sold, specific construction work done, products produced, or services provided.

**18** Has the applicant entity shown on line 1 ever applied for and received an EIN?    ☐ Yes    ☐ No
If "Yes," write previous EIN here ▶

**Third Party Designee**

Complete this section **only** if you want to authorize the named individual to receive the entity's EIN and answer questions about the completion of this form.

Designee's name

Designee's telephone number (include area code)
(    )

Address and ZIP code

Designee's fax number (include area code)
(    )

Under penalties of perjury, I declare that I have examined this application, and to the best of my knowledge and belief, it is true, correct, and complete.

Name and title (type or print clearly) ▶

Applicant's telephone number (include area code)
(    )

Signature ▶                Date ▶

Applicant's fax number (include area code)
(    )

**For Privacy Act and Paperwork Reduction Act Notice, see separate instructions.**    Cat. No. 16055N    Form **SS-4** (Rev. 7-2007)

# Do I Need an EIN?

File Form SS-4 if the applicant entity does not already have an EIN but is required to show an EIN on any return, statement, or other document.[1] See also the separate instructions for each line on Form SS-4.

| IF the applicant... | AND... | THEN... |
|---|---|---|
| Started a new business | Does not currently have (nor expect to have) employees | Complete lines 1, 2, 4a–8a, 8b–c (if applicable), 9a, 9b (if applicable), and 10–14 and 16–18. |
| Hired (or will hire) employees, including household employees | Does not already have an EIN | Complete lines 1, 2, 4a–6, 7a–b (if applicable), 8a, 8b–c (if applicable), 9a, 9b (if applicable), 10–18. |
| Opened a bank account | Needs an EIN for banking purposes only | Complete lines 1–5b, 7a–b (if applicable), 8a, 8b–c (if applicable), 9a, 9b (if applicable), 10, and 18. |
| Changed type of organization | Either the legal character of the organization or its ownership changed (for example, you incorporate a sole proprietorship or form a partnership)[2] | Complete lines 1–18 (as applicable). |
| Purchased a going business[3] | Does not already have an EIN | Complete lines 1–18 (as applicable). |
| Created a trust | The trust is other than a grantor trust or an IRA trust[4] | Complete lines 1–18 (as applicable). |
| Created a pension plan as a plan administrator[5] | Needs an EIN for reporting purposes | Complete lines 1, 3, 4a–5b, 9a, 10, and 18. |
| Is a foreign person needing an EIN to comply with IRS withholding regulations | Needs an EIN to complete a Form W-8 (other than Form W-8ECI), avoid withholding on portfolio assets, or claim tax treaty benefits[6] | Complete lines 1–5b, 7a–b (SSN or ITIN optional), 8a, 8b–c (if applicable), 9a, 9b (if applicable), 10, and 18. |
| Is administering an estate | Needs an EIN to report estate income on Form 1041 | Complete lines 1–6, 9a, 10–12, 13–17 (if applicable), and 18. |
| Is a withholding agent for taxes on non-wage income paid to an alien (i.e., individual, corporation, or partnership, etc.) | Is an agent, broker, fiduciary, manager, tenant, or spouse who is required to file Form 1042, Annual Withholding Tax Return for U.S. Source Income of Foreign Persons | Complete lines 1, 2, 3 (if applicable), 4a–5b, 7a–b (if applicable), 8a, 8b–c (if applicable), 9a, 9b (if applicable), 10 and 18. |
| Is a state or local agency | Serves as a tax reporting agent for public assistance recipients under Rev. Proc. 80-4, 1980-1 C.B. 581[7] | Complete lines 1, 2, 4a–5b, 9a, 10 and 18. |
| Is a single-member LLC | Needs an EIN to file Form 8832, Classification Election, for filing employment tax returns, **or** for state reporting purposes[8] | Complete lines 1–18 (as applicable). |
| Is an S corporation | Needs an EIN to file Form 2553, Election by a Small Business Corporation[9] | Complete lines 1–18 (as applicable). |

[1] For example, a sole proprietorship or self-employed farmer who establishes a qualified retirement plan, or is required to file excise, employment, alcohol, tobacco, or firearms returns, must have an EIN. A partnership, corporation, REMIC (real estate mortgage investment conduit), nonprofit organization (church, club, etc.), or farmers' cooperative must use an EIN for any tax-related purpose even if the entity does not have employees.

[2] However, do not apply for a new EIN if the existing entity only (a) changed its business name, (b) elected on Form 8832 to change the way it is taxed (or is covered by the default rules), or (c) terminated its partnership status because at least 50% of the total interests in partnership capital and profits were sold or exchanged within a 12-month period. The EIN of the terminated partnership should continue to be used. See Regulations section 301.6109-1(d)(2)(iii).

[3] Do not use the EIN of the prior business unless you became the "owner" of a corporation by acquiring its stock.

[4] However, grantor trusts that do not file using Optional Method 1 and IRA trusts that are required to file Form 990-T, Exempt Organization Business Income Tax Return, must have an EIN. For more information on grantor trusts, see the Instructions for Form 1041.

[5] A plan administrator is the person or group of persons specified as the administrator by the instrument under which the plan is operated.

[6] Entities applying to be a Qualified Intermediary (QI) need a QI-EIN even if they already have an EIN. See Rev. Proc. 2000-12.

[7] See also *Household employer* on page 4 of the instructions. **Note.** State or local agencies may need an EIN for other reasons, for example, hired employees.

[8] Most LLCs do not need to file Form 8832. See *Limited liability company (LLC)* on page 4 of the instructions for details on completing Form SS-4 for an LLC.

[9] An existing corporation that is electing or revoking S corporation status should use its previously-assigned EIN.

# BANKING RESOLUTION OF

_____

The undersigned, being the
☐ corporate secretary of the above corporation,
☐ member of the above limited liability company,
☐ manager of the above limited liability company

hereby certifies that on the \_\_\_\_\_ day of _____, _____, the company duly adopted the following resolution:

RESOLVED that the company open bank accounts with _____ _____ and that the ☐ officers of the corporation or ☐ members ☐ managers of the limited liability company are authorized to take such action as is necessary to open such accounts; that the bank's printed form of resolution is hereby adopted and incorporated into these minutes by reference and shall be placed in the minute book; that any \_\_\_\_ of the following persons shall have signature authority over the account:

_____        _____

_____        _____

and that said resolution has not been modified or rescinded.

Date: _____

_____
☐ Corporate Secretary
☐ Member
☐ Manager

*This page intentionally blank.*

# RESOLUTION TO REIMBURSE EXPENSES
of
_____

      RESOLVED that the company shall reimburse the following parties for the organizational expenses of the organizers of this company and that the company shall amortize or deduct these expenses as allowed by IRS regulations.

| Name | Expense | Amount |
|------|---------|--------|
| _____ | _____ | $_____ |
| _____ | _____ | $_____ |
| _____ | _____ | $_____ |
| _____ | _____ | $_____ |
| _____ | _____ | $_____ |
| _____ | _____ | $_____ |
| _____ | _____ | $_____ |

Date:_____

_____

_____

_____

_____

_____

*This page intentionally blank.*

# BILL OF SALE

The undersigned, in consideration of

hereby grants, bargains, sells, transfers, and delivers unto said corporation the following goods and chattels:

To have and to hold the same forever.

And the undersigned, their heirs, successors, and administrators, covenant and warrant that they are the lawful owners of the said goods and chattels and that they are free from all encumbrances. That the undersigned have the right to sell this property and that they will warrant and defend the sale of said property against the lawful claims and demands of all persons.

IN WITNESS whereof the undersigned have executed this Bill of Sale this _____ day of _____, _____.

_____

_____

_____

*This page intentionally blank.*

# NEVADA BUSINESS REGISTRATION FORM INSTRUCTIONS

Completion of this form will provide the common information needed and/or required by participating state and local government agencies. Important details are included to help you provide the necessary information. It is important to respond to all items. Any omission could cause a delay in processing your registration.

**WHO ACCEPTS THIS FORM?** The Nevada Department of Taxation and the Nevada Employment Security Division (ESD). Also, most local governments accept the form.

**WHAT OTHER INFORMATION MUST I PROVIDE?** When applying to **Department of Taxation:** All businesses must complete a Supplemental Application (APP-01.01) to determine correct fees. When applying to **Employment Security Division:** If you employ agricultural or domestic workers, or are a non-profit agency you must complete a Supplemental Registration (NUCS-4058).

**WHO MAY USE THIS FORM?** Any person or corporation who is: opening a new business; opening additional locations; changing locations; changing owners, corporate officers or members; or changing a mailing address.

**WHERE IS THIS FORM AVAILABLE?** This form is available at the participating state and local agencies or by visiting the agency websites listed below. Forms may also be available at Chambers of Commerce and state and local economic development agencies.

## LINE-BY-LINE INSTRUCTIONS FOR COMPLETING THE NEVADA BUSINESS REGISTRATION - PLEASE COMPLETE IN ENGLISH.

1. **I Am Applying For:** Check the boxes that apply. Nevada has no central database for business registration. You are required to submit a copy to each agency that is applicable to your business. Keep a copy for your records.
2. **Check All Box(es) That Apply.**
3. **Business Entity Type:** Indicate the structure and type of ownership of your business.
4. **Corporate/Entity Name:** If incorporated, enter the name as registered with the Secretary of State. Include a telephone number.
5. **Federal Tax Identification Number:** Enter your Federal Identification Number. For information regarding a Federal Identification Number, contact the Internal Revenue Service at 1-800-829-1040. If you have applied for your number and have not received it, write "PENDING." If your Federal Identification Number changes, you must complete a new Nevada Business Registration.
6. **Corporate/Entity Address:** Enter the complete address of the corporation and the state of incorporation.
7. **Doing Business in Nevada As:** Enter the name as it will be known to the public. Include a business telephone and fax number.
8. **E-mail Address and Website Address:** Enter your business e-mail and website addresses if appropriate.
9. **Mailing Address:** This address will be used to mail any licenses, reports, tax returns, and correspondence.
10. **Location(s) of Business Operations:** Enter the complete location of the business including suite numbers, apartment numbers, and street direction (N, S, E, and W). If there are additional locations in Nevada, please attach a list of all locations.
11. **Location of Business Records:** Enter the complete address where business records are maintained during normal working hours. Include the telephone number of this location, if different from the business telephone number.
12. **List All Owners, Partners, Corporate Officers, and Members:** Include the full name, home address (street, city, state, and zip code), Social Security number, date of birth, title, percentage of business owned, and telephone number. If the business is incorporated, list all corporate officers. If the business is a partnership, list all partners. If the business is comprised of two corporations or other entities, list the officers/members/partners, etc. for each entity. Attach additional sheets if needed.
13. **Dates and Amounts Regarding Your Nevada Business:** Enter the date the business started or will start Nevada operations. If adding a location enter the date your additional location will begin Nevada operations. Enter the date the first worker was hired in Nevada. Enter the date and amount of the first Nevada payroll. If this is a new business, enter the estimated number of employees you will have. If the business is currently operating, list the number of employees on the payroll.
14. **Please Check All That Apply to Your Business:** If you check the box marked "Regulated by Federal/State Permit Number," attach a list that identifies the issuing entity and permit number.
15. **Nature of Your Business:** Describe your business activities, goods, products, or services in Nevada. State the approximate percentage of sales or revenues resulting from each item. Example: Retail sale of major appliances to public 60%; repair 40%.
16. **Acquired, Changed, or Have a New Federal Tax Number:** On the first line, enter the date the business was acquired; check the boxes that apply to how the business was acquired; and the portion of the business you acquired. On the second line, list the name of the previous owner and the business name of the previous owner. On the third line, indicate the physical address of the business you acquired. On the fourth line, list your previous Nevada Sales/Use Tax Permit Number and the Employment Security Division (ESD) Account Number of the previous owner. If there is more than one previous owner, attach an additional sheet.
17. **Signature Instructions:** Make copies first and then sign each copy. Original signatures are required by each state and local agency. Legal signatures include: sole proprietor-owner, corporate officer, and managing member.

| | | |
|---|---|---|
| Toll Free (In State) for All State of Nevada Agencies................................................................. | | **800-992-0900** |
| **Nevada Department of Taxation:** | Website: www.tax.state.nv.us | |
| Las Vegas.................. | 555 E. Washington Avenue, Suite 1300 • Las Vegas, Nevada 89101................ | (702) 486-2300 |
| Reno....................... | 4600 Kietzke Lane, Building L, Suite 235 • Reno, Nevada 89502.................... | (775) 688-1295 |
| Carson City............... | 1550 E. College Parkway, Suite 115 • Carson City, Nevada 89706.................. | (775) 684-2000 |
| **Nevada Employment Security Division (ESD):** | Website: www.nvdetr.org | |
| Las Vegas.................................................................................................................. | | (702) 486-0250 |
| Reno........................................................................................................................ | | (775) 688-2663 |
| Statewide (Mailing)..... | 500 E. Third Street • Carson City, Nevada 89713-0030................................ | (775) 687-4545 |

If your business has or may have a discharge to the environment or needs a water appropriation permit, the following telephone numbers should be used for information concerning exemptions and to acquire applications:

| | |
|---|---|
| **Nevada Department of Conservation and Natural Resources:** Website: www.dcnr.nv.gov | |
| Environmental Protection Division ........................................................................... | (775) 687-4670 |
| Water Resources Division (Water Appropriation) ....................................................... | (775) 687-4380 |
| **Nevada Department of Wildlife:** (Industrial Artificial Pond Permit) Website: www.ndow.org ........... | (775) 688-1500 |

**Local Business License Departments:** To obtain the telephone numbers for local license departments check the white pages of the telephone directory under the government name, i.e., Clark County, Reno.

# NEVADA BUSINESS REGISTRATION

Important details are included in the instructions. Please type or print in black ink. Each agency may request additional information depending on your type of business. Completing this form does not relieve you of any statutory or regulatory requirements relating to your business.

| 1 | I Am Applying For: | ☐ Unemployment Insurance (Employment Security Division - ESD) | ☐ State Business License, Sales/Use Tax Permit, Modified Business Tax (Department of Taxation) | ☐ Local Business License | SEND A COPY TO EACH AGENCY |
|---|---|---|---|---|---|

| 2 | ☐ New Business | ☐ Change in Ownership/ Business Entity | ☐ Change in Location | ☐ Change in Name | ☐ Change in Corporate Officers | ☐ Change in Mailing Address | ☐ Other |
|---|---|---|---|---|---|---|---|

| 3 | Business Entity Type: | ☐ Sole Proprietor | ☐ S Corp. | ☐ Publicly Traded Corp. | ☐ Privately Held Corp. | ☐ Association | ☐ Partnership | ☐ Limited Liability Partnership | ☐ Limited Liability Company | ☐ Government Entity | ☐ Other |
|---|---|---|---|---|---|---|---|---|---|---|---|

| 4 | Corporate/Entity Name: | Corporate/Entity Telephone ( ) | **5** Federal Tax Identification Number |
|---|---|---|---|

| 6 | Corporate/Entity Address: | Street Number, Direction (N, S, E, W) and Name  Suite, Unit or Apt # | City, State, and Zip Code +4 | State of Incorporation or Formation |
|---|---|---|---|---|

| 7 | Doing Business in Nevada As: | | Business Telephone ( ) | Fax ( ) |
|---|---|---|---|---|

| 8 | E-mail Address: | Website Address: |
|---|---|---|

| 9 | Mailing Address: | Street Number, Direction (N, S, E, W) and Name  Suite, Unit or Apt # | City, State, and Zip Code +4 |
|---|---|---|---|

| 10 | Location(s) of Business Operations: | Street Number, Direction (N, S, E, W) and Name  Suite, Unit or Apt # | City, State, and Zip Code +4 |
|---|---|---|---|

| 11 | Location of Business Records: | Street Number, Direction (N, S, E, W) and Name  Suite, Unit or Apt # | City, State, and Zip Code +4 | Telephone Number: ( ) |
|---|---|---|---|---|

**12** List All Owners, Partners, Corporate Officers, Members, etc. Attach Additional Sheets if Needed. (If individual ownership, list only one owner.)

| Owner, Partner, Officer, Member, etc. (Last, First, MI): | Residence Address (Street) | SSN: | Date of Birth |
|---|---|---|---|
| Title | Percent Owned | City, State, Zip +4 | Residence Telephone |

| Owner, Partner, Officer, Member, etc. (Last, First, MI): | Residence Address (Street) | SSN: | Date of Birth |
|---|---|---|---|
| Title | Percent Owned | City, State, Zip +4 | Residence Telephone |

| Owner, Partner, Officer, Member, etc. (Last, First, MI): | Residence Address (Street) | SSN: | Date of Birth |
|---|---|---|---|
| Title | Percent Owned | City, State, Zip +4 | Residence Telephone |

| Responsible Local Contact ( Last, First, MI & Title ): | Residence Address (Street), City, State, Zip +4 | SSN: | Residence Telephone |
|---|---|---|---|

| 13 | Date Business Started in Nevada | Date Business Location Opened | Date First Worker Hired in Nevada | Date of First Nevada Payroll | Amount of First Nevada Payroll | Number of Employees |
|---|---|---|---|---|---|---|

**14** PLEASE CHECK ALL THAT APPLY TO YOUR BUSINESS

| | | | | | |
|---|---|---|---|---|---|
| ☐ Mining | ☐ Domestics | ☐ Outside Dining | ☐ Water Appropriation | ☐ Adult Materials/Activity | ☐ Amusement Machines | ☐ Resident Agent |
| ☐ Service | ☐ Agriculture | ☐ Home Occupation | ☐ Hazardous Material | ☐ Leased or Leasing Employees | ☐ Alcohol | ☐ Financial Institutions |
| ☐ Tobacco | ☐ Manufacturing | ☐ Retail Sales—New | ☐ Construction/Erection | ☐ Leasing (Other than Employees) | ☐ Gaming | ☐ Mortgage Brokers |
| ☐ Delivery | ☐ Transportation | ☐ Retail Sales—Used | ☐ Telephone Solicitation | ☐ Supply/Use Temporary Workers | ☐ Health Services | ☐ Banker |
| ☐ Wholesale | ☐ Not for Profit | ☐ Live Entertainment | ☐ Environmental Discharge | ☐ Regulated by Federal/State Permit Number _____ | | ☐ Other _____ |

**15 Describe in Detail the Nature of Your Business in Nevada. Include Product Sold, Labor Performed and/or Services Rendered.**
State the approximate percentage of sales or revenues resulting from each item. Example: Retail sale of major appliances to public 60%; repair 40%.

**16 If You Have Acquired A Nevada Business, Changed Ownership/Business Entity, or Have a New Federal Tax Number, Complete This Section:**

| Date Acquired/Changed: | Acquired/Changed by: ☐ Purchase ☐ Lease ☐ Other | Portion Acquired/Changed: ☐ In Whole ☐ In Part |
|---|---|---|
| Name(s) of Previous Owner(s) | Previous Owner(s) Business Name | |
| Address (Street) | City | State | Zip Code +4 |
| Enter Your Previous Nevada Sales/Use Tax Permit Number, if applicable: | Enter Previous Owner(s) ESD Account Number: | |

**17** I CERTIFY THE INFORMATION PROVIDED IS TRUE, CORRECT AND COMPLETE TO THE BEST OF MY KNOWLEDGE AND BELIEF.
**\*\*Signatures must be original and that of a responsible party. If a general partnership or joint venture, more than one signature is required. Legal signatures include: sole proprietor-owner, corporate officer, and managing member.**

| \*\*Signature Responsible Party / Original | Print Name And Title | Date |
|---|---|---|
| \*\*Signature Responsible Party / Original | Print Name And Title | Date |

**ORIGINAL SIGNATURES REQUIRED BY AGENCIES-KEEP COPY FOR YOUR RECORDS** APP-01.00 Rev 07-12-04

## NEVADA DEPARTMENT OF TAXATION
# SUPPLEMENTAL INFORMATION
Please print clearly — use black or blue ink only.
Please mark applicable type(s)   (see instructions).

| **For Dept. Use Only** |
|---|
| Permit/License No. |
| Dept. of Taxation Representative accepting application: |

☐ Sales/Use Permit    ☐ Consumers Certificate    ☐ Certificate of Authority    ☐ Nevada Business License    ☐ Live Entertainment Tax    ☐ Modified Business Tax

| **1.** | DBA (as indicated on Nevada Business Registration Form): |
|---|---|
| **2.** | Business telephone number:    **3.**    If corporation, STATE of incorporation or formation: |

## FEES AND SECURITY DEPOSIT

| **4.** | Estimated total monthly receipts:    **5.**    Estimated total Nevada monthly TAXABLE receipts: |
|---|---|
| **6.** | ☐ I do not purchase tangible personal property for storage, use or other consumption in Nevada.<br>☐ Corporation with no employees (other than resident agent in Nevada) |
| **7.** | Home-based businesses — indicate last year's NET INCOME or estimate the current year's NET INCOME if this a new business: |

**8.** Reporting cycle (check choice of reporting)
Sales Tax Accounts with over $10,000 a month in TAXABLE sales must report monthly:

|  | Monthly | Quarterly | Annual |
|---|---|---|---|
| Sales/Use Tax | ☐ | ☐ | ☐ |
| Use Tax | ☐ | ☐ | ☐ |
| Live Entertainment Tax ☐ Under 7,500 Seating ☐ 7,500 or More Seating | ☐ | | |
| Modified Business Tax ☐ General Business ☐ Financial Institution | | ☐ | |
| Business Tax (for accounts prior to 10/01/03) | | ☐ | |
| Business License | | | ☐ |

| **9.** | Security (see instructions)<br>☐ Cash<br>$_____    ☐ Surety # _____    ☐ CD    # _____    **10.**    Total Nevada business locations: |
|---|---|
| **11.** | Sales Tax fees (see instructions):    **12.**    Business License Fee (see instructions): |

## 13.    OTHER INFORMATION

| Name of spouse/relative: | Address of spouse/relative: | Phone number of spouse/relative: |
|---|---|---|
| Name of other contact: | Address of other contact: | Phone number of other contact: |
| Accountant/bookkeeper: | Address of accountant/bookkeeper: | Phone number of accountant/bookkeeper: |

Name of bank/financial institution – location / account number:    Other employment (If applicable):

Business account: _____    Company name: _____
Personal account: _____    Company name: _____

## FOR DEPARTMENT USE ONLY

ST/UT No.: _____    BT / BL No.: _____
Combine Accts: ☐ Yes ☐ No
Previous Acct:    Previous Acct Cancelled: ☐ Yes    ☐ No

Comments:

☐ Cash    ☐ Check    ABA #:    Bank:    Branch:

APP SUPPLEMENTAL-01.01
REV 05/25/04

# SUPPLEMENTAL INFORMATION INSTRUCTIONS

**Sales/Use Tax** — A business which sells tangible personal property at retail or wholesale, and has a physical location in Nevada or enters Nevada to conduct business, must pay a $15.00 permit fee for EACH in-state business location. If the business does not have a physical location in Nevada, it must still pay a minimum fee of $15.00.

**Security** — A sales/use tax permit will not be issued until applicable security is submitted. In order to determine the security requirement, compute your average monthly taxable sales. Multiply taxable Nevada sales by applicable tax rate of the county in which business is located. This is your estimated average monthly tax liability. Security is required equal to three times your monthly tax liability for monthly reporting or six times monthly tax liability for quarterly reporting. There is a minimum security deposit requirement. There is no maximum security. After three full years of perfect reporting, you may apply for a waiver of the security requirement.

**Certificate of Authority** — This permit is available to out-of-state businesses having no jurisdiction or nexus in Nevada. The permit allows an out-of-state business, who is not required to hold a Nevada sales/use tax permit, to voluntarily register in order to collect and remit use tax as a convenience for it's Nevada customers. This permit does not require payment of a fee, nor does it require security.

**Consumer's Certificate (Use Tax)** — This registration allows a Nevada business, not required to hold a Nevada sales/use tax permit, to pay use tax directly to the State on tangible personal property purchased from a vendor not registered to collect Nevada sales tax. Example: Contractors who do not make sales and only purchase building materials for their own use from out of state. All businesses required to register for the State Business License that purchase tangible personal property for storage, use or other consumption in Nevada must register for use tax. Registering for use tax does not require payment of a fee, nor does it require security.

**Business License Fee** — Businesses, Nevada corporations, foreign corporations, partnerships and proprietorships operating in Nevada must pay a $100.00 business license fee which is renewable annually on the anniversary date. Nonprofit 501(C) organizations and all governmental entities are not required to obtain a state business license or pay the $100.00 fee. Businesses with employees prior to 10/01/03 are subject to Business Tax.

**Modified Business Tax (MBT) / Modified Business Tax on Financial Institutions (MBTFI)** — Quarterly tax based on gross payroll. You must be registered with Employment Security Division.

**Live Entertainment Tax (LET)** — Monthly tax based on admission charges to facilities providing live entertainment to non-gaming establishments. If the maximum seating capacity is under 300, no tax liability exists. Seating capacities that meet or exceed 300 must register for Live Entertainment Tax. Maximum seating capacity means the maximum occupancy of the facility as determined by the State Fire Marshal or local governmental agency.

## MUST BE SUBMITTED WITH NEVADA BUSINESS REGISTRATION FORM

APP SUPPLEMENTAL-01.01
REV 05/25/04

**ROSS MILLER**
Secretary of State
202 North Carson Street
Carson City, Nevada 89701-4201
(775) 684 5708
Website: secretaryofstate.biz

# Customer Order Instructions

## Service Requested:  ☐ Regular   ☐ 24-Hour Expedite (additional fee included)

SUBMIT THIS COMPLETED FORM WITH YOUR FILING          USE BLACK INK ONLY - DO NOT HIGHLIGHT

Name of Entity: _____   Date: _____

Return to: _____

Contact Name: _____   Phone: _____

**Return Delivery** (mark one):   ☐ FedEx: Account # _____
☐ Hold for Pick Up   ☐ Mail to Address Above  ☐ Other (explain below)

_____

Order Description (include items being ordered and fee breakdown)*:

_____

* **PLEASE NOTE:** this office keeps the original paperwork. The first file
stamped copy ordered at the time of filing is at no charge. Each
additional copy is **$2.00** per page (plus **$30.00** for each certification.)

Total Amount: _____

Method of Payment:
☐ Check/Money Order   ☐ Credit Card (attach checklist)   ☐ Trust Account _____
☐ Use balance remaining in job # _____

*This page intentionally blank.*

**ROSS MILLER**
Secretary of State
206 North Carson Street
Carson City, Nevada 89701-4299
(775) 684 5708
Website: secretaryofstate.biz

# 2 Hour Expedite
## Customer Order Instructions

SUBMIT THIS COMPLETED FORM WITH YOUR FILING                    USE BLACK INK ONLY - DO NOT HIGHLIGHT

Date: [          ]                    2-Hour Expedite Service Requested: **$500.00** Fee Included

Return to: [                              ]

Address: [                              ]

Phone: [              ]

Contact Person: [                    ]

**Return Delivery** (mark one):   ☐ FedEx: Account # [              ]

☐ Hold for Pick Up     ☐ Mail to Address Above     ☐ Other

[                              ]

Confirmation Fax Number: [          ] Confirmation E-mail Address: [          ]

**Name of Entity:**

[                              ]

**Order Description** (include items being ordered and fee breakdown)*:

[                              ]

* **PLEASE NOTE:** this office keeps the original paperwork. The first file
stamped copy ordered at the time of filing is at no charge. *Each
additional copy is $2.00 per page (plus $30.00 for each certification.)*          Total Amount: [          ]

**Method of Payment:**

☐ Check/Money Order     ☐ Credit Card (attach checklist)     ☐ Trust Account [          ]

☐ Use balance remaining in job # [                    ]

*This page intentionally blank.*

**ROSS MILLER**
Secretary of State
206 North Carson Street
Carson City, Nevada 89701-4299
(775) 684 5708
Website: secretaryofstate.biz

# 1 Hour Expedite
# Customer Order Instructions

SUBMIT THIS COMPLETED FORM WITH YOUR FILING          USE BLACK INK ONLY - DO NOT HIGHLIGHT

Date: [          ]          1-Hour Expedite Service Requested: **$1000.00** Fee Included

Return to: [                                  ]

Address: [                                  ]

Phone: [                    ]

Contact Person: [                    ]

**Return Delivery** (mark one):  ☐  FedEx: Account # [                    ]

☐ Hold for Pick Up     ☐ Mail to Address Above     ☐ Other (explain below)

[                                  ]

Confirmation Fax Number: [          ]  Confirmation E-mail Address: [          ]

**Name of Entity:**

[                                  ]

**Order Description** (include items being ordered and fee breakdown)*:

[                                  ]

* **PLEASE NOTE:** this office keeps the original paperwork. The first file
stamped copy ordered at the time of filing is at no charge. *Each
additional copy is **$2.00** per page (plus **$30.00** for each certification.)*          Total Amount: [          ]

**Method of Payment:**

☐ Check/Money Order     ☐ Credit Card (attach checklist)     ☐ Trust Account [          ]

☐ Use balance remaining in job # [                    ]

*This page intentionally blank.*

**ROSS MILLER**
Secretary of State
202 North Carson Street
Carson City, Nevada 89701-4201
(775) 684 5708
Website: secretaryofstate.biz

# Resident Agent Acceptance

**General instructions for this form:**

ABOVE SPACE IS FOR OFFICE USE ONLY

1. Please print legibly or type; Black Ink Only
2. Complete all fields.  Do not highlight.
3. Ensure that document is signed in signature field.

*In the matter of*

(Name of business entity)

I,

(Name of resident agent)

hereby state that on [_____] I accepted the appointment as resident agent
(Date)

for the above named business entity. The street address of the resident agent in this

state is as follows:

**(MANDATORY)**  Physical Street Address

Suite number

City                                              NEVADA

Zip Code

Optional: (address where mail will be sent)

**(OPTIONAL)**  Additional Mailing Address

Suite number

City                                              State

Zip Code

Signature:

**X** _____

**Authorized Signature of R.A. or  On Behalf of R.A. Company**

Date

*This page intentionally blank.*

**ROSS MILLER**
Secretary of State
206 North Carson Street
Carson City, Nevada 89701-4299
(775) 684 5708
Website: secretaryofstate.biz

# Articles of Incorporation

(PURSUANT TO NRS 78)

USE BLACK INK ONLY - DO NOT HIGHLIGHT                    ABOVE SPACE IS FOR OFFICE USE ONLY

| | |
|---|---|
| **1.** *Name of Corporation:* | |
| **2.** *Resident Agent Name and Street Address:* (must be a Nevada address where process may be served) | Name <br> **(MANDATORY)** Physical Street Address — City — Nevada — Zip Code <br> **(OPTIONAL)** Mailing Address — City — State — Zip Code |
| **3.** *Shares:* (number of shares corporation is authorized to issue) | Number of shares with par value: ____  Par value per share: $ ____  Number of shares without par value: ____ |
| **4.** *Names & Addresses of the Board of Directors/Trustees:* (each Director/Trustee must be a **natural person** at least 18 years of age; attach additional page if more than 3 directors/trustees) | 1. ____ Name <br> Street Address — City — State — Zip Code <br> 2. ____ Name <br> Street Address — City — State — Zip Code <br> 3. ____ Name <br> Street Address — City — State — Zip Code |
| **5.** *Purpose:* (optional - see instructions) | The purpose of this Corporation shall be: |
| **6.** *Name, Address and Signature of Incorporator:* (attach additional page if more than 1 incorporator) | Name    **X** Signature <br> Address — City — State — Zip Code |
| **7.** *Certificate of Acceptance of Appointment of Resident Agent:* | I hereby accept appointment as Resident Agent for the above named corporation. <br> **X** _____ Authorized Signature of R. A. or On Behalf of R. A. Company    Date |

*This form must be accompanied by appropriate fees.*

Nevada Secretary of State Form: 78 Articles 2007
Revised on: 01/01/07

**ROSS MILLER**
Secretary of State
206 North Carson Street
Carson City, Nevada 89701-4299
(775) 684 5708
Website: secretaryofstate.biz

# Instructions for
# Articles of Incorporation
### (PURSUANT TO NRS 78)

## IMPORTANT:  READ ALL INSTRUCTIONS CAREFULLY BEFORE COMPLETING FORM.

1.  *Name of the Corporation:*  A name appearing to be that of a natural person and containing a given name or initials must not be used as a corporate name except with the addition of a corporate ending such as Incorporated, Inc., Limited, Ltd., Company, Co., Corporation, Corp. or other words that identifies it as not being a natural person. The name must be distinguishable from the names of corporations, limited-liability companies, limited partnerships, limited-liability limited partnerships, business trusts or limited-liability partnerships on file in the office of the Secretary of State.  A name may be reserved, if available, for 90 days by submitting a name reservation form with a $25.00 filing fee.  For details you may call (775) 684-5708, visit www.secretaryofstate.biz, or write to the Secretary of State, 206 North Carson Street, Carson City NV. 89701-4201.

2.  *Resident Agent:*  Persons wishing to incorporate in the State of Nevada must designate a person as a resident agent who resides or is located in this state.  Every resident agent must have a street address in this state for the service of process, and may have a separate mailing address such as a post office box, which may be different from the street address.

3.  State the number of shares the corporation shall have the authority to issue with par value and its par value in appropriate space provided.  State the number of shares without par value in the space provided for shares without par value.

4.  State the names and addresses of the first governing board.  Use a separate 8 ½ x 11 sheet as necessary for additional members.  Directors or trustees must be at least 18 year of age.

5.  If it appears from the name and/or purpose of the entity being formed that it is to be regulated by the Financial Institutions Division, Insurance Division, State Board of Professional Engineers and Land Surveyors, State Board of Accountancy or Real Estate Division, the application will need to be approved by the regulating agency before it is filed with the Office of the Secretary of State.

6.  Names and addresses of the incorporators are required.  Each incorporator must sign.  Additional 8 ½ x 11 white sheet will be necessary if more than 1 incorporator.

7.  Resident agent must complete and sign certificate of acceptance at bottom of form or attach a separate signed certificate of acceptance.

8.  On a separate 8 ½ x 11, white sheet you may state additional information you wish to be part of the articles.  This is an optional provision.

### ***IMPORTANT***

*INITIAL LIST OF OFFICERS:*  Pursuant to NRS 78.150, each corporation organized under the laws of this state shall, on or before the last day of the first month after the filing of its articles of incorporation, and annually thereafter, file its list of officers, directors and resident agent.  The initial list fee is $125.00.  Forms will be mailed to you upon the organization of your corporation and annually thereafter to the corporation's resident agent.

*COPIES:*  One file stamped copy of the articles will be returned at no additional charge.  To receive a certified copy, enclose an additional $30.00 per certification.  A copy fee of $2.00 per page is required for each additional copy generated when ordering 2 or more file stamped or certified copies.  Appropriate instructions must accompany your order.  NRS 78.105 requires that a corporation receive at least one certified copy to be kept in the office of the resident agent.  The Secretary of State keeps the original filing.

*FILING FEE:* Filing fee is based on the number of shares authorized.  Please see the attached fee schedule. Filing may be expedited for an additional $125.00 expedite fee.

Filing may be submitted at the office of the Secretary of State or by mail at the following addresses:

| | |
|---|---|
| Secretary of State | (This Office Accepts Expedited Filings Only) |
| New Filings Division | Secretary of State-Satellite Office |
| 206 N. Carson Street | Commercial Recordings Division |
| Carson City, NV  89701-4299 | 555 E. Washington Avenue, Suite 4000 |
| 775-684-5708  Fax 775-684-7138 | Las Vegas, NV  89101 |
| | 702-486-2880  Fax 702-486-2888 |

# BYLAWS OF

## A NEVADA CORPORATION

### ARTICLE I—OFFICES

The principal office of the Corporation shall be located in the City of _____
and the State of Nevada. The Corporation may also maintain offices at such other places as the Board of
Directors may, from time to time, determine.

### ARTICLE II—SHAREHOLDERS

Section 1—Annual Meetings: The annual meeting of the shareholders of the Corporation shall be held each
year on _____ at _____m. at the principal office of the Corporation or at such other
places as the Board may authorize, for the purpose of electing directors and transacting such other business as may properly come before the meeting.

Section 2—Special Meetings:  Special meetings of the shareholders may be called at any time by the
Board, the President, or by the holders of 25% of the shares then outstanding and entitled to vote.

Section 3—Place of Meetings: All meetings of shareholders shall be held at the principal office of the
Corporation, or at such other places as the board shall designate in the notice of such meetings.

Section 4—Notice of Meetings: Written or printed notice stating the place, day, and hour of the meeting
and, in the case of a special meeting, the purpose of the meeting, shall be delivered personally or by mail
not less than ten days, nor more than sixty days, before the date of the meeting. Notice shall be given to
each Member of record entitled to vote at the meeting. If mailed, such notice shall be deemed to have been
delivered when deposited in the United States Mail with postage paid and addressed to the Member at
his or her address as it appears on the records of the Corporation.

Section 5—Waiver of Notice:  A written waiver of notice signed by a Member, whether before or after a
meeting, shall be equivalent to the giving of such notice. Attendance of a Member at a meeting shall
constitute a waiver of notice of such meeting, except when the Member attends for the express purpose of
objecting, at the beginning of the meeting, to the transaction of any business because the meeting is not
lawfully called or convened.

Section 6—Quorum: Except as otherwise provided by Statute, or the Articles of Incorporation, at all meetings of shareholders of the Corporation, the presence at the commencement of such meetings in person or
by proxy of shareholders of record holding a majority of the total number of shares of the Corporation then
issued and outstanding and entitled to vote, but in no event less than one-third of the shares entitled to
vote at the meeting, shall constitute a quorum for the transaction of any business. If any shareholder
leaves after the commencement of a meeting, this shall have no effect on the existence of a quorum, after
a quorum has been established at such meeting.

Despite the absence of a quorum at any annual or special meeting of shareholders, the shareholders, by a majority of the votes cast by the holders of shares entitled to vote thereon, may adjourn the
meeting. At any such adjourned meeting at which a quorum is present, any business may be transacted
at the meeting as originally called as if a quorum had been present.

Section 7—Voting: Except as otherwise provided by Statute or by the Articles of Incorporation, any corporate action, other than the election of directors, to be taken by vote of the shareholders, shall be authorized
by a majority of votes cast at a meeting of shareholders by the holders of shares entitled to vote thereon.

Except as otherwise provided by Statute or by the Articles of Incorporation, at each meeting of shareholders, each holder of record of stock of the Corporation entitled to vote thereat, shall be entitled to one vote for each share of stock registered in his or her name on the stock transfer books of the Corporation.

Each shareholder entitled to vote may do so by proxy; provided, however, that the instrument authorizing such proxy to act shall have been executed in writing by the shareholder him- or herself. No proxy shall be valid after the expiration of eleven months from the date of its execution, unless the person executing it shall have specified therein the length of time it is to continue in force. Such instrument shall be exhibited to the Secretary at the meeting and shall be filed with the records of the corporation.

Any resolution in writing, signed by all the shareholders entitled to vote thereon, shall be and constitute action by such shareholders to the effect therein expressed, with the same force and effect as if the same had been duly passed by unanimous vote at a duly called meeting of shareholders and such resolution so signed shall be inserted in the Minute Book of the Corporation under its proper date.

## ARTICLE III—BOARD OF DIRECTORS

Section 1—Number, Election, and Term of Office: The number of the directors of the Corporation shall be ____. This number may be increased or decreased by the amendment of these bylaws by the Board but shall in no case be less than ____ director(s). The Members of the Board, who need not be shareholders, shall be elected by a majority of the votes cast at a meeting of shareholders entitled to vote in the election. Each director shall hold office until the annual meeting of the shareholders next succeeding his or her election, and until his or her successor is elected and qualified, or until his or her prior death, resignation, or removal.

Section 2—Vacancies: Any vacancy in the Board shall be filled for the unexpired portion of the term by a majority vote of the remaining directors, though less than a quorum, at any regular meeting or special meeting of the Board called for that purpose. Any such director so elected may be replaced by the shareholders at a regular or special meeting of shareholders.

Section 3—Duties and Powers: The Board shall be responsible for the control and management of the affairs, property, and interests of the Corporation, and may exercise all powers of the Corporation, except as limited by statute.

Section 4—Annual Meetings: An annual meeting of the Board shall be held immediately following the annual meeting of the shareholders, at the place of such annual meeting of shareholders. The Board, from time to time, may provide by resolution for the holding of other meetings of the Board, and may fix the time and place thereof.

Section 5—Special Meetings: Special meetings of the Board shall be held whenever called by the President or by one of the directors, at such time and place as may be specified in the respective notice or waivers of notice thereof.

Section 6—Notice and Waiver: Notice of any special meeting shall be given at least five days prior thereto by written notice delivered personally, by mail, or by telegram to each Director at his or her address. If mailed, such notice shall be deemed to be delivered when deposited in the United States Mail with postage prepaid. If notice is given by telegram, such notice shall be deemed to be delivered when the telegram is delivered to the telegraph company.

Any Director may waive notice of any meeting, either before, at, or after such meeting, by signing a waiver of notice. The attendance of a Director at a meeting shall constitute a waiver of notice of such meeting and a waiver of any and all objections to the place of such meeting, or the manner in which it has been called or convened, except when a Director states at the beginning of the meeting any objection to the transaction of business because the meeting is not lawfully called or convened.

Section 7—Chairman: The Board may, at its discretion, elect a Chairman. At all meetings of the Board, the Chairman of the Board, if any and if present, shall preside. If there is no Chairman, or he or she is absent, then the President shall preside, and in his or her absence, a Chairman chosen by the directors shall preside.

Section 8—Quorum and Adjournments: At all meetings of the Board, the presence of a majority of the entire Board shall be necessary and sufficient to constitute a quorum for the transaction of business, except as otherwise provided by law, by the Articles of Incorporation, or by these bylaws. A majority of the directors present at the time and place of any regular or special meeting, although less than a quorum, may adjourn the same from time to time without notice, until a quorum shall be present.

Section 9—Board Action: At all meetings of the Board, each director present shall have one vote, irrespective of the number of shares of stock, if any, that he or she may hold. Except as otherwise provided by Statute, the action of a majority of the directors present at any meeting at which a quorum is present shall be the act of the Board. Any action authorized, in writing, by all the Directors entitled to vote thereon and filed with the minutes of the Corporation shall be the act of the Board with the same force and effect as if the same had been passed by unanimous vote at a duly called meeting of the Board. Any action taken by the Board may be taken without a meeting if agreed to in writing by all members before or after the action is taken and if a record of such action is filed in the minute book.

Section 10—Telephone Meetings: Directors may participate in meetings of the Board through use of a telephone if such can be arranged so that all Board members can hear all other members. The use of a telephone for participation shall constitute presence in person.

Section 11—Resignation and Removal: Any director may resign at any time by giving written notice to another Board member, the President, or the Secretary of the Corporation. Unless otherwise specified in such written notice, such resignation shall take effect upon receipt thereof by the Board or by such officer, and the acceptance of such resignation shall not be necessary to make it effective. Any director may be removed with or without cause at any time by the affirmative vote of shareholders holding of record in the aggregate at least a majority of the outstanding shares of the Corporation at a special meeting of the shareholders called for that purpose, and may be removed for cause by action of the Board.

Section 12—Compensation: No stated salary shall be paid to directors, as such for their services, but by resolution of the Board a fixed sum and/or expenses of attendance, if any, may be allowed for attendance at each regular or special meeting of the Board. Nothing herein contained shall be construed to preclude any director from serving the Corporation in any other capacity and receiving compensation therefor.

## ARTICLE IV—OFFICERS

Section 1—Number, Qualification, Election, and Term: The officers of the Corporation shall consist of a President, a Secretary, a Treasurer, and such other officers as the Board may from time to time deem advisable. Any officer may be, but is not required to be, a director of the Corporation. The officers of the Corporation shall be elected by the Board at the regular annual meeting of the Board. Each officer shall hold office until the annual meeting of the Board next succeeding his or her election, and until his or her successor shall have been elected and qualified, or until his or her death, resignation, or removal.

Section 2—Resignation and Removal: Any officer may resign at any time by giving written notice of such resignation to the President or the Secretary of the Corporation or to a Member of the Board. Unless otherwise specified in such written notice, such resignation shall take effect upon receipt thereof by the Board member or by such officer, and the acceptance of such resignation shall not be necessary to make it effective. Any officer may be removed, either with or without cause, and a successor elected by a majority vote of the Board at any time.

Section 3—Vacancies: A vacancy in any office may at any time be filled for the unexpired portion of the term by a majority vote of the Board.

Section 4—Duties of Officers: Officers of the Corporation shall, unless otherwise provided by the Board, each have such powers and duties as generally pertain to their respective offices, as well as such powers and duties as may from time to time be specifically decided by the Board. The President shall be the chief executive officer of the Corporation.

Section 5—Compensation: The officers of the Corporation shall be entitled to such compensation as the Board shall from time to time determine.

Section 6—Delegation of Duties: In the absence or disability of any Officer of the Corporation or for any other reason deemed sufficient by the Board of Directors, the Board may delegate his or her powers or duties to any other Officer or to any other Director.

Section 7—Shares of Other Corporations: Whenever the Corporation is the holder of shares of any other Corporation, any right or power of the Corporation as such shareholder (including the attendance, acting, and voting at shareholders' meetings and execution of waivers, consents, proxies, or other instruments) may be exercised on behalf of the Corporation by the President, any Vice President, or such other person as the Board may authorize.

## ARTICLE V—COMMITTEES

The Board of Directors may, by resolution, designate an Executive Committee and one or more other committees. Such committees shall have such functions and may exercise such power of the Board of Directors as can be lawfully delegated, and to the extent provided in the resolution or resolutions creating such committee or committees. Meetings of committees may be held without notice at such time and at such place as shall from time to time be determined by the committees. The committees of the corporation shall keep regular minutes of their proceedings, and report these minutes to the Board of Directors when required.

## ARTICLE VI—BOOKS, RECORDS, AND REPORTS

Section 1—Annual Report:   The Corporation shall send an annual report to the Members of the Corporation not later than _____ months after the close of each fiscal year of the Corporation. Such report shall include a balance sheet as of the close of the fiscal year of the Corporation and a revenue and disbursement statement for the year ending on such closing date. Such financial statements shall be prepared from and in accordance with the books of the Corporation, and in conformity with generally accepted accounting principles applied on a consistent basis.

Section 2—Permanent Records: The corporation shall keep current and correct records of the accounts, minutes of the meetings, and proceedings and membership records of the corporation. Such records shall be kept at the registered office or the principal place of business of the corporation. Any such records shall be in written form or in a form capable of being converted into written form.

Section 3—Inspection of Corporate Records: Any person who is a Voting Member of the Corporation shall have the right at any reasonable time, and on written demand stating the purpose thereof, to examine and make copies from the relevant books and records of accounts, minutes, and records of the Corporation. Upon the written request of any Voting Member, the Corporation shall mail to such Member a copy of the most recent balance sheet and revenue and disbursement statement.

## ARTICLE VII—SHARES OF STOCK

Section 1—Certificates: Each shareholder of the Corporation shall be entitled to have a certificate representing all shares that he or she owns. The form of such certificate shall be adopted by a majority vote of the Board of Directors and shall be signed by the President and Secretary of the Corporation and sealed with the seal of the corporation. No certificate representing shares shall be issued until the full amount of consideration therefore has been paid.

Section 2—Stock Ledger: The Corporation shall maintain a ledger of the stock records of the Corporation. Transfers of shares of the Corporation shall be made on the stock ledger of the Corporation only at the direction of the holder of record upon surrender of the outstanding certificate(s). The Corporation shall be entitled to treat the holder of record of any share or shares as the absolute owner thereof for all purposes and, accordingly, shall not be bound to recognize any legal, equitable, or other claim to, or interest in, such share or shares on the part of any other person, whether or not it shall have express or other notice thereof, except as otherwise expressly provided by law.

## ARTICLE VIII—DIVIDENDS

Upon approval by the Board of Directors, the corporation may pay dividends on its shares in the form of cash, property, or additional shares at any time that the corporation is solvent and if such dividends would not render the corporation insolvent.

## ARTICLE IX—FISCAL YEAR

The fiscal year of the Corporation shall be the period selected by the Board of Directors as the tax year of the Corporation for federal income tax purposes.

## ARTICLE X—CORPORATE SEAL

The Board of Directors may adopt, use, and modify a corporate seal. Failure to affix the seal to corporate documents shall not affect the validity of such document.

## ARTICLE XI—AMENDMENTS

The Articles of Incorporation may be amended by the shareholders as provided by Nevada statutes. These Bylaws may be altered, amended, or replaced by the Board of Directors, provided, however, that any Bylaws or amendments thereto as adopted by the Board of Directors may be altered, amended, or repealed by vote of the shareholders. Bylaws adopted by the Members may not be amended or repealed by the Board.

## ARTICLE XII—INDEMNIFICATION

Any officer, director, or employee of the Corporation shall be indemnified to the full extent allowed by the laws of the State of Nevada.

Certified to be the Bylaws of the corporation adopted by the Board of Directors on _____, _____.

_____
Secretary

*This page intentionally blank.*

# BYLAWS OF

## A NEVADA PROFESSIONAL ASSOCIATION

### ARTICLE I—OFFICES

The principal office of the Corporation shall be located in the City of _____
and the State of Nevada. The Corporation may also maintain offices at such other places as the Board of
Directors may, from time to time, determine.

### ARTICLE II—PURPOSES

The business purpose of the Corporation shall be to engage in all aspects of the practice of _____
_____ and its fields of specialization. The Corporation shall render professional
services only through its legally authorized officers, agents, and employees.

### ARTICLE III—SHAREHOLDERS

Section 1—Qualifications: Only persons who are duly licensed and in good standing in the profession by
the State of Nevada may be shareholders of the Corporation. Neither the Corporation nor the shareholders may transfer any shares to persons who are not duly licensed. All share certificates of the
corporation shall contain a notice that the transfer is restricted by the bylaws of the Corporation. If any
shareholder shall become disqualified to practice the profession, he or she shall immediately make
arrangements to transfer his or her shares to a qualified person or to the Corporation and shall no longer
participate in the profits of the Corporation related to the profession.

Section 2—Annual Meetings: The annual meeting of the shareholders of the Corporation shall be held
each year on _____ at _____m. at the principal office of the Corporation or at
such other places as the Board may authorize, for the purpose of electing directors and transacting such
other business as may properly come before the meeting.

Section 3—Special Meetings: Special meetings of the shareholders may be called at any time by the Board,
the President, or by the holders of 25% of the shares then outstanding and entitled to vote.

Section 4—Place of Meetings: All meetings of shareholders shall be held at the principal office of the
Corporation, or at such other places as the Board shall designate in the notice of such meetings.

Section 5—Notice of Meetings: Written or printed notice stating the place, day, and hour of the meeting
and, in the case of a special meeting, the purpose of the meeting, shall be delivered personally or by mail
not less than ten days, nor more than sixty days, before the date of the meeting. Notice shall be given to
each Member of record entitled to vote at the meeting. If mailed, such notice shall be deemed to have been
delivered when deposited in the United States Mail with postage paid and addressed to the Member at
his or her address as it appears on the records of the Corporation.

Section 6—Waiver of Notice: A written waiver of notice signed by a Member, whether before or after a
meeting, shall be equivalent to the giving of such notice. Attendance of a Member at a meeting shall
constitute a waiver of notice of such meeting, except when the Member attends for the express purpose of
objecting, at the beginning of the meeting, to the transaction of any business because the meeting is not
lawfully called or convened.

Section 7—Quorum: Except as otherwise provided by Statute, or by the Articles of Incorporation, at all
meetings of shareholders of the Corporation, the presence at the commencement of such meetings of
shareholders of record holding a majority of the total number of shares of the Corporation then issued and

outstanding and entitled to vote, but in no event less than one-third of the shares entitled to vote at the meeting, shall constitute a quorum for the transaction of any business. If any shareholder leaves after the commencement of a meeting, this shall have no effect on the existence of a quorum, after a quorum has been established at such meeting.

Despite the absence of a quorum at any annual or special meeting of shareholders, the shareholders, by a majority of the votes cast by the holders of shares entitled to vote thereon, may adjourn the meeting. At any such adjourned meeting at which a quorum is present, any business may be transacted at the meeting as originally called as if a quorum had been present.

Section 8—Voting: Except as otherwise provided by Statute or by the Articles of Incorporation, any corporate action, other than the election of directors, to be taken by vote of the shareholders, shall be authorized by a majority of votes cast at a meeting of shareholders by the holders of shares entitled to vote thereon.

Except as otherwise provided by Statute or by the Articles of Incorporation, at each meeting of shareholders, each holder of record of stock of the Corporation entitled to vote thereat shall be entitled to one vote for each share of stock registered in his or her name on the stock transfer books of the corporation.

Any resolution in writing, signed by all the shareholders entitled to vote thereon, shall be and constitute action by such shareholders to the effect therein expressed, with the same force and effect as if the same had been duly passed by unanimous vote at a duly called meeting of shareholders and such resolution so signed shall be inserted in the Minute Book of the Corporation under its proper date.

Section 9—Proxies: Shareholders may not at any time vote by proxy or enter into any voting trust or other agreement vesting another person with the voting power of his or her stock.

## ARTICLE IV—BOARD OF DIRECTORS

Section 1—Qualifications: Only persons who are duly licensed and in good standing in the profession by the State of Nevada may be directors of the Corporation. If any director shall become disqualified from practicing the profession, he or she shall immediately resign his or her directorship and any other employment with the Corporation.

Section 2—Number, Election, and Term of Office: The number of the directors of the Corporation shall be ____. This number may be increased or decreased by the amendment of these bylaws by the Board but shall in no case be less than one director. The members of the Board, who need not be shareholders, shall be elected by a majority of the votes cast at a meeting of shareholders entitled to vote in the election. Each director shall hold office until the annual meeting of the shareholders next succeeding his or her election, and until his or her successor is elected and qualified, or until his or her prior death, resignation, or removal.

Section 3—Vacancies: Any vacancy in the Board shall be filled for the unexpired portion of the term by a majority vote of the remaining directors, though less than a quorum, at any regular meeting or special meeting of the Board called for that purpose. Any such director so elected may be replaced by the shareholders at a regular or special meeting of shareholders.

Section 4—Duties and Powers: The Board shall be responsible for the control and management of the affairs, property, and interests of the Corporation, and may exercise all powers of the Corporation, except as limited by statute.

Section 5—Annual Meetings: An annual meeting of the Board shall be held immediately following the annual meeting of the shareholders, at the place of such annual meeting of shareholders. The Board, from time to time, may provide by resolution for the holding of other meetings of the Board, and may fix the time and place thereof.

Section 6—Special Meetings: Special meetings of the Board shall be held whenever called by the President or by one of the directors, at such time and place as may be specified in the respective notice or waivers of notice thereof.

Section 7—Notice and Waiver: Notice of any special meeting shall be given at least five days prior thereto by written notice delivered personally, by mail or by telegram to each director at his or her address. If mailed, such notice shall be deemed to be delivered when deposited in the United States Mail with postage prepaid. If notice is given by telegram, such notice shall be deemed to be delivered when the telegram is delivered to the telegraph company.

Any director may waive notice of any meeting, either before, at, or after such meeting, by signing a waiver of notice. The attendance of a director at a meeting shall constitute a waiver of notice of such meeting and a waiver of any and all objections to the place of such meeting, or the manner in which it has been called or convened, except when a director states at the beginning of the meeting any objection to the transaction of business because the meeting is not lawfully called or convened.

Section 8—Chairman: The Board may, at its discretion, elect a Chairman. At all meetings of the Board, the Chairman of the Board, if any and if present, shall preside. If there is no Chairman, or he or she is absent, then the President shall preside, and in his or her absence, a Chairman chosen by the directors shall preside.

Section 9—Quorum and Adjournments: At all meetings of the Board, the presence of a majority of the entire Board shall be necessary and sufficient to constitute a quorum for the transaction of business, except as otherwise provided by law, by the Articles of Incorporation, or by these bylaws. A majority of the directors present at the time and place of any regular or special meeting, although less than a quorum, may adjourn the same from time to time without notice, until a quorum shall be present.

Section 10—Board Action: At all meetings of the Board, each director present shall have one vote, irrespective of the number of shares of stock, if any, that he or she may hold. Except as otherwise provided by Statute, the action of a majority of the directors present at any meeting at which a quorum is present shall be the act of the Board. Any action authorized, in writing, by all the Directors entitled to vote thereon and filed with the minutes of the Corporation shall be the act of the Board with the same force and effect as if the same had been passed by unanimous vote at a duly called meeting of the Board. Any action taken by the Board may be taken without a meeting if agreed to in writing by all members before or after the action is taken and if a record of such action is filed in the Minute Book.

Section 11—Telephone Meetings: Directors may participate in meetings of the Board through use of a telephone if such can be arranged so that all Board members can hear all other members. The use of a telephone for participation shall constitute presence in person.

Section 12—Resignation and Removal: Any director may resign at any time by giving written notice to another Board member, the President, or the Secretary of the Corporation. Unless otherwise specified in such written notice, such resignation shall take effect upon receipt thereof by the Board or by such officer, and the acceptance of such resignation shall not be necessary to make it effective. Any director may be removed with or without cause at any time by the affirmative vote of shareholders holding of record in the aggregate at least a majority of the outstanding shares of the Corporation at a special meeting of the shareholders called for that purpose, and may be removed for cause by action of the Board.

Section 13—Compensation: No stated salary shall be paid to directors, as such for their services, but by resolution of the Board a fixed sum and/or expenses of attendance, if any, may be allowed for attendance at each regular or special meeting of the Board. Nothing herein contained shall be construed to preclude any director from serving the Corporation in any other capacity and receiving compensation therefor.

## ARTICLE V—OFFICERS

Section 1—Qualifications: Only persons who are duly licensed and in good standing in the profession by the State of Nevada may be officers of the Corporation. If any director shall become disqualified from practicing the profession, he or she shall immediately resign his or her directorship and any other employment with the corporation.

Section 2—Number, Election, and Term: The officers of the Corporation shall consist of a President, a Secretary, a Treasurer, and such other officers as the Board may from time to time deem advisable. Any officer may be, but is not required to be, a director of the Corporation. Any two or more offices may be held by the same person. The officers of the Corporation shall be elected by the Board at the regular annual meeting of the Board. Each officer shall hold office until the annual meeting of the Board next succeeding his or her election, and until his or her successor shall have been elected and qualified, or until his or her death, resignation, or removal.

Section 3—Resignation and Removal: Any officer may resign at any time by giving written notice of such resignation to the President or the Secretary of the Corporation or to a member of the Board. Unless otherwise specified in such written notice, such resignation shall take effect upon receipt thereof by the Board member or by such officer, and the acceptance of such resignation shall not be necessary to make it effective. Any officer may be removed, either with or without cause, and a successor elected by a majority vote of the Board at any time.

Section 4—Vacancies: A vacancy in any office may at any time be filled for the unexpired portion of the term by a majority vote of the Board.

Section 5—Duties of Officers: The officers of the Corporation shall, unless otherwise provided by the Board, each have such powers and duties as generally pertain to their respective offices as well as such powers and duties as may from time to time be specifically decided by the Board. The President shall be the chief executive officer of the Corporation.

Section 6—Compensation: The officers of the Corporation shall be entitled to such compensation as the Board shall from time to time determine.

Section 7—Delegation of Duties: In the absence or disability of any Officer of the Corporation or for any other reason deemed sufficient by the Board of Directors, the Board may delegate his or her powers or duties to any other Officer or to any other director.

Section 8—Shares of Other Corporations: Whenever the Corporation is the holder of shares of any other Corporation, any right or power of the Corporation as such shareholder (including the attendance, acting, and voting at shareholders' meetings and execution of waivers, consents, proxies, or other instruments) may be exercised on behalf of the Corporation by the President, any Vice President, or such other person as the Board may authorize.

## ARTICLE VI—COMMITTEES

The Board of Directors may, by resolution, designate an Executive Committee and one or more other committees. Such committees shall have such functions and may exercise such power of the Board of Directors as can be lawfully delegated, and to the extent provided in the resolution or resolutions creating such committee or committees. Meetings of committees may be held without notice at such time and at such place as shall from time to time be determined by the committees. The committees of the corporation shall keep regular minutes of their proceedings, and report these minutes to the Board of Directors when required.

## ARTICLE VII—BOOKS, RECORDS, AND REPORTS

Section 1—Annual Report: The Corporation shall send an annual report to the Members of the Corporation not later than four months after the close of each fiscal year of the Corporation. Such report shall include a balance sheet as of the close of the fiscal year of the Corporation and a revenue and disbursement statement for the year ending on such closing date. Such financial statements shall be prepared from and in accordance with the books of the Corporation, and in conformity with generally accepted accounting principles applied on a consistent basis.

Section 2—Permanent Records: The Corporation shall keep current and correct records of the accounts, minutes of the meetings, and proceedings and membership records of the Corporation. Such records shall be kept at the registered office or the principal place of business of the Corporation. Any such records shall be in written form or in a form capable of being converted into written form.

Section 3—Inspection of Corporate Records: Any person who is a Voting Member of the Corporation shall have the right at any reasonable time, and on written demand stating the purpose thereof, to examine and make copies from the relevant books and records of accounts, minutes, and records of the Corporation. Upon the written request of any Voting Member, the Corporation shall mail to such Member a copy of the most recent balance sheet and revenue and disbursement statement.

## ARTICLE VIII—SHARES OF STOCK

Section 1—Authorized Shares: The Corporation shall be authorized to issue _____ shares of stock in one class only, each with a par value of $_____.

Section 2—Certificates: Each shareholder of the Corporation shall be entitled to have a certificate representing all shares that he or she owns. The form of such certificate shall be adopted by a majority vote of the Board of Directors and shall be signed by the President and Secretary of the Corporation and sealed with the seal of the Corporation. No certificate representing shares shall be issued until the full amount of consideration therefore has been paid.

Section 3—Stock Ledger: The Corporation shall maintain a ledger of the stock records of the Corporation. Transfers of shares of the Corporation shall be made on the stock ledger of the Corporation only at the direction of the holder of record upon surrender of the outstanding certificate(s). The Corporation shall be entitled to treat the holder of record of any share or shares as the absolute owner thereof for all purposes and, accordingly, shall not be bound to recognize any legal, equitable, or other claim to, or interest in, such share or shares on the part of any other person, whether or not it shall have express or other notice thereof, except as otherwise expressly provided by law.

## ARTICLE IX—DIVIDENDS

Upon approval by the Board of Directors, the corporation may pay dividends on its shares in the form of cash, property, or additional shares at any time that the Corporation is solvent and if such dividends would not render the Corporation insolvent.

## ARTICLE X—FISCAL YEAR

The fiscal year of the Corporation shall be the period selected by the Board of Directors as the tax year of the Corporation for federal income tax purposes.

## ARTICLE XI—CORPORATE SEAL

The Board of Directors may adopt, use, and modify a corporate seal. Failure to affix the seal to corporate documents shall not affect the validity of such document.

## ARTICLE XII—AMENDMENTS

The Articles of Incorporation may be amended by the shareholders as provided by Nevada statutes. These bylaws may be altered, amended, or replaced by the Board of Directors, provided, however, that any bylaws or amendments thereto as adopted by the Board of Directors may be altered, amended, or repealed by vote of the shareholders. Bylaws adopted by the Members may not be amended or repealed by the Board.

## ARTICLE XIII—INDEMNIFICATION

Any officer, director, or employee of the Corporation shall be indemnified to the full extent allowed by the laws of the State of Nevada.

Certified to be the bylaws of the corporation adopted by the Board of Directors on _____, _____.

_____
Secretary

Form **2553**
(Rev. December 2007)
Department of the Treasury
Internal Revenue Service

## Election by a Small Business Corporation
(Under section 1362 of the Internal Revenue Code)
► **See Parts II and III on page 3 and the separate instructions.**
► **The corporation can fax this form to the IRS (see separate instructions).**

OMB No. 1545-0146

**Note.** This election to be an S corporation can be accepted only if all the tests are met under **Who May Elect** on page 1 of the instructions; all shareholders have signed the consent statement; an officer has signed below; and the exact name and address of the corporation and other required form information are provided.

| **Part I** | **Election Information** | | |

**Type or Print**

| Name (see instructions) | **A** Employer identification number |
|---|---|
| Number, street, and room or suite no. (If a P.O. box, see instructions.) | **B** Date incorporated |
| City or town, state, and ZIP code | **C** State of incorporation |

**D** Check the applicable box(es) if the corporation, after applying for the EIN shown in **A** above, changed its ☐ name or ☐ address

**E** Election is to be effective for tax year beginning (month, day, year) (see instructions) . . . . . ► ___/___/___

**Caution.** A corporation (entity) making the election for its first tax year in existence will usually enter the beginning date of a short tax year that begins on a date other than January 1.

**F** Selected tax year:

(1) ☐ Calendar year

(2) ☐ Fiscal year ending (month and day) ► _____

(3) ☐ 52-53-week year ending with reference to the month of December

(4) ☐ 52-53-week year ending with reference to the month of ► _____

If box (2) or (4) is checked, complete Part II

**G** If more than 100 shareholders are listed for item J (see page 2), check this box if treating members of a family as one shareholder results in no more than 100 shareholders (see test 2 under **Who May Elect** in the instructions) ► ☐

| **H** Name and title of officer or legal representative who the IRS may call for more information | **I** Telephone number of officer or legal representative ( ) |

If this S corporation election is being filed with Form 1120S, I declare that I had reasonable cause for not filing Form 2553 timely, and if this election is made by an entity eligible to elect to be treated as a corporation, I declare that I also had reasonable cause for not filing an entity classification election timely. See below for my explanation of the reasons the election or elections were not made on time (see instructions).

------------------------------------------------------------

------------------------------------------------------------

------------------------------------------------------------

------------------------------------------------------------

------------------------------------------------------------

------------------------------------------------------------

------------------------------------------------------------

------------------------------------------------------------

**Sign Here** ►

Under penalties of perjury, I declare that I have examined this election, including accompanying schedules and statements, and to the best of my knowledge and belief, it is true, correct, and complete.

| Signature of officer | Title | Date |
|---|---|---|

**For Paperwork Reduction Act Notice, see separate instructions.**      Cat. No. 18629R      Form **2553** (Rev. 12-2007)

Form 2553 (Rev. 12-2007)                                                                                          Page **2**

## Part I | Election Information (continued)

| J<br>Name and address of each shareholder or former shareholder required to consent to the election. (See the instructions for column K.) | K<br>Shareholders' Consent Statement.<br>Under penalties of perjury, we declare that we consent to the election of the above-named corporation to be an S corporation under section 1362(a) and that we have examined this consent statement, including accompanying schedules and statements, and to the best of our knowledge and belief, it is true, correct, and complete. We understand our consent is binding and may not be withdrawn after the corporation has made a valid election. (Sign and date below.) | | L<br>Stock owned or percentage of ownership<br>(see instructions) | | M<br>Social security number or employer identification number<br>(see instructions) | N<br>Shareholder's tax year ends (month and day) |
|---|---|---|---|---|---|---|
| | Signature | Date | Number of shares or percentage of ownership | Date(s) acquired | | |
| | | | | | | |
| | | | | | | |
| | | | | | | |
| | | | | | | |
| | | | | | | |
| | | | | | | |
| | | | | | | |
| | | | | | | |

Form **2553** (Rev. 12-2007)

## Part II  Selection of Fiscal Tax Year (see instructions)

**Note.** All corporations using this part must complete item O and item P, Q, or R.

**O**  Check the applicable box to indicate whether the corporation is:

**1.** ☐ A new corporation **adopting** the tax year entered in item F, Part I.

**2.** ☐ An existing corporation **retaining** the tax year entered in item F, Part I.

**3.** ☐ An existing corporation **changing** to the tax year entered in item F, Part I.

**P**  Complete item P if the corporation is using the automatic approval provisions of Rev. Proc. 2006-46, 2006-45 I.R.B. 859, to request **(1)** a natural business year (as defined in section 5.07 of Rev. Proc. 2006-46) or **(2)** a year that satisfies the ownership tax year test (as defined in section 5.08 of Rev. Proc. 2006-46). Check the applicable box below to indicate the representation statement the corporation is making.

**1. Natural Business Year ▶** ☐ I represent that the corporation is adopting, retaining, or changing to a tax year that qualifies as its natural business year (as defined in section 5.07 of Rev. Proc. 2006-46) and has attached a statement showing separately for each month the gross receipts for the most recent 47 months (see instructions). I also represent that the corporation is not precluded by section 4.02 of Rev. Proc. 2006-46 from obtaining automatic approval of such adoption, retention, or change in tax year.

**2. Ownership Tax Year ▶** ☐ I represent that shareholders (as described in section 5.08 of Rev. Proc. 2006-46) holding more than half of the shares of the stock (as of the first day of the tax year to which the request relates) of the corporation have the same tax year or are concurrently changing to the tax year that the corporation adopts, retains, or changes to per item F, Part I, and that such tax year satisfies the requirement of section 4.01(3) of Rev. Proc. 2006-46. I also represent that the corporation is not precluded by section 4.02 of Rev. Proc. 2006-46 from obtaining automatic approval of such adoption, retention, or change in tax year.

**Note.** If you do not use item P and the corporation wants a fiscal tax year, complete either item Q or R below. Item Q is used to request a fiscal tax year based on a business purpose and to make a back-up section 444 election. Item R is used to make a regular section 444 election.

**Q**  Business Purpose—To request a fiscal tax year based on a business purpose, check box Q1. See instructions for details including payment of a user fee. You may also check box Q2 and/or box Q3.

**1. Check here ▶** ☐ if the fiscal year entered in item F, Part I, is requested under the prior approval provisions of Rev. Proc. 2002-39, 2002-22 I.R.B. 1046. Attach to Form 2553 a statement describing the relevant facts and circumstances and, if applicable, the gross receipts from sales and services necessary to establish a business purpose. See the instructions for details regarding the gross receipts from sales and services. If the IRS proposes to disapprove the requested fiscal year, do you want a conference with the IRS National Office?

☐ Yes    ☐ No

**2. Check here ▶** ☐ to show that the corporation intends to make a back-up section 444 election in the event the corporation's business purpose request is not approved by the IRS. (See instructions for more information.)

**3. Check here ▶** ☐ to show that the corporation agrees to adopt or change to a tax year ending December 31 if necessary for the IRS to accept this election for S corporation status in the event (1) the corporation's business purpose request is not approved and the corporation makes a back-up section 444 election, but is ultimately not qualified to make a section 444 election, or (2) the corporation's business purpose request is not approved and the corporation did not make a back-up section 444 election.

**R**  Section 444 Election—To make a section 444 election, check box R1. You may also check box R2.

**1. Check here ▶** ☐ to show that the corporation will make, if qualified, a section 444 election to have the fiscal tax year shown in item F, Part I. To make the election, you must complete **Form 8716**, Election To Have a Tax Year Other Than a Required Tax Year, and either attach it to Form 2553 or file it separately.

**2. Check here ▶** ☐ to show that the corporation agrees to adopt or change to a tax year ending December 31 if necessary for the IRS to accept this election for S corporation status in the event the corporation is ultimately not qualified to make a section 444 election.

## Part III  Qualified Subchapter S Trust (QSST) Election Under Section 1361(d)(2)*

| Income beneficiary's name and address | Social security number |
|---|---|
|  |  |
| Trust's name and address | Employer identification number |
|  |  |

Date on which stock of the corporation was transferred to the trust (month, day, year) . . . . . . . . . . ▶ ___ / ___ / ___

In order for the trust named above to be a QSST and thus a qualifying shareholder of the S corporation for which this Form 2553 is filed, I hereby make the election under section 1361(d)(2). Under penalties of perjury, I certify that the trust meets the definitional requirements of section 1361(d)(3) and that all other information provided in Part III is true, correct, and complete.

_____    _____
Signature of income beneficiary or signature and title of legal representative or other qualified person making the election        Date

*Use Part III to make the QSST election only if stock of the corporation has been transferred to the trust on or before the date on which the corporation makes its election to be an S corporation. The QSST election must be made and filed separately if stock of the corporation is transferred to the trust **after** the date on which the corporation makes the S election.

# Instructions for Form 2553
## (Rev. December 2007)

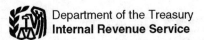
Department of the Treasury
Internal Revenue Service

**Election by a Small Business Corporation**

Section references are to the Internal Revenue Code unless otherwise noted.

## What's New

For tax years ending on or after December 31, 2007, certain corporations (entities) with reasonable cause for not timely filing Form 2553 can request to have the form treated as timely filed by filing Form 2553 as an attachment to Form 1120S, U.S. Income Tax Return for an S Corporation. An entry space for an explanation of reasonable cause was added to page 1 of the form. See *Relief for Late Elections.*

## General Instructions

### Purpose of Form

A corporation or other entity eligible to elect to be treated as a corporation must use Form 2553 to make an election under section 1362(a) to be an S corporation. An entity eligible to elect to be treated as a corporation that meets certain tests discussed below will be treated as a corporation as of the effective date of the S corporation election and does not need to file Form 8832, Entity Classification Election.

The income of an S corporation generally is taxed to the shareholders of the corporation rather than to the corporation itself. However, an S corporation may still owe tax on certain income. For details, see *Tax and Payments* in the Instructions for Form 1120S.

### Who May Elect

A corporation or other entity eligible to elect to be treated as a corporation may elect to be an S corporation only if it meets all the following tests.

1. It is (a) a domestic corporation, or (b) a domestic entity eligible to elect to be treated as a corporation, that timely files Form 2553 and meets all the other tests listed below. If Form 2553 is not timely filed, see *Relief for Late Elections* on page 2.

2. It has no more than 100 shareholders. You can treat a husband and wife (and their estates) as one shareholder for this test. You can also treat all members of a family (as defined in section 1361(c)(1)(B)) and their estates as one shareholder for this test. For additional situations in which certain entities will be treated as members of a family, see Notice 2005-91, 2005-51 I.R.B. 1164. All others are treated as separate shareholders. For details, see section 1361(c)(1).

3. Its only shareholders are individuals, estates, exempt organizations described in section 401(a) or 501(c)(3), or certain trusts described in section 1361(c)(2)(A).

For information about the section 1361(d)(2) election to be a qualified subchapter S trust (QSST), see the instructions for Part III. For information about the section 1361(e)(3) election to be an electing small business trust (ESBT), see Regulations section 1.1361-1(m). For guidance on how to convert a QSST to an ESBT, see Regulations section 1.1361-1(j)(12). If these elections were not timely made, see Rev. Proc. 2003-43, 2003-23 I.R.B. 998.

4. It has no nonresident alien shareholders.

5. It has only one class of stock (disregarding differences in voting rights). Generally, a corporation is treated as having only one class of stock if all outstanding shares of the corporation's stock confer identical rights to distribution and liquidation proceeds. See Regulations section 1.1361-1(l) for details.

6. It is not one of the following ineligible corporations.

a. A bank or thrift institution that uses the reserve method of accounting for bad debts under section 585.

b. An insurance company subject to tax under subchapter L of the Code.

c. A corporation that has elected to be treated as a possessions corporation under section 936.

d. A domestic international sales corporation (DISC) or former DISC.

7. It has or will adopt or change to one of the following tax years.

a. A tax year ending December 31.

b. A natural business year.

c. An ownership tax year.

d. A tax year elected under section 444.

e. A 52-53-week tax year ending with reference to a year listed above.

f. Any other tax year (including a 52-53-week tax year) for which the corporation establishes a business purpose.

For details on making a section 444 election or requesting a natural business, ownership, or other business purpose tax year, see the instructions for Part II.

8. Each shareholder consents as explained in the instructions for column K.

See sections 1361, 1362, and 1378, and their related regulations for additional information on the above tests.

A parent S corporation can elect to treat an eligible wholly-owned subsidiary as a qualified subchapter S subsidiary. If the election is made, the subsidiary's assets, liabilities, and items of income, deduction, and credit generally are treated as those of the parent. For details, see Form 8869, Qualified Subchapter S Subsidiary Election.

### When To Make the Election

Complete and file Form 2553:
- No more than two months and 15 days after the beginning of the tax year the election is to take effect, or
- At any time during the tax year preceding the tax year it is to take effect.

For this purpose, the 2 month period begins on the day of the month the tax year begins and ends with the close of the day before the numerically corresponding day of the second calendar month following that month. If there is no corresponding day, use the close of the last day of the calendar month.

**Example 1. No prior tax year.** A calendar year small business corporation begins its first tax year on January 7. The two month period ends March 6 and 15 days after that is March 21. To be an S corporation beginning with its first tax year, the corporation must file Form 2553 during the period that begins January 7 and ends March 21. Because

Cat. No. 49978N

the corporation had no prior tax year, an election made before January 7 will not be valid.

**Example 2. Prior tax year.** A calendar year small business corporation has been filing Form 1120 as a C corporation but wishes to make an S election for its next tax year beginning January 1. The two month period ends February 28 (29 in leap years) and 15 days after that is March 15. To be an S corporation beginning with its next tax year, the corporation must file Form 2553 during the period that begins the first day (January 1) of its last year as a C corporation and ends March 15th of the year it wishes to be an S corporation. Because the corporation had a prior tax year, it can make the election at any time during that prior tax year.

**Example 3. Tax year less than 2 1/2 months.** A calendar year small business corporation begins its first tax year on November 8. The two month period ends January 7 and 15 days after that is January 22. To be an S corporation beginning with its short tax year, the corporation must file Form 2553 during the period that begins November 8 and ends January 22. Because the corporation had no prior tax year, an election made before November 8 will not be valid.

## Relief for Late Elections

A late election to be an S corporation generally is effective for the tax year following the tax year beginning on the date entered on line E of Form 2553. However, relief for a late election may be available if the corporation can show that the failure to file on time was due to reasonable cause.

To request relief for a late election when the tax year beginning on the date entered on line E ends on or after December 31, 2007, a corporation that meets the following requirements can explain the reasonable cause in the designated space on page 1 of Form 2553.
• The corporation fails to qualify to elect to be an S corporation (see *Who May Elect* on page 1) solely because of the failure to timely file Form 2553.
• The corporation has reasonable cause for its failure to timely file Form 2553.
• The corporation has not filed a tax return for the tax year beginning on the date entered on line E of Form 2553.
• The corporation files Form 2553 as an attachment to Form 1120S no later than 6 months after the due date of Form 1120S (excluding extensions) for the tax year beginning on the date entered on line E of Form 2553.
• No taxpayer whose tax liability or tax return would be affected by the S corporation election (including all shareholders of the S corporation) has reported inconsistently with the S corporation election on any affected return for the tax year beginning on the date entered on line E of Form 2553.
Similar relief is available for an entity eligible to elect to be treated as a corporation (see the instructions for Form 8832) electing to be treated as a corporation as of the date entered on line E of Form 2553. For more details, see Rev. Proc. 2007-62, 2007-41 I.R.B. 786.

To request relief for a late election when the above requirements are not met, the corporation generally must request a private letter ruling and pay a user fee in accordance with Rev. Proc. 2008-1, 2008-1 I.R.B. 1 (or its successor). However, the ruling and user fee requirements may not apply if relief is available under the following revenue procedures.
• If an entity eligible to elect to be treated as a corporation (a) failed to timely file Form 2553, and (b) has not elected to be treated as a corporation, see Rev. Proc. 2004-48, 2004-32 I.R.B. 172.
• If a corporation failed to timely file Form 2553, see Rev. Proc. 2003-43, 2003-23 I.R.B. 998.

• If Form 1120S was filed without an S corporation election and neither the corporation nor any shareholder was notified by the IRS of any problem with the S corporation status within 6 months after the return was timely filed, see Rev. Proc. 97-48, 1997-43 I.R.B. 19.

## Where To File

Generally, send the original election (no photocopies) or fax it to the Internal Revenue Service Center listed below. If the corporation files this election by fax, keep the original Form 2553 with the corporation's permanent records. However, certain late elections can be filed attached to Form 1120S. See *Relief for Late Elections* above.

| If the corporation's principal business, office, or agency is located in: | Use the following address or fax number: |
|---|---|
| Connecticut, Delaware, District of Columbia, Illinois, Indiana, Kentucky, Maine, Maryland, Massachusetts, Michigan, New Hampshire, New Jersey, New York, North Carolina, Ohio, Pennsylvania, Rhode Island, South Carolina, Vermont, Virginia, West Virginia, Wisconsin | Department of the Treasury Internal Revenue Service Center Cincinnati, OH 45999 Fax: (859) 669-5748 |
| Alabama, Alaska, Arizona, Arkansas, California, Colorado, Florida, Georgia, Hawaii, Idaho, Iowa, Kansas, Louisiana, Minnesota, Mississippi, Missouri, Montana, Nebraska, Nevada, New Mexico, North Dakota, Oklahoma, Oregon, South Dakota, Tennessee, Texas, Utah, Washington, Wyoming | Department of the Treasury Internal Revenue Service Center Ogden, UT 84201 Fax: (801) 620-7116 |

## Acceptance or Nonacceptance of Election

The service center will notify the corporation if its election is accepted and when it will take effect. The corporation will also be notified if its election is not accepted. The corporation should generally receive a determination on its election within 60 days after it has filed Form 2553. If box Q1 in Part II is checked, the corporation will receive a ruling letter from the IRS that either approves or denies the selected tax year. When box Q1 is checked, it will generally take an additional 90 days for the Form 2553 to be accepted.

Care should be exercised to ensure that the IRS receives the election. If the corporation is not notified of acceptance or nonacceptance of its election within 2 months of the date of filing (date faxed or mailed), or within 5 months if box Q1 is checked, take follow-up action by calling 1-800-829-4933.

If the IRS questions whether Form 2553 was filed, an acceptable proof of filing is (a) a certified or registered mail receipt (timely postmarked) from the U.S. Postal Service, or its equivalent from a designated private delivery service (see Notice 2004-83, 2004-52 I.R.B. 1030 (or its successor)); (b) Form 2553 with an accepted stamp; (c) Form 2553 with a stamped IRS received date; or (d) an IRS letter stating that Form 2553 has been accepted.

*Do not file Form 1120S for any tax year before the year the election takes effect. If the corporation is now required to file Form 1120, U.S. Corporation Income Tax Return, or any other applicable tax return, continue filing it until the election takes effect.*

## End of Election

Once the election is made, it stays in effect until it is terminated or revoked. IRS consent generally is required for another election by the corporation (or a successor corporation) on Form 2553 for any tax year before the 5th tax year after the first tax year in which the termination or revocation took effect. See Regulations section 1.1362-5 for details.

## Specific Instructions

### Part I

#### Name and Address

Enter the corporation's true name as stated in the corporate charter or other legal document creating it. If the corporation's mailing address is the same as someone else's, such as a shareholder's, enter "C/O" and this person's name following the name of the corporation. Include the suite, room, or other unit number after the street address. If the Post Office does not deliver to the street address and the corporation has a P.O. box, show the box number instead of the street address. If the corporation changed its name or address after applying for its employer identification number, be sure to check the box in item D of Part I.

#### Item A. Employer Identification Number (EIN)

Enter the corporation's EIN. If the corporation does not have an EIN, it must apply for one. An EIN can be applied for:
• Online—Click on the EIN link at *www.irs.gov/businesses/small*. The EIN is issued immediately once the application information is validated.
• By telephone at 1-800-829-4933.
• By mailing or faxing Form SS-4, Application for Employer Identification Number.

If the corporation has not received its EIN by the time the return is due, enter "Applied For" and the date you applied in the space for the EIN. For more details, see the Instructions for Form SS-4.

#### Item E. Effective Date of Election

 *Form 2553 generally must be filed no later than 2 months and 15 days after the date entered for item E. For details and exceptions, see* When To Make the Election *on page 1.*

A corporation (or entity eligible to elect to be treated as a corporation) making the election effective for its first tax year in existence should enter the earliest of the following dates: (a) the date the corporation (entity) first had shareholders (owners), (b) the date the corporation (entity) first had assets, or (c) the date the corporation (entity) began doing business.

 *When the corporation (entity) is making the election for its first tax year in existence, it will usually enter the beginning date of a tax year that begins on a date other than January 1.*

A corporation (entity) not making the election for its first tax year in existence that is keeping its current tax year should enter the beginning date of the first tax year for which it wants the election to be effective.

A corporation (entity) not making the election for its first tax year in existence that is changing its tax year and wants to be an S corporation for the short tax year needed to switch tax years should enter the beginning date of the short tax year. If the corporation (entity) does not want to be an S corporation for this short tax year, it should enter the beginning date of the tax year following this short tax year and file Form 1128, Application To Adopt, Change, or Retain a Tax Year. If this change qualifies as an automatic approval request (Form 1128, Part II), file Form 1128 as an attachment to Form 2553. If this change qualifies as a ruling request (Form 1128, Part III), file Form 1128 separately. If filing Form 1128, enter "Form 1128" on the dotted line to the left of the entry space for item E.

#### Item F

Check the box that corresponds with the S corporation's selected tax year. If box (2) or (4) is checked, provide the additional information about the tax year, and complete Part II of the form.

#### Signature

Form 2553 must be signed and dated by the president, vice president, treasurer, assistant treasurer, chief accounting officer, or any other corporate officer (such as tax officer) authorized to sign.

If Form 2553 is not signed, it will not be considered timely filed.

#### Column K. Shareholders' Consent Statement

For an election filed before the effective date entered for item E, only shareholders who own stock on the day the election is made need to consent to the election.

For an election filed on or after the effective date entered for item E, all shareholders or former shareholders who owned stock at any time during the period beginning on the effective date entered for item E and ending on the day the election is made must consent to the election.

If the corporation timely filed an election, but one or more shareholders did not timely file a consent, see Regulations section 1.1362-6(b)(3)(iii). If the shareholder was a community property spouse who was a shareholder solely because of a state community property law, see Rev. Proc. 2004-35, 2004-23 I.R.B. 1029.

Each shareholder consents by signing and dating either in column K or on a separate consent statement. The following special rules apply in determining who must sign.
• If a husband and wife have a community interest in the stock or in the income from it, both must consent.
• Each tenant in common, joint tenant, and tenant by the entirety must consent.
• A minor's consent is made by the minor, legal representative of the minor, or a natural or adoptive parent of the minor if no legal representative has been appointed.
• The consent of an estate is made by the executor or administrator.
• The consent of an electing small business trust (ESBT) is made by the trustee and, if a grantor trust, the deemed owner. See Regulations section 1.1362-6(b)(2)(iv) for details.
• If the stock is owned by a qualified subchapter S trust (QSST), the deemed owner of the trust must consent.
• If the stock is owned by a trust (other than an ESBT or QSST), the person treated as the shareholder by section 1361(c)(2)(B) must consent.

*Continuation sheet or separate consent statement.* If you need a continuation sheet or use a separate consent statement, attach it to Form 2553. It must contain the name, address, and EIN of the corporation and the information requested in columns J through N of Part I.

## Column L

Enter the number of shares of stock each shareholder owns on the date the election is filed and the date(s) the stock was acquired. Enter -0- for any former shareholders listed in column J. An entity without stock, such as a limited liability company (LLC), should enter the percentage of ownership and date(s) acquired.

## Column M

Enter the social security number of each individual listed in column J. Enter the EIN of each estate, qualified trust, or exempt organization.

## Column N

Enter the month and day that each shareholder's tax year ends. If a shareholder is changing his or her tax year, enter the tax year the shareholder is changing to, and attach an explanation indicating the present tax year and the basis for the change (for example, an automatic revenue procedure or a letter ruling request).

## Part II

Complete Part II if you checked box (2) or (4) in Part I, Item F.

**Note.** Corporations cannot obtain automatic approval of a fiscal year under the natural business year (box P1) or ownership tax year (box P2) provisions if they are under examination, before an appeals (area) office, or before a federal court without meeting certain conditions and attaching a statement to the application. For details, see section 7.03 of Rev. Proc. 2006-46, 2006-45 I.R.B. 859.

## Box P1

A corporation that does not have a 47-month period of gross receipts cannot automatically establish a natural business year.

## Box Q1

For examples of an acceptable business purpose for requesting a fiscal tax year, see section 5.02 of Rev. Proc. 2002-39, 2002-22 I.R.B. 1046, and Rev. Rul. 87-57, 1987-2 C.B. 117.

Attach a statement showing the relevant facts and circumstances to establish a business purpose for the requested fiscal year. For details on what is sufficient to establish a business purpose, see section 5.02 of Rev. Proc. 2002-39.

If your business purpose is based on one of the natural business year tests provided in section 5.03 of Rev. Proc. 2002-39, identify which test you are using (the 25% gross receipts, annual business cycle, or seasonal business test). For the 25% gross receipts test, provide a schedule showing the amount of gross receipts for each month for the most recent 47 months. For either the annual business cycle or seasonal business test, provide the gross receipts from sales and services (and inventory costs, if applicable) for each month of the short period, if any, and the three immediately preceding tax years. If the corporation has been in existence for less than three tax years, submit figures for the period of existence.

If you check box Q1, you will be charged a user fee of $3,200 ($1,500 if your request is received before February 2, 2008) (subject to change by Rev. Proc. 2009-1 or its successor). Do not pay the fee when filing Form 2553. The service center will send Form 2553 to the IRS in Washington, DC, who, in turn, will notify the corporation that the fee is due.

## Box Q2

If the corporation makes a back-up section 444 election for which it is qualified, then the section 444 election will take effect in the event the business purpose request is not approved. In some cases, the tax year requested under the back-up section 444 election may be different than the tax year requested under business purpose. See Form 8716, Election To Have a Tax Year Other Than a Required Tax Year, for details on making a back-up section 444 election.

## Boxes Q3 and R2

If the corporation is not qualified to make the section 444 election after making the item Q2 back-up section 444 election or indicating its intention to make the election in item R1, and therefore it later files a calendar year return, it should write "Section 444 Election Not Made" in the top left corner of the first calendar year Form 1120S it files.

## Part III

In Part III, the income beneficiary (or legal representative) of certain qualified subchapter S trusts (QSSTs) may make the QSST election required by section 1361(d)(2). Part III may be used to make the QSST election only if corporate stock has been transferred to the trust on or before the date on which the corporation makes its election to be an S corporation. However, a statement can be used instead of Part III to make the election. If there was an inadvertent failure to timely file a QSST election, see the relief provisions under Rev. Proc. 2003-43.

**Note.** Use Part III only if you make the election in Part I. Form 2553 cannot be filed with only Part III completed.

The deemed owner of the QSST must also consent to the S corporation election in column K of Form 2553.

**Paperwork Reduction Act Notice.** We ask for the information on this form to carry out the Internal Revenue laws of the United States. You are required to give us the information. We need it to ensure that you are complying with these laws and to allow us to figure and collect the right amount of tax.

You are not required to provide the information requested on a form that is subject to the Paperwork Reduction Act unless the form displays a valid OMB control number. Books or records relating to a form or its instructions must be retained as long as their contents may become material in the administration of any Internal Revenue law. Generally, tax returns and return information are confidential, as required by section 6103.

The time needed to complete and file this form will depend on individual circumstances. The estimated average time is:

| | |
|---|---|
| **Recordkeeping** . . . . . . . . . . . . . . . . . . . . . . | 9 hr., 48 min. |
| **Learning about the law or the form** . . . . . . . . | 2 hr., 33 min. |
| **Preparing, copying, assembling, and sending the form to the IRS** . . . . . . . . . . . . . . . . . . | 4 hr., 1 min. |

If you have comments concerning the accuracy of these time estimates or suggestions for making this form simpler, we would be happy to hear from you. You can write to Internal Revenue Service, Tax Products Coordinating Committee, SE:W:CAR:MP:T:T:SP, 1111 Constitution Ave. NW, IR-6526, Washington, DC 20224. Do not send the form to this address. Instead, see *Where To File* on page 2.

-4-

# WAIVER OF NOTICE

# OF THE ORGANIZATIONAL MEETING

OF

_____

We, the undersigned incorporators named in the certificate of incorporation of the above-named corporation, hereby agree and consent that the organization meeting of the corporation be held on the date and time and place stated below, and hereby waive all notice of such meeting and of any adjournment thereof.

Place of meeting: _____

Date of meeting: _____

Time of meeting: _____

Dated: _____

_____
Incorporator

_____
Incorporator

_____
Incorporator

*This page intentionally blank.*

# MINUTES OF THE ORGANIZATIONAL MEETING OF

# INCORPORATORS AND DIRECTORS OF

_____

The organization meeting of the above corporation was held on _____, _____, at _____ at ____ o'clock __m.

The following persons were present:

_____          _____

_____          _____

_____          _____

The Waiver of Notice of this meeting was signed by all directors and incorporators named in the Articles of Incorporation and filed in the minute book.

The meeting was called to order by _____, an Incorporator named in the Articles of Incorporation. _____ was nominated and elected Chairman and acted as such until relieved by the president. _____ was nominated and elected temporary secretary, and acted as such until relieved by the permanent secretary.

A copy of the Articles of Incorporation, which was filed with the secretary of state of the State of _____ on _____, _____, was examined by the Directors and Incorporators and filed in the minute book.

The election of officers for the coming year was then held and the following were duly nominated and elected by the Board of Directors to be the officers of the corporation, to serve until such time as their successors are elected and qualified:

President:            _____
Vice President:       _____
Secretary:            _____
Treasurer:            _____

The proposed Bylaws for the corporation were then presented to the meeting and discussed. Upon motion duly made, seconded, and carried, the Bylaws were adopted and added to the minute book.

A corporate seal for the corporation was then presented to the meeting and upon motion duly made, seconded, and carried, it was adopted as the seal of the corporation. An impression thereof was then made in the margin of these minutes.

The necessity of opening a bank account was then discussed and upon motion duly made, seconded, and carried, the following resolution was adopted:

RESOLVED that the corporation open bank accounts with _____ _____ and that the officers of the corporation are authorized to take such action as is necessary to open such accounts; that the bank's printed form of resolution is hereby adopted and incorporated into these minutes by reference and shall be placed in the minute book; that any ____ of the following persons shall have signature authority over the account:

_____     _____

_____     _____

_____     _____

Proposed stock certificates and a stock transfer ledger were then presented to the meeting and examined. Upon motion duly made, seconded, and carried, the stock certificates and ledger were adopted as the certificates and transfer book to be used by the corporation. A sample stock certificate marked "VOID" and the stock transfer ledger were then added to the minute book. Upon motion duly made, seconded, and carried, it was then resolved that the stock certificates, when issued, would be signed by the President and the Secretary of the corporation.

The tax status of the corporation was then discussed and it was moved, seconded, and carried that the stock of the corporation be issued under §1244 of the Internal Revenue Code and that the officers of the corporation take the necessary action to:

1.  obtain an employer tax number by filing form SS-4

2.  ☐ become an S Corporation for tax purposes
    ☐ remain a C Corporation for tax purposes

The expenses of organizing the corporation were then discussed and it was moved, seconded, and carried that the corporation pay in full from the corporate funds the expenses and reimburse any advances made by the incorporators upon proof of payment.

The Directors named in the Articles of Incorporation then tendered their resignations, effective upon the adjournment of this meeting. Upon motion duly made, seconded, and carried, the following named persons were elected as Directors of the corporation, each to hold office until the first annual meeting of shareholders, and until a successor of each shall have been elected and qualified.

_____

_____

_____

There were presented to the corporation the following offer(s) to purchase shares of capital stock:

| FROM | NO. OF SHARES | CONSIDERATION |
|---|---|---|
| _____ | _____ | _____ |
| _____ | _____ | _____ |
| _____ | _____ | _____ |
| _____ | _____ | _____ |

The offers were discussed and after motion duly made, seconded, and carried, were approved. It was further resolved that the Board of Directors has determined that the consideration was valued at least equal to the value of the shares to be issued and that upon tender of the consideration, fully paid nonassessable shares of the corporation be issued.

There being no further business before the meeting, on motion duly made, seconded, and carried, the meeting adjourned.

DATED: _____

_____

President

_____

Secretary

*This page intentionally blank.*

# OFFER TO PURCHASE STOCK

**PART A: OFFER TO PURCHASE STOCK**

Date: _____

To the Board of Directors of

_____

    The undersigned hereby offers to purchase _____ shares of the _____ stock of your corporation at a total purchase price of _____.

Very truly yours,

_____

**PART B: OFFER TO SELL STOCK**
Pursuant to Sec. 1244 I.R.C.

Date: _____

To: _____

Dear _____,

    The corporation hereby offers to sell to you _____ shares of its common stock at a price of $_____ per share. These shares are issued pursuant to Section 1244 of the Internal Revenue Code.

    Your signature below shall constitute an acceptance of our offer as of the date it is received by the corporation.

Very truly yours,

_____

By: _____

Accepted:

_____

*This page intentionally blank.*

# RESOLUTION
of

_____

## A NEVADA CORPORATION

 RESOLVED that the corporation elects "S Corporation" status for tax purposes under the Internal Revenue Code and that the officers of the corporation are directed to file IRS Form 2553 and to take any further action necessary for the corporation to qualify for S corporation status.

Shareholders' Consent

The undersigned shareholders being all the shareholders of the above corporation, a Nevada corporation, hereby consent to the election of the corporation to obtain S corporation status.

| Name and Address of Shareholder | Shares Owned | Date Acquired |
|---|---|---|
| _____ | _____ | _____ |
| _____ | _____ | _____ |
| _____ | _____ | _____ |

Date: _____


_____

_____

_____

_____

*This page intentionally blank.*

# STOCK LEDGER

## Certificates Issued

| Cert. No. | No. of Shares | Date of Acquisition | Shareholder Name and Address | From Whom Transferred | Amount Paid |
|---|---|---|---|---|---|
|  |  |  |  |  |  |
|  |  |  |  |  |  |
|  |  |  |  |  |  |
|  |  |  |  |  |  |
|  |  |  |  |  |  |
|  |  |  |  |  |  |
|  |  |  |  |  |  |
|  |  |  |  |  |  |
|  |  |  |  |  |  |
|  |  |  |  |  |  |

## Transfer of Shares

| Date of Transfer | To Whom Transferred | Cert. No. Surrendered | No. of Shares Transferred | Cert. No. |
|---|---|---|---|---|
|  |  |  |  |  |
|  |  |  |  |  |
|  |  |  |  |  |
|  |  |  |  |  |
|  |  |  |  |  |
|  |  |  |  |  |
|  |  |  |  |  |
|  |  |  |  |  |
|  |  |  |  |  |
|  |  |  |  |  |

*This page intentionally blank.*

The shares represented by this certificate have not been registered under state or federal securities laws. Therefore, they may not be transferred until the corporation determines that such transfer will not adversely affect the exemptions relied upon.

Shares

Certificate No.

Organized under the laws of the State of Nevada

This certifies that _____ is the holder of record of

_____ shares of _____ stock of

transferable only on the books of the corporation by the holder hereof in person or by Attorney upon surrender of this certificate properly endorsed.

In witness whereof, the said corporation has caused this certificate to be signed by its duly authorized officers and its corporate seal to be hereto affixed this _____ day of _____.

_____

*For value received, _____ hereby sell, assign, and transfer unto _____,*
*_____,*
*_____ shares represented by this certificate and do hereby irrevocably constitute and*
*appoint _____ attorney to transfer the said shares on the*
*books of the corporation with full power of substitution in the premises.*

*Dated _____*

_____

*Witness:*

_____

The shares represented by this certificate have not been registered under state or federal securities laws. Therefore, they may not be transferred until the corporation determines that such transfer will not adversely affect the exemptions relied upon.

Certificate No.

Shares

Organized under the laws of the State of Nevada

This certifies that _____

is the holder of record of

_____ shares of _____ stock of

transferable only on the books of the corporation by the holder hereof in person or by Attorney upon surrender of this certificate properly endorsed.

In witness whereof, the said corporation has caused this certificate to be signed by its duly authorized officers and its corporate seal to be hereto affixed this _____ day of _____.

_____

_____

*For value received, _____ hereby sell, assign, and transfer unto _____,*
*_____,*
*_____ shares represented by this certificate and do hereby irrevocably constitute and*
*appoint _____ attorney to transfer the said shares on the*
*books of the corporation with full power of substitution in the premises.*

*Dated _____*

_____

*Witness:*

_____

The shares represented by this certificate have not been registered under state or federal securities laws. Therefore, they may not be transferred until the corporation determines that such transfer will not adversely affect the exemptions relied upon.

Shares

Certificate No.

Organized under the laws of the State of Nevada

This certifies that

is the holder of record of

_____ shares of _____ stock of

transferable only on the books of the corporation by the holder hereof in person or by Attorney upon surrender of this certificate properly endorsed.

In witness whereof, the said corporation has caused this certificate to be signed by its duly authorized officers and its corporate seal to be hereto affixed this _____ day of _____.

*For value received, _____ hereby sell, assign, and transfer unto _____,*
*_____,*
*_____ shares represented by this certificate and do hereby irrevocably constitute and*
*appoint _____ attorney to transfer the said shares on the*
*books of the corporation with full power of substitution in the premises.*

*Dated _____*

_____

*Witness:*

_____

The shares represented by this certificate have not been registered under state or federal securities laws. Therefore, they may not be transferred until the corporation determines that such transfer will not adversely affect the exemptions relied upon.

Certificate No.

Shares

Organized under the laws of the State of Nevada

This certifies that

_____ is the holder of record of

_____ shares of _____ stock of

transferable only on the books of the corporation by the holder hereof in person or by Attorney upon surrender of this certificate properly endorsed.

In witness whereof, the said corporation has caused this certificate to be signed by its duly authorized officers and its corporate seal to be hereto affixed this _____ day of _____.

*For value received, _____ hereby sell, assign, and transfer unto _____,*

*_____,*

*_____ shares represented by this certificate and do hereby irrevocably constitute and appoint _____ attorney to transfer the said shares on the books of the corporation with full power of substitution in the premises.*

*Dated _____*

_____

Witness:

_____

# (PROFIT) ANNUAL LIST OF OFFICERS, DIRECTORS AND RESIDENT AGENT OF

FILE NUMBER

(Name of Corporation)

FOR THE FILING PERIOD OF _____ TO _____

The corporation's duly appointed resident agent in the State of Nevada upon whom process can be served is:

A FORM TO CHANGE RESIDENT AGENT INFORMATION CAN BE FOUND ON OUR WEBSITE:  secretaryofstate.biz

*Important: Read instructions before completing and returning this form.*

USE BLACK INK ONLY - DO NOT HIGHLIGHT

ABOVE SPACE IS FOR OFFICE USE ONLY

☐ **Return one file stamped copy.  (If filing not accompanied by order instructions, file stamped copy will be sent to resident agent.)**

1. Print or type names and addresses either residence or business, for all officers and directors. A **President, Secretary, Treasurer, or equivalent of and all Directors** and all directors must be named. Have an **Officer** sign the form. *FORM WILL BE RETURNED IF UNSIGNED*
2. If there are additional directors attach a list of them to this form.
3. Return the completed form with the filing fee. Fee is based upon the current total authorized stock as explained on the Annual List Fee Schedule for Profit Corporations.  A $75.00 penalty must be added for failure to file this form by the deadline.  An annual list received more than 90 days before its due date shall be deemed an amended list for the previous year.
4. Make your check payable to the Secretary of State. Your canceled check will constitute a certificate to transact business.
5. Ordering Copies: If requested above, one file stamped copy will be returned at no additional charge.  To receive a certified copy, enclose an additional $30.00 per certification.  A **copy fee** of  $2.00 per page is required for each additional copy generated when ordering 2 or more file stamped or certified copies.  Appropriate instructions must accompany your order.
6. Return the completed form to: Secretary of State, 202 North Carson Street, Carson City, NV 89701-4201, (775) 684-5708.
7. Form must be in the possession of the Secretary of State on or before the last day of the month in which it is due.  (Postmark date is not accepted as receipt date.)  Forms received after due date will be returned for additional fees and penalties.

## CHECK ONLY IF APPLICABLE

☐ This corporation is a publicly traded corporation. The Central Index Key number is: _____

☐ This publicly traded corporation is not required to have a Central Index Key number.

| NAME | TITLE(S) | | | |
|------|----------|---|---|---|
| | PRESIDENT (OR EQUIVALENT OF) | | | |
| ADDRESS | CITY | ST | ZIP | |

| NAME | TITLE(S) | | | |
|------|----------|---|---|---|
| | SECRETARY (OR EQUIVALENT OF) | | | |
| ADDRESS | CITY | ST | ZIP | |

| NAME | TITLE(S) | | | |
|------|----------|---|---|---|
| | TREASURER (OR EQUIVALENT OF) | | | |
| ADDRESS | CITY | ST | ZIP | |

| NAME | TITLE(S) | | | |
|------|----------|---|---|---|
| | DIRECTOR | | | |
| ADDRESS | CITY | ST | ZIP | |

I declare, to the best of my knowledge under penalty of perjury, that the above mentioned entity has complied with the provisions of NRS 360.780 and acknowledge that pursuant to NRS 239.330, it is a category C felony to knowingly offer any false or forged instrument for filing in the Office of the Secretary of State.

X_____
**Signature of Officer**

Title _____   Date _____

ROSS MILLER
Secretary of State
202 North Carson Street
Carson City, Nevada 89701-4201
(775) 684 5708
Website: secretaryofstate.biz

## Instructions for Annual List and Resident Agent Form

_ATTENTION:_  You may now file your initial or annual list online at http://secretaryofstate.biz

IMPORTANT:  READ ALL INSTRUCTIONS CAREFULLY BEFORE COMPLETING FORM.

_ATTENTION:_  Pursuant to NRS, the Annual List and Resident Agent form _MUST_ be in the care, custody and control of the Secretary of State by the close of business on the last day of the anniversary month of the original filing.  Example:  If the entity organized on October 15, 1997 the list must be filed by October 31st of each year.  (Postmark date is _not_ accepted as receipt date in the Office of the Secretary of State.)

_As of November 1, 2003 the annual filing fee will be based on the total number of shares provided for in the articles.  Annual lists for nonprofit corporations without shares are $25.00.  See fee schedule or contact our office._

TYPE or PRINT the following information on the Annual List:

1. The _FILE NUMBER_ and _NAME_ of the entity _EXACTLY_ as it is registered with this office.

2. The _FILING PERIOD_ is the month and year of filing TO the month and year 12 months from that date.  Example: if the entity date was 1/12/99 the filing period would be 1/1999 to 1/2000.

3. The name and address of the _RESIDENT AGENT and OTHER_ names and addresses as required on the list should be entered in the boxes provided on the form.  Limited-Liability Companies **MUST** indicate whether _MANAGER or MANAGING MEMBER_ is being listed.

4. The _SIGNATURE_, including his/her title and date signed MUST be included in the areas provided at the bottom of the form.

5. Completed _FORM, FEES and applicable PENALTIES_ must be returned to the Secretary of State. Pursuant to NRS 225.085, all Initial and Annual Lists must be in the care, custody and control of the Secretary of State by the close of the business on the due date.  Lists received after the due date will be returned unfiled, and will require any associated fees and penalties as a result of being late. Trackable delivery methods such as Express Mail, Federal Express, UPS Overnight may be acceptable if the package was guaranteed to be delivered on or before the due date yet failed to be timely delivered.

_ADDITIONAL FORMS_  may be obtained on our website at http://secretaryofstate.biz or by calling 775-684-5708.

_FILE STAMPED COPIES:_  To receive one file stamped copy, please mark the appropriate check box on the list. Additional copies require $2.00 per page and appropriate order instructions.

_CERTIFIED COPIES:_  To order a certified copy, enclose an additional $30.00 and appropriate instructions.  A copy fee of $2.00 per page is required for each copy generated when ordering 2 or more certified copies.

_EXPEDITE FEE:_  Filing may be expedited for an additional $75.00 fee.

_NOTE:_  The Las Vegas Satellite Office will only accept _expedited_ filings.  Regular filings should be sent to the Carson City address.

Filing may be submitted at the office of the Secretary of State or by mail at the following addresses:

| | |
|---|---|
| Secretary of State | (This Office Accepts Expedited Filings Only) |
| Status Division | Secretary of State-Satellite Office |
| 202 N. Carson Street | Commercial Recordings Division |
| Carson City, NV 89701-4201 | 555 E. Washington Avenue, Suite 4000 |
| 775-684-5708  Fax 775-684-7123 | Las Vegas, NV 89101 |
| | 702-486-2880  Fax 702-486-2888 |

# WAIVER OF NOTICE OF THE ANNUAL MEETING OF
# THE BOARD OF DIRECTORS OF

_____

The undersigned, being all the Directors of the Corporation, hereby agree and consent that an annual meeting of the Board of Directors of the Corporation be held on the _____ day of _____, _____, at ___ o'clock ___m. at _____ _____ and do hereby waive all notice whatsoever of such meeting and of any adjournment or adjournments thereof.

We do further agree and consent that any and all lawful business may be transacted at such meeting or at any adjournment or adjournments thereof as may be deemed advisable by the Directors present. Any business transacted at such meeting or at any adjournment or adjournments thereof shall be as valid and legal as if such meeting or adjourned meeting were held after notice.

Date: _____

_____
Director

_____
Director

_____
Director

_____
Director

*This page intentionally blank.*

# MINUTES OF THE ANNUAL MEETING OF
# THE BOARD OF DIRECTORS OF

_____

The annual meeting of the Board of Directors of the Corporation was held on the date and at the time and place set forth in the written waiver of notice signed by the directors, and attached to the minutes of this meeting.

The following were present, being all the directors of the Corporation:

_____        _____

_____        _____

The meeting was called to order and it was moved, seconded, and unanimously carried that _____ act as Chairman and that _____ act as Secretary.

The minutes of the last meeting of the Board of Directors that was held on _____, _____, were read and approved by the Board.

Upon motion duly made, seconded, and carried, the following were elected officers for the following year and until their successors are elected and qualify:

President: _____
Vice President:_____
Secretary: _____
Treasurer:_____

There being no further business to come before the meeting, upon motion duly made, seconded, and unanimously carried, it was adjourned.

_____
Secretary

Directors:

_____

_____

_____

_____

*This page intentionally blank.*

# WAIVER OF NOTICE OF THE ANNUAL MEETING OF
# THE SHAREHOLDERS OF

_____

The undersigned, being all the shareholders of the Corporation, hereby agree and consent that an annual meeting of the shareholders of the Corporation be held on the _____ day of _____, _____, at _____ o'clock _____m. at _____ _____ and do hereby waive all notice whatsoever of such meeting and of any adjournment or adjournments thereof.

We do further agree and consent that any and all lawful business may be transacted at such meeting or at any adjournment or adjournments thereof. Any business transacted at such meeting or at any adjournment or adjournments thereof shall be as valid and legal as if such meeting or adjourned meeting were held after notice.

Date: _____

_____
Shareholder

_____
Shareholder

_____
Shareholder

_____
Shareholder

*This page intentionally blank.*

# MINUTES OF THE ANNUAL MEETING OF
## SHAREHOLDERS OF

_____

The annual meeting of Shareholders of the Corporation was held on the date and at the time and place set forth in the written waiver of notice signed by the shareholders, and attached to the minutes of this meeting.

There were present the following shareholders:

Shareholder                                    No. of Shares

_____          _____

_____          _____

_____          _____

_____          _____

The meeting was called to order and it was moved, seconded, and unanimously carried that _____ act as Chairman and that _____ act as Secretary.

A roll call was taken and the Chairman noted that all the outstanding shares of the Corporation were represented in person or by proxy. Any proxies were attached to these minutes.

The minutes of the last meeting of the shareholders, which was held on _____, _____, were read and approved by the shareholders.

Upon motion duly made, seconded, and carried, the following were elected directors for the following year:

_____          _____

_____          _____

There being no further business to come before the meeting, upon motion duly made, seconded, and unanimously carried, it was adjourned.

_____
Secretary

Shareholders:

_____

_____

_____

_____

*This page intentionally blank.*

# WAIVER OF NOTICE OF SPECIAL MEETING OF
# THE BOARD OF DIRECTORS OF

_____

The undersigned, being all the Directors of the Corporation, hereby agree and consent that a special meeting of the Board of Directors of the Corporation be held on the ____ day of _____, _____, at ____ o'clock ___m. at _____ _____ and do hereby waive all notice whatsoever of such meeting and of any adjournment or adjournments thereof.

The purpose of the meeting is:

We do further agree and consent that any and all lawful business may be transacted at such meeting or at any adjournment or adjournments thereof as may be deemed advisable by the Directors present. Any business transacted at such meeting or at any adjournment or adjournments thereof shall be as valid and legal as if such meeting or adjourned meeting were held after notice.

Date: _____

_____
Director

_____
Director

_____
Director

_____
Director

*This page intentionally blank.*

# MINUTES OF SPECIAL MEETING OF
# THE BOARD OF DIRECTORS OF

_____

A special meeting of the Board of Directors of the Corporation was held on the date and at the time and place set forth in the written waiver of notice signed by the directors, and attached to the minutes of this meeting.

The following were present, being all the directors of the Corporation:

_____    _____

_____    _____

The meeting was called to order and it was moved, seconded, and unanimously carried that _____ act as Chairman and that _____ act as Secretary.

The minutes of the last meeting of the Board of Directors, which was held on _____, _____, were read and approved by the Board.

Upon motion duly made, seconded, and carried, the following resolution was adopted:

There being no further business to come before the meeting, upon motion duly made, seconded, and unanimously carried, it was adjourned.

_____
Secretary

Directors:

_____

_____

_____

_____

*This page intentionally blank.*

# WAIVER OF NOTICE OF SPECIAL MEETING OF
# THE SHAREHOLDERS OF

_____

The undersigned, being all the shareholders of the Corporation, hereby agree and consent that a special meeting of the shareholders of the Corporation be held on the ____ day of _____, _____, at ____ o'clock ___m. at _____ _____ and do hereby waive all notice whatsoever of such meeting and of any adjournment or adjournments thereof.

The purpose of the meeting is:

We do further agree and consent that any and all lawful business may be transacted at such meeting or at any adjournment or adjournments thereof. Any business transacted at such meeting or at any adjournment or adjournments thereof shall be as valid and legal as if such meeting or adjourned meeting were held after notice.

Date: _____

_____
Shareholder

_____
Shareholder

_____
Shareholder

_____
Shareholder

*This page intentionally blank.*

# MINUTES OF SPECIAL MEETING OF
# SHAREHOLDERS OF

_____

A special meeting of shareholders of the Corporation was held on the date and at the time and place set forth in the written waiver of notice signed by the shareholders, and attached to the minutes of this meeting.

There were present the following shareholders:

| Shareholder | No. of Shares |
| --- | --- |
| _____ | _____ |
| _____ | _____ |
| _____ | _____ |
| _____ | _____ |

The meeting was called to order and it was moved, seconded, and unanimously carried that _____ act as Chairman and that _____ act as Secretary.

A roll call was taken and the Chairman noted that all the outstanding shares of the Corporation were represented in person or by proxy. Any proxies were attached to these minutes.

The minutes of the last meeting of the shareholders, which was held on _____, _____, were read and approved by the shareholders.

Upon motion duly made, seconded, and carried, the following resolution was adopted:


There being no further business to come before the meeting, upon motion duly made, seconded, and unanimously carried, it was adjourned.

_____
Secretary

Shareholders:

_____

_____

_____

_____

*This page intentionally blank.*

**ROSS MILLER**
Secretary of State
206 North Carson Street
Carson City, Nevada 89701-4299
(775) 684 5708
Website: secretaryofstate.biz

# Articles of Organization
# Limited-Liability Company
### (PURSUANT TO NRS 86)

USE BLACK INK ONLY - DO NOT HIGHLIGHT                    ABOVE SPACE IS FOR OFFICE USE ONLY

| | |
|---|---|
| **1. _Name of Limited-Liability Company:_** <br> _(must contain approved limited-liability company wording; see instructions)_ | Check box if a Series Limited-Liability Company ☐ |
| **2. _Resident Agent Name and Street Address:_** <br> _(must be a Nevada address where process may be served)_ | Name <br> **(MANDATORY)** Physical Street Address — City — Nevada — Zip Code <br> **(OPTIONAL)** Mailing Address — City — State — Zip Code |
| **3. _Dissolution Date:_** <br> _(OPTIONAL; see instructions)_ | Latest date upon which the company is to dissolve (if existence is not perpetual): |
| **4. _Management:_** | Company shall be managed by ☐ Manager(s) **OR** ☐ Members <br> _(check only one box)_ |
| **5. _Name and Address of each Manager or Managing Member:_** <br> _(attach additional page if more than 3)_ | Name <br> Address — City — State Zip Code <br> Name <br> Address — City — State Zip Code <br> Name <br> Address — City — State Zip Code |
| **6. _Name, Address and Signature of Organizer:_** <br> _(attach additional page if more than 1)_ | Name — X Signature <br> Address — City — State Zip Code |
| **7. _Certificate of Acceptance of Appointment of Resident Agent:_** | I hereby accept appointment as Resident Agent for the above named limited-liability company. <br> X _____ <br> **Authorized Signature of R.A. or On Behalf of R.A. Company** — Date |

_This form must be accompanied by appropriate fees._

Nevada Secretary of State Form LLC Arts 2007
Revised on 01/01/07

**ROSS MILLER**
Secretary of State
206 North Carson Street
Carson City, Nevada 89701-4299
(775) 684 5708
Website: secretaryofstate.biz

> # Instructions for Limited-Liability Company Articles of Organization
> ### (PURSUANT TO NRS 86)

## IMPORTANT: READ ALL INSTRUCTIONS CAREFULLY BEFORE COMPLETING FORM.

1. *Name of the Limited-Liability Company:*   The name must contain the words Limited-Liability Company, Limited Company or Limited or the abbreviations Ltd., L.L.C., LLC or LC .  The word "company" may also be abbreviated.  The name must be distinguishable from the name of a limited-liability company, limited partnership, limited-liability limited partnership, limited-liability partnership, business trust or corporation already on file in this office.  A name may be reserved, if available, for 90 days by submitting a name reservation form with a $25.00 filing fee to the office of the Secretary of State.  For details you may call (775) 684-5708, visit www.secretaryofstate.biz, or write to the Secretary of State, 206 North Carson Street, Carson City NV. 89701-4201.  If it appears from the name and/or purpose of the entity being formed that it is to be regulated by the Financial Institutions Division, Insurance Division, State Board of Professional Engineers and Land Surveyors, State Board of Accountancy or Real Estate Division, the application will need to be approved by the regulating agency before it is filed with the Office of the Secretary of State.

2. *Resident Agent:*  Persons wishing to file articles of organization in the State of Nevada must designate a person as a resident agent who resides or is located in this state.  Every resident agent must have a street address in the state of Nevada for the service of process, and may have a separate mailing address such as a post office box, which may be different from the street address

3. *Dissolution Date:*  State the latest date upon which the company is to dissolve. This provision is optional.

4.  Limited-liability companies may be managed by one or more manager(s) or one or more members.  Please state whether the company is managed by members or managers.  If the company is to be managed by one or more managers, the name and post office or street address, either resident or business, of each manager must be set forth.  If the company is to be managed by the members, the name and post office or street address, either residence or business, of each member must be set forth.

5.  One or more persons may organize a limited-liability company.  Indicate the names and addresses of the organizers executing the articles.

6.  Resident agent must complete and sign certificate of acceptance at bottom of form or attach a separate signed certificate of acceptance.

7.  On a separate 8 ½" x 11" sheet, state any other provisions which the members elect to set out in the articles of organization for the regulation of the internal affairs of the company, including any provisions which under NRS Chapter 86 are required or permitted to be set out in the operating agreement of the company.

### ***IMPORTANT***

*INITIAL LIST OF MANAGERS OR MEMBERS:* Pursuant to NRS 86.263, each limited-liability company organized under the laws of this state shall, on or before the last day of the first month after the filing of its articles of organization, and annually thereafter, file its list of officers, directors and resident agent.  The initial list fee is $125.00.  Forms will be mailed to you upon the filing of your limited-liability company and annually thereafter to the entity's resident agent.

*COPIES:* One file stamped copy of the articles will be returned at no additional charge.  To receive a certified copy, enclose an additional $30.00 per certification.  A copy fee of $2.00 per page is required for each additional copy generated when ordering 2 or more file stamped or certified copies.  Appropriate instructions must accompany your order.  NRS 86.241 requires that a limited liability company have at least one certified copy to be kept in the office of the resident agent. The Secretary of State keeps the original filing.

*FILING FEE:* $75.00 Filing fee is required.  Filing may be expedited for an additional $125.00 expedite fee.

Filing may be submitted at the office of the Secretary of State or by mail at the following addresses:

|  |  |
|---|---|
| Secretary of State | (This Office Accepts Expedited Filings Only) |
| New Filings Division | Secretary of State-Satellite Office |
| 206 N. Carson Street | Commercial Recordings Division |
| Carson City, NV 89701-4299 | 555 E. Washington Avenue, Suite 4000 |
| 775-684-5708 Fax 775-684-7138 | Las Vegas, NV 89101 |
|  | 702-486-2880 Fax 702-486-2888 |

Nevada Secretary of State Form LLC Instructions 2007
Revised on: 06/05/07

Form **8832**
(Rev. March 2007)
Department of the Treasury
Internal Revenue Service

## Entity Classification Election

OMB No. 1545-1516

**Type or Print**

| Name of eligible entity making election | Employer identification number |
|---|---|

Number, street, and room or suite no. If a P.O. box, see instructions.

City or town, state, and ZIP code. If a foreign address, enter city, province or state, postal code and country. Follow the country's practice for entering the postal code.

► Check if: ☐ Address change

---

**1   Type of election** (see instructions):

**a** ☐ Initial classification by a newly-formed entity. Skip lines 2a and 2b and go to line 3.
**b** ☐ Change in current classification. Go to line 2a.

**2a** Has the eligible entity previously filed an entity election that had an effective date within the last 60 months?

   ☐ **Yes.** Go to line 2b.
   ☐ **No.** Skip line 2b and go to line 3.

**2b** Was the eligible entity's prior election for initial classification by a newly formed entity effective on the date of formation?

   ☐ **Yes.** Go to line 3.
   ☐ **No.** Stop here. You generally are not currently eligible to make the election (see instructions).

**3** Does the eligible entity have more than one owner?

   ☐ **Yes.** You can elect to be classified as a partnership or an association taxable as a corporation. Skip line 4 and go to line 5.
   ☐ **No.** You can elect to be classified as an association taxable as a corporation or disregarded as a separate entity. Go to line 4.

**4** If the eligible entity has only one owner, provide the following information:
   **a** Name of owner ► ----------------------------------------------------------------------------
   **b** Identifying number of owner ► ------------------------------------------------------------

**5** If the eligible entity is owned by one or more affiliated corporations that file a consolidated return, provide the name and employer identification number of the parent corporation:
   **a** Name of parent corporation ► ------------------------------------------------------------
   **b** Employer identification number ► ---------------------------------------------------------

---

**For Paperwork Reduction Act Notice, see instructions.**          Cat. No. 22598R          Form **8832** (Rev. 3-2007)

**6   Type of entity** (see instructions):

**a** ☐ A domestic eligible entity electing to be classified as an association taxable as a corporation.

**b** ☐ A domestic eligible entity electing to be classified as a partnership.

**c** ☐ A domestic eligible entity with a single owner electing to be disregarded as a separate entity.

**d** ☐ A foreign eligible entity electing to be classified as an association taxable as a corporation.

**e** ☐ A foreign eligible entity electing to be classified as a partnership.

**f** ☐ A foreign eligible entity with a single owner electing to be disregarded as a separate entity.

**7**   If the eligible entity is created or organized in a foreign jurisdiction, provide the foreign country of organization ▶ ...........................................................................................................

**8**   Election is to be effective beginning (month, day, year) (see instructions) . . . . . . . . . . . . ▶ ___ / ___ / ___

| **9** Name and title of contact person whom the IRS may call for more information | **10** Contact person's telephone number |
|---|---|
| | ( ) |

## Consent Statement and Signature(s) (see instructions)

Under penalties of perjury, I (we) declare that I (we) consent to the election of the above-named entity to be classified as indicated above, and that I (we) have examined this consent statement, and to the best of my (our) knowledge and belief, it is true, correct, and complete. If I am an officer, manager, or member signing for all members of the entity, I further declare that I am authorized to execute this consent statement on their behalf.

| Signature(s) | Date | Title |
|---|---|---|
| | | |
| | | |
| | | |
| | | |
| | | |
| | | |
| | | |
| | | |
| | | |
| | | |
| | | |
| | | |
| | | |

# General Instructions

Section references are to the Internal Revenue Code unless otherwise noted.

## What's New

This revision of the Form 8832 instructions reflects an update to the filing locations. Our previous revision (December 2006) stated that all entity classification elections were sent to the service center in Ogden, UT. *This is no longer the case.* Now the form is filed either in Cincinnati or Ogden depending upon your principal business location. See *Where To File* on page 4 for your filing location.

● You are not required to sign the copy of Form 8832 filed with your tax return. See *Consent statement and signature(s)* on page 6.

● New questions on lines 2a and 2b highlight the general rule which limits an eligible entity's ability to change its classification by election again during the 60 months after the effective date of making an earlier entity classification election.

● All single-owner eligible entities electing either corporate or disregarded entity status must provide the name and identifying number of their owner on lines 4a and 4b. Previously this requirement applied only to single-owner eligible entities electing disregarded entity status.

● All eligible entities owned by one or more affiliated corporations that file a consolidated return must provide the name and employer identification number (EIN) of their parent corporation on lines 5a and 5b. Previously this requirement applied only to single-owner eligible entities electing disregarded entity status.

● All foreign eligible entities making an entity classification election, including those also organized under domestic law, must provide the name of the foreign country in which they are organized on line 7. Previously this requirement applied only to single-owner foreign eligible entities electing disregarded entity status.

## Purpose of Form

An eligible entity uses Form 8832 to elect how it will be classified for federal tax purposes, as a corporation, a partnership, or an entity disregarded as separate from its owner. An eligible entity is classified for federal tax purposes under the default rules described below unless it files Form 8832 or Form 2553, Election by a Small Business Corporation, to elect a classification or change its current classification. See *Who Must File* on page 4.

 *A new eligible entity should not file Form 8832 if it will be using its default classification (see* Default Rules *below).*

**Eligible entity.** An eligible entity is a business entity that is not included in items 1, or 3 through 9, under the definition of **corporation** provided under *Definitions.*

Eligible entities include limited liability companies (LLCs), partnerships, and any foreign entity that is not identified as a corporation under Regulations section 301.7701-2(b)(8) (see item 3 below).

Generally, corporations are not eligible entities. However, the following types of corporations are treated as eligible entities:

**1.** An eligible entity that previously elected to be an association taxable as a corporation by filing Form 8832. An entity that elects to be classified as a corporation by filing Form 8832 can make another election to change its classification (see the *60-month limitation rule* discussed below in the instructions for lines 2a and 2b).

**2.** A foreign eligible entity that became an association taxable as a corporation under the foreign default rule described below.

**3.** A foreign corporation that is not identified as a corporation under Regulations section 301.7701-2(b)(8). If a foreign corporation is not identified on the list included in these regulations, it qualifies as an eligible entity. See the list of *Foreign Entities Classified as Corporations for Federal Tax Purposes* under this regulation on page 6. Refer to the regulations for any changes to the list made after these instructions were printed.

The IRS will use the information entered on this form to establish the entity's filing and reporting requirements for federal tax purposes.

## Default Rules

**Existing entity default rule.** Certain domestic and foreign entities that were in existence before January 1, 1997, and have an established federal tax classification generally do not need to make an election to continue that classification. If an existing entity decides to change its classification, it may do so subject to the 60-month limitation rule. See the instructions for lines 2a and 2b. See Regulations sections 301.7701-3(b)(3) and 301.7701-3(h)(2) for more details.

**Domestic default rule.** Unless an election is made on Form 8832, a domestic eligible entity is:

**1.** A partnership if it has two or more members.

**2.** Disregarded as an entity separate from its owner if it has a single owner.

A change in the number of members of an eligible entity classified as an **association** (defined below) does not affect the entity's classification. However, an eligible entity classified as a partnership will become a disregarded entity when the entity's membership is reduced to one member and a disregarded entity will be classified as a partnership when the entity has more than one member.

**Foreign default rule.** Unless an election is made on Form 8832, a foreign eligible entity is:

**1.** A partnership if it has two or more members and at least one member does not have limited liability.

**2.** An association taxable as a corporation if all members have limited liability.

**3.** Disregarded as an entity separate from its owner if it has a single owner that does not have limited liability.

## Definitions

**Association.** For purposes of this form, an association is an eligible entity taxable as a corporation by election or, for foreign eligible entities, under the default rules (see Regulations section 301.7701-3).

**Business entity.** A business entity is any entity recognized for federal tax purposes that is not properly classified as a trust under Regulations section 301.7701-4 or otherwise subject to special treatment under the Code regarding the entity's classification. See Regulations section 301.7701-2(a).

**Corporation.** For federal tax purposes, a corporation is any of the following:

**1.** A business entity organized under a federal or state statute, or under a statute of a federally recognized Indian tribe, if the statute describes or refers to the entity as incorporated or as a corporation, body corporate, or body politic.

**2.** An association (as determined under Regulations section 301.7701-3).

**3.** A business entity organized under a state statute, if the statute describes or refers to the entity as a joint-stock company or joint-stock association.

**4.** An insurance company.

**5.** A state-chartered business entity conducting banking activities, if any of its deposits are insured under the Federal Deposit Insurance Act, as amended, 12 U.S.C. 1811 et seq., or a similar federal statute.

**6.** A business entity wholly owned by a state or any political subdivision thereof, or a business entity wholly owned by a foreign government or any other entity described in Regulations section 1.892-2T.

**7.** A business entity that is taxable as a corporation under a provision of the Code other than section 7701(a)(3).

**8.** A foreign business entity listed on page 6. See Regulations section 301.7701-2(b)(8) for any exceptions and inclusions to items on this list and for any revisions made to this list since these instructions were printed.

**9.** An entity created or organized under the laws of more than one jurisdiction (business entities with multiple charters) if the entity is treated as a corporation with respect to any one of the jurisdictions. See Regulations section 301.7701-2(b)(9) for examples.

**Disregarded entity.** A disregarded entity is an eligible entity that is treated as an entity not separate from its single owner. Its separate existence will be ignored for federal tax purposes unless it elects corporate tax treatment.

**Limited liability.** A member of a foreign eligible entity has limited liability if the member has no personal liability for any debts of or claims against the entity by reason of being a member. This determination is based solely on the statute or law under which the entity is organized (and, if relevant, the entity's organizational documents). A member has personal liability if the creditors of the entity may seek satisfaction of all or any part of the debts or claims against the entity from the member as such. A member has personal liability even if the member makes an agreement under which another person (whether or not a member of the entity) assumes that liability or agrees to indemnify that member for that liability.

**Partnership.** A partnership is a business entity that has at least two members and is not a corporation as defined on page 3 under *Corporation.*

## Who Must File

File this form for an eligible entity that is one of the following:

● A domestic entity electing to be classified as an association taxable as a corporation.

● A domestic entity electing to change its current classification (even if it is currently classified under the default rule).

● A foreign entity that has more than one owner, all owners having limited liability, electing to be classified as a partnership.

● A foreign entity that has at least one owner that does not have limited liability, electing to be classified as an association taxable as a corporation.

● A foreign entity with a single owner having limited liability, electing to be an entity disregarded as an entity separate from its owner.

● A foreign entity electing to change its current classification (even if it is currently classified under the default rule).

Do not file this form for an eligible entity that is:

● Tax-exempt under section 501(a);

● A real estate investment trust (REIT), as defined in section 856; or

● Electing to be classified as an S corporation. An eligible entity that timely files Form 2553 to elect classification as an S corporation and meets all other requirements to qualify as an S corporation is deemed to have made an election under Regulations section 301.7701-3(c)(v) to be classified as an association taxable as a corporation.

All three of these entities are deemed to have made an election to be classified as an association.

## Effect of Election

The federal tax treatment of elective changes in classification as described in Regulations section 301.7701-3(g)(1) is summarized as follows:

● If an eligible entity classified as a partnership elects to be classified as an association, it is deemed that the partnership contributes all of its assets and liabilities to the association in exchange for stock in the association, and immediately thereafter, the partnership liquidates by distributing the stock of the association to its partners.

● If an eligible entity classified as an association elects to be classified as a partnership, it is deemed that the association distributes all of its assets and liabilities to its shareholders in liquidation of the association, and immediately thereafter, the shareholders contribute all of the distributed assets and liabilities to a newly formed partnership.

● If an eligible entity classified as an association elects to be disregarded as an entity separate from its owner, it is deemed that the association distributes all of its assets and liabilities to its single owner in liquidation of the association.

● If an eligible entity that is disregarded as an entity separate from its owner elects to be classified as an association, the owner of the eligible entity is deemed to have contributed all of the assets and liabilities of the entity to the association in exchange for the stock of the association.

**Note.** For information on the federal tax consequences of elective changes in classification, see Regulations section 301.7701-3(g).

## When To File

An election specifying an eligible entity's classification cannot take effect more than 75 days prior to the date the election is filed, nor can it take effect later than 12 months after the date the election is filed.

*Late election relief.* A newly formed entity may be eligible for late election relief under Rev. Proc. 2002-59, 2002-39 I.R.B. 615 if:

● The entity failed to obtain its desired classification solely because Form 8832 was not timely filed,

● The due date for the entity's desired classification tax return (excluding extensions) for the tax year beginning with the entity's formation date has not passed, and

● The entity has reasonable cause for its failure to make a timely election.

To obtain relief, a newly formed entity must file Form 8832 on or before the due date of the first federal tax return (excluding extensions) of the entity's desired classification. The entity must also write "FILED PURSUANT TO REV. PROC. 2002-59" at the top of the form. The entity must attach a statement to the form explaining why it failed to file a timely election. If Rev. Proc. 2002-59 does not apply, an entity may seek relief for a late entity election by requesting a private letter ruling and paying a user fee in accordance with Rev. Proc. 2006-1, 2006-1 I.R.B. 1 (or its successor).

## Where To File

File Form 8832 with the Internal Revenue Service Center for your state listed below.

Attach a copy of Form 8832 to the entity's federal tax return for the tax year of the election. If the entity is not required to file a return for that year, a copy of its Form 8832 must be attached to the federal tax returns of all direct or indirect owners of the entity for the tax year of the owner that includes the date on which the election took effect. Failure to attach a copy of Form 8832 will not invalidate an otherwise valid election, but penalties may be assessed against persons who are required to, but do not, attach Form 8832.

Each member of the entity is required to file their return consistent with the entity election. Penalties apply to returns filed inconsistent with the entity's election.

| If the entity's principal business, office, or agency is located in: | Use the following Internal Revenue Service Center address: |
|---|---|
| Connecticut, Delaware, District of Columbia, Illinois, Indiana, Kentucky, Maine, Maryland, Massachusetts, Michigan, New Hampshire, New Jersey, New York, North Carolina, Ohio, Pennsylvania, Rhode Island, South Carolina, Vermont, Virginia, West Virginia, Wisconsin | Cincinnati, OH 45999 |

| If the entity's principal business, office, or agency is located in: | Use the following Internal Revenue Service Center address: |
| --- | --- |
| Alabama, Alaska, Arizona, Arkansas, California, Colorado, Florida, Georgia, Hawaii, Idaho, Iowa, Kansas, Louisiana, Minnesota, Mississippi, Missouri, Montana, Nebraska, Nevada, New Mexico, North Dakota, Oklahoma, Oregon, South Dakota, Tennessee, Texas, Utah, Washington, Wyoming | Ogden, UT 84201 |
| A foreign country or U.S. possession | Ogden, UT 84201-0023 |

**Note.** Also attach a copy to the entity's federal income tax return for the tax year of the election.

## Acceptance or Nonacceptance of Election

The service center will notify the eligible entity at the address listed on Form 8832 if its election is accepted or not accepted. The entity should generally receive a determination on its election within 60 days after it has filed Form 8832.

Care should be exercised to ensure that the IRS receives the election. If the entity is not notified of acceptance or nonacceptance of its election within 60 days of the date of filing, take follow-up action by calling 1-800-829-0115, or by sending a letter to the service center to inquire about its status. Send any such letter by certified or registered mail via the U.S. Postal Service, or equivalent type of delivery by a designated private delivery service (see Notice 2004-83, 2004-52 I.R.B. 1030 (or its successor)).

If the IRS questions whether Form 8832 was filed, an acceptable proof of filing is:

- A certified or registered mail receipt (timely postmarked) from the U.S. Postal Service, or its equivalent from a designated private delivery service;
- Form 8832 with an accepted stamp;
- Form 8832 with a stamped IRS received date; or
- An IRS letter stating that Form 8832 has been accepted.

## Specific Instructions

**Name.** Enter the name of the eligible entity electing to be classified.

**Employer identification number (EIN).** Show the EIN of the eligible entity electing to be classified.

**Caution.** Do not put "Applied For" on this line.

**Note.** Any entity that has an EIN will retain that EIN even if its federal tax classification changes under Regulations section 301.7701-3.

If a disregarded entity's classification changes so that it becomes recognized as a partnership or association for federal tax purposes, and that entity had an EIN, then the entity must continue to use that EIN. If the entity did not already have its own EIN, then the entity must apply for an EIN and not use the identifying number of the single owner.

A foreign person that makes an election under Regulations section 301.7701-3(c) and (d) must also use its own taxpayer identifying number. See sections 6721 through 6724 for penalties that may apply for failure to supply taxpayer identifying numbers.

If the entity electing to be classified using Form 8832 does not have an EIN, it must apply for one on Form SS-4, Application for Employer Identification Number. If the filing of Form 8832 is the only reason the entity is applying for an EIN, check the "Other" box on line 9 of Form SS-4 and enter "Form 8832" to the right of that box. The entity must have received an EIN by the time Form 8832 is filed in order for the form to be processed. An election will not be accepted if the eligible entity does not provide an EIN. **Caution.** Do not apply for a new EIN for an existing entity that is changing its classification if the entity already has an EIN.

**Address.** Enter the address of the entity electing a classification. All correspondence regarding the acceptance or nonacceptance of the election will be sent to this address. Include the suite, room, or other unit number after the street address. If the Post Office does not deliver mail to the street address and the entity has a P.O. box, show the box number instead of the street address. If the electing entity receives its mail in care of a third party (such as an accountant or an attorney), enter on the street address line "C/O" followed by the third party's name and street address or P.O. box.

**Address change.** If the eligible entity has changed its address since filing Form SS-4 or the entity's most recently-filed return (including a change to an "in care of" address), check the box for an address change.

**Note.** If a change of address occurs after the later of the filing of Form SS-4 or the most recently-filed return, use Form 8822, Change of Address, to notify the IRS of the new address. A new address shown on Form 8832 will not update the entity's address of record with the IRS.

**Line 1.** Check box 1a if the entity is choosing a classification for the first time (i.e., the entity does not want to be classified under the applicable default classification). Do not file this form if the entity wants to be classified under the default rules.

Check box 1b if the entity is changing its current classification.

**Lines 2a and 2b. 60-month limitation rule.** Once an eligible entity makes an election to *change* its classification, the entity generally cannot change its classification by election again during the 60 months after the effective date of the election. However, the IRS may (by private letter ruling) permit the entity to change its classification by election within the 60-month period if more than 50% of the ownership interests in the entity, as of the effective date of the election, are owned by persons that did not own any interests in the entity on the effective date or the filing date of the entity's prior election.

**Note.** The 60-month limitation does not apply if the previous election was made by a *newly formed* eligible entity and was effective on the date of formation.

**Line 4.** If an eligible entity has only one owner, provide the name of its owner on line 4a and the owner's identifying number (social security number, or individual taxpayer identification number, or EIN) on line 4b. Enter "DE" if the owner is a disregarded entity that does not have an identifying number. If the owner is a foreign person or entity and does not have a U.S. identifying number, enter "none" on line 4b.

**Line 5.** If the eligible entity is owned by one or more members of an affiliated group of corporations that file a consolidated return, provide the name and EIN of the parent corporation.

**Line 6.** Check the appropriate box if you are changing a current classification (no matter how achieved), or are electing out of a default classification. Do not file this form if you fall within a default classification that is the desired classification for the new entity.

**Line 7.** If the entity making the election is created or organized in a foreign jurisdiction, enter the name of the foreign country in which it is organized. This information must be provided even if the entity is also organized under domestic law.

**Line 8.** Generally, the election will take effect on the date you enter on line 8 of this form, or on the date filed if no date is entered on line 8. An election specifying an entity's classification for federal tax purposes can take effect no more than 75 days prior to the date the election is filed, nor can it take effect later than 12 months after the date on which the election is filed. If line 8 shows a date more than 75 days prior to the date on which the election is filed, the election will default to 75 days before the date it is filed. If line 8 shows an effective date more than 12 months from the filing date, the election will take effect 12 months after the date the election is filed.

**Consent statement and signature(s).**
Form 8832 must be signed by:

**1.** Each member of the electing entity who is an owner at the time the election is filed; or

**2.** Any officer, manager, or member of the electing entity who is authorized (under local law or the organizational documents) to make the election. The elector represents to having such authorization under penalties of perjury.

If an election is to be effective for any period prior to the time it is filed, each person who was an owner between the date the election is to be effective and the date the election is filed, must sign.

If you need a continuation sheet or use a separate consent statement, attach it to Form 8832. The separate consent statement must contain the same information as shown on Form 8832.

**Note.** Do not sign the copy that is attached to your tax return.

## Paperwork Reduction Act Notice

We ask for the information on this form to carry out the Internal Revenue laws of the United States. You are required to give us the information. We need it to ensure that you are complying with these laws and to allow us to figure and collect the right amount of tax.

You are not required to provide the information requested on a form that is subject to the Paperwork Reduction Act unless the form displays a valid OMB control number. Books or records relating to a form or its instructions must be retained as long as their contents may become material in the administration of any Internal Revenue law. Generally, tax returns and return information are confidential, as required by section 6103.

The time needed to complete and file this form will vary depending on individual circumstances. The estimated average time is:

**Recordkeeping** . . . . 1 hr., 49 min.

**Learning about the law or the form** . . . . 2 hr., 7 min.

**Preparing and sending the form to the IRS** . . . . . 23 min.

If you have comments concerning the accuracy of these time estimates or suggestions for making this form simpler, we would be happy to hear from you. You can write to the Internal Revenue Service, Tax Products Coordinating Committee, SE:W:CAR:MP:T:T:SP, 1111 Constitution Ave. NW, IR-6406, Washington, DC 20224. Do not send the form to this address. Instead, see *Where To File* on page 4.

*Foreign Entities Classified as Corporations for Federal Tax Purposes:*

**American Samoa**—Corporation
**Argentina**—Sociedad Anonima
**Australia**—Public Limited Company
**Austria**—Aktiengesellschaft
**Barbados**—Limited Company
**Belgium**—Societe Anonyme
**Belize**—Public Limited Company
**Bolivia**—Sociedad Anonima
**Brazil**—Sociedade Anonima
**Canada**—Corporation and Company
**Chile**—Sociedad Anonima
**People's Republic of China**—Gufen Youxian Gongsi
**Republic of China (Taiwan)**—Ku-fen Yu-hsien Kung-szu
**Colombia**—Sociedad Anonima
**Costa Rica**—Sociedad Anonima
**Cyprus**—Public Limited Company
**Czech Republic**—Akciova Spolecnost
**Denmark**—Aktieselskab
**Ecuador**—Sociedad Anonima or Compania Anonima
**Egypt**—Sharikat Al-Mossahamah
**El Salvador**—Sociedad Anonima
**Estonia**—Aktsiaselts
**European Economic Area/European Union**—Societas Europaea
**Finland**—Julkinen Osakeyhtio/ Publikt Aktiebolag
**France**—Societe Anonyme
**Germany**—Aktiengesellschaft
**Greece**—Anonymos Etairia
**Guam**—Corporation
**Guatemala**—Sociedad Anonima
**Guyana**—Public Limited Company
**Honduras**—Sociedad Anonima
**Hong Kong**—Public Limited Company
**Hungary**—Reszvenytarsasag
**Iceland**—Hlutafelag
**India**—Public Limited Company
**Indonesia**—Perseroan Terbuka
**Ireland**—Public Limited Company
**Israel**—Public Limited Company
**Italy**—Societa per Azioni
**Jamaica**—Public Limited Company
**Japan**—Kabushiki Kaisha
**Kazakstan**—Ashyk Aktsionerlik Kogham
**Republic of Korea**—Chusik Hoesa
**Latvia**—Akciju Sabiedriba
**Liberia**—Corporation
**Liechtenstein**—Aktiengesellschaft
**Lithuania**—Akcine Bendroves
**Luxembourg**—Societe Anonyme

**Malaysia**—Berhad
**Malta**—Public Limited Company
**Mexico**—Sociedad Anonima
**Morocco**—Societe Anonyme
**Netherlands**—Naamloze Vennootschap
**New Zealand**—Limited Company
**Nicaragua**—Compania Anonima
**Nigeria**—Public Limited Company
**Northern Mariana Islands**—Corporation
**Norway**—Allment Aksjeselskap
**Pakistan**—Public Limited Company
**Panama**—Sociedad Anonima
**Paraguay**—Sociedad Anonima
**Peru**—Sociedad Anonima
**Philippines**—Stock Corporation
**Poland**—Spolka Akcyjna
**Portugal**—Sociedade Anonima
**Puerto Rico**—Corporation
**Romania**—Societe pe Actiuni
**Russia**—Otkrytoye Aktsionernoy Obshchestvo
**Saudi Arabia**—Sharikat Al-Mossahamah
**Singapore**—Public Limited Company
**Slovak Republic**—Akciova Spolocnost
**Slovenia**—Delniska Druzba
**South Africa**—Public Limited Company
**Spain**—Sociedad Anonima
**Surinam**—Naamloze Vennootschap
**Sweden**—Publika Aktiebolag
**Switzerland**—Aktiengesellschaft
**Thailand**—Borisat Chamkad (Mahachon)
**Trinidad and Tobago**—Limited Company
**Tunisia**—Societe Anonyme
**Turkey**—Anonim Sirket
**Ukraine**—Aktsionerne Tovaristvo Vidkritogo Tipu
**United Kingdom**—Public Limited Company
**United States Virgin Islands**—Corporation
**Uruguay**—Sociedad Anonima
**Venezuela**—Sociedad Anonima or Compania Anonima

*See Regulations section 301.7701-2(b)(8) for any exceptions and inclusions to items on this list and for any revisions made to this list since these instructions were printed.*

# LIMITED LIABILITY COMPANY
## MEMBER-MANAGED OPERATING AGREEMENT OF

_____

THIS AGREEMENT is made effective as of _____, _____, among the member(s) and the company.

**1. Formation.** A limited liability company of the above name has been formed under the laws of the state of Nevada by filing articles of organization with the secretary of state. The purpose of the business shall be to carry on any act or activity lawful under the jurisdiction in which it operates. The company may operate under a fictitious name or names as long as the company is in compliance with applicable fictitious name registration laws. The term of the company shall be perpetual or until dissolved as provided by law or by vote of the member(s) as provided in this agreement. Upon dissolution, the remaining members shall have the power to continue the operation of the company as long as necessary and allowable under state law until the winding up of the affairs of the business has been completed.

**2. Members.** The initial member(s) shall be listed on Schedule A, which shall accompany and be made a part of this agreement. Additional members may be admitted to membership upon the unanimous consent of the current members. Transfer or pledge of a member's interest may not be made except upon consent of all members.

**3. Contributions.** The initial capital contribution(s) shall be listed on Schedule A, which shall accompany and be made a part of this agreement. No member shall be obligated to contribute any more than the amount set forth on Schedule A unless agreed to in writing by all the members and no member shall have any personal liability for any debt, obligation, or liability of the company other than for full payment of his or her capital contribution. No member shall be entitled to interest on the capital contribution. Member voting rights shall be in proportion to the amount of their contributions.

**4. Profit and Loss.** The profits and losses of the business, and all other taxable or deductible items, shall be allocated to the members according to the percentages on Schedule A, which shall accompany and be made a part of this agreement.

**5. Distributions.** The company shall have the power to make distributions to its members in such amounts and at such intervals as a majority of the members deem appropriate according to law.

**6. Management.** The limited liability company shall be managed by its members listed on Schedule A. In the event of a dispute between members, final determination shall be made with a vote by the members, votes being proportioned according to capital contributions.

**7. Registered Agent.** The company shall at all times have a registered agent and registered office. The initial registered agent and registered office shall be listed on Schedule A, which shall accompany and be made a part of this agreement.

**8. Assets.** The assets of the company shall be registered in the legal name of the company and not in the names of the individual members.

**9. Records and Accounting.** The company shall keep an accurate accounting of its affairs using any method of accounting allowed by law. All members shall have a right to inspect the records during normal business hours. The members shall have the power to hire such accountants as they deem necessary or desirable.

**10. Banking.** The members of the company shall be authorized to set up bank accounts as in their sole discretion are deemed necessary and are authorized to execute any banking resolutions provided by the institution in which the accounts are being set up.

**11. Taxes.** The company shall file such tax returns as required by law. The company shall elect to be taxed as a majority of the members decide is in their best interests. The *tax matters partner*, as required by the Internal Revenue Code, shall be listed on Schedule A, which shall accompany and be made a part of this agreement.

**12. Separate Entity.** The company is a legal entity separate from its members. No member shall have any separate liability for any debts, obligations, or liability of the company except as provided in this agreement.

**13. Indemnity and Exculpation.** The limited liability company shall indemnify and hold harmless its members, managers, employees, and agents to the fullest extent allowed by law for acts or omissions done as part of their duties to or for the company. Indemnification shall include all liabilities, expenses, attorney and accountant fees, and other costs reasonably expended. No member shall be liable to the company for acts done in good faith.

**14. Meetings.** The members shall have no obligation to hold annual or any other meeting, but may hold such meetings if they deem them necessary or desirable.

**15. Amendment of this Agreement.** This agreement may not be amended except in writing signed by all the members.

**16. Conflict of Interest.** No member shall be involved with any business or undertaking that competes with the interests of the company except upon agreement in writing by all the members.

**17. Deadlock.** In the event that the members cannot come to an agreement on any matter, the members agree to submit the issue to mediation to be paid for by the company. In the event the mediation is unsuccessful, they agree to seek arbitration under the rules of the American Arbitration Association.

**18. Dissociation of a Member.** A member shall have the right to discontinue membership upon giving thirty days' notice. A member shall cease to have the right to membership upon death, court-ordered incapacity, bankruptcy, or expulsion. The company shall have the right to buy the interest of any dissociated member at fair market value.

**19. Dissolution.** The company shall dissolve upon the unanimous consent of all the members or upon any event requiring dissolution under state law. In the event of the death, bankruptcy, permanent incapacity, or withdrawal of a member, the remaining members may elect to dissolve or to continue the continuation of the company.

**20. General Provisions.** This agreement is intended to represent the entire agreement between the parties. In the event that any party of this agreement is held to be contrary to law or unenforceable, said party shall be considered amended to comply with the law and such holding shall not affect the enforceability of other terms of this agreement. This agreement shall be binding upon the heirs, successors, and assigns of the members.

**21. Miscellaneous.** _____

_____

_____

_____

_____

**IN WITNESS whereof, the members of the limited liability company sign this agreement and adopt it as their operating agreement this _____ day of _____, _____.**

_____        _____

_____        _____

_____        _____

# LIMITED LIABILITY COMPANY
# MANAGEMENT AGREEMENT OF

_____

THIS AGREEMENT is made effective as of _____, _____, among the member(s) and the company.

**1. Formation.** A limited liability company of the above name has been formed under the laws of the state of Nevada by filing articles of organization with the secretary of state. The purpose of the business shall be to carry on any act or activity lawful under the jurisdiction in which it operates. The company may operate under a fictitious name or names as long as the company is in compliance with applicable fictitious name registration laws. The term of the company shall be perpetual or until dissolved as provided by law or by vote of the member(s) as provided in this agreement. Upon dissolution, the remaining members shall have the power to continue the operation of the company as long as necessary and allowable under state law until the winding up of the affairs of the business has been completed.

**2. Members.** The initial member(s) shall be listed on Schedule A, which shall accompany and be made a part of this agreement. Additional members may be admitted to membership upon the unanimous consent of the current members. Transfer or pledge of a member's interest may not be made except upon consent of all members.

**3. Contributions.** The initial capital contribution(s) shall be listed on Schedule A, which shall accompany and be made a part of this agreement. No member shall be obligated to contribute any more than the amount set forth on Schedule A unless agreed to in writing by all the members. No member shall have any personal liability for any debt, obligation, or liability of the company other than for full payment of his or her capital contribution. No member shall be entitled to interest on the capital contribution. Member voting rights shall be in proportion to the amount of their contributions.

**4. Profit and Loss.** The profits and losses of the business, and all other taxable or deductible items, shall be allocated to the members according to the percentages on Schedule A, which shall accompany and be made a part of this agreement.

**5. Distributions.** The company shall have the power to make distributions to its members in such amounts and at such intervals as a majority of the members deem appropriate according to law.

**6. Management.** The limited liability company shall be managed by the managers listed on Schedule A, which shall accompany and be made a part of this agreement. These managers may or may not be members of the company and each manager shall have an equal vote with other managers as to management decisions. Managers shall serve until resignation or death or until they are removed by a majority vote of the members. Replacement managers shall be selected by a majority vote of the members. Managers shall have no personal liability for expenses, obligations, or liabilities of the company.

**7. Registered Agent.** The company shall at all times have a registered agent and registered office. The initial registered agent and registered office shall be listed on Schedule A, which shall accompany and be made a part of this agreement.

**8. Assets.** The assets of the company shall be registered in the legal name of the company and not in the names of the individual members.

**9. Records and Accounting.** The company shall keep an accurate accounting of its affairs using any method of accounting allowed by law. All members shall have a right to inspect the records during normal business hours. The members shall have the power to hire such accountants as they deem necessary or desirable.

**10. Banking.** The members of the company shall be authorized to set up bank accounts as in their sole discretion are deemed necessary and are authorized to execute any banking resolutions provided by the institution in which the accounts are being set up.

**11. Taxes.** The company shall file such tax returns as required by law. The company shall elect to be taxed as a majority of the members decide is in their best interests. The *tax matters partner*, as required by the Internal Revenue Code, shall be listed on Schedule A, which shall accompany and be made a part of this agreement.

**12. Separate Entity.** The company is a legal entity separate from its members. No member shall have any separate liability for any debts, obligations, or liability of the company except as provided in this agreement.

**13. Indemnity and Exculpation.** The limited liability company shall indemnify and hold harmless its members, managers, employees, and agents to the fullest extent allowed by law for acts or omissions done as part of their duties to or for the company. Indemnification shall include all liabilities, expenses, attorney and accountant fees, and other costs reasonably expended. No member shall be liable to the company for acts done in good faith.

**14. Meetings.** The members shall have no obligation to hold annual or any other meeting, but may hold such meetings if they deem them necessary or desirable.

**15. Amendment of this Agreement.** This agreement may not be amended except in writing signed by all the members.

**16. Conflict of Interest.** No member shall be involved with any business or undertaking that competes with the interests of the company except upon agreement in writing by all the members.

**17. Deadlock.** In the event that the members cannot come to an agreement on any matter, the members agree to submit the issue to mediation to be paid for by the company. In the event the mediation is unsuccessful, they agree to seek arbitration under the rules of the American Arbitration Association.

**18. Dissociation of a Member.** A member shall have the right to discontinue membership upon giving thirty days' notice. A member shall cease to have the right to membership upon death, court-ordered incapacity, bankruptcy, or expulsion. The company shall have the right to buy the interest of any dissociated member at fair market value.

**19. Dissolution.** The company shall dissolve upon the unanimous consent of all the members or upon any event requiring dissolution under state law. In the event of the death, bankruptcy, permanent incapacity, or withdrawal of a member, the remaining members may elect to dissolve or to continue the continuation of the company.

**20. General Provisions.** This agreement is intended to represent the entire agreement between the parties. In the event that any party of this agreement is held to be contrary to law or unenforceable, said party shall be considered amended to comply with the law and such holding shall not affect the enforceability of other terms of this agreement. This agreement shall be binding upon the heirs, successors, and assigns of the members.

**21. Miscellaneous.** _____

_____

_____

_____

_____

**IN WITNESS whereof, the members of the limited liability company sign this agreement and adopt it as their operating agreement this _____ day of _____, _____.**

_____          _____

_____          _____

_____          _____

# SCHEDULE A TO
# LIMITED LIABILITY COMPANY
# OPERATING OR MANAGEMENT AGREEMENT OF

_____

1. **Initial Member(s).** The initial member(s) are:

2. **Capital Contribution(s).** The capital contribution(s) of the member(s) is/are:

3. **Profits and Losses.** The profits, losses, and other tax matters shall be allocated among the members in the following percentages:

4. **Management.** The company shall be managed by:

5. **Registered Agent.** The initial registered agent and registered office of the company are:

6. **Tax Matters.** The tax matters partner is:

*This page intentionally blank.*

# ANNUAL LIST OF MANAGERS OR MANAGING MEMBERS AND RESIDENT AGENT OF

FILE NUMBER

(Name of Limited-Liability Company)

FOR THE FILING PERIOD OF _____ TO _____

The corporation's duly appointed resident agent in the State of Nevada upon whom process can be served is:

A FORM TO CHANGE RESIDENT AGENT INFORMATION CAN BE FOUND ON OUR WEBSITE:  secretaryofstate.biz

**Important: Read instructions before completing and returning this form.**

**USE BLACK INK ONLY - DO NOT HIGHLIGHT**                    ABOVE SPACE IS FOR OFFICE USE ONLY

☐ Return one file stamped copy.  (If filing not accompanied by order instructions, file stamped copy will be sent to resident agent.)

1. Print or type names and addresses, either residence or business, for all managers or managing members. A **Manager**, or if none, **a Managing Member** of the LLC must sign the form. *FORM WILL BE RETURNED IF UNSIGNED*
2. If there are additional managers or managing members, attach a list of them to this form.
3. Return the completed form with the $125.00 filing fee. A $75.00 penalty must be added for failure to file this form by the deadline. An annual list received more than 90 days before its due date shall be deemed an amended list for the previous year.
4. Make your check payable to the Secretary of State. Your canceled check will constitute a certificate to transact business.
5. **Ordering Copies:**  If requested above, one file stamped copy will be returned at no additional charge.  To receive a certified copy, enclose an additional $30.00 per certification.  A **copy fee** of  $2.00 per page is required for each additional copy generated when ordering 2 or more file stamped or certified copies.  Appropriate instructions must accompany your order.
6. Return the completed form to: Secretary of State, 202 North Carson Street, Carson City, NV 89701-4201, (775) 684-5708.
7. Form must be in the possession of the Secretary of State on or before the last day of the month in which it is due.  (Postmark date is not accepted as receipt date.)  Forms received after due date will be returned for additional fees and penalties.

FILING FEE $125 00        LATE PENALTY: $75.00

| NAME | (DOCUMENT WILL BE REJECTED IF TITLE NOT INDICATED) | | |
|------|-----------------------------------------------------|---|---|
|      | ☐ MANAGER        ☐ MANAGING MEMBER | | |
| ADDRESS | CITY | ST | ZIP |

| NAME | (DOCUMENT WILL BE REJECTED IF TITLE NOT INDICATED) | | |
|------|-----------------------------------------------------|---|---|
|      | ☐ MANAGER        ☐ MANAGING MEMBER | | |
| ADDRESS | CITY | ST | ZIP |

| NAME | (DOCUMENT WILL BE REJECTED IF TITLE NOT INDICATED) | | |
|------|-----------------------------------------------------|---|---|
|      | ☐ MANAGER        ☐ MANAGING MEMBER | | |
| ADDRESS | CITY | ST | ZIP |

| NAME | (DOCUMENT WILL BE REJECTED IF TITLE NOT INDICATED) | | |
|------|-----------------------------------------------------|---|---|
|      | ☐ MANAGER        ☐ MANAGING MEMBER | | |
| ADDRESS | CITY | ST | ZIP |

| NAME | (DOCUMENT WILL BE REJECTED IF TITLE NOT INDICATED) | | |
|------|-----------------------------------------------------|---|---|
|      | ☐ MANAGER        ☐ MANAGING MEMBER | | |
| ADDRESS | CITY | ST | ZIP |

I declare, to the best of my knowledge under penalty of perjury, that the above mentioned entity has complied with the provisions of NRS 360.780 and acknowledge that pursuant to NRS 239.330, it is a category C felony to knowingly offer any false or forged instrument for filing in the Office of the Secretary of State.

**X** _____        Title _____        Date _____

**Signature of Manager or Managing Member**

**ROSS MILLER**
Secretary of State
202 North Carson Street
Carson City, Nevada 89701-4201
(775) 684 5708
Website: secretaryofstate.biz

---

# Instructions for
# Annual List and Resident Agent
# Form

---

*ATTENTION:* You may now file your initial or annual list online at
http://secretaryofstate.biz

IMPORTANT: READ ALL INSTRUCTIONS CAREFULLY BEFORE COMPLETING FORM.

*ATTENTION:* Pursuant to NRS, the Annual List and Resident Agent form *MUST* be in the care, custody and control of the Secretary of State by the close of business on the last day of the anniversary month of the original filing. Example: If the entity organized on October 15, 1997 the list must be filed by October 31st of each year. (Postmark date is *not* accepted as receipt date in the Office of the Secretary of State.)

*As of November 1, 2003 the annual filing fee will be based on the total number of shares provided for in the articles. Annual lists for nonprofit corporations without shares are $25.00. See fee schedule or contact our office.*

TYPE or PRINT the following information on the Annual List:

1. The *FILE NUMBER* and *NAME* of the entity *EXACTLY* as it is registered with this office.

2. The *FILING PERIOD* is the month and year of filing TO the month and year 12 months from that date. Example: if the entity date was 1/12/99 the filing period would be 1/1999 to 1/2000.

3. The name and address of the *RESIDENT AGENT and OTHER* names and addresses as required on the list should be entered in the boxes provided on the form. Limited-Liability Companies **MUST** indicate whether *MANAGER or MANAGING MEMBER* is being listed.

4. The *SIGNATURE*, including his/her title and date signed MUST be included in the areas provided at the bottom of the form.

5. Completed *FORM, FEES and applicable PENALTIES* must be returned to the Secretary of State. Pursuant to NRS 225.085, all Initial and Annual Lists must be in the care, custody and control of the Secretary of State by the close of the business on the due date. Lists received after the due date will be returned unfiled, and will require any associated fees and penalties as a result of being late. Trackable delivery methods such as Express Mail, Federal Express, UPS Overnight may be acceptable if the package was guaranteed to be delivered on or before the due date yet failed to be timely delivered.

*ADDITIONAL FORMS* may be obtained on our website at http://.secretaryofstate.biz or by calling 775-684-5708.

*FILE STAMPED COPIES:* To receive one file stamped copy, please mark the appropriate check box on the list. Additional copies require $2.00 per page and appropriate order instructions.

*CERTIFIED COPIES:* To order a certified copy, enclose an additional $30.00 and appropriate instructions. A copy fee of $2.00 per page is required for each copy generated when ordering 2 or more certified copies.

*EXPEDITE FEE:* Filing may be expedited for an additional $75.00 fee.

*NOTE:* The Las Vegas Satellite Office will only accept *expedited* filings. Regular filings should be sent to the Carson City address.

Filing may be submitted at the office of the Secretary of State or by mail at the following addresses:

| | |
|---|---|
| Secretary of State | (This Office Accepts Expedited Filings Only) |
| Status Division | Secretary of State-Satellite Office |
| 202 N. Carson Street | Commercial Recordings Division |
| Carson City, NV 89701-4201 | 555 E. Washington Avenue, Suite 4000 |
| 775-684-5708  Fax 775-684-7123 | Las Vegas, NV 89101 |
| | 702-486-2880  Fax 702-486-2888 |

# MINUTES OF A MEETING OF MEMBERS OF

_____

A meeting of the members of the company was held on _____, _____, at _____.

The following were present, being all the members of the limited liability company:

_____     _____

_____     _____

_____     _____

The meeting was called to order and it was moved, seconded, and unanimously carried that _____ act as Chairman and that _____ act as Secretary.

After discussion and upon motion duly made, seconded, and carried, the following resolution(s) were adopted:

There being no further business to come before the meeting, upon motion duly made, seconded, and unanimously carried, it was adjourned.

_____
Secretary

Members:

_____

_____

_____

_____

*This page intentionally blank.*

# CERTIFICATE OF AUTHORITY

FOR

_____

This is to certify that the above limited liability company is managed by its

&#9633; members

&#9633; managers

who are listed below and that each of them is authorized and empowered to transact business on behalf of the company.

Name                                          Address

_____        _____

_____        _____

_____        _____

_____        _____

_____        _____

                                              _____

Date: _____

Name of company:

_____

By: _____

Position: _____

# Index

# W

# Z